AUG 19 2019

D0769361

The Mexican Mission

In the sixty years following the Spanish conquest, indigenous communities in central Mexico suffered the equivalent of three Black Deaths, a demographic catastrophe that prompted them to rebuild under the aegis of Spanish missions. Where previous histories have framed this process as an epochal spiritual conversion, *The Mexican Mission* widens the lens to examine its political and economic history, revealing a worldly enterprise that both remade and colonized Mesoamerica. The mission exerted immense temporal power in struggles over indigenous jurisdictions, resources, and people. Competing communities adapted the mission to their own designs; most notably, they drafted labor to raise ostentatious monastery complexes in the midst of mass death. While the mission fostered indigenous recovery, it also grounded Spanish imperial authority in the legitimacy of local native rule. The Mexican mission became one of the most extensive in early modern history, with influences reverberating on Spanish frontiers from New Mexico to Mindanao.

Ryan Dominic Crewe is Associate Professor of History at the University of Colorado, Denver.

CAMBRIDGE LATIN AMERICAN STUDIES

General Editors
KRIS LANE, Tulane University
MATTHEW RESTALL, Pennsylvania State University

Editor Emeritus
HERBERT S. KLEIN
Gouverneur Morris Emeritus Professor of History, Columbia University
and Hoover Research Fellow, Stanford University

Other Books in the Series

(Continued after the Index)

The Mexican Mission

Indigenous Reconstruction and Mendicant
Enterprise in New Spain, 1521–1600

RYAN DOMINIC CREWE

University of Colorado, Denver

3 9075 05404586 6

CAMBRIDGE
UNIVERSITY PRESS

CAMBRIDGE
UNIVERSITY PRESS

University Printing House, Cambridge CB2 8BS, United Kingdom

One Liberty Plaza, 20th Floor, New York, NY 10006, USA

477 Williamstown Road, Port Melbourne, VIC 3207, Australia

314–321, 3rd Floor, Plot 3, Splendor Forum, Jasola District Centre,
New Delhi – 110025, India

79 Anson Road, #06–04/06, Singapore 079906

Cambridge University Press is part of the University of Cambridge.

It furthers the University's mission by disseminating knowledge in the pursuit of
education, learning, and research at the highest international levels of excellence.

www.cambridge.org
Information on this title: www.cambridge.org/9781108492546
DOI: 10.1017/9781108602310

© Ryan Dominic Crewe 2019

This publication is in copyright. Subject to statutory exception
and to the provisions of relevant collective licensing agreements,
no reproduction of any part may take place without the written
permission of Cambridge University Press.

First published 2019

Printed in the United Kingdom by TJ International Ltd, Padstow Cornwall

A catalogue record for this publication is available from the British Library.

Library of Congress Cataloging-in-Publication Data
NAMES: Crewe, Ryan Dominic, 1977- author.
TITLE: The Mexican mission : indigenous reconstruction and mendicant enterprise in
New Spain, 1521-1600 / Ryan Dominic Crewe, University of Colorado, Denver.
DESCRIPTION: 1 [edition]. | New York : Cambridge University Press, 2019. |
SERIES: Cambridge Latin American studies
IDENTIFIERS: LCCN 2018051120 | ISBN 9781108492546 (hardback) |
ISBN 9781108462921 (pbk.)
SUBJECTS: LCSH: Mexico–History–Spanish colony, 1540-1810–Missions. |
Mexico–History–Spanish colony, 1540-1810–Church history.
CLASSIFICATION: LCC BV2835.3 .C74 2019 | DDC 266/.27209031–dc23
LC record available at https://lccn.loc.gov/2018051120

ISBN 978-1-108-49254-6 Hardback

Cambridge University Press has no responsibility for the persistence or accuracy of
URLs for external or third-party internet websites referred to in this publication
and does not guarantee that any content on such websites is, or will remain,
accurate or appropriate.

For my mother and father

Contents

Figures

Maps

Tables

Acknowledgments

Some two decades ago, two professors at the University of California at Davis lent their support and encouragement to an undergraduate student who had just returned from study abroad in Spain with a head full of questions about Spanish colonization. I was fascinated by the transition from late-medieval medieval Spain to colonial expansion in the Americas. At Davis, Charles Walker and the late Arnold J. Bauer lent their unflagging support, hours of conversation that I remember fondly, and unswerving guidance as I made my way through a lengthy senior thesis. Books begin like this: not solely with the curiosity of the student, but with the generosity and listening skills of the mentor. Even after many twists and turns, this book is very much the result of those initial questions, those initial conversations over coffee. I shall be eternally grateful: Chuck, thank you for your guidance that long ago set me on this path. And to Arnie: *pardiez, el zagal por fin cumplió.*

At Yale University, I found the ideal environment for examining the history of New Spain in a global context. I shall forever be indebted to my advisor, Stuart B. Schwartz, for his guidance and inspiration over all these years – first in coursework, then the dissertation, and recently as I revised the dissertation and produced this book. Stuart brings a sense of wonder to the study of the past, as well as an unflagging insistence to never lose sight of the humanity of our historical subjects – lessons that guide me to this day. I would also like to thank Gilbert Joseph for his advice and encouragement over all these years. Their guidance and inspiration made all of this possible. I am also grateful to Rolena Adorno, whose courses introduced me to the works of sixteenth-century chroniclers and critics, and to Mary Miller and Jaime Lara, whose course in sixteenth-century Mexican art and architecture planted the seeds that led me to explore the history of Mexican "fortress monasteries" in the archives and in the field.

Along the way, as this project proceeded through dissertation, post-doc, and production phases, several institutions provided generous support for research. I thank the Fulbright-Hays Doctoral Dissertation Research Abroad Program, the John F. Enders Foundation, the Andrew M. Mellon Foundation, the Yale Council for International and Area Studies, the Tinker Foundation, the Consejo Superior de Investigaciones Científicas, and the Graduate School of Arts and Sciences of Yale University. I am also grateful to Daniel Chua at the University of Hong Kong's Society of Scholars in the Humanities, whose support for my second project on the Pacific world also provided me with time – and a broader global perspective on the early modern period – to begin revising a dissertation that was all too unwieldy. Finally, the University of Colorado at Denver has also supported my research and writing. In particular, the Office of Research Services under the leadership of Bob Damrauer, the College of Letters and Science, and the Department of History have generously supported research trips and the final production funding for this book.

During the course of research, the staffs of several institutions provided the documents, assisted me in following enticing leads, ran the photocopies, and helped me to contemplate the mysteries of *tramitología*. In Spain, these include the Archivo Histórico Nacional, the Biblioteca Nacional de España, the Biblioteca de la Real Academia de la Historia, the Archivo General de Simancas, and above all, the Archivo General de Indias. In the United States, the staffs of the Huntington Library and the Nettie Lee Benson Library at the University of Texas at Austin also provided their assistance. In Mexico, I would like to thank the staffs of the Instituto Nacional de Antropología e Historia, the Biblioteca Nacional de México-Fondo Reservado, the Universidad Iberoamericana, the Archivo Provincial de la Orden Agustina de México, and the Instituto Mora. Most importantly, however, I appreciate the labors of the staff of the Archivo General de la Nación in Mexico City, especially in Galería Cuatro, who delivered the documentation that forms the core of this study.

I am also grateful to my colleagues, whose comments and suggestions have been extremely helpful: William Taylor, Jonathan Truitt, Ana Pulido Rull, Robert Ferry, Jorge Cañizares Esguerra, Joaquín Rivaya Martínez,

Kevin Gosner, Ignacio Martínez, Alex Hidalgo, and José Carlos de la Puente. At the Cambridge Latin American Series, I thank Kris Lane and Matthew Restall for all their support, which made publishing a seamless process. I am also grateful to Peter Anthamatten and Cody J. Peterson, who designed the maps for this book. My eternal thanks also go to my editor, Debbie Gershenowitz, who has helped me navigate this book from manuscript to publication with great patience and excellent advice. I also counted on the great help of the production team at Cambridge University Press, as well as Rudy León, who produced the index and provided great feedback, and Carolyn Holleyman, who copy-edited this book and was a tremendous help in the final phases.

Over the years friends have helped me, most of them unknowingly, through this seemingly unending process of research, writing, and revision. María Willstedt, since the beginnings of this project, has always listened, provided insight, and assisted with revisions. I will always be grateful to Louise Walker for her support and advice through the many stages of the graduate career – with great laughs and insights along the way. I also would like to thank Martin Nesvig, who has provided invaluable advice and support. In New Haven, tremendous intellects enlivened my first years there with debates about nearly everything: Manuella Meyer, David Assouline, Haralampos Stratigopoulos, Luís Martín Cabrera, Daniel Noemi, Tatiana Seijas, and Nefeli Misuraca. In Mexico, my fellow inmates at Lecumberri also provided great company and conversation as we navigated the legajos and defined our projects: José Barragán and Heather Peterson, who never resisted a call to head over to VIPs for coffee and some *molletes*. In Hong Kong, long conversations with Rajeev Balasubramanyam, Divya Ghelani, and Victor Zatsepine brought me great inspiration. In London, Father Vincent Crewe, my uncle, and the late Father David Roderick at Sunbury parish widened my perspectives and did so with only the finest bourdeaux. And at the University of Colorado, Denver, I have been lucky to have the good friendship and support of my colleagues. I am especially grateful to Gabriel Finkelstein, who read the entire manuscript multiple times and provided invaluable advice. Finally, I want to thank Carmela Romanov for accompanying me on this long journey, seeing one sixteenth-century church after another, supporting me through the endless hours of writing – above all, I thank her for her lessons on *lo que viene siendo México*.

My eternal gratitude will forever go to my family for their support for every single step, every milestone, of this seemingly-endless project: my brothers John and Gregory, and my late grandmother, Clara Freschi. My parents, Dominic and Carolyn Crewe, are my greatest teachers. Through lessons and example they taught the importance of empathy and wonder, and a sense of social justice. And for as far back as my memory can take me, they have always inspired me to follow my curiosity.

For their love, I dedicate this book to them.

Ryan Dominic Crewe

Introduction

> Therefore I cannot refrain from speaking about the city of this world, a city which aims at dominion, which holds nations in enslavement, but is itself dominated by the very lust of domination.
>
> Augustine, *City of God*, Book I, Preface.

Across the highlands of central Mexico, hundreds of stone churches stand as a testament to the turbulent history of sixteenth-century Mexico. Austere and windowless, their massive walls of dark red stone propped by pyramidal buttresses, the largest of these missions are among the most imposing erected in the Spanish Empire. In bustling provincial towns and near-abandoned villages these edifices are still imposing, with gothic arches and barrel vaults often rising as high as eighty feet. Closer up these structures lose their severe appearance as their details come into view. In delicately-carved façades, and on murals inside the churches and their adjoining monasteries, native artists left lavish evidence of Mesoamerica's encounter with the European Renaissance. Surrounding these structures, vast churchyards attest to the multitudes that once assembled for masses and instruction. The scale of these missions seems outsize for the handful of mendicant friars who used them as their bases. Yet between 1521 and 1590, indigenous communities undertook monumental campaigns in the wake of conquest and in spite of four catastrophic epidemics, each of which was on the magnitude of the Black Death. Stone by stone, laborers built the infrastructure for one of the most extensive mission enterprises in global history. Amid these stout cloisters and churches that still echo with murmured prayers, questions arise: What motivated native communities to raise these complexes while they sought to recover from conquest and epidemics? Are these walls a testament to Spanish power? Or are they monuments to indigenous persistence?

This book addresses these questions by exploring the social history of the mission enterprise in sixteenth-century Mexico: a story of upheaval, recovery, and the costs of rebuilding. Long studied principally through the lens of religion, missions were also a political force that reinforced colonizers and colonized alike: it was not only a spiritual encounter, but also a worldly enterprise whose transcultural power both colonized and remade Mesoamerica. Amid demographic crises, disruptive social change, and shifting indigenous and Spanish politics, this hybrid enterprise held sway over the indigenous politics of the Viceroyalty of New Spain for seventy years.

At first glance, the Mexican mission epitomized the epochal ambitions of Spanish imperialism. After all, Spaniards – especially missionaries – doggedly pursued an ideal of establishing a universal Christian *imperium*, a new order in which Augustine's city of man would do the work of the city of God. A messianic, exclusivist Christianity shaped their imaginations of the lands that suddenly fell within the perimeters of their world. In like manner, sixteenth-century missionaries viewed the violence of conquest and the colonial regime as instruments of conversion. Preaching alone would not complete their task, and the asymmetry of colonialism offered them a means of implanting the Church on a scale unseen since Charlemagne. To build churches, force recantations, and impose Christian governance, missionaries embraced temporal powers: primarily that of the king of Spain, but also the authority of local native rulers. With the authorization of the Crown and Papacy, the mendicant Orders – Franciscans, Augustinians, and Dominicans – established the Mexican mission as a system of spiritual and temporal rule over native communities. Each colossal church was an ostentatious affirmation of their aim.

Natives had a more urgent mission of their own: that of recovering from demographic, social, and political catastrophe. Rulers in over two hundred city-states used missions to legitimize their rule and consolidate their territories under Spanish sovereignty. Around mission bases known as *doctrinas*, indigenous rulers and missionaries reconstituted local native governments and communities, each with its own church, council, treasury, jurisdiction, and partial autonomy. For even while missions contributed to the violence of colonial rule, they offered indigenous nobles the means to reassert their claims to sovereignty in the wake of losses of at least a third of their population. Survivors of the *hueycocolixtli* epidemic of 1545–1547 actually *doubled* the construction of monasteries in the decade that followed the catastrophe, evidence that these churches arose less from obedience to custom or piety than from the intention to rebuild polities around church structures that would preserve the life and force of their Mesoamerican forebears, the *teocallis* (temples). The mission was a vehicle of native survival and social reconstitution.

The Mexican mission therefore comprised two missions: one was an apostolic enterprise that legitimized Spanish sovereignty over the New World, while the other was a program of native recovery that legitimized local polities. The Mexican mission expanded across the map of Mesoamerican politics, which consisted of a complex web of interdependent but competing polities. Over two hundred local states, each with their own alliances and rivalries, as well as two moribund empires, the Aztec Triple Alliance and the Kingdom of Michoacán, populated this terrain. In just thirty years, the mission enterprise achieved something that the Aztec Empire had never accomplished: it united the length and breadth of sedentary Central Mexico from Jalisco to Veracruz and from the Río Pánuco to Southern Oaxaca under the sway of Spanish-ruled Tenochtitlán. By the 1570s, a constellation of nearly three hundred doctrinas extended across the highlands of Central Mexico. Alongside their associated indigenous governments, these doctrinas formed the very sinews of colonial governance. For Spaniards, doctrinas instilled *policía* – rational temporal rule – as much as they enabled the spiritual enterprise. This book traces the social construction of the mission on this continental scale, something lacking in a field that has fragmented into studies defined by place and ethnicity.[1] It examines the expansion of this transcultural institution in polities across several ethnic regions, arguing that similar sedentary patterns of settlement and economy laid the basis for this broad network of missions.[2] In 277 doctrinas in indigenous communities, each with its own history and desire for autonomy, the mission enterprise derived its power from its capacity to align, however unequally, the interests of local native leaders with those of Spanish colonizers.[3]

---

[1] The last major region-wide works on the mission enterprise were those of Robert Ricard, *The Spiritual Conquest of Mexico*, trans. and ed. Lesley Byrd Simpson (Berkeley, CA: University of California Press, 1966); and George Kubler, *Mexican Architecture in the Sixteenth Century* (New Haven, CN: Yale University Press, 1948). More recently, Mark Christensen has used native devotional texts to compare central Mexico with Yucatan, in *Nahua and Maya Catholicisms: Texts and Religion in Colonial Central Mexico and Yucatan* (Stanford, CA: Stanford University Press, 2013).

[2] Based on archival data and printed primary sources, this work traces the foundation and development of 277 *doctrinas*. See Appendix for data on *doctrina* foundations and construction projects of mission churches.

[3] Given its focus on native city-states, this study does not examine indigenous urban parishes where Spanish settlement predominated. On indigenous parishes in Tenochtitlán, see Jonathan G. Truitt, *Sustaining the Divine in Mexico Tenochtitlan: Nahuas and Catholicism, 1523–1700* (Norman, OK: University of Oklahoma Press, 2018).

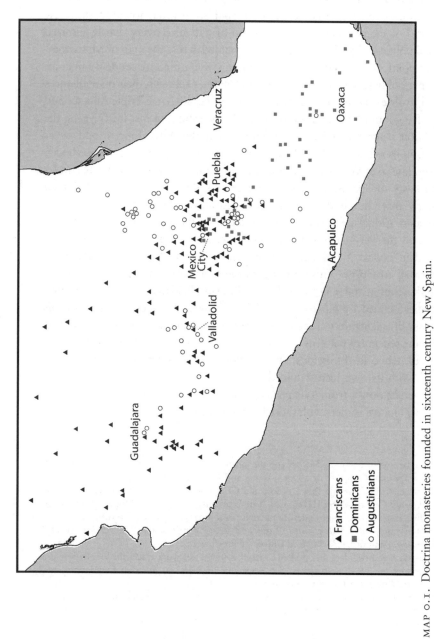

MAP 0.1. Doctrina monasteries founded in sixteenth century New Spain.
Drawn by Peter Anthamatten and Cody J. Peterson. Based on Elena Vázquez, Distribución geográfica del Arzobispado de México, siglo XVI (Mexico City: Biblioteca enciclopédica del Estado de México, 1968).

Legend:
▲ Franciscans
■ Dominicans
○ Augustinians

Map labels: Veracruz, Oaxaca, Puebla, Mexico City, Acapulco, Valladolid, Guadalajara

DEFINING THE MISSION

Of all the popular images of Spanish colonialism, the mission certainly is one of the most enduring. Yet in academic studies the mission has been a fluid concept, subject to changing ideas and approaches. For much of the twentieth century, and indeed for centuries before that, mission history was an extension of the missionaries' worldviews. Apologetic narratives located missions within a broader story of missionary action and native reaction. More recently, indigenous ethnography has reoriented this relationship by paying attention to long-ignored patterns of indigenous agency. The encounter, in their telling, was anything but passive.[4]

As interpretations of the mission shifted, so too did Mexico's place in mission history. In early mission scholarship, central Mexico stood out like a jewel in a Spanish prelate's miter – it embodied what a Spanish mission was about.[5] This changed, however, with indigenous ethnography. Most influential was James Lockhart's argument that the apostolic labor of Spanish priests among the sedentary cultures of Mexico should not be considered a mission nor should the Spanish priests who preached in this foreign land be considered missionaries. The essence of this argument is linguistic: sixteenth-century Spaniards did not generally use the terms "mission" or "missionary." *Misión* and *misionero*, in the Spanish language of the time, referred to evangelism on the frontier in the seventeenth and eighteenth centuries. Spanish priests working in sixteenth-century Mexico were typically called *doctrineros*, or instructors of Christian doctrine. Accordingly, the sites where they worked and resided were called *doctrinas*. That these more pedagogical terms reflect a cultural reality is the second part of Lockhart's argument. In contrast to frontier missions among nomadic peoples, he states, the sedentary peoples of Mesoamerica "needed less to be converted than instructed." Early Christianity in Mesoamerica was exceptional because European and central

---

[4] Charles E. Dibble, "The Nahuatlization of Christianity," in *Sixteenth-Century Mexico: The Work of Sahagún*, ed. Munro S. Edmundson (Albuquerque, NM: University of New Mexico Press, 1974), 225–33; Louise M. Burkhart, *The Slippery Earth: Nahua-Christian Moral Dialogue in Sixteenth-Century Mexico* (Tucson: University of Arizona Press, 1989); Osvaldo V. Pardo, *The Origins of Mexican Catholicism: Nahua Rituals and Christian Sacraments in Sixteenth-Century Mexico* (Ann Arbor, MI: University of Michigan Press, 2005); Christensen, *Nahua and Maya*.

[5] Mariano Cuevas, *Historia de la Iglesia en México*, 3 vols. (Mexico City: Patricio Sanz, 1921); Ricard, *Spiritual Conquest*; Lino Gómez Canedo, *Evangelización y conquista: Experiencia franciscana en Hispanoamérica* (Mexico City: Porrúa, 1977).

Mexican societies were fundamentally compatible.[6] Having sounded the alarm regarding anachronism, Lockhart's argument ends up mirroring the very anthropological categories that missionary authors like Acosta and Las Casas had used to rank native cultures according to their perceived degree of advancement relative to Europe.[7]

Nevertheless, the fact that contemporary Spaniards did not employ the term *misión* does not negate its usefulness as a concept. The mission is of central importance to the history of Christianity and European imperial expansion. It denotes a frontier relationship between priest and native neophyte that is entirely applicable to the history of sixteenth-century Mexico. "Mission" refers to a delegation of people sent abroad to propagate a faith and to the stations where missionaries and natives interacted. By insisting on an untranslated Spanish term for such an important institution, we risk using language to segregate colonial Mesoamerica from global history. The term allows historians of places as different as Quebec or Goa to compare and contrast the varying experiences of a mobile Christianity that advanced in tandem with early modern colonization, trade, and cross-cultural interactions.[8] It speaks to the spiritual ambiguities of a transoceanic apostolate, as well as to the temporal power that missions acquired in the Spanish Empire. Additionally, thanks to the dynamic work of historians of Spanish frontiers in Northern New Spain and South America, studies of missions have also come to address secular factors like demography, ecology, and native politics.[9]

The Mexican mission was both noun and verb. It was, of course, a frontier institution that had its own organizational schema, systems of financing, police forces, schools, and protocols for cooperation between

---

[6] James Lockhart, *The Nahuas after the Conquest* (Stanford, CA: Stanford University Press, 1992), 203. See also Susan Deeds, *Defiance and Deference in Mexico's Colonial North: Indians under Spanish Rule un Nueva Vizcaya* (Austin, TX: University of Texas Press, 2003), 4.

[7] José de Acosta, *Natural and Moral History of the Indies*, trans. and ed. Jane Mangan (Durham: Duke University Press, 2002); Bartolomé de Las Casas, *Apologética historia sumaria*, ed. Edmundo O'Gorman (Mexico City: UNAM, 1967).

[8] Alan Greer and Kenneth Mills, "A Catholic Atlantic," in *The Atlantic in Global History*, eds. Jorge Cañizares-Esguerra and Erik R. Seeman (Upper Saddle River, NJ: Prentice Hall, 2007), 3–19.

[9] See Deeds, *Defiance*; Steven W. Hackel, *Children of Coyote, Missionaries of Saint Francis: Indian-Spanish Relations in Colonial California, 1769–1850* (Chapel Hill, NC: University of North Carolina Press, 2003); Cynthia Radding, *Wandering Peoples: Colonialism, Ethnic Spaces, and Ecological Frontiers in Northwestern Mexico, 1700–1850* (Durham, NC: Duke University Press, 1997); Barbara Ganson, *The Guaraní under Spanish Rule in Río de la Plata* (Stanford, CA: Stanford University Press, 2006).

missionaries and native officials. Each mission was a space of political negotiation, economic production, and social relations that reflected contending interests and demographic pressures. Its infrastructure could not be missed. A good number of its churches overshadowed all others in Mexico, save the cathedral in the colonial capital. Indeed many still overshadow their towns and villages to this day. This was intentional: missionaries and native rulers, for their distinct reasons, wanted the mission to be tangible, visible, and imposing, a thing to be ignored at one's peril. But the mission was also a verb, a practice, a sum of actions that both bridged and marked the divides of culture and class. For Spaniards, it was an act of crossing seas and cultural boundaries, of learning and translation, and above all of preaching, persuading, and converting. For natives, it involved recovering, regrouping, gaining recognition, and restoring order. These actions built an institution that ordered its participants into asymmetrical relations of power, and the repeating rhythms of rituals, preaching, and almsgiving sanctified and routinized it to the point that it became a hegemonic force in native politics.[10] In many ways the Mexican mission epitomized sixteenth-century Spanish colonialism. It was a Church born in violence and raised on a bounty of native tributes; it was a Church of appearances, a structure quickly built for political ends, whose very success in the mundane – in the city of this world – left lingering doubts in the spirit and sowed jealousy among all those who did not profit from it.

REMAKING MESOAMERICA

"The day the Spaniards arrived was when Our Lord began to punish us." So responded a group of Mixtec elders in 1580 to Spanish queries about their lives since the Spanish conquest.[11] The scale and pace of the calamities that they witnessed had been nearly unfathomable. The war of conquest of 1519–1521, though certainly disruptive, paled in comparison to the

---

[10] William F. Hanks draws upon Bourdieu to define these two crucial political aspects of the mission as "field," the mission's "schematic structure," and "habitus," the habits of thought and action that reproduce the mission as a core part of the colonial social order. See *Converting Words: Maya in the Age of the Cross* (Berkeley, CA: University of California Press, 2010), 93–6.

[11] Kevin Terraciano, *The Mixtecs of Colonial Oaxaca: Ñadzahui History, Sixteenth through Eighteenth Centuries* (Stanford, CA: Stanford University Press, 2001), 362; René Acuña, ed. *Relaciones geográficas del siglo XVI* (Mexico City: UNAM, 1982); See also Barbara Mundy, *Mapping New Spain: Indigenous Cartography and the Relaciones Geográficas* (Chicago, IL: University of Chicago Press, 2000).

devastation of the smallpox epidemic that accompanied it.[12] Over the remainder of the century three more demographic catastrophes followed in 1545, 1575, and the 1590s. Each one of these epidemics claimed at least a third of the population; by the end of the century, roughly ninety percent of the preconquest population had been lost. Lack of immunity to European diseases undoubtedly triggered these disasters, but the losses incurred by each epidemic were magnified by the "socially-mediated catastrophe" of colonialism. Communities that were already straining to sustain themselves still had to meet unrelenting demands for tributes and labor from Spaniards and the native rulers whom they recognized. While natives buried their dead and gathered the survivors, they faced an avaricious colonial system that only mourned their mortality as an economic loss.[13] This vicious cycle of disease and exploitation resulted in widespread famine, malnutrition, and depopulation. Towns and city-states across the region survived these existential threats by fusing local systems of governance with the mission enterprise. They directed the mission towards their urgent task of rebuilding and remaking their world in this century of death.

The mission's role in social reconstruction has largely been overlooked by a historiography that has focused on the more intangible dimensions of the enterprise. The spiritual encounter, not politics and society, has garnered the most attention. Classic studies, especially those of Robert Ricard and George Kubler, spoke of a "spiritual conquest" of the natives.[14] Subsequent historians challenged these triumphal narratives by calling attention to indigenous agency in adopting and engaging Christianity.[15] Following ethnohistorian Charles Dibble's call to view the mission encounter as a process of *nahuatlization* of Christianity, historians advanced our understanding the ways in which natives assimilated and translated Catholicism as a means of preserving their own cultural world. These scholars

---

[12] Thomas M. Whitmore, *Disease and Death in Early Colonial Mexico: Simulating Amerindian Depopulation* (Boulder, CO: Westview Press, 1992); Hans J. Prem, "Disease Outbreaks in Central Mexico during the Sixteenth Century," in *Secret Judgments of God: Old World Disease in Colonial Spanish America*, eds. Noble David Cook and W. George Lowell (Norman, OK: University of Oklahoma Press, 1992), 20–48; B. H. Slicher Van Bath, "The Calculation of the Population of New Spain, Especially for the Period before 1570." *Boletín de estudios latinoamericanos y del Caribe*, vol. 24 (1978), 67–95.

[13] Slavoj Zizek, *Violence* (New York: Picador, 2008), 94; Massimo Livi Bacci, *Conquest: The Destruction of the American Indios* (Cambridge: Polity Press, 2008), 140–55.

[14] Ricard, *Spiritual Conquest*; Cuevas, *Historia*.

[15] Matthew Restall, "A History of the New Philology and the New Philology in History." *Latin American Research Review*, vol. 38, no. 1 (2003), 114–15.

drew upon native-language sermons, *confesionarios*, confraternity constitutions, and liturgical texts. Instead, they argued, natives in central Mexico "Nahuatlized" Christianity, and the "missionary was missionized" by indigenous culture.[16] By bringing native-language sources into the study of the mission enterprise, ethnohistorical scholarship has greatly advanced our understanding the ways in which natives assimilated, shaped, and translated Catholicism as a means of preserving their own culture.

Yet in its mission to place indigenous spiritual and intellectual life at the center of early colonial religion, the 'cultural turn' has let questions of power and class fade into the background. This is especially the case regarding the increasingly asymmetrical relations between Spanish colonizers and indigenous peoples, and between nobles and commoners within indigenous communities.[17] The ambiguities of native translations have received more attention in the mission history of central Mexico than the social history of demographic catastrophes and colonization. Moreover, the very provenance of ethnohistorical sources calls into question any native counter-conquest of Christianity. Indigenous ecclesiastical texts, whether in Spanish or native languages, were produced mainly by a minority of lettered indigenous elites who received their education at mission schools. The records of a native confraternity in Tula, for example, reveal that its membership represented just three percent of the local population in 1570.[18] Indigenous nobles and

---

[16] Dibble, "Nahuatlization"; Burkhart, *Slippery Earth*, 15–24; Pardo, *Origins*; Christensen, *Nahua and Maya*; Louise M. Burkhart ed. and trans., *Holy Wednesday: A Nahua Drama from Early Colonial Mexico* (Philadelphia: University of Pennsylvania Press, 1996); Bartolomé de Alva, *A Guide to Confession Large and Small in the Mexican Language: 1634*, trans. and eds. Barry D. Sell, John Frederick Schwaller, and Lu Ann Homza (Norman, OK: University of Oklahoma Press, 1999); Alonso de Molina, *Nahua Confraternities in Early Colonial Mexico: The 1552 Nahuatl Ordinances of Fray Alonso de Molina, OFM*, trans. and eds. Barry D. Sell, Larissa Taylor and Asunción Lavrín (Berkeley, CA: American Academy of Franciscan History, 2002); Barry D. Sell and Louise M. Burkhart, eds. *Nahuatl Theater*, 2 vols. (Norman, OK: University of Oklahoma Press, 2004).

[17] There are notable exceptions. Studies of culture and linguistics that address colonial power directly include: Viviana Díaz Balsera, *The Pyramid under the Cross: Franciscan Discourses of Evangelization and the Nahua Christian Subject in Sixteenth-century Mexico* (Tucson: University of Arizona Press, 2005); Hanks, *Converting Words*.

[18] Barry D. Sell, "The Molina Confraternity Rules of 1552," in *Nahua Confraternities in Early Colonial Mexico: The 1552 Nahuatl Ordinances of Fray Alonso de Molina, OFM*, trans. and eds. Alonso de Molina, Barry D. Sell, Larissa Taylor, and Asunción Lavrín (Berkeley, CA: American Academy of Franciscan History, 2002), 53–5. Recent analyses of these small but influential circles of *letrados* have gone beyond the *nahuatlization* thesis: Rosend Rovira Morgado, *San Francisco Padremeh: El temprano cabildo indio y las cuatro parcialidades de México-Tenochtitlán (1549–1599)* (Madrid: CSIC, 2017); Hanks, *Converting Words*.

pious converts voluntarily marched in processions, performed charity, and produced texts and art, but as Eric Van Young has warned, we risk distorting the mission enterprise if we assume that elite records reveal a "hegemonic status they may not have in fact enjoyed."[19] Privileging elite collaborators and voluntary participants risks losing sight of the fact that the mission was a political institution that governed over anyone who made their life in a polity reduced to Spanish rule. It encompassed sincere converts, secret devotees and practitioners of native rites, and many others who freely drew elements from both traditions that they felt empowered them.[20] Drawing conclusions about missions solely from elite spiritual records effectively means writing the majority of native commoners out of the story – the very social group that hauled the mission's stones, built its walls, and furnished its upkeep.

This book widens the lens on the mission enterprise. It draws from a variety of archival records that bear witness to the role of the mission enterprise in adjudicating territories, policing natives, regulating conflicts, and mobilizing laborers. Based on *mandamientos* (viceregal responses that summarize petitions from indigenous and ecclesiastical actors), civil and inquisitorial trials, correspondence, and viceregal account books, this study documents the everyday struggles that raged within the mission enterprise: commoners protesting against overwork in friars' kitchens, witnesses recalling the construction of a monastery, or native rulers ordering the demolition of rival churches. These political and material contingencies set the parameters for religious change in post-conquest Mexico. As such, these civil records lay the foundation for a new social history of the mission.

In ways great and small, from matters as momentous as the foundation of a new mission to details as small as a barrio's contribution of lumber for scaffolding, civil sources document a mission enterprise that helped reorder a world in crisis. Precisely because it was a means of survival and reconstitution, the mission was also a pawn in the intensifying rivalries, class struggles, and factional divisions of indigenous politics in the years after the conquest. Like the colonial legal system, the mission enterprise served as an arena for indigenous struggles over land, resources, and power. Ambitious native rulers drove its expansion for the better part of six decades, drawing upon its rituals and architecture to reconstitute local governments and reaffirm hierarchies of deference in the eyes of their

---

[19] Eric Van Young, "The New Cultural History Comes to Old Mexico." *The Hispanic American Historical Review*, vol. 79, no. 2 (May 1999), 236.

[20] David Tavárez, *The Invisible War: Indigenous Devotions, Discipline, and Dissent in Colonial Mexico* (Stanford, CA: Stanford University Press, 2011).

intended native subjects and their Spanish overlords. Contrary to widespread assumptions that natives uniformly supported their rulers' collaborations, there was in fact considerable dissent: commoners resisted the terms of labor, denounced forced marches to mass, and boycotted mission projects when notions of reciprocity were broken.[21] Yet their protest was not aimed at the mission itself; on the contrary, many of these dissident groups sought to secede from their rulers precisely by erecting missions and hosting friars. These local indigenous struggles to control jurisdictions, resources, and people was one of the principal means by which the mission enterprise acquired power in New Spain.

For several decades, catastrophic loss provoked vitality. By arguing, governing, punishing, praying, seceding, singing, and protesting, natives made this enterprise their own. Regardless of whether they believed the friars' doctrine, indigenous peoples built this institution to serve their own worldly and spiritual ends. Rituals, laws, and infrastructure – both the material and the political edifice – were "made [to] function in another register."[22] Their actions compel us to reconsider debates surrounding indigenous agency in colonial encounters. On the one hand, the Mexican indigenous mission of recovery issues a powerful riposte to the deterministic theses of decline so common to histories of indigenous peoples, whether we are speaking of Mexico, Tahiti, or Australia, among many other contact zones. The "fatal impact" of disease and invasion was indeed destructive, but it is also true that native communities did not succumb to despair.[23] Indigenous peoples in Mexico built the most extensive mission church in the early modern period. But by the same token, historians have often underestimated the toll of demographic crises, conquest, and colonial power relations. These studies have taken pains to emphasize the continuity of indigenous culture against those who have

---

[21] Lockhart, *Nahuas*, 421; Eleanor Wake, *Framing the Sacred: The Indian Churches of Early Colonial Mexico* (Norman, OK: University of Oklahoma Press, 2010), 88–92.

[22] Michel de Certeau, *The Practice of Everyday Life* (Berkeley: University of California Press, 1988), 32.

[23] Such fatalistic histories include: Alfred W. Crosby, *The Columbian Exchange* (Westport, CT: Greenwood Press, 1972); Alan Moorehead, *The Fatal Impact: An Account of the Invasion of the South Pacific, 1767–1840* (New York: Harper & Row, 1966). Contrasting this literature, post-contact histories around the globe have found indigenous agency and creative responses to disruptions. See, for example, David Igler, *The Great Ocean: Pacific Worlds from Captain Cook to the Gold Rush* (Oxford: Oxford University Press, 2013); Hackel, *Children*; Richard White, *The Middle Ground: Indians, Empires, and Republics in the Great Lakes Region, 1650–1815* (Cambridge: Cambridge University Press, 1991).

argued that indigenous societies underwent irreversible decline and "culture-loss."[24] The viceregal records that I have examined – petitions, testimonies, and protests – make it apparent that indigenous peoples navigated a channel between structure and agency. They sought to reconcile the impact of tragedy with their desire to overcome it. Neither hapless victims nor captains – or conquistadors – of their destinies, natives redirected the mission to the service of their own recovery. In our own twenty-first century, which augurs to be tumultuous, it behooves us to listen with humility to their stories of upheaval and rebuilding.

THE TROPICS OF CONVERSION

The history of the mission in Mexico is not only relevant to Mesoamerica, for the vast edifice that Mesoamerican communities built through their staggering efforts also influenced global history. The overseas connections of the enterprise, especially its influences on subsequent frontiers, have largely been overlooked. Contemporaries, however, made note of the mission's connections to other parts of the globe. Missionaries, royal officials, and even indigenous chroniclers like Domingo Chimalpahin, viewed the mission enterprise as essential to a broader global process of Christian expansion.[25] From its very inception, the Mexican mission was globally connected – not solely to other missions in the New World or to Iberia, but also across the Pacific to later Spanish missions in the Philippines and East Asia. The mission thus spanned the histories of the

---

[24] Lockhart, *Nahuas*; Burkhart, *Slippery Earth*; Susan Schroeder, "The Genre of Conquest Studies," in *Indian Conquistadors: Indigenous Allies in the Conquest of Mesoamerica*, eds. Laura E. Matthew and Michel R. Oudjik (Norman: University of Oklahoma Press, 2007), 5–27; On cultural and social decline, see: Serge Gruzinski, *The Conquest of Mexico: The Incorporation of Indian Societies into the Western World, 16th–18th Centuries*, trans. and ed. Eileen Corrigan (London: Polity Press, 1993); Margarita Menegus, "El gobierno de los indios en la Nueva España, siglo XVI. Señores o Cabildo." *Revista de Indias*, vol. 59, no. 217 (1999), 599–617; Charles Gibson, *The Aztecs under Spanish Rule: A History of the Indians in the Valley of Mexico* (Stanford: Stanford University Press, 1964).

[25] See Domingo Chimalpáhin, *Annals of His Time: Don Domingo de San Anton Muñón Chimalpahin Quauhtlehuanitzin*, trans. and eds. James Lockhart, Susan Schroeder and Doris Namala (Stanford: Stanford University Press, 2006); Antonio de Remesal, *Historia de la prouincia de S. Vicente de Chyapa y Guatemala* (Madrid, 1629), 680–90; Gerónimo de Mendieta, *Historia eclesiástica indiana*, ed. Joaquín García Icazbalceta (Mexico City, 2002), vol. II, 281; Bernardino de Sahagún, *Florentine Codex: General History of the Things of New Spain*, trans. and eds. Charles E. Dibble and Arthur J. O. Anderson (Salt Lake City: University of Utah Press, 1982).

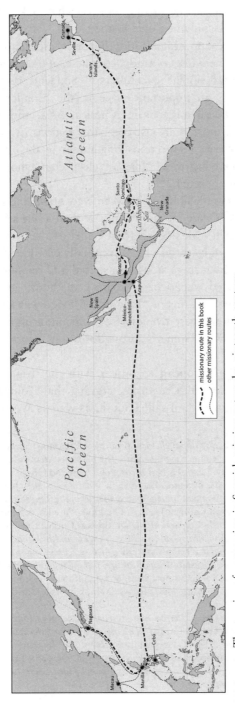

MAP O.2. The tropics of conversion in Spanish mission networks, sixteenth century. Drawn by Peter Anthamatten and Cody J. Peterson.

Atlantic, Mesoamerican, and Pacific worlds. This makes the Mexican mission an ideal case study in global history.

Global history presupposes that local histories, especially at the crossroads of expanding networks of trade, conquest, and evangelization, are comparable to other similar encounters.[26] Sixteenth-century Mexico therefore commands an important place in the broader comparative history of early modern missions in America, Asia, and Africa.[27] Yet global history does more than just compares regions; it also privileges synchronicity, recovering connections long hidden by the blinkers of Area Studies and national histories, "like an electrician who repairs what historians have disconnected."[28]

This book recovers the linkages between New Spain and the sixteenth-century world, which were far more complex than a line simply connecting Mexico with Seville. Mexico lay at the center of a network of missions that, carried westward by trade winds, eventually extended from Spain to the Philippines. At each stage along this spatial and temporal trajectory, missions accumulated experiences, refined methods, and sharpened anthropological classifications of "Indians." Mexico was key to the progress of missions along these tropics of conversion, a phrase that draws inspiration from Wey Gómez's groundbreaking work on colonial exploration.[29]

Gómez traces the European encounter with the tropics in the late-fifteenth and early sixteenth centuries, arguing that Columbus and the Europeans who followed him sailed South, as well as West, in search of

---

[26] Sebastian Conrad, *What is Global History?* (Princeton: Princeton University Press, 2016); Ryan Dominic Crewe, "Connecting the Indies: The Hispano-Asian Pacific World in Early Modern Global History." *Estudos Históricos*, vol. 20, no. 60 (2017), 17–34.

[27] Hackel, *Children*; Deeds, *Defiance*; Radding, *Wandering Peoples*; Juliana Barr, *Peace Came in the Form of a Woman: Indians and Spaniards in the Texas Borderlands* (Chapel Hill: University of North Carolina Press, 2007); Oona Paredes, *A Mountain of Difference: The Lumad in Early Colonial Mindanao* (Ithaca: Cornell University Press, 2013); Ines G. Županov, *Disputed Mission: Jesuit Experiments and Brahmanical Knowledge in Seventeenth-Century India* (Oxford: Oxford University Press, 1999); Cécile Fromont, *The Art of Conversion: Christian Visual Culture in the Kingdom of the Kongo* (Chapel Hill, NC: University of North Carolina Press, 2014); Anthony Reid, *Southeast Asia in the Age of Commerce, 1450–1680, vol. II* (New Haven, CN: Yale University Press, 1993), 132–200.

[28] Serge Gruzinski, *Las cuatro partes del mundo: Historia de una mundialización* (Mexico City: Fondo de Cultura Económica, 2010), 44. See also Sanjay Subrahmanyam, "Holding the World in Balance: The Connected histories of the Iberian Overseas Empires, 1500–1600." *American Historical Review*, vol. 112, no. 5 (2007), 1359–85.

[29] Wey Gómez, *The Tropics of Empire: Why Columbus Sailed South to the Indies* (Cambridge, MA: MIT Press, 2008).

bounty in a region that classical geography had written off as uninhabitable and sterile. While European explorers praised the Torrid Zone as "unexpectedly vast and productive," they still retained views rooted in an older geography that deemed inhabitants uncivilized.[30] The tropics were thus "teeming" but "barbarous," an "incubator of life" that nonetheless required European discipline, steeled in temperate climes to become profitable.[31] Spaniards promoted the tropics as a vast region of potential wealth that nonetheless lay at "Europe's moral periphery."[32]

Likewise, early modern Catholic missionaries imagined the tropics of conversion as a region whose spiritual wealth lay in millions of potential converts. Most missionaries saw native peoples in the tropics in the same contradictory terms as their secular counterparts: as a multitude to be brought to the faith, on the one hand, and as a horde that could be led all too easily into sin.[33] They could be saved, but they also would need the missionaries' tutelage and protection for an indefinite period.[34]

Rapidly-developing crises quickly frustrated the missionaries' plans, for disease and colonial exploitation ruined missions in the Canaries and the Caribbean. But the trade winds – in the belt between the 15th and the 25th parallel – that pushed Spaniards ever westward soon brought them to Mexico. Here the Spaniards encountered social structures, political and religious institutions, cities, and economies that they recognized as sophisticated. Mexico epitomized the spiritual promise of the tropics. The Franciscan missionary Fray Jerónimo de Mendieta declared that the capabilities of Mexican natives were such that with proper Christian guidance and an end to exploitation they could well turn Mexico into "the most prosperous republic in the world...where Christian life would flourish most abundantly."[35] In the missionaries' anthropological schema, the highland societies of Mexico lay between the hamlets of the

---

[30] ibid., 48–53, 434.   [31] ibid., 434, 53.   [32] ibid., 53.

[33] Anthony Pagden, *The Fall of Natural Man: The American Indian and the Origins of Comparative Ethnology* (Cambridge: Cambridge University Press, 1982), 20–4. See: Mendieta, *Historia ecclesiástica indiana*, vol. I, 110–7; Francisco de Burgoa, *Geográfica descripción*, 2 vols. (Mexico City: Talleres Gráficos de la Nación, 1934), vol. I, 19–24; Mathias de Escobar, *Americana Thebaida: vitus patrum de los religiosos hermitaños de nuestro padre San Agustín, de la Provincia de San Nicolás Tolentino de Michoacán*, ed. Nicolás P. Navarrete (Morelia: Universidad Michoacana de San Nicolás de Hidalgo, 2008), 30–61.

[34] Acosta, *Natural and Moral History*, 256–8; Mendieta, *Historia eclesiástica indiana*, vol. I, 118–21.

[35] Mendieta to Archbishop of Mexico (1589), in *Códice Franciscano*, ed. Joaquín García Icazbalceta (Mexico City, 1892), 81–2.

Circum-Caribbean and the empires of East Asia, which were considered the closest non-Christian societies to Europe.[36] But the same Mexican natives who built the largest missions in the Atlantic world also needed the guidance of missionaries in order to advance. Mendieta envisioned New Spain not as a kingdom or colony, but as one vast classroom wherein natives would be eternal pupils under the direction of the friars.[37] The very structures that indigenous peoples raised in order to preserve their communities only empowered missionaries to intervene further in their lives.

The spiritual harvests that missionaries reaped in Mexico, it turns out, were not their only ambition. Trade winds tempted the more adventurous of the conquistadors and missionaries to entertain the old dream of reaching the Orient. After 1565, the course of empire brought them from Mexico to the Philippines, at the very doorstep to China and Japan.[38] Though Mexico was the "most populated and well-appointed part of these West Indies," Fray Bernardino de Sahagún declared, it was "but a stepping-stone on the way to China...where there are people of great capabilities, public order (*policía*), and wisdom."[39] For Spanish missionaries – even for Sahagún, whose ethnographic work with native students helped preserve knowledge of pre-conquest Mesoamerica – Mexico was a dress rehearsal for a bigger stage. Midway between the benighted missions of the Atlantic basin and the expected spiritual bonanzas of Asia, Mexico was the crucible for a mission system that openly relied on raw temporal power, and it provided a useful practice in how to Christianize a vast civilization. That Chinese mandarins and Japanese shoguns proved such assumptions to be dead wrong only illustrates the sudden reverses of global history.

The Mexican mission occupied a central position in the tropics of conversion that stretched from the Canaries to the Philippines. Ensconced in Mesoamerican society, it had roots in late-medieval Iberia and the early

---

[36] Acosta, *Natural and Moral History*, 163–4.   [37] Icazbalceta, *Códice Franciscano*, 82.

[38] Already in the 1530s leaders in the Franciscan and Dominican Orders sought to abandon New Spain to pursue their dreams of reaching China: Mendieta, *Historia ecclesiástica indiana*, vol. II, 280–3; Ryan Dominic Crewe, "Pacific Purgatory: Spanish Dominicans, Chinese Sangleys, and the Entanglement of Mission and Commerce in Manila, 1580–1604." *Journal of Early Modern History*, vol. 19 (2015), 337–44; Acosta, *Natural and Moral History*, 108.

[39] Bernardino de Sahagún, *Historia general de las cosas de Nueva España*, eds. Alfredo López Austin and Josefina García Quintana (Madrid: Alianza Editorial, 1988), vol. II, 813.

Atlantic, it tied together the northern half of Spain's American empire, and it was a base for Pacific expansion. For all who regarded it, supporters as well as detractors, Mexico exemplified a mission model in which the spiritual end justified the temporal means.

A VISIBLE CHURCH

Saints and hypocrites alike intermingled in Augustine's "visible church," a community of professed but not necessarily devout Christians. By virtue of Spanish imperial policy, which justified the employment of temporal power in the service of propagating the Gospel, the mission enterprise emerged as a visible church that swept all into its ranks. In practice, the mission was as much a project of worldly governance as it was a spiritual program. Missionary veterans of the Mexico stated this succinctly at the Synod of Manila in 1582, as they applied New World experience to Luzón and the Visayas: "in order for the faith to gain entry among these peoples, it is necessary to put in place a new government."[40] Spanish authorities integrated Christianized native polities into their legal and moral universe as *pueblos de indios*, spaces where political, spatial, and spiritual transformation were to go hand-in-hand.[41] Christian temporal power – both of the Spanish Empire and of native polities under its sway – was an effective tool in excluding other religions and building a community in which the faith would eventually flourish. Political conquest would make Christianity enforceable in the temporal world, which would then set into place the *habitus* of Christian actions and beliefs. Spaniards pragmatically accepted that a sincere faith might develop only gradually in the wake of violence and invasion. As King Ferdinand remarked in 1501 of the newly converted Granadan Moors, the first conquest in the long campaign of Spanish evangelism: "if they do not become true Christians, then their sons or their grandchildren will."[42] This logic applied to Jews in fifteenth-century Seville, to natives in the seventeenth-century Philippines, or, as in our case here, to indigenous people in sixteenth-century Mexico. What mattered first was the *apparent* conversion of the non-Christian populace, which meant introducing monogamy, christening sacred spaces, and extirpating allegiances to

---

[40] Synod of Manila (1582), in ed. Valentín Marín y Morales, *Ensayo de una síntesis de los trabajos realizados por las corporaciones religiosas* (Manila, 1901), 199.

[41] Margarita Menegus, *Del señorío indígena a la república de indios: El caso de Toluca, 1500–1600* (Mexico City: Conaculta, 1994), 16.

[42] Miguel Ángel Ladero Quesada, *Los mudéjares de Castilla en tiempos de Isabel I* (Valladolid: Instituto Isabel la Católica de Historia Eclesiástica, 1969), 81.

other gods, spirits, or natural forces. Christianity was to be the sole religion: with its exclusivity enforced in the public domain, it would set the conditions for sincere sentiments, devotions and ultimately faith. Nearly all missionaries in this effort wholeheartedly embraced the idea that temporal power – of the Spanish Crown as well as of indigenous polities – existed in order to enforce this transformation.

The Mexican mission, then, was one in which doctrine was constantly overshadowed by political and social concerns. Its power derived from its capacity to join the native project of rebuilding community with the Spanish project of Christian *imperium*. This enterprise did not emerge, as some would explain it, by way of the haphazard misreadings, sometimes called "double mistaken identity," in which Spaniards and natives viewed each other solely from their own perspectives.[43] Instead, natives and Spaniards took stock of one another, established relationships, and collaborated on matters of shared interest in order to gain leverage against rivals in their own societies. They were aware of the double meaning – and dual political value – of the vast enterprise that they raised together. Spaniards understood that the mission consolidated their colonial regime by stabilizing indigenous governments. In this vein the first viceroy of Mexico candidly remarked that "just one foot-soldier of these friars is worth more than all the lances that the Castilians used to subjugate this land."[44] At the same time, indigenous polities used the mission to carve out a space for themselves in the Spanish Empire. So important was the mission Church to the survival of pueblos that, for centuries, communities would mark the building of their local church as the legal foundation of the pueblo itself. Even today the church edifice is the embodiment of the community.[45] The mission provided indigenous communities with a means of asserting their autonomy, but each stone that they set into its infrastructure also cemented a colonial order predicated on their own subordination.

---

[43] See Lockhart's theory of "Double Mistaken Identity," in *Nahuas*, 442–6.

[44] Joaquín García Icazbalceta, ed. *Códice Mendieta* (Mexico City, 1892), vol. II, 187–8.

[45] Stephanie Wood, *Transcending Conquest: Nahua Views of Spanish Colonial Mexico* (Norman, OK: University of Oklahoma Press, 2003); Robert S. Haskett, *Visions of Paradise: Primordial Titles and Mesoamerican History in Cuernavaca* (Norman: Oklahoma University Press, 2005); Paula López Caballero, ed. *Los títulos primordiales del centro de México* (Mexico City: Conaculta, 2003); Margarita Menegus, "Los títulos primordiales de los pueblos de indios," in *Dos décadas de investigación en la historia económica comparada en América*, ed. Margarita Mengus (Mexico City: El Colegio de México, 1999), 137–61.

Because it was able to align disparate and sometimes conflicting interests in both the indigenous and Spanish worlds, the mission dominated indigenous politics for as long as demographic and economic factors permitted. At its core, its wealth depended upon the vast numbers of natives that distinguished Mesoamerica from previous colonial experiences in the Atlantic world. Friars saw divine promise in what they called the "multitudes of Indians," whose conversion seemed to foretell the divine promise of a new Church untainted by the ills of Europe. For their part, native governments adapted the mission enterprise to their tribute economy and arrangements of governance, deploying millions of hands to lay stone and raise beams in the construction of a network of missions. The reputation of this enterprise as a vehicle of social reconstitution only increased with the misfortunes of native communities continually beset by losses and instability. Political intrigues, territorial rivalries, and unrelenting epidemics eventually strained the capacity of the mission to meet native demands. By then the sixteenth century mission enterprise had come close to ruling supreme over New Spain. Vast, powerful, and wealthy, but also controversial, contested, and fallible, the Mexican mission allowed for a rich exchange of ideas and beliefs. But in the end, it was more a city of man than a city of God.

PART I

CONVERSION

I

The Burning Temple

Religion and Conquest in Mesoamerica and the Iberian Atlantic, circa 1500

In 1535, an indigenous painter-scribe (*tlacuilo*) in the former Aztec capital of México-Tenochtitlán recorded the history of the Aztec Empire for the Spaniards who had defeated it (*Fig. 1.1*). The first viceroy, Don Antonio de Mendoza, had recently arrived, and in order to rule over New Spain more efficiently, he had requested a record of the conquests and tributes of the former empire. In the pictographic language of indigenous codices that he had likely learned in temple schools (*calmecac*), the tlacuilo listed Aztec conquests by year, from the foundation of the empire around 1428 until the arrival of the Spaniards in 1519. Page after page marks the subjugation of one *altepetl* (city-state, pl. *altepeme*) after another with the same glyph: a burning *teocalli* (temple), its thatch roof toppled, with grey volutes indicating smoke. Next to each burning teocalli is the place-glyph identifying the conquered polity: for example, in the bottom right corner of the image below, an eagle denotes Cuauhtitlán, or *place of the eagles*, an ancient city-state in the Valley of Mexico that had rebelled against the emperor.[1] The image lists the final conquests of Emperor Axayacatl, around 1481, a typical year of geostrategic challenges in which imperial armies were tied up in reconquering rebel city-states close to the capital while they sought to expand the northern frontiers ever further into the distant lands of the Huaxteca.[2]

[1] Elizabeth Hill Boone, *Stories in Red and Black: Pictorial Histories of the Aztecs and Mixtecs* (Austin: University of Texas Press, 2000), 33–5.
[2] Robert Hayward Barlow, "Conquistas de los antiguos mexicanos." *Journal de la Société des Américanistes*, vol. 36 (1947), 215–22.

FIGURE 1.1 List of towns conquered by Emperor Axayácatl.
Anon. Indigenous tlacuilos, c. 1535, Codex Mendoza. Oxford Bodleian Library, Ms. Arch.
Selden, A. 1, f. 10v. Photo courtesy of Bodleian Libraries.

The burning temple represented an altepetl's loss of autonomy in the
profoundest sense. The act "signified," David Carrasco writes, "that the
structure, symbols, gods, energy and essences of a community have been
destroyed."[3] More than just a symbol, the temple was an edifice raised by
the labor and contributions of all communities that formed part of the
city-state. It was thus a tangible marker of a community's legitimate
place among the city-states and confederations of Mesoamerica.
Atop its frustum – the stone platform with steep steps popularly called
"pyramids" – thatched chapels housed the patron gods, who embodied
the distinct history of the city-state and sacralized the territorial claims of
its local rulers. Conquering invaders would immediately set fire to this
symbol of autonomy and seize the local patron gods, as if to appropriate
the powers of those whom they had just vanquished.[4]

---

[3] David Carrasco, *City of Sacrifice: The Aztec Empire and the Role of Violence in Civiliza-
tion* (Boston: Beacon Press, 1999), 25; Fernando de Alva Ixtlilxóchitl, *Obras históricas*, ed.
Edmundo O'Gorman, 2 vols. (Mexico City: UNAM, 1977), vol. II, 103–4; Alonso de
Zorita, *Relación de los señores de la Nueva España*, ed. Germán Vázquez (Madrid:
Historia 16, 1992), 95.

[4] Frances F. Berdan, Patricia Rieff Anawalt, eds., *The Essential Codex Mendoza* (University
of California Press, 1997); Eloise Quiñones Keber, *Codex Telleriano-Remensis: Ritual,
Divination, and History in a Pictorial Aztec Manuscript* (Austin: University of Texas Press,
1995); Frances F. Berdan, *The Aztecs of Central Mexico: An Imperial Society* (Belmont,
CA: Thomson Wadsworth, 2005), 116; Richard F. Townsend, *The Aztecs* (London:
Thames and Hudson, 2009), 80–3.

Across Mesoamerica and the Iberian world in the fifteenth century, sacred structures – mosques, synagogues, animist godheads, and teocallis – went up in flames on frontiers of imperial expansion and marked a transfer of sovereignty. These acts and legacies of conquest, unconnected prior to the conquest of Mexico, converged there and shaped the development of the mission enterprise. That one should insist upon the importance of both Mesoamerican and Iberian legacies to understanding the mission in colonial Mexico is of obvious importance. But a third historical thread gets far less attention: the advancing, deadly wave of Spanish invasion, slave raiding, ecological crises, and demographic collapses that extended from the Canaries to the Caribbean, and then onward the American mainland. These early Atlantic encounters shaped Mexican missions as much as the politics of the Aztec Empire and late-medieval Iberia.

This chapter examines these three simultaneous histories of religion as a tool of conquest: the role of religion as an affirmation of Mesoamerican sovereignty, as an act of conquest in late-medieval Spain, and as a fragile legal sanctuary on the earliest Atlantic frontiers. Like a satellite hovering above the late-fifteenth and early-sixteenth century Atlantic world, it examines the ways in which these instances of religion and conquest came to influence the Mexican mission.

CLAIMING A CORNER OF THE EARTH

Templo Mayor (Great Temple), Tenochtitlán, 1487. High above his proud imperial capital, Aztec Emperor Ahuitzotl ascended the steep steps of the Great Temple of Tenochtitlán and led a celebration that would go down in memory for the unsurpassed scale of its pageantry and bloodshed. A year had passed since his coronation, and Ahuitzotl had a debt of victories to pay with the blood of his war captives. When Ahuitzotl had returned from his frontier conquests, he distributed these prisoners to the wards of the city, where, for a time, they were treated like gods. But their enjoyment was short-lived. On the occasion of the rededication of the Great Temple, whose expansion he had overseen, Ahuitzotl decided to sacrifice them all. The emperor sent invitations to friends and foes alike to witness the ceremony. The spectacle astonished his guests: over four days, we are told, thousands of captives made their way in orderly lines through the city and up the staircase of the Great Temple, where Ahuitzotl and his high priests plunged obsidian knives into their chests, ripped out their hearts, and rolled their corpses down the sides of the pyramid. The blood of sacrificial victims pooled and flowed over the steps, encrusting between its stones. After the sacrifice was complete, Ahuitzotl lavished his guests with gifts and sent them home, no doubt with a new sense of dread of the Mexica.[5]

The dedication of the Great Temple in 1487 exemplifies the overlap of religion and imperialism in Mesoamerica prior to the Spanish conquest. The Mesoamerican teocalli, or "god-house" in Náhuatl, represented an *axis mundi* that united the heavens with the earth. It was a recreation of Coatepec, the sacred mountain where their tribal god of war, Huitzilipochtli, was born.[6] Huitzilipochtli was honored at the top of the structure, along with Tlaloc, the god of rain. Together they indicated the two vital forces of the Aztec world, warfare and agriculture.[7] The Great Temple portrayed Aztecs as rulers in the "present moment," presiding over a world whose days were numbered, destined to be cut short by the cosmic cycle. But the present world could be prolonged, Aztecs claimed, through wars and sacrifices.[8] This immense sacred structure grew in tandem with the empire, feeding upon the ever-rising numbers of captives and tributes that flowed from the frontiers towards the institutions at the core of Tenochtitlán. The Great Temple was thus an expression of both worldly and spiritual power: it anchored an empire that saw itself, in the words of the Texcocan King Nezahualpilli the Elder, as "the root, navel, and heart of this entire apparatus of the world."[9] It embodied Aztec efforts to rule over a corner of the earth and over an epoch that dangled on the precipice of cataclysm.[10]

As the Great Temple grew with each generation, the structure show-cased how far the Mexica had come. Their beginnings were humble. They arrived in central Mexico sometime in the twelfth century as outsiders, one of several tribes that had abandoned the deserts of the north for the sedentary comforts of the altiplano city-states.[11] These nomads moved

[5] Diego Durán, *History of the Indians of New Spain*, trans. and ed. Doris Hayden (Norman: University of Oklahoma Press, 1994), 328–43; Nigel Davies, *The Aztecs* (Norman, OK: University of Oklahoma Press, 1980), 165–7.

[6] Carrasco, *City of Sacrifice*, 59–60; Eduardo Matos Moctezuma, *Tenochtitlán* (Mexico City: Fondo de Cultura Económica, 2010), 87–9.

[7] Matos Moctezuma, ibid., 90.

[8] Richard F. Townsend, *State and Cosmos in the Art of Tenochtitlán* (Washington, DC: Dumbarton Oaks Research Library and Collection, 1979), 56; Townsend, *The Aztecs*, 138–43.

[9] Matos Moctezuma, *Tenochtitlán*, 81.   [10] Carrasco, *City of Sacrifice*.

[11] I refer to the ethnic group that founded Tenochtitlán and its subsequent empire as the Mexica, but I use the term "Aztec" to denote the empire, its officials, and its bureaucracy

with their patron gods safely stored in sacred bundles under the leadership of rulers, many of whom would later be deified.[12] The Mexica took full advantage of the collapse of the Toltec Empire as central Mexico fragmented into dozens of warring city-states, entering the breech and stepping into Mesoamerican history. They first hired themselves out as mercenaries, but over time the hereditary leaders of kinship groups within the tribe intermarried with Toltec elites. This produced a noble class with a mixed nomadic and imperial heritage, and as the Mexica gained influence they developed this legacy into a claim to rule.[13] In 1325, they established their altepetl at Tenochtitlán, a low-lying island in Lake Texcoco, by erecting a temple to their patron god. According to Mexica myth, they settled there after seeing the divine sign that their priests had foretold centuries earlier: they found an eagle perched on a cactus, devouring a serpent. Over the following decades they fought innumerable wars as mercenaries and allies, and their rulers married into regional dynasties. Then, in 1428, they conquered Azcapotzalco, their former masters. This marked the foundation of the Aztec Empire.[14] The Mexica thus passed from the "hunger, poverty, and suffering" of migration to the indignity of "[having] to pay tribute to other provinces," to ruling over a "free and prosperous city…the queen of all cities, all of which pay tribute to her."[15]

Itzcoatl, the founding Aztec Emperor, consolidated his authority by setting fire to codices that recorded inconvenient precedents of Mexica commoners having a say in the affairs of the polity.[16] He replaced these

since the empire incorporated a vast array of ethnic groups. "Aztec" derives from "Aztlán," the mythical homeland of the tribe. "Mexica" derives from "Mezitin" or "Meçitl," a priest who initiated the migration. Durán, *History*, 3–30; Rudolph van Zantwijk, *The Aztec Arrangement: The Social History of Pre-Spanish Mexico* (Norman, TX: University of Oklahoma Press, 1985), 38–43; Sahagún, *Florentine Codex*, vol. XI, 189–91.

[12] Guilhem Olivier, "Les paquets sacrés ou la mémoire cachée des indiens du Mexique central (XV–XVI siècles)." *Journal de la Société des Américanistes*, vol. 81 (1995), 105–41; Alfredo López Austin, *Hombre-dios: Religión y política en el mundo náhuatl* (Mexico City: UNAM, 1998), 106–60; Geoffrey Conrad and Arthur A. Demarest, *Religion and Empire: The Dynamics of Aztec and Inca Expansionism* (Cambridge: Cambridge University Press, 1998), 26–8.

[13] Townsend, *State and Cosmos*, 10–1; Conrad and Demarest, *Religion and Empire*, 24–7.

[14] Davies, *Aztecs*, 35–9; Van Zantwijk, *Aztec Arrangement*, 57–82; Conrad and Demarest, *Religion and Empire*, 59–61.

[15] This tale of the Mexicas' transformation appears in a chapter of Diego Durán's chronicle that narrates an expedition to the northern deserts sent by Moctezuma to find Aztlán in the fifteenth century. Durán, *History*, 218. See also Townsend, *State and Cosmos*, 12, 22.

[16] Sahagún, *Florentine Codex*, bk. 10, ch. 29.

local histories with an imperial narrative that paralleled his tribe's ascent to power with the tale of their tribal god's ascent to solar deification. Around Huitzilipochtli, and the Great Temple dedicated to him, the Aztec regime built a state religion that served expansion by conquest.[17] The central tenet of this imperial cult "held that the Mexica must relentlessly take captives in warfare and sacrifice them ... [in order to] strengthen the sun and stave off its inevitable destruction by the forces of darkness."[18] By anointing themselves the foremost "mortal collaborators" with the gods, the Mexica turned practices long extant in Mesoamerican agricultural rites into a tool of subjugation.[19]

Aztec imperialism might have been as sharp-edged as the obsidian blades that cut into its war captives, but in administrative terms it was complex web of overlapping sovereignties. In many respects the Aztec Empire was an extended family, for the ruling dynasties of the city-states that were incorporated into it, whether by force or through alliances, intermarried with the Mexica elite.[20] The empire was a vast elite network that made the gap between nobles and commoners ever starker.[21] Local ruling elites had wide berth to rule over their jurisdictions according to their customs on condition that they served in imperial wars, paid tributes regularly, delivered war captives, and heeded royal invitations.[22] Set to consume these offerings of subject populations, the empire became overextended. Its rulers had to unceasingly pursue conquest without paying sufficient attention to consolidating their power in order to maintain this imperial economy of tributes and sacrifices.[23]

If we look beyond the imperial elite and their capital, the Aztec Empire presented a fragmented political landscape of several hundred semi-autonomous altepetls. Like the Mexica altepetl of Tenochtitlán, each

---

[17] Conrad and Demarest, *Religion and Empire*, 32–4, 38; Townsend, *State and Cosmos*, 54.

[18] Conrad and Demarest, ibid., 38.

[19] Townsend, *State and Cosmos*, 53–4; Conrad and Demarest, *Religion and Empire*, 48.

[20] Frances F. Berdan and Michael E. Smith, "Imperial Strategies and Core-Periphery Relations," in *Aztec Imperial Strategies*, eds. Frances F. Berdan, Richard E. Blanton, et al. (Washington, DC: Dumbarton Oaks, 1996), 211.

[21] Michael E. Smith, "The Role of Social Stratification in the Aztec Empire: A View from the Provinces." *American Anthropologist*, vol. 88 (1986), 70–91; Michael E. Smith, *Aztec City-State Capitals* (Gainesville: University of Florida Press, 2008), 11–2; Ross Hassig, *Aztec Warfare: Imperial Expansion and Political Control* (Norman, OK: University of Oklahoma Press, 1988), 201–3.

[22] Davies, *Aztecs*, 110–2; Michael E. Smith, *The Aztecs* (Malden, MA: Wiley-Blackwell, 2012), 153–65.

[23] Conrad and Demarest, *Religion and Empire*, 53.

altepetl also boasted its own hereditary rulers (*tlatoque*, sing. *tlatoani*), a class of nobles (*pipiltin*, sing. *pilli*), palace (*tecpan*), market (*tianquiztli*), and temple (*teocalli*).[24] Each altepetl told its own story of exceptionalism, but for all their diversity they drew upon a common source of Mesoamerican origin histories and foundational narratives.[25] Each altepetl also boasted its own patron gods, carefully borne in sacred bundles during their migrations from the deserts: Mexica carried turquoise (*chalchihuite*) and kindling in memory of their patron god's gift of fire, while the Texcocans bore Tezcatlipoca's obsidian mirror, which aided in foretelling the future.[26] In the Mixtec city-state (*ñuu*) of Tlaxiaco in Oaxaca, a collection of figures of green gemstone were held in such reverence that a Dominican friar in the sixteenth century referred to them as the *corazón del pueblo* – "the heart of the town," or put another way, "the heart of the people."[27]

The history of many central Mexican altepeme spoke of migration, intermarriage with local inhabitants, and the founding of their permanent settlement, a seminal event that marked their exodus from nomadism to sedentary life. They built temples for their patron gods, marking a new permanent home for the tribe and its divine protectors.[28] But each altepetl was also a sacred kingdom. In Náhuatl, altepetl means "water-mountain," a term more far-reaching than *urbs* (the fabric of the city) or even *civitas* (the society dwelling within it). The altepetl was a *rinconada*, a corner of the earth where the mountain – which was sacred because it drew rain from the heavens – met the alluvial plain, the place of

[24] Smith, *Aztecs*, 153–4; Lockhart, *Nahuas*, 14–5; Susan Schroeder, *Chimalpahin and the Kingdom of Chalco* (Tucson: University of Arizona Press, 1991), 119–53.

[25] López Austin, *Hombre-dios*, 52.

[26] López Austin, ibid., 58–9; Townsend, *State and Cosmos*, 34.

[27] Burgoa, *Geográfica descripción*, vol. I, 332–3.

[28] Schroeder, *Chimalpahin*, 121; Smith, *Aztec City-State Capitals*, 74–83; Pablo Escalante Gonzalbo, "El patrocinio del arte indocristiano en el siglo XVI. La iniciativa de las autoridades indígenas en Tlaxcala y Cuauhtinchan," in *Patrocinio, colección, y circulación de las artes*, ed. Gustavo Curiel (Mexico City: UNAM, 1997), 218–9; David Carrasco and Scott Sessions, ed. *Cave, City, and Eagle's Nest: An Interpretive Journey through the Mapa de Cuauhtinchan no. 2* (Albuquerque: University of New Mexico Press, 2007). On sacred bundles, see: Olivier, "Les paquets"; Werner Stenzel, "The sacred bundles in Mesoamerican religion," *Thirty-eighth International Congress of Americanists*, vol. 2 (1968), 347–52. Despite significant cultural variations, in general terms this political structure also characterized local native polities in other sedentary societies in Central Mexico such as the Mixtecan *ñuu* of Oaxaca and the Purhépecha *ireta* in the Kingdom of Michoacán. On the Mixteca, see Terraciano, *Mixtecs*, 347–8; for Michoacán under the Tarascan Empire, see Rodrigo Martínez Baracs, *Convivencia y utopía: El gobierno indio de la "ciudad de Mechuacan"* (Mexico City: Fondo de Cultura Económica, 2005), 56.

abundance, agriculture, and settlement. At the core of the altepetl, the teocalli marked sovereign claims over surrounding lands.[29] Its solidity represented a struggle against impermanence, for the inhabitants were attached to their land not solely because their roots extended back to time immemorial, but also because their collective memory recalled the pains of migration, hunger, and poverty. They were determined not to return to those periods of want and wandering. The temple, and later the community church, was an expression of this will.

In its internal composition, each altepetl consisted of wards called *calpoltin* (sing. *calpolli*). In general, calpoltin were made of "groups of families that lived near one another, were subject to a local lord, controlled a block of land, and often shared a common occupation."[30] In some areas they were formed by ethnic minorities within an altepetl.[31] This was the most basic social unit in central Mexican society, arguably the most vital site in the economic and political lives of commoners (*macehualtin*, sing. *macehual*). Membership in the calpolli gave them the right to cultivate a plot of land in usufruct in exchange for tributes and draft labor.[32] Each calpolli was thus like a miniature altepetl, boasting its own hereditary nobility, palace, and teocalli dedicated to its patron-god (*calpulteotl*).[33] In principle, all calpoltin had equal weight within their altepetl, but in practice the wealthier calpulli tended to dominate the others.[34] Prior to Aztec expansionism, commoners had carried greater influence in their calpoltin, electing their rulers and extracting concessions for their labor and tribute. Class differences

---

[29] María Elena Bernal García and Ángel Julián García Zambrano, "El altepetl colonial y sus antecedents prehispánicos: contexto teórico-historiográfico," in *Territorialidad y paisaje en el altepetl del siglo XVI*, eds. Federico Fernández Christlieb and Ángel Julián García Zambrano (Mexico City: Fondo de Cultura Económica, 2006), 46–8, 99–101; Van Zantwijk, *Aztec Arrangement*, 200–1.

[30] Smith, *The Aztecs*, 135; Matos Moctezuma, *Tenochtitlán*, 77.

[31] Lockhart, *Nahuas*; Dana Leibsohn, *Script and Glyph: Pre-Hispanic History, Colonial Bookmaking, and the Historia Tolteca-Chichimeca* (Washington, DC: Dumbarton Oaks Research Library and Collection, 2009), 19–23.

[32] Smith, *The Aztecs*, 135–6; Rebecca Horn, *Postconquest Coyoacan: Nahua-Spanish Relations in Central Mexico, 1519–1650* (Stanford: Stanford University Press, 1997), 20–2.

[33] Matos Moctezuma, *Tenochtitlán*, 77; Smith, *Aztec City-State Capitals*, 90; Conrad and Demarest, *Religion and Empire*, 23; López Austin, *Hombre-dios*, 47–52.

[34] Lockhart, *Nahuas*; Conrad and Demarest, *Religion and Empire*, 24; Pedro Carrasco, "Social Organization of Ancient Mexico," in eds. R. Wauchope et al., *Handbook of Middle American Indians*, vol. 10, 366.

rigidified, however, as Aztec imperialism widened the gap between nobles and commoners.[35] Ultimately, the authority of an altepetl – and by extension, of the empire – consisted in the ability of local and imperial elites to mobilize calpoltin in the tasks of farming, taxpaying, and soldiering.[36]

Like a matryoshka doll, each unit in Mesoamerican politics shared the same fundamental characteristics. Each calpolli and altepetl was anchored by a teocalli, which represented the history of the local group. Long after Spaniards physically demolished the teocalli, they would still have to reckon with its afterlife – with the ways in which these sacred structures defined relations, identities, and territorial claims in hundreds of calpoltin and altepeme. Within each unit, tribute payments and participation in religious rites confirmed political authority. Local rulers, in turn, distributed tributes to reward their subjects and pay respect to their overlords. And in order to bring the rains down from the sacred mountain to irrigate their crops, priests made offerings of copal, sage, and blood. Native students of fray Bernardino de Sahagún eloquently explained this religious system of serving gods and life-forces:

> It was the doctrine of the elders
> that there is life because of the gods;
> with their sacrifice, they gave us life.
>
> It was their doctrine
> that the gods provide our subsistence,
> all that we eat and drink,
> that which maintains life: maize, beans,
> amaranth, sage.
>
> To them do we pray
> for water, for rain
> which nourish things on earth.[37]

The scale of the sacrifice to keep the world in balance only grew from one level to the next, from humble calpoltin to proud altepeme to the all-consuming imperial capital.

---

[35] Conrad and Demarest, *Religion and Empire*, 36–8; Elizabeth M. Brumfiel, "Aztec State Making: Ecology, Structure, and the Origin of the State." *American Anthropologist*, vol. 85 (1983), 269–71.

[36] Smith, *Aztec City-State Capitals*, 91; Escalante Gonzalbo, "El patrocinio," 217; Berdan and Smith, "Imperial Strategies," 215–17.

[37] Miguel León Portilla, *Aztec Thought and Culture*, trans. ed. J. E. Davis (Norman, OK: University of Oklahoma Press, 1963), 158–66.

Aztec imperialism derived its power from the life forces of its subject populations. Tribute payments in commodities fed the residents of the growing capital, while payments in luxury goods – feathers, gold lip plugs, bracelets, jade stones, and ocelot skin garments – adorned temples, priests, and warriors. These precious goods also provided Mexica rulers with a currency of power, since they redistributed these goods as rewards and diplomatic gifts.[38] Altepeme also demonstrated their subjugation to the empire by channeling the labor of their commoners to construction projects like the vast hydraulic programs that desalinated Lake Texcoco and reclaimed new lands for cultivation.[39] Most significant, however, was the labor that subject altepeme provided for construction in the imperial capital. Building temples served "as a measure of political fealty" as much as it was a display of "piety."[40] When Emperor Moctezuma I erected his temple to Huitzilipochtli, he called upon surrounding altepeme to provide materials and labor: Texcoco built the front, Tacuba the back, Otomí communities provided sand, and lowland communities brought lime.[41] To refuse such demands effectively amounted to a declaration of independence that invited certain war, as befell Chalco after it rejected one such invitation from Moctezuma.[42]

Aztec conquests not only consumed the things of this world; they also absorbed the sacred forces of conquered and subject peoples. The toppling of temples in the heat of war may have marked conquest, but this violence was not necessarily iconoclastic. On the contrary: Aztec conquerors tended to appropriate foreign gods and thereby absorb their forces. They seized sacred relics and brought them to Tenochtitlán, where the Mexica placed them in the *coateocalli*, a pantheon where "all the gods could be adored."[43] On some occasions Aztec conquerors even captured local priesthoods in conquered areas and took them to Tenochtitlán to serve in the *coateocalli*. After the Aztecs conquered the Toluca Valley in

---

[38] Berdan, *Aztecs of Central Mexico*, 41–7.

[39] Brumfiel, "Aztec State-Making," 275; Berdan, *Aztecs of Central Mexico*, 42; Hodge, "Political Organization of the Central Provinces," in ed. Berdan, Blanton et al., *Aztec Imperial Strategies*," 26.

[40] Hassig, *Aztec Warfare*, 159; Berdan, *Aztecs of Central Mexico*, 113.   [41] Hodge, ibid.

[42] Hassig, ibid.; See also Durán, *History*, 105.

[43] Hassig, *Aztec Warfare*, 105. In many cases local populations hid their sacred bundles to avoid seizure of their gods, as occurred after the Spanish conquest. See Patricia Lopes Don, *Bonfires of Culture: Franciscans, Indigenous Leaders, and Inquisition in Early Mexico, 1524–1540* (Norman: University of Oklahoma Press, 2010), 111–45. Durán, *History*, 431.

the 1490s, the conquerors erected a temple in Tenochtitlán dedicated to the god of the defeated Matlatzincas, where he "received sacrifices."[44] Thus, while Spanish conquerors and missionaries had the goal of annihilating all deities and forms of worship other than their own, the Mexica – and Mesoamericans in general – were accustomed to incorporate foreign gods into their religion.[45] Fray Toribio de Benevente Motolinía, one of the first Franciscan missionaries in Mexico, despaired of this difference when he found images of the Virgin Mary placed next to idols during his first years in Mexico: "Since they had a hundred gods before, now they wanted a hundred-and-one."[46]

The tale of the birth of the Mexicas' patron god Huitzilipochtli encapsulates Aztec politics. Atop the sacred mountain of Coatepec, the earth goddess Coatlicue found herself under attack by her children at the moment she was going into labor. Vowing revenge inside the womb, Huitzilipochtli cut himself out of his mother and immediately donned battle dress. He swept down on his sister Coyolxauhqui, who had incited his siblings to rebel, chopped her to pieces, and tossed her down from the sacred mountain. He then stripped his other siblings of their ornaments, seized their holy relics, and massacred them all. Huitzilipochtli thus "transformed their obliteration into his own power."[47] In similar fashion, precious objects from the far corners of the Aztec empire were arrayed throughout the Great Temple so that the Mexica who served the gods could increase their sacred and temporal powers.[48] So sang Huitzilipochtli:

> When I came forth, when I was sent here,
> I was given arrows and a shield,
> For battle is my work.
> And with my belly, with my head,
> I shall confront cities everywhere.
> I shall join battle with them,
> I shall provide the gods with drink,
> I shall provide the gods with food!
> Here I shall bring together the diverse peoples,

---

[44] Emily Umberger, "Art and Imperial Strategy in Tenochtitlán," in ed. Berdan et al., *Aztec Imperial Strategies*, 93; Conrad and Demarast, *Religion and Empire*, 44–8; Townsend, *State and Cosmos*, 42–3; Van Zantwijk, *Aztec Arrangement*, 112; Smith, *Aztec City-State Capitals*, 203.

[45] Townsend, *State and Cosmos*, 36.

[46] Toribio de Benevente Motolinía, *Historia de los indios de la Nueva España*, ed. Edmundo O'Gorman (Mexico City: Porrúa, 2001), 29.

[47] Carrasco, *City of Sacrifice*, 63.   [48] Carrasco, ibid., 58–63.

And not in vain, for I shall conquer them,
That I may see the house of jade, the house of gold,
The house of quetzal feathers. . .[49]

ALL THE MOSQUES ARE NOW CHURCHES

Parish Church of Santa Fé de Granada, December 20, 1499. In the late afternoon, around the hour of the winter sunset, a Muslim woman named Fatima slowly inched forward in line toward the altar of the church. There, one by one, Granadan Muslims renounced their religion and were inducted into the Christian faith by the most powerful churchman in Spain, Cardinal Fray Francisco Jiménez de Cisneros, the Archbishop of Toledo. It was an improvised affair. Old Christian godparents took turns to sponsor the masses of converts, and scribes hastily recorded the head of each household's Muslim and new Christian names, their dependents, domicile, and trade. Like many of the other women in line that day, Fatima was listed in the baptismal record as the head of a household, perhaps because she had been widowed during Granada's war against the Spaniards that had concluded with the final defeat of this last Muslim kingdom on Iberian soil in 1492. She joined a diverse array of Granadan society. Granadan royalty, African slaves, tradesmen, and farmers all waited to receive a baptism that, by all appearances, none desired.[50]

For seven years, Castilian conquerors and local Muslim *alguaciles* (*al-wazir*, community leaders) had been promising that defeat would not lead to the heartbreaking scene that Fatima now beheld: a panicked rush to the baptismal font.[51] Over the previous weeks the pressures to convert had been mounting. Cardinal Cisneros had arrived in the city with a cadre of militant Franciscans under the pretext of investigating *elches*, Christian renegades who had been living as Muslims for decades.[52] The Franciscans

---

[49] Timothy J. Knab, ed. *A Scattering of Jades: Stories, Poems, and Prayers of the Aztecs*, trans. Thelma D. Sullivan (Tucson, AZ: University of Arizona Press, 1994), 87.

[50] Cisneros papers, AHN Universidades, leg. 720, ff. 48r–240v and 297r–340v. Over eight thousand names are listed over a three-month period from November 1499 to February 1500. This description of the baptism of Dec. 20 1499 is drawn from ff. 68r–72v. Ladero Quesada points out the large number of women listed as heads of households – scars of the devastating war that only concluded nine years before. See "Nóminas de conversos granadinos (1499–1500)," in *Estudios sobre Málaga y el Reino de Granada en el V centenario de la Conquista* (Málaga, 1987), 296–303.

[51] Miguel Ángel Ladero Quesada, *Granada después de la conquista: repobladores y mudéjares* (Granada: Diputación Provincial de Granada, 1988).

[52] Investigation into *elches* (1499), AHN Universidades, leg. 720, f. 282r.

quickly went beyond their original task and started to preach in Muslim quarters. Ecclesiastical authorities arrested local Muslim leaders who protested, which provoked rioting throughout the city.[53] Spanish Christians declared the street violence a rebellion, and soon Granadan Muslims found themselves facing the choice of conversion or expulsion. Whatever duress Fatima confronted that tense December was enough to send her to the baptismal font on the fourth day of mass conversions that would continue for another three months. She joined a hundred and forty others in line. When the Cardinal or one of his attendants sprinkled holy water over her at the altar, Fatima became Catalina. Afterwards she stepped back out into a city that, like her, was being converted through force and fear to Christianity.[54]

If Ahuitzotl's line of war captives fed and enlarged his empire, Cisneros' line of sorrowful converts was a step towards reducing the world to "one faith and one baptism."[55] The mass conversion of Granadan Muslims of 1499–1500, and the subsequent expulsion of those who refused to convert, was a watershed in Castilian Christian efforts to end the multi-religious coexistence, known as *convivencia*, that had shaped medieval Iberia for hundreds of years. This was a plural, interdependent, but also antagonistic coexistence of Muslims, Jews, and Christians.[56] Contrary to the optimistic views of some, convivencia was born more of necessity than of cosmopolitanism. Both Muslim and Christian conquerors were willing to set aside their desires to convert the rival faiths in exchange for payments of tribute from them. In 1086 the Almoravid conqueror Yusuf Ibn Tasufin made such an offer when he gave defeated Christians and Jews the option of either converting to Islam or paying the *jizya*, a tax guaranteeing protection to monotheists, or "people of the book."[57] When Christian kings conquered

---

[53] Luís del Mármol Carvajal, *Rebelión y castigo de los moriscos* (Málaga: Editorial Arguval, 1991), 61; Ladero Quesada, "Nóminas," 228, 255; Juan Vallejo, *memorial*, AHN Universidades, leg. 716, f. 9r.

[54] AHN Universidades, leg. 720, f. 71v.

[55] Jesús Suberbiola Martínez, *El Real Patronato de Granada: El Arzobispo Talavera, la Iglesia, y el estado moderno* (Granada: Caja General de Ahorros y Monte de Piedad de Granada, 1985), 189.

[56] David Nirenberg, *Communities of Violence: Persecution of Minorities in the Middle Ages* (Princeton: Princeton University Press, 1996); Charles J. Halperin, "The Ideology of Silence: Prejudice and Pragmatism on the Medieval Religious Frontier." *Comparative Studies in Society and History*, vol. 26, no. 3 (July 1984), 443–9. For a foundational – if rose tinted – examination of *convivencia*, see Américo Castro, *La realidad histórica de España* (Mexico City: Porrúa, 1987).

[57] Emilio García Gómez, "Novedades sobre la batalla llamada de Al-Zallaqa (1086), una versión oficial de la batalla." *Al Andalus*, vol. 15 (1950), 127–33.

Muslim territories, they followed Muslim precedents by levying similar taxes on Muslims and Jews.[58] Doing so was the path of least resistance, but it flew in the face of Christian hope for the triumph of the faith over infidels.

Convivencia unraveled over the course of the fifteenth century amid rising social tensions. In Castilian cities, Christian populations launched pogroms against religious minorities. On the streets, in synagogues, and in mosques, convivencia was preached, legislated, beaten, and burned out of existence. In 1476 and 1480, representatives at the Castilian parliament abolished the last remaining legal protections for Jews and Muslims that dated to the thirteenth century.[59] Shortly thereafter civil and ecclesiastical authorities created the Inquisition to police Christian orthodoxy and guard its boundaries against the influences of Islam and Judaism. The end of convivencia reflected a desire, among nobles and commoners alike, to see Christianity triumph at the cost of its competitors. It was a notion of religious exclusivism that would soon make its way across two oceans.

Although the Catholic Kings conquered Granada in the same year that they expelled all Jews who refused to convert to Christianity, their initial policies towards native Muslims in the former Nasrid kingdom reprised convivencia. Set high in the sierras of Eastern Andalucía, the kingdom was a vast Muslim land that was at once foreign and familiar. For the moment prudence outweighed evangelism. In the pacts of surrender signed in 1492, the Crown guaranteed Muslim rights to their own religion and law on condition that they paid a head-tax. The capitulations abolished the native Nasrid monarchy, but they maintained local power structures in the *aljamas,* parish-sized districts that oversaw the administration of justice and tax-collection.[60] During the 1490s this social order preserved the delicate peace between Christian colonists and Muslim

---

[58] The *Siete Partidas,* the thirteenth-century Castilian legal code, replicated Islamic laws concerning *dhimmis* (Jews and Christians, or "people of the Book"). According to the Pact of 'Umar, the integrity of *dhimmi* communities, including the rights to worship and autonomous regulation, were guaranteed on condition that the community paid a community tax (*jizya*). See Norman A. Stillman, *The Jews of Arab Lands: A History and Source Book* (Philadelphia: Jewish Publication Society of America, 1979), 158; Gregorio López, *Siete Partidas* (Madrid: Boletín Oficial del Estado, 1974 [1555]), 6:7:2.

[59] Manuel Colmeiro, ed. *Cortes de los antiguos reinos de León y de Castilla* (Madrid, 1883), vol. II, 49, 63.

[60] Ángel Galán Sánchez, "Poder cristiano y 'colaboracionismo' mudéjar en el Reino de Granada (1485–1501)," in *Estudios sobre Málaga y el Reino de Granada en el V Centenario de la Conquista,* ed. José Enrique López de Coca Castañer (Málaga: Diputación Provincial, 1987), 272, 285.

natives. As Queen Isabel assured *aljama* leaders, "our will is that no Moor will be forced to become Christian."[61] Shortly thereafter Cisneros arrived in Granada with his campaign of provocation.

After the mass baptisms of thousands like Fatima came the symbolic reordering of city life: Cisneros marked the end of the public presence of Islam in Granada with a bonfire of all the Korans that could be found.[62] As Muslim leaders had either converted or fled, clergymen consecrated the mosques. "All of the mosques are now churches," Cisneros proudly reported to his colleagues in Toledo, "and the same infidels who were our enemies are now witnesses."[63] Cisneros urged royal officials to make conversion to Christianity the primary condition of vassalage to the Crown; accordingly, in 1502, Fernando and Isabel declared that Christianity would be the sole legal religion in Castile. For Cisneros, the order in which peace was to be made was clear. When Castilian captains and missionaries entered negotiations with Muslim rebels in the Alpujarra Mountains, he stated: "Pray to the Lord that first their souls make peace with God, because without this there will be little advantage in ruling over their bodies."[64]

Making conversion a condition of surrender laid a precedent for subsequent Spanish conquests. Cisneros and his Franciscans knew of the injunctions of canon law that required clerics to instruct nonbelievers prior to conversion, but they justified mass baptism by invoking an emergency procedure, known as "urgent need," which allowed them to redeem infidels without prior indoctrination in times of war or duress. Instruction would come later, under the aegis of a colonial regime whose entire *raison d'être* would be to support evangelization with arms and treasure. Over the following decades missionaries converted multitudes under the presumption that conquest aided their project of conversion.[65] This informed those who set policy for new Spanish conquests in the Caribbean. Eleven years after the completion of the Granada campaign, one of Cisneros' collaborators in the councils of state, Juan López de Palacios Rubios, institutionalized the practices that had been emerging on

[61] Ladero Quesada, *Los Mudejares*, 128.
[62] AGS Cédulas de la Cámara, libro 27, f. 22r.
[63] Cisneros to Cathedral Chapter of Toledo (1500), in Ladero Quesada, *Los mudéjares*, 236.
[64] Cisneros to Dean of the Cathedral of Toledo (1500), BNE, ms. 13020, f. 94.
[65] *Parecer sobre si los infieles pueden ser atraídos a la fee, pusiendolos en necesidad*, AHN Universidades, leg. 720, f. 7r–v; for papal approval of this method as practiced in Granada, AGS Patronato Real, leg. 65, exp. 95.

Spanish frontiers.[66] The most notable of these was the *requerimiento*, or "requirement," that made the acceptance of missionaries a fundamental condition of subjection to the Spanish Crown.

Palacios Rubios intended for conquistadors to read the *requerimiento* to natives before they initiated hostilities against them. The text explained the reasons why Spaniards were entitled to make "just war": unbeknownst to them, the Pope had "donated" native lands to the Catholic Kings in 1494, ostensibly as an act of grace. Natives faced two choices which they would be allowed to deliberate for an "appropriate amount of time." If they desired peace, they would have to acknowledge the Church as "lord of the universal world," submit to the king of Spain as their temporal lord, and allow priests into their communities. But if they did not accept, the text warned, "and if they "maliciously" delayed their response,

I swear to you that with the help of God we will enter with force against you and make war upon you everywhere ... and we will subject you to the yoke and obedience to the Church and his Majesty, and we will take you, your wives and your children, and we will sell them as slaves and dispose of them as their Majesties command, and we will take your goods and do all of the terrible things and damages that we can do to vassals who do not obey nor want to receive their lord.

The message ended with an extraordinary disclaimer: "And we vow that the deaths and damages resulting from that shall be your fault and not of their Highnesses nor of these gentlemen that came here with us."[67] Conquistadors infamously read the protocol without interpreters before sacking native villages, solely to make sure that the record of their warfare was unassailable. With good reason the text has been dismissed as a legal absurdity for half a millennium. Fray Bartolomé de las Casas famously remarked that he was not sure whether to laugh or cry when he first heard of it.[68]

Absurd though it was, however, the requerimiento provides a snapshot of how the end of convivencia in Iberia shaped Spanish conditions of peace and war in the New World. The primary Spanish condition of peace in the

---

[66] Manuel Giménez Fernández, *Bartolomé de las Casas: Delegado de Cisneros para la reformación de las Indias* (Seville: Escuela Superior de Estudios Hispano-Americanos, 1953), 66, 141.

[67] Bartolomé de las Casas, see *Historia de las Indias*, ed. Agustín Millares Carlo (Mexico City: Fondo de Cultura Económica, 1951), vol. III, 27. Three other versions can be found in Francisco Morales Padrón, *Teoría y leyes de la conquista* (Madrid: Ediciones Cultura Hispánica del Centro Iberoamericano de Cooperación, 1979), 338–45.

[68] Las Casas, *Historia*, vol. III, 31.

requerimiento is the native reception of preachers, followed by the natives' conversion to Christianity. While the emissary does state that "they [Spanish soldiers and missionaries] will not force you to become Christians" – a nod to theologians who insisted that true faith was only voluntary – the text clearly states that conversion to Christianity is the only insurance of personal freedom and private property.[69] Peace depended upon the indigenous community's willingness to receive preachers. But in the longer term, delay was also grounds for just war. In his treatise *De las islas del mar océano* a few years prior to the requerimiento, Palacios Rubios wrote: "The natives are obliged to admit preachers of our holy faith so that they can explain in detail all of its mysteries to them. And if, after a prudent period to decide, they decide not to do it, they can be invaded."[70] These terms clearly contrasted with the agreements of convivencia, which allotted a space for conquered religions at the price of paying tribute (*jizya*).[71] Granadan Muslims, Canary Islanders, Caribbean natives, and the Mexica of Tenochtitlán met with far starker terms than most conquered peoples in medieval Iberia. After 1500, the condition of peace was to extinguish native faiths, publicly accept Christianity, *and* pay tribute to new rulers.

The aggressive policies that brought about the conversion of natives like the Granadan widow Fatima allowed Spaniards to entertain achieving a long-unattainable ideal of Christian universalism. Christians had prayed for the conversion of the infidels in their midst and at the edges of the world during convivencia, but political conditions and habits militated against serious evangelization. Theologians, especially Hostiensis, had long argued that Christendom, with the Pope as its head, enjoyed *de jure* authority over the globe.[72] These arguments informed the Alexandrine Bulls, which granted the Spanish Crown sovereignty over the New World on condition

---

[69] ibid., 27.

[70] Juan López de Palacios Rubios, *De las islas del mar océano*, trans. eds. A. Millares Carlo and Silvio Zavala (Mexico City: Fondo de Cultura Económica, 1963).

[71] Patricia Seed, *Ceremonies of Possession in Europe's Conquest of the New World, 1492–1640* (New York: Cambridge University Press, 1995); Annie Marie Lemistre, "Les origines du *Requerimiento*." *Mélanges de la Casa de Velasquez*, vol. 6 (1970), 166–81.

[72] The arguments of medieval theologian Hostiensis regarding the universal dominion of the Papacy influenced Palacios Rubios and many later interpreters of the papal donations. Lemistre, "Les origines"; Bartolomé de las Casas, *Del único modo de atraer a todos los pueblos a la verdadera religión*, ed. Agustín Millares Carlo (Mexico City: Fondo de Cultura Económica, 1975); Las Casas, *Historia*, vol. III, 28. See also Silvio Zavala, *The Political Philosophy of the Conquest of America* (Mexico City: Editorial Cultura, 1953), 55–7.

that it actively Christianize native populations.[73] The expanding horizons of the late fifteenth century suddenly turned this abstract claim into a tangible possibility. Triumphs of the faith at home seemed to connect to the dramatic news brought by Columbus, Vespucci, and da Gama. As Spaniards removed the last constraints of convivencia by ordering Jews and Muslims to convert or go into exile, they conjured up old dreams, never fully repressed, of redeeming the world under "one monarch, one empire, and one sword."[74] In his memoirs, Cisneros' assistant, Juan Vallejo, inserted a song that Morisco children allegedly sang in the streets of Granada during the conversions. Mocking their broken Spanish, Vallejo's ditty parodied the combination of coercion and incentives that Spaniards employed to get Muslims to convert, since the "bonnet" – *caperuza* in Spanish – given in exchange for baptism could refer either to a gift or a blow to the head. Such was the attitude that was reigning in the governing circles of the Castilian Church and Monarchy in those years: the ends justified the means.

> Now come King Fernando to win all of world ...
> Archbishop of Toleto, you give bonnet and me Christian later
> To win all of world.[75]

SEEKING A SANCTUARY

Gáldar, Canary Islands, 1484. After two years of captivity in Spain, Tenesor Semidan was finally returning to his native island of Gran Canaria. It was undoubtedly a bittersweet homecoming. As the native

---

[73] Anthony Pagden, *Lords of all the World: Ideologies of Empire in Spain, Britain, and France, c. 1500–c. 1800* (New Haven: Yale University Press, 1995), 31–2.

[74] Hernando de Acuña's poem in praise of Charles V upon the seizure of Tunis in 1535. As translated in David Brading, *The First America: The Spanish Monarchy, Creole Patriots, and the Liberal State* (New York: Cambridge University Press, 1991), 22; original in Hernando de Acuña, *Varias poesías*, ed. E. Catena de Vindel (Madrid, 1954), 342.

[75]

> "Agora venir el Rey fernando a ganar a todo lo mundo
> Arçobispo de garanata cara de oveja y carne de cabra
> Arçobispo de toleto dar *caperuça* y cristiano luego
> Para ganar a todo lo mundo."

According to the Diccionario de la Real Academia, *caperuza* translates to "bonnet," but "*dar en caperuza*" can also mean "to hit someone in the head; to hurt someone; or to frustrate one's designs or cut one off in the middle of a dispute." *Memorial*, Juan Vallejo, AHN Universidades, leg. 716, f. 9v.

ruler (*guanarteme*) of Gáldar, a fertile chiefdom on the northern side of
the island, Semidan had resisted the Spanish invasion of 1482, but surrendered after hopes of expelling the foreigners faded.[76] Lacking iron
except for what they managed to pilfer from Spaniards, Canary Islanders
had been fighting at a technological disadvantage.[77] The Spanish conqueror Pedro de Vera promptly dispatched him as a royal hostage to
Spain. Semidan soon found himself at the royal court of the Catholic
Kings in Madrid, where he asked to be baptized. With King Fernando
himself serving as his godfather, Semidan took the name don Fernando
Guanarteme, a name that signaled his spiritual kinship with the king of
Aragon as well as his royal status among the Guanches, the Canary Island
natives. In a typical gesture to elite converts representing their incorporation into Christendom, the Catholic King dressed him in new Castilian
clothes.[78] Guanarteme's conversion sealed a pact between his people and
the Spanish monarchy: while the Canarian ruler promised to comply with
missionaries, the monarchs of Spain promised to protect native converts
from enslavement, safeguard their personal property, and give them rights
to "pass like Christians" and trade "without fear of captivity" in any part
of Spain.[79] Yet everywhere there were signs of the Spaniards' bad faith.
On his way back to the Canaries, Guanarteme despaired at seeing hundreds his countrymen abused and sold at the docks of Seville. He protested to his new godparents, who promised to intervene.[80]

Upon his return to Gáldar, Don Fernando Guanarteme sought to turn
his indigenous communities into sanctuaries from colonial violence. Spanish authorities praised him for lining up his natives to receive baptism.[81]
He served as a mediator in nearby Telde, a jurisdiction where Spaniards
faced stiff resistance, convincing the holdouts "with assuaging words"

---

[76] Chronicler Andrés Bernáldez equated *guanarteme* with *rey*: *Memorias del reinado de los Reyes Católicos*, eds. Manuel Gómez Moreno and Juan de M. Carriazo (Madrid: Real Academia de la Historia, 1962), 141; Juan de Abreu Galindo, *Historia de la conquista de las siete islas de Gran Canaria* (Santa Cruz de Tenerife: Librería Isleña, 1848), 142–3.

[77] Bernáldez, *Memorias*, 138.

[78] Bernáldez, ibid.; Antonio Rumeu de Armas, *La política indigenista de Isabel la Católica* (Valladolid: Insituto Isabel la Católica de Historia Eclesiástica, 1969, 51; Abreu Galindo, ibid.

[79] Abreu Galindo, ibid.; Lawsuit by Canarians Juan Beltrán and Juan Cabello (1515), Rumeu de Armas, *Política indigenista*, 222; Fray Juan de Frías against Pedro de Vera (1495), Rumeu, ibid., 308.

[80] Royal Provision against abuses of Canary Islanders (1485), Rumeu de Armas, *Política indigenista*, 231.

[81] Felipe Fernández-Armesto, *Before Columbus: Exploration and Colonisation from the Mediterranean to the Atlantic 1229–1492* (London: Macmillan, 1987), 208–9.

that their fight was over and that their only hope was to surrender and convert.[82] The Christians would treat them well, respect their persons and possessions, and help them rebuild their community. Most of the residents surrendered, but others, including a local ruler's son, instead hurled themselves from cliffs to their deaths to avoid surrender.[83] Shortly thereafter the bishop of the Canaries, Fray Juan de Frías, presided over a mass baptism of the newly subjected population.[84] Guanarteme was not the sole collaborator in those years. On the island of La Palma, a native noblewoman named Francisca Gazmira also led native communities to the baptismal font.[85] In the face of military defeat, slave raids, inexplicable diseases, and dwindling numbers, Canarians accepted the price of survival: the terms of the unarmed Spaniards among them – the missionaries – who at least promised to protect them under Spanish rule.

In many respects, the colonial history of America began not with Columbus' landfall at Guanahaní but with the conquests of these seven arid islands off the coast of West Africa. It was here, on this unpredictable and dangerous frontier, where Spanish politics of conversion shifted from spiritual warfare against known enemies to a mission of protecting gentiles hitherto unknown to Europeans. Canary Islanders faced Castilian invasions, technological disadvantages, slave raiding, and devastating epidemics. War, disease, and exploitation changed societies in the Canaries and the Caribbean so rapidly and profoundly that natives found themselves in a crisis that could only be described as existential. Amidst the chaos they encountered the missionaries, the only unarmed group among the Spaniards, who showed a willingness to dialogue and negotiate peace. Indigenous engagement with missionaries was inseparable from their efforts to restore order, halt slave raids, and end the downward cycle of mass mortality. For missionaries, too, the unprecedented destruction that they witnessed transformed their mission into something more than just an instrument of spiritual warfare against infidels or a lonely apostolic legation in faraway lands.[86] Where convivencia ended and the

---

[82] Abreu, *Historia*, 148–50.   [83] Abreu, *Historia*, 150.   [84] Bernáldez, *Memorias*, 142.
[85] "Proceso de las yslas de Canaria." AGS Consejo Real, leg. 106, f. 12; Castilians-indigenous alliance, La Palma (1495), Rumeu de Armas, *Política indigenista*, 310; Fernández-Armesto, *Before Columbus*, 210.
[86] Pedro de Leturia, *Relaciones entre la Santa Sede e Hispano-America*, 3 vols. (Caracas: 1959), 172; Antonio Rubial García, *La hermana pobreza. El franciscanismo: de la Edad Media a la evangelización novohispana* (Mexico City: UNAM, 1996), 22; Fernández-Armesto, *Before Columbus*, 236; Rumeu de Armas, *Política indigenista*, 20.

Atlantic World began, the mission gained power because both Spaniards and natives began to associate this institution with peacemaking.

European mariners first voyaged to the Canaries in the late thirteenth century. Castilians, Portuguese, and Normans searched for gold, slaves, and souls. Europeans noted the islanders' animistic religion and their lack of iron; natives noted the invaders' weapons, boats, and icons.[87] The first missionaries in the archipelago were Franciscan Minorites from Mallorca, strict adherents of the Rule of Saint Francis who viewed their work at the edge of the known world as a form of hermitage.[88] Few records survive of their contact with Canarian natives. A fourteenth-century chronicle stated that the friars learned native languages, indoctrinated natives, and promoted settlement in this pastoral society: "They have been reduced to the mildness of civilized men and a human way of life, and their young men have been brought by practice to the knowledge of letters."[89] But the Minorite mission was short-lived. Missionaries had to compete with slavers, and they lacked the ability to defend natives. With warfare between natives and Europeans intensifying, the Minorites left the islands in the 1390s.

The failure of the Minorite mission taught an important lesson to the next missionaries who arrived in the archipelago: the mission would need to embrace worldly power if it was to found a new Church. Fifteenth-century missionaries in the Canaries were Observant Franciscans, a reform that co-opted the Minorites' asceticism but pledged full obedience to papal and secular authority.[90] In effect, the Observants both rejected the world and yet acquired power in it.[91] They managed to convert a handful of native leaders to Christianity in the 1420s, but slave raids ravaged native communities and undercut their legitimacy. The Observants understood that unless they could protect converts natives would have little incentive to convert. To protest the slave raids against

---

[87] Bernáldez, *Memorias*, 138, 135–9; José Rodríguez Moure, *Historia de la devoción del pueblo canario a la Virgen de Candelaria* (Tenerife, 1913), 15–40.

[88] Fernández-Armesto, *Before Columbus*, 236; Rumeu de Armas, *Política indigenista*, 20.

[89] Fernández-Armesto, ibid., 234, cites an anonymous Franciscan chronicle inserted in a fourteenth-century work by a Canon in Zurich.

[90] Minorite missions incorporated themselves into the Observant movement, which received papal recognition at the Council of Costanza in 1415. Rubial García, *Hermana pobreza*, 26.

[91] García Oro, *Prehistoria y primeros capítulos de la evangelización de América* (Caracas: Ediciones Trípode, 1988), 60–1; Rumeu de Armas, *Política indigenista*, 29.

their converts, a group of missionaries sailed to Rome with two native converts in 1434.[92]

The visit by the Canarian converts prompted Pope Eugenius IV to establish a vital legal precedent for subsequent transoceanic missions. The bull *Regimini Gregis* exempted all Canarian converts from enslavement. To enforce the policy, the Papacy resorted to its moral economy of indulgence and excommunication: all those who manumitted Canarian slaves received a plenary indulgence, while anyone who enslaved Canarians in mission areas were to be cast out of the Church.[93] Shortly thereafter several native leaders signed peace treaties with the missionaries. In 1462, Pope Pius II recognized these pacts with the bull *Pastor Bonis*, which granted protection to all native communities that agreed to receive missionaries. In practice these policies had the unintended effect of distinguishing zones of legal enslavement, or *bandos de guerra*, from protected mission zones called *bandos de paz*. Thus in a cruel circular logic, the presence of the mission clarified the areas where European slavers could lawfully capture Canarians to sell in Andalusian ports, a threat that induced Canarians to ask for friars and baptism. Slaving and missionizing were thus antithetical but symbiotic, and after the papal bulls of the 1460s and 1470s, both activities intensified.[94]

In this context, a reinvigorated Spanish Crown under Fernando and Isabel asserted royal authority over the archipelago in the 1470s. Co-opting papal policies, they issued decrees that reinterpreted the bulls in their favor. In 1476, after Pope Sixtus VI banned the enslavement of Canarian converts, Fernando and Isabel seconded the ban but added that Castilians could legally enslave all unconverted natives as infidels.[95] At the same time, they also made clear the incentive of conversion by declaring that all native Christians were their free vassals with full rights under Castilian law.[96] The royal legislation thus made conversion a fundamental condition of peace. In this way frontier violence induced natives to convert. Without qualms Fernando and Isabel defined their new policy without qualms: "the conquest proceeds by preaching as much as by force of arms."[97]

---

[92] Fernández-Armesto, *Before Columbus*, 236.

[93] Rumeu de Armas, *Política indigenista*, 32.   [94] García Oro, *Prehistoria*, 92.

[95] Rumeu de Armas, ibid., 40.

[96] Reyes Católicos to Pedro Osorio, Alcaide de Palos (1477), Rumeu de Armas, ibid., 163.

[97] Royal Provision to Andrés de Zumis, apostolic nuncio (1479), Rumeu de Armas, ibid., 190.

In 1478, the Catholic Kings forged an alliance with Observant missionaries in the conquest of the densely-populated islands of Gran Canaria, La Palma, and Tenerife. Over the protests of some missionaries who feared that royal sponsorship would compromise their apostolic ideals, the Catholic Kings assumed control over the missionaries' funds of indulgence raised in the streets and churches of Spain. They named the Bishop of the Canaries, the Franciscan Fray Juan de Frías, as the commander of the conquest of Gran Canaria. The extraordinary appointment confirmed the incorporation of the Observant mission enterprise, which the monarchs now funded and regulated, into their project "to submit the island to the Crown, and to expel ... all superstition and heresies of the Canarians and other pagans of those islands."[98] Frías coordinated military incursions and negotiated with native leaders like Tenesor Semidan, soon to be baptized as don Fernando Guanarteme.

By the time Columbus sailed through the Canaries on his first voyage across the Atlantic, conversion had already become a legal foundation for relations between overseas indigenous populations and Spaniards. We see this in the Alexandrine Bulls, which lent themselves to be read as an injunction to protect all native converts.[99] This was the opinion of Queen Isabel herself, who took offense at Columbus' trafficking in enslaved Caribbean natives in Spanish ports and at Court. Isabel also commanded that all natives in the Caribbean, especially those who received Christianity, were to be protected from enslavement and dispossession.[100] Some years later, the Laws of Burgos reaffirmed that all natives in the Caribbean were free vassals of the Crown, which committed itself to supporting their instruction in Christianity.[101]

Yet the promise of peace turned out to be evanescent, especially when it was more profitable for Spaniards to remain at war. When Spaniards conquered the last island in the Canaries, Tenerife (1493–1497), they flatly rejected native offers to convert. Their reason, according to royal

---

[98] Accord between Catholic Kings and Bishop of Rubicón (Canary Islands), Fray Juan de Frías (1478), Rumeu de Armas, ibid., 178.

[99] Pagden, *Lords of all the World*, 32, 52.

[100] Frank Moya Pons, *La Española en el siglo XVI* (Santo Domingo: Editorial Taller, 1978), 251–3; Pagden, *Fall of Natural Man*, 31.

[101] Johannes Meier, "The Beginnings of the Catholic Church in the Caribbean," in *Christianity in the Caribbean: Essays on Church History*, ed. Armando Lampe (Kingston: University of the West Indies Press, 2001), 7–8; Pedro Fernández Rodríguez, *Los dominicos en la primera evangelización de México* (Salamanca: Editorial San Esteban, 1994), 59–61.

chronicler Andrés Bernáldez, was "the tremendous cost" that the conquerors had incurred in the conquest: conversions would have narrowed the pool of slaves, and thus it was more profitable to keep the natives as infidels marked for enslavement.[102]

These tensions between spiritual and material profit appear to have riven the dual monarchy of the Catholic Kings. Isabel issued edicts and held councils of theologians to strengthen the protection of the new converts, whereas her husband Fernando defended his rights to employ slaves.[103] Conquistadors like Pedrias Dávila read the requerimiento solely as a pretext for enslaving native populations before they had time to consider the option of conversion.[104] Moreover, although royal legislation outlawed enslaving converts, it still allowed Spanish colonial officials to compel them to labor as long as this did not impede their indoctrination.[105] Spaniards in the Canaries and the Caribbean never resolved these conflicts between slaving and conversion before populations in both archipelagos fell victim to perilous cycles of disease and exploitation.[106] Even Peter Martyr, the Italian humanist who spent three decades publicizing Spanish exploits in the New World for European readers, despaired of the collapse of societies in the Caribbean.[107]

The principal challenge for native rulers after surrender and conversion was keeping Spaniards to their word. Canarians saw their children sold into slavery, Caribbean converts suffered the burden of forced labor, and the children of Iberian converts from Islam and Judaism faced constant doubts regarding the sincerity of their Christianity.[108] Time and again, natives discovered the limits of Christian sanctuary from colonial violence. Yet they struggled on, defending the sincerity of their baptisms in order to hold on to their titles, lands, and homelands. The question that a Granadan imam raised in a clandestine gathering to converted Moors some years after their mass conversion would no doubt echo in similar

---

[102] Bernáldez, *Memorias*, 340.   [103] Pagden, *Fall of Natural Man*, 30–1.

[104] BRAH Col. Muñoz, vol. 57, signatura 9/4837, ff. 423–32v; Meier, ibid., 10–2; Fernández Rodríguez, ibid., 47–54.

[105] Fernández Rodríguez, *Los dominicos*, 54–5.

[106] Las Casas, *Historia*, vol. III, 270–3; Moya Pons, *La Española*, 251–3; 10–2, 14–20; Massimo Livi-Bacci, "The Depopulation of Hispanic America after the Conquest." *Population and Development Review*, vol. 32, no. 2 (2006), 200. Minutes of discussions at Court (1524), BRAH, Col. Muñoz, vol. 57, signatura 9/4837, f. 377v.

[107] Brading, ibid., 17.

[108] AGS Patronato Real, leg. 68, f. 64; AGS, Cámara – Cédulas, lib. 263; AHN Universidades: f. 28.

gatherings on Atlantic islands, in the altepeme of central Mexico, and under the distant skies of the Pacific:

> If the King of the Conquest does not keep his good faith,
>   what are we to expect of his successors?[109]

CONVERGING HISTORIES

Not long after Cortés made landfall on Mexican shores in 1519, missionaries and natives raised a new mission Church that had roots in the Mesoamerican, Iberian, and early Atlantic experiences of religion and conquest: religion as a marker of sovereignty, religion as conquest, and religion as sanctuary. These attributes coincided, often uneasily, in the mission enterprise. A web of Mesoamerican communities accustomed to absorbing foreign deities engaged the Iberian mission, an heir to evangelical violence, a feeble protector of native gentiles, and a tired witness to their enslavement and destruction. The tropics of conversion – the Canaries, the Caribbean, and the lowlands of the American continent – had thus far succumbed to disease and greed. In Central Mexico missionaries would try again, joining with indigenous communities determined to bring an end to the chaos.

The news of Mexico was electric in the Caribbean. Settlers abandoned the islands in search of worldly riches and missionaries hastened towards the spiritual promise of the Mesoamerican highlands. They carried with them experiences in the alleys of Andalusia, the crags of the Canaries, and the islands of the Caribbean. When Cortés climbed the bloodstained staircase of Ahuitzotl's Great Temple, he insisted that an image of the Virgin Mary be given a special place next to Huitzilipochtli in the main shrine. The Mexica complied and incorporated the Castilians' "goddess" into their pantheon. The conquistador, however, could not hold back his disdain for Mexicas' patron god, and in a fit of rage he took up a bar and shattered the statue. When he reported the incident in his letters, he searched for the right word to describe this foreign place of worship. He settled on *mezquita*: mosque.[110]

---

[109] L. P. Harvey, "Yuçe Banigas, un moro en la Granada de los Reyes Católicos," *Al-Andalus* (1953).

[110] Cortés, Second Letter of Relation (1520), *Cartas de relación* (Mexico City: Porrúa, 2005), 79–80.

2

Christening Colonialism

The Politics of Conversion in Post-Conquest Mexico

Se vogliamo che tutto rimanga com'è, bisogna che tutto cambi.
If we want everything to stay the same, everything must change.

Lampedusa, *Il Gattopardo*

In 1524, around a campfire somewhere in the jungles of northeastern Guatemala, the lord of Tacuba is said to have declared to his Mexican peers: "Since the world is upside down, let it all be for me."[1] Appearing decades later in a chronicle by the indigenous historian Fernando de Alva Ixtlilxóchitl, the lord's apocryphal pronouncement is revealing. Three years had passed since the fall of the Aztec Empire, and the most powerful lords of central Mexico found themselves in this dark wood as participants in Hernán Cortés' ill-fated expedition to Honduras. Each perilous river crossing, native ambush, and struggle against incessant mosquitos on this frustrating journey was but one more collaborative gesture in their unceasing efforts to prove their political relevance in rapidly changing circumstances. Among these rulers was the chronicler's ancestor, Don Fernando Ixtlilxóchitl, lord of Texcoco, who survived the war of conquest and the smallpox epidemic of 1519–1521 and saw opportunity in the ruins of Aztec imperialism.[2] Ixtlilxóchitl and his fellow rulers claimed

---

[1] Fernando de Alva Ixtlilxóchitl, *The Native Conquistador: Alva Ixtlilxóchitl's Account of the Conquest of New Spain*, trans. and eds. Amber Brian, Bradley Benton, and Pablo García Loaeza (University Park, PA: Pennsylvania State University Press, 2015), 89.

[2] Matthew Restall, "The New Conquest History." *History Compass*, vol. 10, no. 2 (2012), 151–60; Matthew Restall, *Seven Myths of the Spanish Conquest* (New York: Oxford University Press, 2003), 44–54; Schroeder, "Conquest Studies," 1–9.

power for themselves and their local states. Yet, the tumult of post-conquest politics consumed some of its greatest native strategists. One morning, not long after the lord of Tacuba embraced the chaos, Hernan Cortés had him unceremoniously executed along with all but one of his compatriots. Most notably, the former Aztec emperor Cuauhtémoc was among those found dangling from a *ceiba* tree.[3] Only Ixtlilxóchitl, Cortés' nervous ally, was spared – but he wasn't out of the woods yet.

Ixtlilxóchitl exemplified the pragmatism of native lords in the conquest era. As he trudged through the jungles of the Petén in 1524, he had already counted five years as one of Hernán Cortés' most steadfast allies. Before the Spaniards arrived, Ixtlilxóchitl had been losing ground in a power struggle against his half-brother, Cacama, Moctezuma's favorite to rule over the powerful kingdom of Texcoco, a key constituent of the Aztec Triple Alliance which controlled vast swathes of the empire.[4] This sibling rivalry was a consequence of royal polygamy, which was a basis for the horizontal and vertical alliances that regional and imperial rulers made with one another. Taking on multiple wives allowed rulers to intermarry with their peers, superiors, and clients. This practice, however, produced internal rivalries and factions that Spaniards could exploit.[5] Such was the case of Ixtlilxóchitl's Texcoco on the eve of conquest. Continual shifts in power affected the standing of royal wives like Ixtlilxóchitl's mother, whose favor was waning at the Texcocan court to the detriment of her ambitious son. Thus in 1519, with little to lose, Ixtlilxóchitl bet on the Spaniards.[6] Even Cortés recognized that for indigenous rulers the war of conquest was more like a dispute within an extended family, fought

---

[3] Hernando Alvarado Tezozómoc, *Crónica Mexicáyotl*, trans. and ed. Adrián León (Mexico City: UNAM, 1949), 165–6; Domingo Chimalpáhin, *Las ocho relaciones y el memorial de Colhuacan [1607–1637]*, trans. and ed. Rafael Tena (Mexico City: Conaculta, 1998), vol. II, 167.

[4] Camilla Townsend, "Polygyny and the Divided Altepetl: The Tetzcocan Key to Pre-Conquest Nahua Politics," in *Texcoco: Prehispanic and Colonial Perspectives*, eds. Jongsoo Lee and Galen Brokaw (Boulder, CO: University Press of Colorado, 2014), 93–116.

[5] Ross Hassig, *Polygamy and the Rise and Demise of the Aztec Empire* (Albuquerque, NM: University of New Mexico Press, 2016).

[6] Townsend, "Polygyny"; Camilla Townsend, "'What in the World Have You Done to Me, My Lover?' Sex Servitude, and Politics among the Pre-Conquest Nahuas as Seen in the Cantares Mexicanos." *The Americas*, vol. 62, no. 3 (2006), 349–89; Lori Boornazian Diel, "Till Death Do Us Part: Unconventional Marriages as Aztec Political Strategy." *Ancient Mesoamerica*, vol. 18 (2007), 259–72; Susan Schroeder, "Chimalpahin and Why Women Matter in History," in *Indigenous Intellectuals: Knowledge, Power, and Colonial Culture in Mexico and the Andes*, eds. Gabriela Ramos and Yanna Yannakakis (Durham, NC: Duke University Press, 2014), 107–31.

largely by "those who had once been friends and vassals, relatives and brothers, even fathers and sons."[7] Ixtlilxóchitl prevailed over his internal rivals in the war of conquest, and then sought to make Texcoco a quasi-imperial power by laying claim over a swathe of territory stretching from the valley of Mexico all the way to the Gulf Coast.[8]

Ixtlilxóchitl quickly came to understand that his alliance with the Castilian intruders extended beyond the initial material exchanges, offers of wives and concubines, gifts of slaves, and payments of tribute. It also included religious demands that burrowed ever deeper into indigenous politics, society, and lives. When Franciscan friars first arrived in Mexico in 1523, he housed them in the palace of his deceased father, King Nezahuacóyotl, perhaps in an effort to integrate the newcomers to his kingdom as his dependents. The friars presented themselves as natural allies of the natives, promising to protect them in this volatile world while they offered eternal salvation in the next. Ixtlilxóchitl cooperated by sending the children of local nobility to the missionaries for instruction.[9] It was also evident, however, that conversion carried considerable costs. While strategic alliances on the Spanish–Mesoamerican frontier had involved exchanges of goods and favors, the more durable alliances with the friars were sealed with more far-reaching demands: to demonstrate fealty, native idols had to be destroyed, deities had to be desecrated, and local priesthoods had to be dismantled. So as not to provoke native priests and their devotees, who still retained power and prestige, Ixtlilxóchitl initially attended to the friars' needs with great caution.

A year after the Franciscans settled into his family's royal palaces, Ixtlilxóchitl converted to Christianity in a solemn ceremony. With Hernán Cortés serving as his godfather, he took the name Fernando in honor of the Catholic King. He then ordered his extended family to follow his example. When his mother refused, he is said to have vowed to "burn her alive if she did not get baptized."[10] The threat worked, and in subsequent purges he prevailed over the rest of his family rivals, leading his chronicler and descendant to tout his role in the conversion of Mexico as "second only to God's."[11] In fact, however, don Fernando Ixtlilxóchitl appears to have soft-pedaled the implementation of the friars' demands, for no mass

[7] Hernán Cortés, *Letters from Mexico*, trans. and ed. Anthony Pagden (New Haven, CT: Yale University Press, 2001), 220.
[8] Ixtlilxóchitl, *Native Conquistador*, 66.   [9] Ixtlilxóchitl, *Native Conquistador*, 75–82.
[10] Ixtlilxóchitl, *Obras históricas*, vol. I, 399–401.
[11] Ixtlilxóchitl, *Native Conquistador*, 78; Miguel León Portilla, "Testimonios nahuas sobre la conquista espiritual." *Estudios de cultura náhuatl*, vol. 11 (1971), 24; Lockhart,

conversions or iconoclastic acts followed his own baptism.[12] Franciscans only launched their assault on native religion after Ixtlilxóchitl left to join Cortés' expedition. While don Fernando marched to Honduras, the very children whom he had placed under the friars' care rampaged through his capital, destroying temples and driving the native priests out of their sacred grounds.[13]

Ixtlilxóchitl had placated the Spaniards with his conversion, but the execution of native lords in the jungle – which had claimed the life of his own half-brother and former rival – also demonstrated that mere baptism did not provide much security. Upon his return to Texcoco, he threw his political weight behind the friars, who proceeded to convert large numbers of commoners in Texcocan dominions to Christianity.[14] To set an example for other nobles – and perhaps in an effort to end the political rivalries stemming from royal polygamy that had so marked his early life – he repudiated his many consorts and achieved notoriety as the first native to marry in the Church.[15] Ixtlilxóchitl had found that his alliance with the friars provided a means of managing a world turned upside down. Conversion had not won him an empire, but it did win him control over a recognized jurisdiction under Spanish sovereignty.[16]

Ixtlilxóchitl's tale attests to the torturous paths that increasing numbers of indigenous people made to the baptismal font after the Spanish conquest. Undoubtedly, a rapid shift took place in indigenous public religious affiliations in the 1520s and 1530s: by all accounts, millions received baptism, often collectively, as makeshift churches began to appear atop temple ruins and young neophytes confiscated and desecrated images of local deities.[17] Each baptism was fraught with

---

Nahuas, 23–5, 29, 205; Chimalpáhin, *Las ocho relaciones*, vol. II, 169; Fray Toribio de Benevente Motolinía, *Memoriales*, ed. Nancy Jo Dyer (Mexico City: El Colegio de México, 1996), 442; Gibson, *Aztecs*, 170. Similarly, in other areas with complex divisions where there was no single *tlatoani*, such as Cuitláhuac and Xochimilco, rulers strengthened their position against internal competitors by cooperating with missionaries. Ross Hassig, *Mexico and the Spanish Conquest* (Norman: University of Oklahoma Press, 1994), 161; Juan de Torquemada, *Monarquía indiana*, ed. Miguel León Portilla (Mexico City: Porrúa, 1967), vol. III, 146.

[12] Ixtlilxóchitl, *Native Conquistador*, ibid.
[13] Mendieta, *Historia eclesiástica indiana*, vol. I, 376.
[14] Motolinía, *Historia de los indios*, 112.
[15] Motolinía, *Historia de los indios*, 139; Townsend, "Polygyny," 109–10.
[16] Ixtlilxóchitl, *Native Conquistador*, 109.
[17] Torquemada, *Monarquía indiana*, vol. III, 145; Éric Roulet, *L'évangelisation des Indiens du Mexique: Impact et réalité de la conquête spirituelle (XVIe siècle)* (Rennes: Presses Universitaires de Rennes, 2008), 39–45.

ambiguities, doubts, and conflicts that were subsequently silenced by
mendicant and indigenous chroniclers, who depicted conversion as a
sudden Christian triumph over an entrenched and bloodthirsty paganism.
Colonial chroniclers, both missionary and indigenous alike, described a
process that was inexorable, collective, and orchestrated, so lightning-fast
it seemed deceptively easy.[18] Their histories have left us with powerful
images of baptisms of thousands by a lone friar, bonfires of rejected
deities, and displays of missionary piety and poverty. Apologist historians
subsequently attributed this rapid "spiritual conquest" to the courage of a
mere handful of mendicant friars, and conversely, to the utter passivity of
native peoples and indeed of the New World itself.[19] In mendicant histories of conversion in Texcoco, for example, Ixtlilxóchitl's role is silenced
and the friars take center stage.[20] Like its secular counterpart in Spanish
conquest histories, the "spiritual conquest" historiography contributed to
a totalizing theory of rupture: a vision of indigenous collapse and
unequivocal Spanish triumph.[21]

  Over the past decades, historians have chopped away at these long-
standing totems of Mexican missionary history. Gone are the heroic
images of mass baptisms and spiritual battles; the militancy of a few
dozen friars has dissolved into a vaster story of ambivalent cross-cultural
encounters. Drawing on native-language sources recovered and valorized
by ethnohistorians, scholars of the early mission years have refocused
attention on native agents of religious change. Revisionists traced the
ambiguities and pitfalls of translating spiritual concepts, used censuses
to show that religious conversion was neither as collective nor as instant-
aneous as missionaries had boasted, and identified coincidences in society

---

[18] Torquemada, *Monarquía indiana*, vol. III, 156; Franciscans to Charles V (1532) in *Cartas de Indias* (Madrid: Atlas, 1974), vol. I, 55; Zumárraga to the General Chapter of Tolouse of 1532, in Joaquín García Icazbalceta, *Don Fray Juan de Zumárraga: Primer Obispo y Arzobispo de México*, 4 vols. (Mexico City: Porrúa, 1947), vol. II, 300–6; Mendieta, *Historia eclesiástica indiana*, vol. II, 347–8; Cuevas, *Historia*, vol. I, 334; Martínez Baracs, *Convivencia y utopia*, 123; Durán, *History*, 562. Similarly, indigenous scribes and historians also developed this narrative of their ancestors' rapid and unanimous embrace of Christianity. See Robert Haskett, "Conquering the Spiritual Conquest in Cuernavaca," in *The Conquest All Over Again: Nahuas and Zapotecs Thinking, Writing, and Painting Spanish Colonialism*, ed. Susan Schroeder (Eastbourne: Sussex University Press, 2010), 226–60; Wood, *Transcending Conquest*.
[19] Cuevas, *Historia*; Ricard, *Spiritual Conquest*; Kubler, *Mexican Architecture*.
[20] Motolinía, *Historia de los indios*; Mendieta, *Historia eclesiástica indiana*; Torquemada, *Monarquía indiana*.
[21] Restall, "New Conquest History," 151–60; Schroeder, "Conquest Studies," 1–9.

and religion that eased native transitions to Christianity.[22] These retellings have swung the pendulum of early mission history from rupture to continuity: by this reckoning, indigenous people like Ixtlilxóchitl converted because elements of Christianity resonated with their own lifeways and religious practices.[23] Susan Schroeder sums up this view: "It turns out that what the natives embraced of Christianity was often what was already known and practiced."[24] What did not change in this shift from apologism to ethnohistory, however, is the centrality of culture and spirituality in this process. Pedagogy, ritual performance, and cross-cultural communitication are privileged as the main indicators of religious change.[25] Apologists and revisionists alike have situated this process squarely in the immaterial realm of spirituality.

If theories of rupture reduced a fraught process to a simple tale of European triumph, then theories of continuity have tended to minimize the existential challenges and traumas that natives confronted after the conquest. Yet, conversion was inseparable from the grim contingencies of the post-conquest world. It was a socio-political process that set parameters for the cultural and spiritual encounters that followed. The expansion and acceleration of native baptisms was the product not solely of a spiritual encounter, or of a clash or melding of mentalities, but was also part and parcel of struggles for power over native communities. As a rite of initiation that carried both legal and religious legitimacy in the emerging colonial regime, baptism marked a shift in what David Tavárez has called the "collective sphere" of indigenous religiosity, the "core of corporate or state ritual practices" that "articulated a claim to legitimate power made by elites" and "reproduced a project of social order."[26] Baptism opened the way for Christian interventions in indigenous

---

[22] Dibble, "Nahuatlization," 225–33; James Lockhart, "Some Nahua Concepts in Postconquest Guise." *History of European Ideas*, vol. 6, no. 4 (1985), 465–82; Sarah Cline, "The Spiritual Conquest Reexamined: Baptism and Christian Marriage in Early Sixteenth Century Mexico." *Hispanic American Historical Review*, vol. 73, no. 3 (1993), 453–80; Burkhart, *Slippery Earth*; Pardo, *Origins*; Christensen, *Nahua and Maya*; Amara Solari, *Maya Ideologies of the Sacred: The Transfiguration of Space in Colonial Yucatan* (Austin, TX: University of Texas Press, 2013); Ronald Spores, *The Mixtecs in Ancient and Colonial Times* (Norman, OK: University of Oklahoma Press, 1984), 142.

[23] Lockhart, "Nahua Concepts," 467; Schroeder, "Conquest Studies"; Burkhart, *Slippery Earth*, 10; Wake, *Framing*, 7.

[24] Schroeder, "Conquest Studies," 8.

[25] Burkhart, *Slippery Earth*, 10; Wake, *Framing*; Pardo, *Origins*; Christensen, *Maya and Nahua*; Solari, *Maya Ideologies*; Hanks, *Converting Words*.

[26] Tavárez differentiates the "collective sphere," linked to public and political rituals, from an "elective sphere," or "personal ritual practices" performed to effect change at the

political life. Considering that the very natives who converted – or refused to do so – acted under duress, as well as the fact that conversion was fundamental to Spanish notions of legitimacy, it follows that the baptism of millions should not be understood solely in spiritual terms. The political contexts and contingencies behind baptism instead reveal it as the result of a series of decisions that indigenous people made in their efforts to mitigate the disruptions that began with the conquest.

This social and political analysis of conversion in Mexico draws upon recent reconsiderations of religiosity in early modern missions around the globe. "Religion" has become something far more amorphous than a container of doctrines and rites, while "conversion" has become something more than an interior process by which one exchanges one container of beliefs for another. Alan Greer, a historian of Iroquois-Jesuit contacts in New France, proposes that religion be understood as "an assemblage of phenomena" – all the observances, rituals, beliefs, and politics that are embedded in human relationships with the supernatural – which can be best understood "within a specific social context, rather than as manifestations of free-floating abstraction."[27] And the contexts are always political: time and again, scholars of early colonial interactions have found indigenous individuals and communities selecting those elements of newly arrived foreign religions that strengthened their hand.[28] Amidst the pervasive disruptions of colonial conquests, affiliation and adoption was one way to manage and at times draw power from radically new circumstances.[29] In the case of post-conquest Mexico, the challenge

individual, communal, or universal levels. See Tavárez, *Invisible War*, 10. See also Hanks, *Converting Words*.

[27] Alan Greer, "Conversion and Identity: Iroquois Christianity in Seventeenth-Century New France," in *Conversion: Old Worlds and New*, eds. Kenneth Mills and Anthony Grafton (Rochester, NY: University of Rochester Press, 2003), 177–8; Kenneth Mills, "Introduction," in Mills and Grafton, eds., *Conversion*, xii; Inge Clendinnen, "Ways to the Sacred: Reconstructing 'Religion' in Sixteenth-Century Mexico." *History and Anthropology*, vol. 5 (1990), 105–41; Rosalba Piazza, *La conciencia oscura de los naturales: Proceses de idolatría en la diócesis de Oaxaca (Nueva España), siglos xvi–xviii* (Mexico City: Colegio de México, 2016), 24–6.

[28] In his study of Southeast Asian conversions to Islam and Christianity in the fifteenth and sixteenth centuries, Anthony Reid calls this "adhesion": the adoption of useful elements of an outsider religion, often in the context of alliance-formation, without the full internalization of its message, institutions, or practices. See *Southeast Asia*, vol. 1; Fromont, *Art of Conversion*; Crewe, "Pacific Purgatory," 337–65; Eugenio Menegon, *Ancestors, Virgins, and Friars: Christianity as a Local Religion in Late Imperial China* (Cambridge, MA: Harvard University Press, 2009); Paredes, *Mountain of Difference*.

[29] Greer, "Conversion and Identity," 177–9; Fromont, *Art of Conversion*, 2–15; Paredes, *Mountain of Difference*; Ganson, *Guaraní*.

lies in understanding the vast scale, speed, and intensity of native affiliation with Christianity. Why did baptism and conversion expand through
the central highlands after the conquest, to the point that the mission
enterprise became nearly hegemonic by the 1540s?[30]

Baptism acquired ever-greater relevance to indigenous efforts to stabilize a world that had been thrown into disorder. In the words of Inga
Clendinnen, natives "strove to accommodate losses in all areas of life."[31]
Invasion, conquest, exploitation, and epidemics shook the very hierarchies, economies, and certainties that bound together lives and communities;
baptism, by contrast, afforded them legitimacy, protection, and status.
The growing crowds around the baptismal font were the result of natives'
growing realizations of the potential that baptism and alliance with friars
had in their urgent tasks of subduing violence, gaining political legitimacy, and rebuilding the community as a sanctuary from the worst excesses
of colonialism. Like don Fernando Ixtlilxóchitl, indigenous people of all
classes sought to redirect the forces of disruption towards shared projects
of survival and reconstruction. Each scene at the font was a grand wager
to change everything in order to change as little as possible.

THE ALLIES AT THE FONT

Far from a spiritual awakening, conversion in post-conquest Mexico was
a social process that was deeply rooted in Mesoamerican politics. The
foreign priests, their paraphernalia like the cross and the font, their single
deity, and their books were all exotic imports, to be sure, but the first
wave of converts soberly received their baptisms for entirely local, indigenous reasons. The pattern had been set years before the first friars set
foot in Mexico. Since the Spaniards first arrived in the Gulf of Mexico, the
internal tensions and open conflicts of Mesoamerican geopolitics eased
the intruders' march inland. The Totonacs, overtaxed and recently conquered, offered crucial early help to Cortés; and famously the Tlaxcalans,
enemies to the death of the Aztecs, formed a vital part of Cortés' victorious army. After the collapse of the Mesoamerican imperial order, long-

---

[30] "Hegemony develops not because people collaborate in their own subjugation but
because a dominating power has been able to institute practices and beliefs that rational
people choose to adhere to, often because of coercive threats, but that over time come to
appear normal, even natural." Susan Kellogg, *Law and the Transformation of Aztec
Culture* 1500–1700 (Norman, OK: University of Oklahoma Press, 1995), xix–xx.
[31] Clendinnen, "Ways," 130.

repressed local ambitions were released as ruling dynasties in city-states jockeyed to assert control and settle scores. This was the political reality that greeted the Spanish missionaries. Spain's most ambitious overseas mission began not with a theological disputation or an inspiring example of Franciscan poverty, but with the power plays of this reduced world of small kingdoms – a web of rivalries, one-upmanship, and ambition. After exchanges of gifts, slaves and concubines sealed initial alliances on the volatile Mesoamerican–Spanish frontier, the bonds of fictive kinship implicit in baptism joined native rulers and Spanish colonizers into the promise of a more permanent and intimate bond.

Micropatriotism determined how empires in Mesoamerica were built and dismantled, as well as the ways in which conquerors' religions were adopted and integrated into local life.[32] The vast and complex patchwork of proud and competing altepeme – and its city-state equivalents in Michoacán and Oaxaca – that extended over the valleys and hills of central Mexico both predated and long outlasted Aztec and Tarascan imperialism.[33] Each of these city-states had its own jurisdiction, ruling dynasties, systems of rotating and collective governance, and patron god. An idea of separateness, nurtured through ethnic origin stories and histories, was such that the altepetl – not the empire – was very much the center of indigenous identity.[34] Aztec and Tarascan imperialism did little to alter this micropatriotism; indeed, these empires simply drew their energies from it. In exchange for their submission, participation in military campaigns, and tribute payments to the empire, local rulers of city-states generally retained their political authority over taxation and land distribution. Submission to the empire also connected local rulers to imperial dynasties, and marriage alliances and polygamy empowered

---

[32] Lockhart, "Nahua Concepts," 274–9; James Lockhart, ed. and trans., *We People Here: Nahuatl Accounts of the Conquest of Mexico* (Eugene, OR: Wipf and Stock, 1993), 30.

[33] Lockhart, *Nahuas*, 14–15. See also Schroeder, *Chimalpahin*, 119–53. Bernal García and García Zambrano add ecological factors to Lockhart's definition in: "El altepetl colonial," 46–8, 99–101. This political structure also characterized local native polities in other sedentary societies in Central Mexico such as the Mixtecan *ñuu* of Oaxaca and the Purhépecha *ireta* in the Kingdom of Michoacán. On the Mixteca, see Terraciano, *Mixtecs*, 347–8; for Michoacán under the Tarascan Empire, see Martínez Baracs, *Convivencia y utopía*, 56. On the Zapotec equivalent of the Central Mexican city-state, the *queche*, see Tavárez, *Invisible War*, 9.

[34] Hodge, "Political Organization," 23, 31–3; Smith, *Aztecs*, 51, 153–5; Frances F. Berdan, "Introduction to Part II," in ed. Berdan, Blanton et al., *Aztec Imperial Strategies*, 109–15.

local city-state dynasties by extending and deepening their networks. By 1519, the Aztec Empire consisted of about 450 city-states.[35]

Indirect rule, however, also came with a heavy dose of imperial interventionism. Starting with Moctezuma Ilhuicamina I in the 1440s, Aztec rulers increasingly removed powers of taxation from city-states, and they tipped the scales in favor of their preferred candidates in dynastic disputes. In rebellious areas, they replaced local rulers with military governors.[36] These pressures were such that whenever the opportunity arose polities frequently withheld their tributes and sought to secede. For example, Cuauhnahuac (present-day Cuernavaca), a major kingdom anchoring the southern quadrant of the Aztec Empire, rebelled on three occasions.[37] Aztecs responded to similar uprisings with spectacular acts of violence that only spurred more resistance in turn.[38] An unresolved contradiction therefore lay at the core of Mesoamerican imperialism: while indirect rule allowed the empire to expand, it also inspired city-states to seek independence.[39]

Such an opportunity opened in 1519 when Cortés' expedition appeared on the Gulf coast of Mexico. Spaniards quickly sensed these tensions between localism and imperial interventionism, and they exploited it to their full advantage. Cortés incited the inhabitants of dissident city-states to overthrow established symbols of authority and to stop paying tribute to the Aztecs. Local rulers evaluated the potential uses of these unknown foreigners with strange technology in light of their own interests.[40] The Totonacs of Cempoala, a province on the Gulf Coast that was among the first to ally with Cortés, had recently been subdued and formed into a tributary province after having risen multiple times against Aztec rule. Cortés offered to assist them, and after initial

---

[35] Hodge, "Political Organization," 20–3, 41–5; Frances F. Berdan, "The Tributary Provinces," in ed. Berdan, Blanton et al., *Aztec Imperial Strategies*, 115–137; Smith, *Aztecs*, 51, 153; Pedro Carrasco, *The Tenochca Empire of Ancient Mexico: The Triple Alliance of Tenochtitlan, Tetzcoco, and Tlacopan* (Norman: University of Oklahoma Press, 1999), 424–37; Conrad and Demarest, *Religion and Empire*, 17–20, 32–44; Gibson, *Aztecs*, 34; Hassig, *Aztec Warfare*, 171.

[36] Smith, *Aztecs*, 51; Carrasco, *Tenochca Empire*, 432–7; Lockhart, *Nahuas*, 27; Gibson, *Aztecs*, 34.

[37] Smith, *Aztecs*, 56; Brigida von Mentz, *Cuauhnáhuac 1450–1675: Su historia indígena y documentos en mexicano: cambio y continuidad de una cultura Nahua* (Mexico City: Porrúa, 2008), 66–76.

[38] Conrad and Demarest, *Religion and Empire*, 57–8; Hassig, *Aztec Warfare*, 20.

[39] Smith, *Aztecs*, 20–2; Hassig, ibid.

[40] Hassig, *Mexico and the Spanish Conquest*, 40–4, 60, 88.

hesitation they joined his Spaniards in attacking the nearby Aztec tribute garrison at Cuetlaxtlán.[41] Similarly, the Tlaxcalans initially resisted the Spaniards, but after a series of embarrassing defeats, they too joined Cortés after deciding that these foreigners could be put to some use against their Aztec enemies.

From the very first contacts between Spaniards and altepetl rulers, religion was inseparable from their negotiations of peace and war. Conquistadors, not missionaries, were the first messengers of Christianity in Mexico. Theirs was a particularly bellicose frontier variant of Christianity, made forever infamous in the Requerimiento.[42] Amid the din of war, the Spanish offered two clear options: accept Christianity and be saved in this world and in the next, or resist it and face damnation in both. Spaniards expected natives to demonstrate their compliance by destroying sacred objects in public.[43] In 1534 Alonso de Villanueva, a veteran conquistador who participated in the conquest, described Spanish readings of the protocol during the war of conquest:

To the Indian rulers and lords of these provinces ... Hernán Cortés always informed them that they were not to follow their rites and ceremonies, nor worship the idols that they worshipped, because this [worship] was all foolishness, and that if they [followed these instructions], that our lord God would give them many gifts. But if they did otherwise, they would be punished.[44]

Over the next decade, native rulers sealed their alliances with the Spaniards by gathering figures of deities that Spaniards called idols, and summarily smashing them to pieces for their guests.[45] If reports of later incidents are any indication, natives probably engaged in a form of triage, selecting the least important figures while sparing the relics of their patron gods.[46] News of this Spanish practice of peace and war must have quickly

---

[41] Bernal Díaz del Castillo, *Historia verdadera de la conquista de la Nueva España*, ed. Joaquín Ramírez Cabañas (Mexico City: Porrúa, 2005), 83–4; Hassig, *Mexico and the Spanish Conquest*, 74–5; Pedro Carrasco, *Estructura politico-territorial del Imperio tenochca* (Mexico City: Fondo de Cultura Económica, 1996), 528–9.

[42] Victor Frankl, "Hernán Cortés y la tradición de las Siete Partidas." *Revista de Historia de América*, vol. 53 (1962), 9–74; Seed, *Ceremonies of Possession*, 88; Antonio Ybot León, *La Iglesia y los eclesiásticos españoles en la empresa de Indias* (Barcelona: Salvat Editores, 1954), vol. I, 128–34; Hassig, *Mexico and the Spanish Conquest*, 60.

[43] Díaz del Castillo, *Historia verdadera*, 165.

[44] Testimonio, Alonso de Villanueva (1534), in *Documentos cortesianos*, ed. José Luís Martínez, 4 vols. (Mexico City: Fondo de Cultura Económica, 1993), vol. II, 313.

[45] Díaz del Castillo, *Historia verdadera*, 85–90.

[46] Tavárez, *Invisible War*, 51; Lopes Don, *Bonfires of Culture*, 211–45; Piazza, *La conciencia oscura*, 50.

circulated through the networks' Mesoamerican diplomacy, for word of the Spaniards' iconoclastic demands moved ahead of the conquistadors themselves. By the time Cortés' Spanish-indigenous contingent reached Honduras in 1525, the sacrifice of idols had become routine wherever Spaniards arrived. In a Mayan town along the way, native rulers greeted Cortés by offering statues for destruction as he entered the town, before he even read them the admonishments that would have instructed them to do so.[47] Symbolic violence thus heralded the Christian mission in Mesoamerica. Its first messages were threats uttered by combatants; it commenced with deities reduced to shards and the whitewashing of temple walls.

These exhortations and acts of symbolic violence were not entirely alien to native rulers, for they vaguely resonated with Mesoamerican diplomacy and warfare. Prior to hostilities it was common practice for imperial envoys to demand recognition of Huitzilipochtli, the Aztec hummingbird-god of war. During combat local deities were either destroyed or carted away to Tenochtitlán for internment in the sacred dungeons of defeated gods, and conquerors sealed their victory by burning and destroying local temples.[48] For this reason, Moctezuma had good reason to be concerned about Cortés' continuous demands that natives destroy their temples.[49] Such coincidences ended there, however: while the destruction of idols signified a transfer of sovereignty and tributes to the conquering power in Mesoamerican politics, natives would soon learn that in the Spanish context it implied a far more sweeping, cosmic transformation.

Before the fall of Tenochtitlán to Spanish forces, however, these iconoclastic acts appear to have had meaning only in the narrower terms of Mesoamerican diplomacy. During the war of conquest native rulers had leverage to resist complying with the invaders' broader demands to destroy native religious institutions and practices. Spaniards depended far too heavily on their hosts and allies to compel them to obey their admonitions.[50] This was the recommendation of Cortés' Mercedarian chaplain,

---

[47] Cortés, Fifth Letter of Relation (1526), *Cartas de Relación*, 291.

[48] Hassig, *Aztec Warfare*, 8–9; Smith, *The Aztecs*, 203–4; Carrasco, *City of Sacrifice*, 25; Lopes Don, *Bonfires of Culture*, 120; Ixtlilxóchitl, *Obras históricas*, vol. II, 103–4; Zorita, *Relación*, 95.

[49] Hassig, *Mexico and the Spanish Conquest*, ibid., 75–7.

[50] Díaz del Castillo, *Historia verdadera*, ibid.; Hassig, *Mexico and the Spanish Conquest*, 87–91; Charles Gibson, *Tlaxcala in the Sixteenth Century* (Stanford, CA: Stanford

who prudently advised the conquistador against forcing the matter.[51]
And Bernal Díaz del Castillo, ever attuned to the more mundane concerns
of the soldier, wrote that more often than not hungry Spanish soldiers
would read their protocol and then promptly settle into a meal prepared
by those whom they had just admonished.[52] The price of seizing Tenochtitlán, then, was a grudging tolerance of native religion.[53] It was not until
the final defeat of the Aztecs that the balance of power shifted decisively in
favor of Spanish proselytization. The war of conquest exacted a heavy
human toll, and even more devastating was a smallpox epidemic that
killed about a third of the population.[54] The consequence was a vacuum
of indigenous political authority across the region.[55] "What are we to do
now, my lords?," asked one group of gathered nobles in the *Relación de
Michoacán* after their overlord died in the epidemic: "How could it be
that this house now lay desolate?"[56]

Amid tragedy, however, there was also opportunity. In city-states that
had relinquished varying degrees of sovereignty to Aztec or Tarascan
imperial rulers or to more powerful neighbors, the unraveling of Mesoamerican empires unleashed the forces of localism. After Tenochtitlán fell,
dozens of resurgent city-states reasserted themselves vis-à-vis their local
rivals as well as the new Spanish rulers in Tenochtitlán. These included
all kinds of polities: former imperial city-states, commercial centers, sacred
cities, independent kingdoms, and repressed ethnicities. Within these polities, dynasties, territorial sub-units, and ethnic groups contended for
power. Rival groups quickly divided into pro- and anti-Spanish factions.[57]
In Yanhuitlán, for example, a faction of local rulers bade their time by
opposing the arrival of mendicant missionaries.[58] As it became ever clearer
that the Spaniards were in Mesoamerica to stay, rulers of altepeme learned

University Press, 1952), 29–37; Andrea Martínez Baracs, *Un gobierno de indios: Tlaxcala, 1519–1750* (Mexico City: Fondo de Cultura Económica, 2008), 49, 110–12.

[51] Díaz del Castillo, *Historia verdadera*, 133, 149.

[52] See, for example, Díaz del Castillo's description of the entry of the Spaniards in Quiahuiztlan and the so-called town of "Castil-blanco" in the Sierra Oriental near Perote,
ibid., 103; Hassig, *Mexico and the Spanish Conquest*, 78.

[53] Gibson, *Tlaxcala*, 29–37; Martínez Baracs, *Un gobierno de indios*, 49, 110–12.

[54] Whitmore, *Disease*, 202–13; Robert McCaa, "Spanish and Nahuatl Views on Smallpox
and Demographic Catastrophe in Mexico." *Journal of Interdisciplinary History*, vol. 25,
no. 3 (1995), 397–430.

[55] Cortés, *Cartas de Relación*, 131; Martínez Baracs, *Un gobierno de indios*, 99, 114.

[56] Martínez Baracs, *Un gobierno de indios*, 115; Jerónimo de Alcalá, *Relación de Michoacán* (Zamora: El Colegio de Michoacán, 2008), 248.

[57] Lopes Don, *Bonfires of Culture*, 33; Hassig, *Mexico and the Spanish Conquest*, ibid.

[58] Piazza, *La conciencia oscura*, 35.

to turn their displays of conversion into political capital. The earliest examples come from the very center of the former Aztec Empire, where noble descendants of emperor Axayacatl in Tenochtitlán requested baptism, collaborated with the Franciscans upon their arrival in 1523 and 1524, and most importantly, provided them with properties for their newly-founded monastery and chapels. By doing so, these members of the Mexica royalty assured themselves a place in the new order of their imperial city.[59]

Such was the political power of baptism, however, that it also served as a tool for the descendants of Axayacatl's victims and other marginalized groups at the bottom of the imperial hierarchy. Alliance and conversion buoyed the resurgence of marginalized ethnicities and city-states across the former Aztec Empire. In the Valley of Toluca, where Matlatzinca and Otomí peoples had been displaced by Mexica colonists after Axayacatl had conquered the area in 1474, the conflict between natives and Mexica colonists opened an opportunity for the Spaniards.[60] When a Spanish-indigenous contingent under Gonzalo de Sandoval arrived in 1521, repressed Otomí and Matlatzinca groups joined the Spaniards and overthrew their Mexica overlords. In order to restore his family's lordship in Toluca and recover his lands and authority, native witnesses declared decades later, a Matlatzinca nobleman named Tuchcoyotzin approached Hernán Cortés and offered to receive baptism, addressing him with same title as the Aztec emperors (*huey tlatoani*) before declaring, "Do with me as you please, for I wish to be Christian."[61] The Matlatzinca ruler was baptized as don Fernando Cortés Tuchcoyotzin and received the markers of Christian affiliation and status: a set of Spanish clothing, a golden sword, a green silk hat, and a white horse from the Spanish conqueror.[62]

---

[59] Rovira Morgado, *San Francisco Padremeh*, 33–5.

[60] Cortés, *Cartas de Relación*, 175, 189–91; Carrasco, *Estructura*, 366–70; Peter Gerhard, *A Guide to the Historical Geography of New Spain* (Norman, OK: University of Oklahoma Press, 1993), 330; Margarita Menegus, *Del señorío indígena a la república de indios: El caso de Toluca (1500–1600)* (Mexico City: Conaculta, 1994), 34–45. Testimony by Alonso González, macegual of Tlacotepeque (1590), AGN Hospital, leg. 277, exp. 2, cuaderno 2, f. 879v.

[61] Deposition of Diego de Haro (1594), AGN Hospital de Jesús, leg. 277, cuad. 2, exp. 2, f. 248v; Francisco Juarez Olit, indio of Çinacantepec (1598) AGN Hospital, ibid., f. 864r; Alonso González, *macegual* of Tlacotepeque (1598), AGN Hospital, ibid., ff. 879r–880r; Juan Colli, principal of Capuluac (1598), AGN Hospital, ibid., ff. 751v, 753r; Pedro Hernández Ytzcuinichinal, principal of Hueytenango (1598), AGN Hospital, ibid., f. 497v.

[62] Testimony of Juan Colli, ibid. AGN Hospital, ibid., f. 753v; Testimony of Nicolás Aguilar, ibid., AGN Hospital, ibid., ff. 763v–4r; Pedro Hernández, indio of Xiquipilco, AGN Hospital, ibid., f. 847r; Testimony of Don Nicolás de Aguilar, *indio mexicano* and

Tuchcoytzin then turned the table on his former rulers: after sealing his alliance with his new godparent, he ordered Mexica residents to pay tribute.[63] Similarly in the Mixteca region of Oaxaca, which likewise suffered direct rule and Mexica colonization, the path to reclaiming local autonomy ran through the baptismal font.[64]

At all levels in the hierarchy of the late Aztec Empire, from Ixtlilxóchitl in imperial Texcoco to Tuchcoyotzin among the marginalized Matlatzinca, rulers adapted the Spaniards' demands for conversion to their circumstances. The gifts of clothes, the establishment of fictive kinship ties through godparentage, and the renaming after victorious godparents or other prominent Spanish figures connected with Mesoamerican political practices. With its element of *compadrazgo* (godparentage), baptism allowed for analogous ties of fictive kinship between the Spanish rulers of Tenochtitlán and newly baptized local rulers.[65] Power in the Aztec Empire was not so much territorial as it was a web of personal obligations and ties of kinship between lesser and greater rulers. Native ruling elites across the region, both friends and foes, were related through marriage. When imperial rulers intervened in local politics of subjugated states, they often chose from among relatives.[66] Like the Aztec rulers before them, Spaniards also leveraged personal ties – now in the form of godparentage – to promote their preferred candidates to local rule. In Chalco, for instance, Cortés imposed the local lordship (*tlatocóyotl*) upon an eight-year-old heir in the wake of the smallpox epidemic. Baptized Don Hernando Cortés Cihuailacatzin, the young newly-converted ruler served at the pleasure of his conquistador godparent who ruled in Tenochtitlán.[67]

---

principal of Xalatlaco (1598), AGN Hospital, ibid., ff. 763v–4r; Deposition of Diego de Haro, AGN Hospital de Jesús, ibid., ff. 248–9. Fray Juan de Torquemada also refers to a 'Don Fernando Cortés' who was the first indigenous convert in the Toluca Valley: *Monaquía indiana*, vol. III, 223. Testimony of Juan Colli, AGN, ibid., f. 754r; Testimony of Don Nicolás de Aguilar, AGN, ibid., f. 764r.

[63] Testimony of Juan Colli, ibid., f. 753r; Testimony of Alonso González, macegual de Tlacotepeque, AGN Hospital de Jesús, ibid., f. 879r.

[64] Teresa Rojas Rabiela, Elsa Leticia Rea López, and Constantino Medina Lima ed. and trans., *Vidas y bienes olvidados* (Mexico City: CIESAS, 1999), vol. I, 72.

[65] Pardo, *Origins*, 25; Lockhart, *Nahuas*, 123; Hugo G. Nutini, Pedro Carrasco, James M. Taggart, eds., *Essays on Mexican Kinship* (Pittsburgh: University of Pittsburgh Press, 1976); Hugo G. Nutini and Betty Bell, *Ritual Kinship* (Princeton, NJ: Princeton University Press, 1980).

[66] Smith, *Aztecs*, 58.

[67] Chimalpáhin, *Las ocho relaciones*, vol. I, 153–5, 333, vol. II, 342–3; Schroeder, *Chimalpahin*, 57–8; René García Castro, "De señoríos a pueblos de indios. La transición en la

In city-states throughout Mesoamerica in the 1520s and 1530s, local rulers stepped into the power vacuum left by imperial collapse, conquest, and smallpox, and those who survived walked out with new Christian names. In imperial cities like Texcoco or Tacuba, tributary states like Tepeaca or Oaxtepec, and resurgent ethnic communities like Toluca or Coixtlahuaca, the names of local elites began to echo those of the men who were turning out to be their overlords rather than their liberators.[68] Native politics, Spanish theological imperialism, and a large dose of expediency had opened the door for missionaries. But the politics of conquest alone were not enough to produce the kind of large-scale conversions that missionaries desired. Indeed, a rare early census made in several indigenous communities in modern-day Morelos in the mid-1530s reveals the limited scope but political centrality of early conversion. In the record, native rulers were nearly all baptized, but many members of their extended families and large swathes of their communities – particularly commoners – were not. Political expedience had influenced local rulers to convert, but Christianity was still far from being the exclusive religion in the indigenous public sphere.[69] To achieve this ambitious goal, missionaries knew they would have to extend Christianity from the realm of high diplomacy into that of everyday politics: to face-to-face confrontations, mobilizations of acolytes and collaborators, and dramatic acts of symbolic and physical violence.

THE ECONOMY OF SALVATION

In 1524, a contingent of twelve Spanish Franciscans – known as *los doce* – disembarked at Veracruz. They were not the first mendicant friars in Mexico, for before them three Flemish Franciscans had already begun low-profile mission work under the protection of don Fernando Ixtlilxóchitl in Texcoco. These humanist friars had quietly ministered to a small number of converts and elite children. *Los doce*, in contrast, arrived with an activism strengthened by years of battling for their ascetic Observant movement in Castile, and they came bearing authorizations to officially

---

región otomiana de Toluca (1521–1550)," in *Gobierno y economía en los pueblos indios del México colonial, ed.* Francisco Gonzalo-Hermosillo Adams (Mexico City: INAH, 2001), 209.

[68] Torquemada, *Monarquía indiana*, vol. III, 25–6.

[69] Cline, "Spiritual Conquest Reexamined."

establish a mission Church in Mexico.[70] They arrived in pomp, albeit of the Franciscan variety: with a dramatic performance of humility. Cortés, who had specifically requested Franciscans to build the Church in New Spain due to their reputation for austerity, played his part. As the friars entered México-Tenochtitlán, Cortés led native rulers and Spanish captains to prostrate themselves before the friars. The conqueror fell to his knees as he approached the bedraggled friars to kiss their hands.[71] The scene must have astonished native observers. This humbling of temporal lords before spiritual authorities signaled the preeminent role that the Franciscan friars would have in the indigenous politics of New Spain.

After the arrival ceremony, however, the Franciscans stepped into a post-conquest reality in which Spaniards and natives coexisted through fragile alliances and mutual dissimulations – a place where military victory dangled on a thread, and where Christianity, though proclaimed at every turn through the routines of Spaniards' communications, was still barely visible. Not unlike the Spanish North African *presidio* of Orán or the Portuguese forts on the coasts of Africa and Asia in those years, the Spanish colony at Tenochtitlán and surrounding towns was still little more than a frontier enclave that survived by adroitly navigating native politics and downplaying its Christian militancy. Vulnerability compelled Spanish colonists and priests to reluctantly tolerate native religion.[72] Franciscans recalled that during their first months in Mexico, "at night they would hear the shouts of the dances, songs, and drunkenness" of indigenous rites in surrounding villages.[73] Such strategic tolerance was unacceptable to the newly-arrived friars. Just two decades earlier, their Order had overseen the end of Iberian *convivencia* in Granada; indeed one of them, Fray Andrés de Córdoba, had served as a missionary in the former Muslim Kingdom.[74] As the heavy copal incense and drumming of

---

[70] Juan Meseguer Fernández, "Contenido misionológico de la obediencia e instrucción de Fray Francisco de los Ángeles a los Doce Apóstoles de México." *The Americas*, vol. 11, no. 3 (1955), 473–500; Pedro Oroz, *The Oroz Codex*, ed. Angelico Chavez (Washington, DC: The Academy of American Franciscan History, 1972), 347–60.

[71] Rovira Morgado, *San Francisco Padremeh*, 33.

[72] Henry Kamen, *Empire: How Spain Became a World Power, 1492–1763* (New York: Harper Collins, 2003), 30–2, 343; Chandra Richard DaSilva, "Beyond the Cape: The Portuguese Encounter with the Peoples of South Asia," in Stuart B. Schwartz, ed., *Implicit Understandings* (Cambridge: Cambridge University Press, 1994), 292–322; Subrahmanyam, "Holding the World in Balance," 1329–58.

[73] Torquemada, *Monarquía indiana*. vol. III, 46.

[74] Kubler, *Mexican Architecture*, vol. I, 7; Motolinía, *Historia de los indios*, 169–83; Rubial García, *Hermana pobreza*, 90–110.

daily rituals enveloped them, the most pressing question now hung over the missionaries: how would twenty missionaries go about converting millions? The ways in which the Franciscans went about solving this problem set patterns and precedents for all subsequent mendicants who would arrive in Mexico over the next decades.

The open politicization of conversion in the Spanish conquest directly affected the friars' administration of baptism. How accessible baptism should be, and what requirements should be met to receive it, were questions that led the friars straight into the thickets of Catholic theology. Their methodological dilemma touched upon fundamental questions regarding the nature and conditions of Christian conversion. After centuries of administering sacraments to newborns in long-standing parishes – among what Spaniards would call "Old Christians" – Catholic theology and liturgy was ponderous regarding adult conversions: catechumens needed to be carefully instructed and tested for their sincerity before they were admitted, and the baptismal rite needed to be observed with all the solemnity befitting one's entry into the Body of Christ. Baptism therefore included an act of exorcism, the recitation of prayers, and the application of oil and chrism. In Mexico, the twelve Franciscans argued that these parts of the ceremony were nonessential accessories that impeded their goal of mass conversion.[75] In order to admit millions of native converts to the faith as quickly as possible, the number of elements in the rite had to be reduced to its bare essentials. Franciscans justified this argument with medieval precedents that authorized ministers to administer rapid baptisms with little more than a prayer and holy water in cases of "urgent need," including shipwrecks, acts of war, or being surrounded by infidels. Post-conquest Mexico, they argued, fell in the latter category.[76] The missionaries sought to quickly resolve this problem before they set out to evangelize. Accordingly, they enacted these liturgical changes at a *junta* (extraordinary council) that brought together missionaries, royal officials, and Hernán Cortés in Ixtlilxóchitl's Texcoco.[77] Together they authorized a streamlined liturgy that would allow

---

[75] Claudio Ceccherelli, "El bautismo y los franciscanos en Méjico (1525–1539)," *Missionalia Hispánica*, vol. 12 (1955), 230; Pardo, *Origins*, 27–8; Gómez Canedo, *Evangelización*, 175; Fray Juan Focher, *Manual del bautismo de adultos y del matrimonio de los bautizandos*, ed. Juan Pascual Guzmán del Álba (Mexico City: Frente de Afirmación Hispanista, 1997), 22; José A. Llaguno, *La personalidad jurídica del indio y el III Concilio Provincial Mexicano (1585)* (Mexico City: Porrúa, 1983), 9.

[76] Ceccherelli, ibid.; Torquemada, *Monarquía indiana*, vol. III, 153–9.

[77] Alva Ixtlilxóchitl, *Native Conquistador*, 78.

them to conduct mass baptisms – indeed, an eighteenth-century summation of the proceedings suggests that the friars even received authorization to baptize *en masse* the masses with a hyssop.[78] The purpose was clear: a handful of friars would admit all natives to the faith that wished to do so, with minimal prior instruction or inquiry into their underlying motives.[79] In the friars' economy of salvation, baptism was to be made available at the lowest cost in terms of doctrinal preparation.

This liturgical reform was no narrow ecclesiastical matter: the Spanish conquest made baptism a political act, and with this reform the Franciscans aligned their theology and practice of conversion with post-conquest realities. Mexican natives had been hearing Spaniards present conversion status as a condition of enslavement and freedom ever since Cortés first landed at Cempoala five years earlier. But what began as words uttered in the protocols of conquest was becoming the primary means of gaining legitimacy under Spanish sovereignty. By offering a simplified liturgy, the Franciscans provided natives with an initiation rite that simplified their entry not only into Christianity, but also the Spanish legal and political universe.[80]

Critics warned that making baptism widely available, even in the exceptional circumstances of conquest, would debase the sacrament.[81] Bartolomé de las Casas, for example, argued that the Franciscans' policies dangerously exposed the Christian mission to the "fatal apparatus of war."[82] By making baptism easily available in a climate of war and terror, in which survival itself required political expedience, converts would convert for all the wrong reasons. "Is it not something to be feared," he asked, "that [natives] do not receive with a tranquil soul the truths that they hear about the Faith, after so much suffering, and that they do not convert to the true God with a true conversion?"[83] For their part,

---

[78] Francisco Antonio Lorenzana, *Concilios provinciales, primero y segundo, celebrados en la muy noble y muy leal Ciudad de México* (Mexico City, 1769), 7; Francisco López de Gómara, *Historia de la conquista de México* (Caracas: Biblioteca Ayacucho, 1979), 258. Torquemada, *Monarquía indiana*, vol. III, 25; Cuevas, *Historia*, vol. I, 171; Ybot León, *La Iglesia*, vol. I, 648; Llaguno, *La personalidad jurídica*, 9.

[79] Ceccherelli, "El bautismo," 211; Torquemada, *Monarquía indiana*, vol. III, 153–4; Pardo, *Origins*.

[80] Ceccherelli, ibid.; Torquemada, *Monarquía indiana*.

[81] As the baptism controversy intensified in the late 1530s, Gaspar de Ávalos, Bishop of Granada, declared, "We do not believe that *aspersión* [performing mass baptisms with the hyssop] is the most secure way." BNE ms. 19419, ff. 240v–41v. See also Pardo, *Origins*, 32–48.

[82] Las Casas, *Del único modo*, 352.   [83] ibid., 397.

Franciscans in Mexico lost little sleep over this because they openly admitted that conquest was itself a divine instrument. Even while they condemned specific acts of cruelty and exploitation, the friars accommodated the systemic violence of colonization. Fray Toribio de Benevente Motolinía, one of the twelve Franciscans, stated, "through [Cortés] God opened the door to preach the Gospel ... and for those who do not wish to hear [the Gospel] willingly, let it be by force. The proverb, 'it is better to be good by force than bad by will,' applies here."[84] The ends thus justified the means: having opened the door to baptism as widely as possible, indigenous catechumens proceeded to pass through it for their own reasons, whether in order to appropriate the foreigners' spiritual powers or to flee violence. Though unpalatable to many of their colleagues in the early Mexican Church, especially Dominicans and Augustinians, the Franciscan approach responded to the missionaries' immediate challenges in Mexico.[85] Dominicans and Augustinians would quietly adapt their high standards to overwhelming demands for baptism, which the Franciscans had helped to drum up in the first place.[86] Ultimately, the Franciscans' baptism policies were partially vindicated in 1539, when Mexican bishops set their skepticism aside and allowed them to continue baptizing "until the multitude of people coming to baptism ends."[87]

At the Franciscans' *junta* in 1524, however, all of this remained hypothetical. There was no multitude of Indians begging for baptism outside Ixtlilxóchitl's palaces. Two years would pass until crowds would line up for baptism in Texcoco, and indigenous priests still officiated nearby in the open. No "urgent need" yet existed other than in the friars' own hopes that the multitudes might soon overwhelm them with their desire for salvation. To drum up the vast crowds that their policy anticipated, a powerful "urgent need" for baptism among the indigenous would have to be produced.

---

[84] Toribio de Benevente Motolinía (1555), in *Colección de documentos inéditos relativos al descubrimiento, conquista y organización de las antiguas posesiones españolas de América y Oceanía*, 42 vols. (Madrid, 1867), vol. VII, 268.

[85] Juan de Grijalva, *Crónica de la orden de N.P.S. Agustín en las provincias de la Nueva España* (Mexico City: Porrúa, 1985), 99–101.

[86] Pardo, *Origins*; Ricard, *Spiritual Conquest*, 164–80.

[87] The Bishops issued this instruction in light of the Papal Bull *Altitudo divinis consilii* of Paul III (1537), which hesitantly acknowledged the Franciscans' right to alter the liturgy in cases of "urgent need." Torquemada, *Monarquía indiana*, vol. III, 153–60; Helen-Rand Parish and Harold E. Weidman, *Las Casas en México: Historia y obra desconocidas* (Mexico City: Fondo de Cultura Económica, 1996), 306–9.

SACRED TERROR: FRIARS AND THEIR PARA-MISSIONARIES

Just as the violence of conquest had opened the door for their mission, Franciscans had few qualms about relying upon violence and terror to induce large-scale conversion. This underside of the Mexican mission has been minimized by arguments that the mendicant friars were either a "largely peaceable lot" or that they had at least started out as such before they sank into nightmares of disillusion and violent projection by the late-1530s – inquisition trials, torture, and the high-profile execution of don Carlos of Texcoco.[88] In fact, it was not long after Franciscans arrived in Mexico that they abandoned their official charge from their Order, which commanded them to "convert with words and example."[89] Fray Francisco Jiménez, a member of *los doce*, admitted as much: in Mexico "apostolic methods" of "condemning only with the word ... produced no results." Far more efficacious on this frontier was Christ's injunction, *compelle eos intrare* (compel them to enter). "We are learning," Jiménez declared, "that the mass of people [is] removed from all principles of virtue…and that they only come to perform virtue through fear."[90] This was no gradual descent into anger and disappointment. By Jiménez's account, the friars had learned all of this by 1526.

Missionary violence spiraled inward from the systemic to the personal and intimate. Having embraced the political realities of conquest and colonization – and even while they criticized the Spanish colonists' worst excesses – Franciscans embarked on their own campaign of symbolic and physical violence with the aim of imposing "a new universe of meaning."[91] This approach gave priority to battling in the public sphere of collective religious observances, with varying results.[92] At this early stage, friars sought nothing less than to discredit native religion and expel it from public life, first by destroying idols and temples, and then by persecuting adherents and practitioners of native rituals. A letter from

---

[88] On the missionaries as a "peaceable lot," see Burkhart, *Slippery Earth*, 11. For studies depicting the missionaries' slide from idealism to disappointment, see Inga Clendinnen, *Ambivalent Conquests: Maya and Spaniard in Yucatan, 1517–1570* (Cambridge: Cambridge University Press, 1987); Clendinnen, "Disciplining the Indians: Franciscan Ideology and Missionary Violence in Sixteenth-Century Yucatan." *Past and Present*, no. 94 (Feb. 1982), 27–48; Ricard, *Spiritual Conquest*; Rubial García, *Hermana pobreza*.

[89] Obedience and Instruction (1523), in Oroz, *Oroz Codex*, 350; Clendinnen, "Disciplining," 29.

[90] Rubial García, *La hermana pobreza*, 246. The provenance of the phrase "compel them to enter" is Luke 14:23.

[91] Zizek, *Violence*, 2.   [92] Tavárez, *Invisible War*, 13.

indigenous nobles to the Spanish crown in 1560, ostensibly written to exalt its pious authors and discredit less-faithful neighbors, succinctly describes this violence in passing: "People of many altepetl were forced and tortured [or] were hanged or burned because they did not want to relinquish idolatry, and unwillingly received the gospel and faith." It was the friars' "good deed," they added, to "teach us to despise, destroy, and burn the stones and wood that we worshipped as gods."[93]

Rather than a "spiritual conquest," with its imagery of conquering friars, this was something more akin to a dirty war: a sordid struggle, instigated and sanctioned by friars, that was directed against proscribed gods and the rituals performed for them. Rumors, torture, and terror fueled this religious violence, the ultimate aim of which was to cast native religiosity as a cosmic enemy and dismantle the social prestige that upheld native priests and shamans at all levels of society. Before preaching, before baptism, was the bonfire of the gods. Fray Toribio de Benevente Motolinía declared that these rituals of destruction preceded preaching the Word and inducting people into the faith.[94] Yet this was mostly a war fought by natives themselves: neophyte provocateurs, investigators, accusers, and anti-Christian counter-preachers were its front-line combatants. Since missionaries were few in number and had a limited personal impact across such a vast territory, they relied on native children whom they sequestered, like janissaries, in mission schools in order to expand their reach throughout the central Mexican altepeme.[95] After receiving intense indoctrination, these acolytes were then deployed as a shock force and served as front-line investigators into ongoing native rites. These actions, in turn, provoked resistence from native priests and people loyal to them. The resulting religious strife opened up new religious divisions in communities, which ultimately served the friars' transformative agenda.

It bears asking, at this point, how the missionaries managed to develop cadres of native neophytes within a few short years. Franciscans – as well as the other mendicant Orders that followed – managed to isolate elite native children by leveraging native-Spanish alliances to their advantage. In the same year as the Franciscans' *junta*, Cortés ordered all indigenous

---

[93] Cabildo of Huexotzinco to Philip II (1560), in Lockhart, *We People Here*, 292–3.

[94] Motolinía, *Memoriales*, 227.

[95] Richard Trexler, "From the Mouth of Babes: Christianization by Children in Sixteenth-Century New Spain," in *Religious Organization and Religious Experience*, ed. J. Davis, (London: Academic Press, 1982), 97–114; Carmen Bernard and Serge Gruzinski, *Historia del Nuevo Mundo: Del descubrimiento a la conquista. La experiencia europea, 1492–1550* (Mexico City: Fondo de Cultura Económica, 2005), 335–9.

rulers to release their sons – especially their heirs – to the friars for indoctrination.[96] Precedents for this sequestration of native children could be found on earlier Iberian frontiers, as well as in theological arguments that allowed for pagan children to be separated from their parents, forcibly if necessary, so that they may be reared as Christians.[97]

This demand to sequester native children would not necessarily have seemed outrageous for native lords. In central Mexico, after all, it had been customary for parents to relinquish their sons to temple priests to "serve the idols until they reached the age of marriage," according to one early colonial account.[98] Elite children, along with some talented children of commoners, entered temple schools known as *calmecac* to receive rigorous training for the upper levels of civil, military, and religious institutions.[99] Meanwhile, lesser schools known as *telpochcalli* trained groups of youth in military formations and manual arts. Both institutions served as caretakers of the deities.[100] Mission schools drew upon these precedents, but with the intention of dismantling the very social-religious world that prehispanic schools had sought to perpetuate.[101] This distinction was not lost on native rulers. According to multiple reports from missionaries, some rulers attempted to send the children of lesser wives, vassals, and even slaves to the mission schools instead of their direct heirs.[102]

---

[96] Cortés, Ordenanzas (1524), Martínez, *Documentos cortesianos*, vol. I, 279. The order was not unique to Mexico: similar orders were issued elsewhere in 1503, 1513, and 1525. Antonio de León Pinelo, *Recopilación de las Indias*, ed. Ismael Sánches Bella (Mexico City: Porrúa, 1992), vol. I, 322.

[97] Justifications for the sequestration of unbaptized children of infidels existed in medieval ecclesiastical precedents. See Juan Focher, *Itinerario del misionero en América*, ed. Antonio Eguiluz (Madrid: Librería General V. Suárez, 1960), 62–74.

[98] Joaquín García Icazbalceta, ed., *Colección de documentos para la historia de México* (Mexico City: Porrúa, 2004), vol. I, 383.

[99] Zorita, *Relación*, 96; Alfredo López Austin, *Educación mexica. Antología de textos sahagunianos* (Mexico City: UNAM, 1985); Georges Baudot, *Utopía e historia en México: Los primeros cronistas de la civilización mexicana (1520–1569)*, trans. Vicente González Loscertales (Madrid: Espasa-Calpe, 1983), 116.

[100] For a synthesis of sixteenth-century chronicle descriptions of indigenous schools before the conquest, see José María Kobayashi, *La educación como conquista: Empresa franciscana en México* (Mexico City: El Colegio de México, 2002), 58–86.

[101] García Icazbalceta, ed. *Colección de documentos*, vol. I, 383; Zorita, *Relación*, 96; Motolinía, *Memoriales*, 430.

[102] Mendieta, *Historia eclesiástica indiana*, vol. I, 365, 388; Torquemada, *Monarquía indiana*, 28. Don Carlos of Texcoco, later burned for preaching against the friars, refused to give his son to Franciscans. See Luís González Obregón, ed., *Proceso inquisitorial del cacique de Tetzcoco* (Mexico City: Archivo General de la Nación, 1910), 37.

Cortés' sequestration orders placed several thousand elite boys in schools attached to the first monasteries in México-Tenochtitlán, Texcoco, Tlaxcala and Huexotzingo.[103] Each school housed between five hundred and a thousand students ruled by strict discipline. Escapees, for example, were placed into stocks.[104] Having received indoctrination from their new spiritual fathers, these students emerged from the mission schools as the *niños de monasterio* – the "monastery boys." These acolytes functioned as a para-missionary group, a shock force that performed the friars' disciplinary work of inflicting summary punishments, intimidating recalcitrant elders, denouncing people – including family members and elders – for idolatry, and destroying all physical signs of native religion.[105] Mission historians have long focused on the linguistic and scholarly advances made at these schools, silencing their more violent purposes.[106] We need only turn to don Pablo Nazareo, a star student who became a noted scholar of Latin, to see the darker side of mission education. In a petition to Philip II in 1566, Nazareo described his early work as a *niño de monasterio*: "Having eradicated the many evils caused by idolaters with not a little labor and by various methods, I pacified these Mexican provinces in the company of others ... with Christian doctrine instead of the Spaniards' sword."[107] By the friars' own admission, they would have achieved little without students like Nazareo – in 1532, in fact, the head of the Franciscans declared that the *niños* were "our most certain and durable result thus far."[108] Behind Nazareo's gentle language of "pacification" by means of much "labor" and "various methods," lies a harsh history of native strife and spiritual warfare.

The friars' war on native religion began on the morning of January 1, 1525. In coordination with an order issued by Hernán Cortés that prohibited the observance of all forms of native religion, the friars and their young acolytes launched an assault on indigenous priests and adherents.[109]

[103] Torquemada, *Monarquía indiana*, vol. III, 25.
[104] Pedro de Gante to Charles V (1532), in *Cartas de Indias*, vol. I, 51–3; Mendieta, *Historia eclesiástica indiana*, vol. I, 362; Torquemada, *Monarquía indiana*, vol. III, 29; Trexler, "From the Mouth of Babes," 119; Testimony of Ruíz de la Mota (1529), in *Colección de documentos inéditos relativos al descrubrimiento*, vol. 40, 495.
[105] Torquemada, *Monarquía indiana*, vol. III, 29, 34.
[106] Kobayashi, *La educación*, 151–6, 285–8; Christensen, *Maya and Nahua*, 54.
[107] Don Pablo Nazareo to Philip II (1566), in Francisco del Paso y Troncoso, ed., *Epistolario de Nueva España, 1505–1818* (Mexico City: Porrúa, 1940), vol. X, 116.
[108] Icazbalceta, *Colección de documentos*, vol. I, 224.
[109] Patricia Lopes Don, "Franciscans, Indian Sorcerers, and the Inquisition in New Spain, 1536–1543." *Journal of World History*, vol. 17, no. 1 (2006), 32.

The friars and their niños de monasterio destroyed the main temples of Tenochtitlán, Texcoco, and Tlaxcala. Franciscan historian Fray juan de Torquemada wrote that in the crowded *tianguez* (marketplace) of Tenochtitlán the natives "watched the temple burn … and they began to cry and scream, as we Christians would if we saw the temples of our true God burned or destroyed by His enemies."[110] In Texcoco, the friars and their students cleared out native priests who were still residing and serving in the Temple of Huitzilipochtli, set fire to the complex – which included the archive of the Texcocan kingdom – and proceeded to destroy idols.[111] The wave of destruction soon fanned out across central Mexico. In Chalco, the historian Chimalpáhin wrote a century later, "all of [the temples] were destroyed; they were burning at dawn."[112] A pattern soon developed: friars or their acolytes would arrive in a town, demand that residents surrender their idols, and the ritual of iconoclasm and corporal punishment would begin. An Augustinian friar, for example, reported that he had natives found hiding "idols" brought before their townsfolk and whipped by his auxiliaries "to instill fear in the others." In violation of Church laws that prohibited the punishment of non-Christians, among the victims was Ollin, an unbaptized native.[113] Friars proudly reported the destruction using biblical scales: twenty thousand idols smashed by a single friar in a day, thousands of local deities delivered to the flames, or five hundred major temples dismantled in just five years.[114]

Before long the niños de monasterio began to work independently, beyond the supervision of the friars and largely outside of the law.[115] Dressed in white surplices that identified them with the Church, they went from town to town.[116] In Yanhuitlán, a native acolyte named Mateo instructed residents to perform the sign of the cross and say the *credo* and *paternoster* in Mixtec.[117] Spaniards doubted the extent to which these youths understood the tenets of Christianity – a viceroy even

---

[110] Torquemada, *Monarquía indiana*, vol. III, 50.

[111] Motolinía, *Historia de los indios*, 26.

[112] Chimalpáhin, *Las ocho relaciones*, vol. II, 169; Charles E. Dibble, ed., *Codex en Cruz* (Salt Lake City: University of Utah Press, 1981); Javier Noguez, ed., *Tira de Tepechpan: Códice colonial procedente del Valle de México* (Mexico City: Biblioteca Enciclopédica del Estado de México, 1978), 107.

[113] AGN Inquisición, tomo 1, no. 6, ff. 5r–7v. On the prohibition of punishing non-Christians, see Piazza, *La conciencia oscura*, 2–3. For more examples of public punishments of "idolatry," see Fray Martín de Valencia (1532), in *Cartas de Indias*, vol. I, 54–61; Cuevas, *Historia*, vol. I, 200–1.

[114] Roulet, *L'évangélisation*, 31–2.   [115] Trexler, "From the Mouth of Babes," 123.

[116] Cuevas, *Historia*, vol. I, 200–1.   [117] Piazza, *La conciencia oscura*, 58.

complained that "some have turned out so bad that it would have been better if they had never studied" – but these early campaigns were more about power than indoctrination.[118] An early inquisition record from the town of Totoltepec, near the mines of Tenancingo (southwest Estado de México), illustrates this. A lone niño de monasterio named Pedro was imparting the Christian doctrine to local lords using "some figures that he had drawn on paper." Evidently unimpressed with the young man, a cacique named Juan then "spat upon" Pedro and "mocked" his doctrine. The ruler refused to attend any more sermons and stopped dressing like a Castilian, prompting rumors that he was still practicing "idolatry." After the niños de monasterio denounced him to Archbishop Zumárraga, the cacique Juan landed in the Inquisition.[119]

As their power expanded, these native acolytes came to act as a kind of religious police that investigated 'idolatry' and executed the friars' justice.[120] They followed up on rumors of indigenous rites and tracked down stashes of idols, many of which had been buried in the hopes that the Spaniards might eventually leave their land.[121] One suspected idolater declared that local people no longer kept idols at a sacred cave since "the niños from Texcoco" frequently showed up to search for them.[122] Acolytes would break into the homes of commoners and rulers alike, and even those of their own families, "turning everything upside down." Accusations of robbery soon surfaced. In an investigation by the First Audiencia, the list of allegedly stolen items included gold, feathers, jewels, corn, and rare birds. Most commonly, however, these surrogates were accused of stealing tribute blankets.[123] Others declared that the niños were raping women during their raids on indigenous homes and their preaching campaigns.[124]

---

[118] Motolinía, *Historia de los indios*, 285; Luís de Velasco to Philip II (1554), in Mariano Cuevas, ed., *Documentos inéditos del siglo XVI para la historia de México* (Mexico City: Porrúa, 1975), 186.

[119] Trial of Juan, cacique del Pueblo de Totoltepec. No date is given for this trial, but it probably took place between 1536 and 1539. AGN Inquisición, tomo 30. exp. 9, ff. 73r–4r, 76r.

[120] Torquemada, *Monarquía indiana*, vol. III, 51.

[121] Trial of Juan, cacique of Totoltepec. AGN Inquisición vol. 30, exp. 9, f. 75r.

[122] AGN Inquisición, tomo 37, exp. 2, f. 18r.

[123] Torquemada, *Monarquía indiana*, vol. III, 34; Nuño de Guzmán against Zumárraga (1529), *Colección de documentos inéditos relativos al descrubtimiento*, vol. 40, 475, 510, 543–4; Nuño de Guzmán (1532), in Paso y Troncoso, *Epistolario*, vol. II, 152; Trial of Pedro, cacique of Totolapan (1540), AGN Inquisición, vol. 212, exp. 7, f. 38v.

[124] García del Pilar, interpreter for the Audiencia, claimed that several local lords in Tenayuca declared that two monastery boys would regularly force several women "to

Admittedly, these accusations come from partisan witnesses, namely Spanish colonists led by the notorious conquistador Nuño de Guzmán who clashed with the Franciscans. Even by the contentious standards of colonial Spanish litigation, it would be hard to find a more rancorous legal battle. No corroborating evidence exists aside from an oblique comment by Bishop Zumárraga a decade later that accusations of sexual abuse ceased as soon as the first generation of monastery boys had married and taken up positions in native governments.[125] In the absence of corroborating evidence, the First Audiencia's trial against the friars could be set aside if not for the considerable ink that mendicant chroniclers spilled, in which they openly admitted and even boasted of their acolytes' violence. Though they represent opposite sides of the friar-settler conflict, the niños' accusers and defenders both indicated that the monastery boys enjoyed the missionaries' wholehearted support for their violent methods.

Mendicant chroniclers cheered on their native students when they murdered native priests, and memorialized them as martyrs when they died at the hands of the native priests' loyalists. The niños de monasterio confronted native priests of all kinds, from state-supported priests attached to temples to freelancing *nahuales* (shape-shifting sorcerers). At the beginning of the missionary campaigns, native priests still felt confident to publicly challenge and even taunt the friars and their acolytes. At the edge of an indigenous town, a shaman named Océlotl taunted a friar who was exiting after delivering a sermon: "Go on, go on, I will go [in] after you."[126] Others even developed an anti-baptism that cleansed natives of the foreigners' ablution.[127] And in Yanhuitlán, according to native witnesses who testified to the Inquisition, resistance to the friars' young acolytes was such that locals assassinated an entire group of them

---

go to a secret place to preach, [and] they laid down with them and did other vile things." *Colección de documentos inéditos relativos al descrubtimiento*, 533–4; Martínez, *Documentos cortesianos*, vol. III, 69–70, 178, 202.

[125] Cuevas *Documentos*, 493–4; *Colección de documentos inéditos relativos al descrubtimiento*, 474, 496, 510, 522.

[126] Trial of Martín Ucelo (1536), in Luís González Obregón ed. *Procesos de idólatras y hechiceros* (Mexico City: Archivo General de la Nación, 1912), 20–1; Lopes Don, *Bonfires of Culture*, 52–80.

[127] In Michmiloyan, an underground native priest in 1566 caused a scandal by preaching against the missionaries and washing the heads of baptized indigenous: Luís Reyes García, ed. *Cómo te confundes? Acaso no somos conquistados? Anales de Juan Bautista* (Mexico City: CIESAS, 2001), 156–7. See also Mendieta, *Historia eclesiástica indiana*, vol. I, 370; Tavárez, *Invisible War*, 53.

in the early 1530s.[128] Missionaries naturally took offense at this hostility, but many understood the socio-political origins of this resistance. Native priests, after all, formed part of a priestly class similar to their own, which saw their status undermined by Christian assaults.[129]

Franciscan chronicles boast that in Tlaxcala niños de monasterio took it upon themselves to stone a priest to death. A *teopixque* (mid-ranking priest) had taken the unusual step of leaving his temple compound to openly denounce the Franciscans in the marketplace. Through the obsidian teeth attached to his mask of the deity Ometochtli, the *teopixque* warned onlookers that ever-worsening calamities would befall them if they heeded the Spanish priests. Shortly thereafter a group of mission acolytes arrived in the plaza and confronted him. As the *teopixque* tried to break away, he tripped and the niños de monasterio stoned him to death. Franciscans displayed the *teopixque*'s corpse to the crowd, a Franciscan chronicler adding that the body "did not seem human, but rather a fuming ember from Hell."[130] Such confrontations marked a rapid shift in the abilities of native priests to marshal resistance to their foreign competitors and the young acolytes pledged to them. The missionaries' violence left them "dumbfounded and terrified," the chronicler Mendieta wrote, "to see that the one who had gone out to frighten others now lay dead."[131] Franciscans in Tlaxcala admitted the stoning did wonders for their efforts. It was, Torquemada wrote, "the cause for which many residents converted to Christianity."[132]

Violence sanctioned by missionaries increasingly drove native priesthoods underground. The public, temple-based cults that had supported a political order were ending. Some priests became peripatetic shamans, their rites focusing on the agricultural cycle.[133] Others fled. One native priest left Texcoco after the mass baptisms and escaped to the crags of the Sierra Norte de Meztitlán, where indigenous church constables found him in a cave two decades later.[134] The stoning of the *teopixque*, along with the persecution of others like him, made it clear how dangerous their vocation had become. Devotion to the gods, once the pillar of political

---

[128] Piazza, *La conciencia oscura*, 62.
[129] Mendieta, *Historia eclesiástica indiana*, vol. I, 383–5.
[130] Mendieta, ibid., 385–6; Torquemada, *Monarquía indiana*, vol. III, 65, 149; León Portilla, "Testimonios nahuas," 25.
[131] Mendieta, ibid.   [132] Torquemada, *Monarquía indiana*, vol. III, 65.
[133] Lopes Don, "Franciscans," 41.   [134] Grijalva, *Crónica*, 175.

and institutional authority, had in brief time become a crypto-religion performed under the cover of darkness.[135]

This religious strife placed indigenous rulers in a conundrum. The wave of repression laid bare the true costs of the political expediency that had driven them to receive baptism. In private, many rulers continued to rely on native priests for their own religious and political needs, but events were also making adherence to Christianity an essential source of political legitimacy under Spanish rule. If they embraced the friars, they risked alienating anti-Spanish factions and priests within their polities; if they embraced native priests, they risked running afoul of the friars and their monastery boys.[136] In Yanhuitlán, two native rulers sought to resolve this dilemma through polygamy, marrying slaves as their second wives in the religion in which they most had to prove their credentials: thus an elder ruler sought to align himself with Christianity by taking a baptized slave as his second wife, while a younger ruler sought to demonstrate his worth to elder loyalists by taking an unbaptized slave as his.[137] For many, however, the tensions and provocations of the anti-idolatry campaign left little time for such solutions. In two high-profile cases, rulers in Cuauhtinchan and Tlaxcala killed monastery boys about to uncover their secret observances of native religion. The rulers died in executions overseen by friars, and the murdered acolytes became martyrs for the missionary cause.[138] Elsewhere native rulers faced draconian punishments for supporting native priests. In Texcoco, Ixtlilxóchitl was punished for drinking *pulque* (which friars associated with native rituals). Another lord nearby died from a brutal punishment he received on the friars' orders.[139] In Chalco, according to the native historian Chimalpáhin, in 1530 don Hernando Cortés Cihuailacatzin, appointed by his

[135] Tavárez, *Invisible War*, ibid.

[136] A royal ordinance in 1546 formalized this understanding as law. Any unbaptized ruler was to be deposed, lashed, and have his hair removed. Edmundo O'Gorman, "Una ordenanza para el gobierno de indios, 1546," *Boletín del Archivo General de la Nación* vol. 11, no. 2 (1940), 185; Charles Gibson, "The Aztec Aristocracy in Colonial Mexico." *Comparative Studies in Society and History*, vol. 2, no. 2 (1960), 173; Stephanie Wood, *Transcending Conquest*, 102.

[137] Piazza, *La conciencia oscura*, 106.

[138] BNAH, Anales antiguos de México, tomo 273, vol. II, ff. 715r, 739r, 914, 983r; Torquemada, *Monarquía indiana*, vol. III, 94–100; Mendieta, *Historia eclesiástica indiana*, vol. I, 388–9.

[139] Testimony of Xoan de Burgos, in *Colección de documentos inéditos relativos al descrubtimiento*, 509.

godfather, was tortured in the testicles for concealing ritual objects.[140] And in Toluca, don Fernando Cortés Tuchcoyotzin, the Matlatzinca ruler who Cortés had restored to power upon his baptism, was banished to a monastery in México-Tenochtitlán for idolatry.[141] These punishments, performed *in situ* by missionaries and their native auxiliaries, were low-profile cases compared to the infamous trial and public execution of don Carlos Chichimecatecuhtli of Texcoco by the Inquisition in 1539.

It is in this grim context of terror, resistance, and retribution that indigenous individuals and families approached the baptismal font in the 1520s and 1530s. Far from being a spiritual conquest – a "myth of completion" as unfounded as that of the Spanish conquest itself – the strife left natives with lingering fears.[142] Terror served the friars' goal of extirpation in an essential yet limited way: iconoclasm and repression silenced the collective religious observances that had maintained community and cosmos, forcing adherents into their private sanctuaries, into small circles of trust, secrets, and hideaways.[143] The friars' totalizing goal of erasing native religion was and would remain unattainable, but their campaigns helped generate a groundswell of baptisms in the 1530s. Inseparable from the sacred terror of the early mission and encroaching colonization, baptism was fast becoming "the remedy against the very threat that it posed."[144]

PROMISES OF PROTECTION

Destructive and terrifying though it was, missionary violence and its resultant strife paled in comparison with the other disruptions ushered in by the Spanish conquest. Wars, epidemics, failed harvests, and famines were accompanied by unrelenting Spanish demands for gold, concubines, and slaves. Such was the scale of this cycle of tragedies that Fray Toribio de Benevente Motolinía declared that they were only rivaled by the biblical plagues of Egypt.[145] Mendicant missionaries feared the violence of conquest and its chaotic aftermath would suffocate the mission Church while it was still in the cradle. In the face of this postconquest crisis, increasing numbers of natives identified mendicant missionaries as the

---

[140] Chimalpáhin, *Las ocho relaciones*, vol. II, 181.
[141] Testimony, Andrés de Santa María (1598), AGN Hospital de Jesús, leg. 277, exp. 2, cuaderno 2, f. 482r.
[142] Restall, *Seven Myths.*   [143] Tavárez, *Invisible War.*   [144] Zizek, *Violence,* 21.
[145] Motolinía, *Memoriales,* 133–4.

least-disruptive subgroup of the invaders: unarmed and promising alliances and protection, the mission laid a potential pathway forward for native recovery efforts. James Axtell, a historian of Puritan missions in colonial New England, aptly described native conversion and alliance with missionaries as a "new answer – however distasteful, grieving, or upsetting – to the urgent and mortal problems that faced them."[146]

Amid the din of conquest and the smoldering remains of the gods – and the public punishments meted out by the niños – the mission also preached a promise of protection that was already clear in Spanish protocols of war and peace. Those who converted to Christianity would maintain their personal freedom, property, and communities. Natives took notice of the fact that missionaries struggled against Spanish settlers, and many acted upon this. This Mexican "struggle for justice" unfolded in missions, church pulpits, courthouses, and local rulers' *tecpans* (palaces).[147] Many native rulers deepened their alliances with friars as they challenged the abuses of Spanish settlers in their search for royal justice. At stake for natives and missionaries alike was the integrity and feasibility of the promise that Christian baptism could preserve personal and communal liberty.

Franciscans made no secret of their contempt for early Spanish settlers. They freely denounced settler violence, even while they condoned that of their acolytes, and they claimed preeminence in all questions concerning indigenous governance. Already by 1526, their disputes with settlers and officials had grown so heated that they threatened to abandon New Spain entirely.[148] Awareness of previous demographic disasters in the Canary Islands and the Caribbean – which many attributed to Spanish practices, not disease – drove their sense of urgency. During their first years the friars turned their attention to unregulated enslavement. They helped secure the promulgation of the royal Ordinances of Granada in 1526, which ordered that unjustly enslaved Indians be immediately freed, and in 1528 they helped draft a decree issued by Charles V that mandated the registration of all enslaved Indians.[149]

---

[146] Axtell, "Some thoughts on the Ethnohistory of Missions," 38.
[147] On the "Spanish struggle for justice" that unfolded in philosophical and legal discussions in universities and at Court in Spain, see: Lewis Hanke, *The Spanish Struggle for Justice in the Spanish Conquest of America* (Boston, MA: Little, Brown and Co., 1965), 86–7, 133–5; Silvio Zavala, *Los esclavos indios de la Nueva España* (Mexico City: El Colegio Nacional, 1994), 5–105.
[148] Peggy Liss, *Mexico under Spain, 1521–1556* (Chicago, IL: University of Chicago Press, 1975), 70.
[149] Gómez Canedo, *Evangelización*, 115.

Years of struggles over indigenous lives polarized Spanish settlers and Franciscans to such an extent that one friar was hauled before the Inquisition for having proclaimed: "I hope to God that He shall do justice against the Spaniards, and that you all see it, because if he does not, I will renounce the Faith."[150]

The foremost missionary in this struggle was Fray Juan de Zumárraga, a Franciscan friar tapped as bishop-elect of the newly-created Diocese of Mexico. Zumarraga arrived from Spain with royal authorization to serve as "protector of the Indians." Indigenous rulers, facing widespread abuse by Spanish colonists who had the legal backing of the pro-settler judges of the recently-created First Audiencia, an executive council and appellate court intended to establish royal authority over New Spain, flocked to Zumárraga's residence to seek his assistance.[151] Franciscans and indigenous rulers found common cause in their struggle against Spanish settler abuses. Their collaboration alerted the missionaries' Spanish opponents: "It is entirely certain," warned Fray Vicente de Santa María, a Dominican ally of Spanish settlers, "that the bishop protects the Indians, but he will never live in peace with the members of the Audiencia if he tries to remove the Indians from their authority."[152]

Soon Zumárraga and the Franciscans found a *cause célèbre* in their struggle. In 1529, a battle broke out over labor, tributes, and the enslavement of natives in Huexotzingo, a large city-state at the foot of Popocatépetl in the Valley of Puebla. Huexotzingo presented Franciscans with a typical case of the instability of the 1520s. Like Tlaxcala, the people of this Nahuatl-speaking altepetl had resisted Aztec expansionism, and they had allied with the Spaniards and Tlaxcalans early in the war of conquest. After the fall of Tenochtitlán, Cortés claimed Huexotzingo as part of his personal fiefdom. When Franciscans first arrived in Mexico in 1524, they established one of their first missions there.[153] In 1526, royal officials seized Cortés' properties and Huexotzingo became a pawn in the chaotic struggles among Spanish factions over indigenous spoils. By 1529, the city-state became a sinecure for the judges of the First Audiencia in Mexico City, who demanded labor and tribute

---

[150] Denunciation against Fray Francisco de Dios (1543), AGN Inquisición, tomo 125, exp. 3, f. 7v.

[151] Zumárraga to Charles V (1529), Icazbalceta, *Zumárraga*, vol. II, 222.

[152] Fray Vicente de Santa María to Bishop of Osma, undated. BRAH Col. Munoz, t. A/105, ff. 70v–3.

[153] Lucas, principal de Huexotzingo (1531), Martínez, *Documentos cortesianos*, vol. III, 207.

without regard for the town's population or resources.[154] The judges demanded exorbitant amounts of gold even though the mineral could not be found nearby, and natives perished making daily deliveries of food and firewood across the frigid passes between the town and in Mexico City.[155] Huexotzingo reached a tipping-point when the conquistador Nuño de Guzmán demanded soldiers for his campaign in Nueva Galicia (modern-day Jalisco). Guzmán also made an exorbitant demand: Huexotzingo was to produce a pennant laced with feathers and gold depicting the Virgin Mary, which would accompany the conquistador into battle. To cover the expenses – especially for the gold and featherwork – local rulers sold town residents into slavery. One of the earliest indigenous images of the Virgin Mary in the Americas thus consumed twenty native lives.[156]

Huexotzingo's rulers brought these travails to Zumárraga's attention, and the Franciscans pledged themselves to the town's defense. The stage was set for a standoff between the friars and Spanish settlers. Zumárraga went to the Audiencia to advocate on their behalf, but the judges threatened to punish him "like the bishop of Zamora," a bishop who had recently been hung for treason during the Comunero revolt in Castile.[157] The Audiencia judges ordered the arrest of Huexotzingo's rulers, but rumors of their warrants ran well ahead of the constables tasked with issuing them, and accordingly the indigenous rulers of Huexotzingo took refuge in the Franciscan monastery.[158] Franciscans mobilized in response. At mass in Mexico City, a friar publicized the dispute in a fiery sermon attended by Audiencia judges. He excommunicated them in their presence. Meanwhile Zumárraga and the head of the Franciscans in Mexico, Fray Martín de Valencia, traveled to Huexotzingo to join the native lords and friars in their showdown with the Audiencia constables. When the constables arrived at the doorway of the monastery to arrest the native

---

[154] Gerhard, *Guide*, 141.

[155] Gerhard, *Guide*, 141; Cabildo of Huexotzingo to Philip II (1560), Lockhart, *We People Here*, 294–5; Zumárraga to Charles V (1529), in Icazbalceta, *Zumárraga* 228; Testimony by Rodrigo de Almonte (1531). Martínez, *Documentos cortesianos*, 218; Cortés to Francisco de Terrazas (1529), in Paso y Troncoso, *Epistolario*, vol. I, 41.

[156] Rodrigo de Albornoz to Charles V (1525), in Joaquín García Icazbalceta, ed. *Colección de documentos*, vol. I, 492–3; Mendieta, *Historia eclesiástica indiana*, vol. I, 478; Lucas, indio principal of Huexotzingo, Martínez, *Documentos cortesianos*, 208; Tochel, indio principal of Huexotzingo, Martínez, ibid., 212–3.

[157] García Icazbalceta, *Colección de documentos*, 228.

[158] Zumárraga to Charles V (1529), in García Icazbalceta, *Zumárraga*, vol. II, 229; Audiencia on Huexotzingo Franciscans (1529), in ibid., 165.

nobles, the Guardian of the monastery threatened to excommunicate them if they proceeded any further.[159] In this instance the risk of eternal damnation sufficed: the officials left the scene and the Franciscan-Huexotzinca alliance prevailed. With typical hyperbole, Spanish settlers warned that the incident demonstrated that the Franciscans intended to overturn royal authority and establish an independent kingdom.[160] In reality, however, the standoff at Huexotzingo had a more prosaic, but no less powerful, result: it sent a message to native communities that a close alliance with mendicants could stave off the worst disruptions of colonization.

Huexotzingo was but a small victory; it did not check the overwhelming trend that had already become clear to natives and Spaniards alike by the late-1520s. In a negative feedback loop that was all too familiar to Spanish veterans of earlier conquests, excessive Spanish demands for labor and treasure were disrupting native community and household economies that were already reeling from virgin soil epidemics. "As we have seen on Hispaniola and Cuba and the other islands," Zumárraga warned, the Spaniards' "lack of moderation" in their tribute and labor demands would be "the end of this land."[161] Spaniards were arbitrarily demanding *tamemes* (human carriers) to haul goods, minerals, and raw materials from their encomiendas, while thousands more were ordered to work in distant mines.[162] Declining populations, failed crops, and rising tribute demands pushed native rulers to make the difficult decision to meet their tribute payments by paying Spaniards in native slaves. As local supplies of slaves diminished, local rulers then moved on to declare free vassals, *naborías* (indentured laborers), or temporary bondsmen to be slaves in order to make their payments. Spanish collectors would then send these slaves to work in mines or they would sell them in a rapidly growing slave trade.[163] The French Franciscan, Fray Jacobo de Testera, exhorted Emperor Charles V to be mindful of his spiritual responsibilities:

[159] García Icazbalceta, ibid. Mendieta states that friars had been preaching against encomendero abuses for several years: *Historia eclesiástica indiana*, vol. I, 478.

[160] García Icazbalceta, ibid., 166.

[161] García Icazbalceta, *Zumárraga*, vol. I, 238; Mendieta, *Historia eclesiástica indiana*, vol. I, 484; Fuenleal to Charles V (1532), *Colección de documentos inéditos relativos al descrubtimiento*, vol. XIII, 256–8.

[162] García Icazbalceta, *Zumárraga*, vol. I, 238.

[163] Contador Rodrigo de Albornoz to Charles V (1525), in García Icazbalceta, *Colección de documentos*, vol. I, 492–3. Mendieta, *Historia eclesiástica indiana*, vol. I, 478.

The branding iron only gives souls ... to our adversary [the devil] ... and they are currently selling at two pesos per soul ... [but] your majesty has rents in the most precious gold in the world; because while the other is mineral gold, yours is spiritual gold.[164]

In the city-states of central Mexico, the branding iron and the overseer's whip were consuming the very souls that the missionaries were seeking to convert. For Testera and the Franciscans, the choice was clear: Spaniards could choose vassalage – tribute-paying native Christians under encomienda labor agreements – or they could allow Indian enslavement to expand, in which case there would only be desolation: "there will be nobody left to preach to, only deserted homes and wild animals, given the haste of this sad trade."[165]

The slaving economy posed an even greater danger to indigenous communities and missionary ambitions beyond the frontiers of colonization, areas that Spanish colonists called the "lands of war." Located far to the north and south of Mexico-Tenochtitlán, these regions had been volatile frontiers of the Aztec empire, and they lay at the edges of the sedentary core of Mesoamerican cultures. In the Pánuco region on the Gulf Coast (about two hundred kilometers north of Mexico City), the conquistador Nuño de Guzmán and his subordinates enslaved thousands and sold them to Spaniards in Mexico City and the Caribbean, where native depopulation spurred demand for slave labor.[166] To the south of Mexico City in the modern state of Guerrero, Spanish conquistadors enslaved entire communities of Impiltzingas. This provided a much-needed supply of slaves for nearby mines in Taxco and Toluca.[167] Slave traders justified this by drawing on the Spanish protocols of conquest, which legitimated the enslavement of all natives who resisted evangelization. To ensure maximum profits, their definition of resistance was loose: after the war of conquest, Hernán Cortés himself justified the mass enslavement of communities "even if they decide not to make war but

[164] Testera to Charles V (1533), in Paso y Troncoso, *Epistolario*, vol. III, 98. See Hanke, *Spanish Struggle*, 95.

[165] Testera, ibid.

[166] Zumárraga estimated that slavers in the Pánuco had already traded between nine and ten thousand indigenous with Spanish buyers in the Caribbean by 1529. García Icazbalceta, *Colección de documentos*, vol. II, 211–2.

[167] Vasco de Quiroga to Indies Council (1531), in Rafael Arguayo Spencer, *Don Vasco de Quiroga: Taumaturgo de la organización social* (Mexico City: Ediciones Oasis, 1970), 81; Zavala, *Esclavos*, 52–3.

do not want to become Christians ... as is done in infidel lands."[168] As occurred decades earlier in the Canaries, in these lands of war there was more profit in selling native "infidels" as slaves than in converting them to Christianity.[169]

It is no wonder, then, that Fray Toribio Benevente de Motolinía famously declared native enslavement and exploitation to be an "eighth plague" in the series of calamities that struck the indigenous population of Mexico after the conquest. "Such was the haste to make slaves in those years," he wrote in his *Memoriales*, "that they brought the Indians from all corners of New Spain like sheep ... branding them on their faces with their owners' names." To enslave freeborn natives and resell them, he declared, amounted to a "civil death."[170] The slave trade also impeded the expansion of the mission enterprise.[171] The enslavement of populations "about to be converted" as if they were taken in "just war against Turks or Moors," Bishop Vasco de Quiroga argued, was morally untenable in a "Christian land" where the Gospel was being preached "without resistance."[172] Even worse, it contradicted the protection that missionaries offered to indigenous converts. Quiroga declared, "...seeing themselves [working in] the mines, with much reason they will suspect, with not a little irreverence and contempt, the sacrament of baptism that they had just received."[173] Enslavement and exploitation threatened the credibility of the mendicant friars' promises of spiritual and temporal salvation. Accordingly, in the 1530s missionaries fought Spanish settler slaving practices on all fronts: in the pulpits of Mexico City, in Spain, and at the Papal Court.[174] Indigenous communities did not fail to notice. When the pugnacious Fray Jacobo de Testera returned to Mexico in 1543 from a long journey to Spain and Rome in which he advocated successfully for native rights, indigenous towns along his path to Mexico City erected triumphal arches in his honor. It was enough to make Spanish colonists grumble that natives had received the old Gallic theologian "as if he were a viceroy."[175]

---

[168] Martínez, *Documentos cortesianos*, vol. I, 83, vol. II, 110, 164, 170, 312; Zavala, *Esclavos*, 2, 102; Díaz del Castillo, *Historia verdadera*, 267–9.

[169] Rodrigo de Albornoz to Charles V (1525), García Icazbalceta, *Colección de documentos*, vol. I, 491; Sebastián Ramírez de Fuenleal to Charles V (1532), in *Colección de documentos inéditos relativos al descrubtimiento*, vol. XIII, 256–8.

[170] Motolinía, *Memoriales*, 143–4.   [171] Cuevas, *Documentos*, 13–6.

[172] Spencer, *Vasco de Quiroga*, 163.   [173] Spencer, *Vasco de Quiroga*, 164.

[174] Zavala, *Esclavos*, 126.

[175] Tastera was a collaborator with Las Casas and was present at the promulgation of the New Laws of 1543. Roulet, *L'évangélisation*, 138; Hanke, *Spanish Struggle*, 95.

Franciscan antislavery activism, however, did not extend to a broader anti-colonialism. While a handful of radical missionaries passionately followed Las Casas' calls to separate the mission from colonial conquests and economies, most Franciscans and other mendicant missionaries believed their mission communities were vital parts of a colonial system whose ultimate purpose on earth, warts and all, was to fund and protect the mission Church. Even while they defended the native lords at the Monastery of Huexotzingo, Franciscans argued forcefully in favor of perpetual encomienda titles.[176] Contrary to settlers' claims that Franciscans were denying them the fruits of conquest, Franciscans argued that their activism against native enslavement preserved the very labor force that was necessary to the emerging colonial economy. Addressing Spanish settlers, Fray Gerónimo de Mendieta posed this question:

Brothers, if we did not defend the Indians, you would not have anyone to serve you. We favor them and work to preserve them so that you have someone to serve you, and in defending and teaching them, we serve you and unburden your consciences. When you took charge of them … you did nothing else other than ensure that they served you and gave you whatever they had, and even what they did not have, without regard for their deaths or diminution. But if you use them up, who would serve you?[177]

Franciscans sought a well-regulated system of indigenous vassalage that would preserve the lives of their converts and still generate sufficient tributes to enrich Spanish colonists and the mission Church. With moderate Spanish exactions, secular and spiritual profits would mutually aid each other. Ultimately, Zumárraga argued, the Franciscans had allied with indigenous rulers to guarantee order, which had been imperiled by Spanish colonists' assaults on native lives.[178]

For indigenous communities, mendicant activism presented the possibility of temporal salvation: a chance to stabilize a world gone awry. Despite their violence, the missionaries still stood out from other Spaniards as the subset of the conquering Spanish altepetl with whom natives could negotiate.[179] Franciscans, as well as the Dominicans and

[176] García Icazbalceta, *Colección de documentos*, vol. I, 234, 260, vol. II, 549.
[177] Mendieta, *Historia eclesiástica indiana*, vol. I, 483.
[178] García Icazbalceta, *Colección de documentos*, vol. I, 232.
[179] García Icazbalceta, *Colección de documentos*, vol. I, 181–2, 232; Fray Pedro de Gante to Charles V (1532), in *Cartas de Indias*, vol. I, 51–3; Liss, *Mexico under Spain*, 78–9; Bernard and Gruzinski, *Historia*, 326.

Augustinians who followed them to Mexico, demonstrated this by consistently triangulating between Spanish settlers, whom they frequently criticized in public, and the native communities that they claimed to protect. Exceptional cases such as Yanhuitlán, where local rulers allied with their encomendero instead of the friars in order to protect native religion from mendicant iconoclasm, only prove the rule: after coming face-to-face with the Inquisition, the rulers reached an understanding with the friars and went on to rule over their city-state with the friars' support.[180] In the long term, the mendicants offered the most feasible path for the native enterprise of survival.

Mendicants quickly garnered a reputation as protectors. On frontiers, for example, rulers of distant towns that were being subjected to slave raids travelled all the way to Mexico City to beg for friars.[181] Conversion status also was becoming renowned for its protective properties. According to Bishop Vasco de Quiroga, natives in remote areas would implore Spanish passersby to teach them the Our Father or the Ave María in exchange for food, in order to claim protection as Christians.[182] Caught between the settlers and missionary violence, indigenous rulers across New Spain followed the example of the nobles of Huexotzingo: they chose the missionaries. Reflecting on these events two decades later, indigenous nobles declared that accepting the friars' protection had saved them from the worst ravages of conquest: "without the Franciscans' actions in their favor, they would be nothing more than slaves."[183] Out of each local alliance between friars and rulers, a sanctuary from the most destructive violence of colonialism had begun to emerge.

CONCLUSION

In communities across post-conquest central Mexico, a rising consensus brought natives in ever-greater numbers to the font to receive baptism. This mass movement towards public affiliation with Christianity had little to do with conversion, at least by its narrow definition as a "spiritual turning." Instead, indigenous people associated the friars' rite of initiation

---

[180] Piazza, *La conciencia oscura*, 55, 104.
[181] Quiroga, ibid., 165; García Icazbalceta, ibid., 180.   [182] Quiroga, ibid.
[183] Roulet, *L'évangélisation*, 138; Esteban de Guzmán, Pedro de Moteuczuma Tlacahuepantli, and alcaldes y regidores of Mexico-Tenochtitlán (1554), in Emma Pérez-Rocha y Rafael Tena, *La nobleza indígena del centro de México después de la conquista* (Mexico City: INAH, 2000), 195; Martínez Baracs, *Convivencia y utopia*, 138.

with their own urgent tasks of safeguarding self, family, and community. From the beginning of the Franciscans' evangelizing campaign in 1525, both the costs and benefits of baptism were evident: while the missionaries' direct violence and exclusivist demands made it clear that baptism was a repudiation of the public presence of native religion, it also was becoming evident that baptism offered a constructive means of managing the multiple threats that beset native communities. Because baptism and affiliation with the Catholic Church was so central to legitimacy and sovereignty in Spanish imperialism, its benefits came to outweigh its costs. The ceremony of ablution and the status it conferred was relevant to the challenges of the post-conquest world and it had the power to mollify the more destructive results of Spanish colonization. Steadily, and then overwhelmingly, native societies came to associate baptism and mission with the urgent task of rebuilding indigenous communities as sanctuaries against the existential threats of colonial violence and exploitation.

This complex interplay of political expedience, sacred terror, and the promise of sanctuary provoked the large-scale collective baptisms that were so glorified in mendicant chronicles. Communities sought baptism in ever-greater numbers during the 1530s.[184] Missionaries, who fanned out beyond the lakeside cities in Valley of Mexico, resorted to biblical numbers in their attempts to report on the gathering multitudes to authorities in Spain. In 1532 the leading Franciscans in Mexico declared that each one of the original twelve friars in Mexico had single-handedly "baptized, as of today, more than a hundred thousand, most of them children" – a total of 1.2 million neophytes in just seven years.[185] When Franciscans visited the altepetl of Tepeaca in 1537, the chronicler Torquemada claimed, a friar baptized sixty-thousand natives in a matter of days.[186] In town after town "those who came [to receive baptism] were so many that they seemed an infinity, and [the friars] could not even find a place nor time to eat."[187] Franciscans publicized these numbers – which they no doubt inflated – to exalt their own charismatic powers. Yet even the more subdued Augustinian and Dominican accounts of baptism, while they emphasize their slower pedagogy, still admit that on the

[184] Cuevas, *Historia*, vol. I, 334.
[185] Fray Martín de Valencia and original twelve missionaries to Charles V (1532), in *Cartas de Indias*, vol. I, 55.
[186] Torquemada, *Monarquía indiana*, vol. III, 156. Sixteenth-century estimates gave a contact-era population of 100,000 tributary families in Tepeaca and its jurisdiction, thus the Franciscans' figure of 60,000 baptisms is not implausible. Gerhard, *Guide*, 280.
[187] Torquemada, *Monarquía indiana*, vol. III, 145.

appointed day entire towns would be inducted into the faith to meet the growing indigenous demand.[188]

Baptism offered a temporal solution to neutralize the violence, exploitation, and danger that beset post-conquest indigenous society. Such motives were not solely material, for in the natives' acceptance of baptism and friars – and its attendant public repudiation of their native rites and priests – there was also a spirituality in preserving one's life, home, and community during radical changes. Over time indigenous communities came to remember these first baptisms as a central act in the political reconstitution of the altepetl in the Spanish colonial order. Indigenous historians would further legitimize their polities and lineages by presenting heroic narratives of conversion, initiated and prompted by native rulers like Ixtlilxóchitl. For Spaniards, these acts not only extended Christendom into the American contintent; they also served to legitimize Spanish dominion over native polities.[189] Yet it was a social pact laden with contradictions, for it bound indigenous desires for continuity within a new status that presupposed their transformation. Mass baptism thus put on display one of the great paradoxes of colonial power: the same disruptive forces that bring down societies can sometimes be redirected towards preserving their underlying foundations, to the modest satisfaction of both intruder and native. As if through a distorting mirror, each party saw what it wished to see in the act of conversion and submission. Where natives saw baptism as a guarantee of protection; missionaries saw a transforming miracle.

---

[188] Pardo, *Origins*; Ricard, *Spiritual Conquest*.
[189] Wood, *Transcending Conquest*, 102.

PART II

CONSTRUCTION

3

The Staff, the Lash, and the Trumpet

The Native Infrastructure of the Mission Enterprise

Missions are hybrid enterprises. On the one hand they are, by definition, the work of religious messengers who travel abroad in order to convert societies different from their own. On the other hand, missionaries must engage local cultures – their laws, their governments, even their rites – in order to remake them. Thus the Jesuit Matteo Ricci famously donned the garb of Confucian literati in the hopes that converts might implant Christianity in the Middle Kingdom, while at the other extreme, Franciscans in Japan decided that it was more convenient for them to incite commoners to rebel against feudal lords.[1] The mission's goal of total transformation always required, to varying degrees, local immersion. Even the most intransigent missionaries, like the sanguinary Fray Diego de Landa in the Yucatán Peninsula, knew that their mission depended upon their ability to preserve some aspects of local culture in order to destroy native religions.[2] Yet assessing the Other went both ways, for indigenous peoples also "counter-explored" the missionaries as much as the missionaries studied them: California natives approached missions in

---

[1] On Iberian missions in China, see: Jonathan Spence, *The Memory Palace of Matteo Ricci* (New York: Penguin Books, 1985); Liam Matthew Brockey, *Journey to the East: The Jesuit Mission to China, 1579–1724* (Cambridge, 2007). On Japan, see: Charles Ralph Boxer, *The Christian Century in Japan, 1549–1650* (Manchester, 2001 [1951]); Juan Gil, *Hidalgos y samurais: España y Japón en los siglos XVI y XVII* (Madrid: Alianza Editorial, 1991). Spanish missionaries in China, particularly Dominicans in Fujian Province, had a methodology similar to their mendicant brethren in Japan: see Menegon, *Ancestors, Virgins, and Friars.*

[2] See Clendinnen, *Ambivalent Conquests*; Fray Diego de Landa, *Relación de las cosas de Yucatan* (Mexico City: Porrúa, 1986).

their struggles against starvation, the Iroquois used Jesuits to expand their autonomy, and Kongolese monarchs drew upon Catholic institutions to strengthen their authority.[3] Each mission was a unique nexus between local interactions and broader forces of change in the early modern world.

The mission enterprise emerged in sixteenth-century Mexico out of several hundred local alliances between the mendicant orders and the elite class of indigenous nobles known in Náhuatl as pipiltin. Mendicant missionaries considered the altepetl (local native city-state), with its social hierarchies and territorial organization, to be the most convenient point of entry into Mesoamerican society, whereas pipiltin used missions to rebuild their polities. Both groups cemented this missionary–pipiltin alliance through the administration of temporal power. From its very beginnings, the mission enterprise was as much an expression of native territorial organization and governing structures as it was the work of missionaries. Recent scholarship based on elite native-language records has recovered the ways in which ruling groups and collaborators co-produced the native Church, as well as the outlooks of those who contravened mission directives.[4] Beyond the spiritual and ritualistic scope of those records, however, lies a far broader history of the mission's role as an institution of daily governance that set the parameters for cultural adaptations and challenges. As a political force, the mission was a compulsory and exclusivist public religion that counted on the backing of both indigenous and Spanish temporal power. It grew out of native policing, taxation, and territorial politics. These more prosaic features of indigenous society proved to be an enduring source of the power that missions held over native societies.

The missionary–pipiltin alliance not only drew its strength from coinciding interests, but also from the compatibility between mendicant and native organizations. Although mendicants went great lengths to favorably compare their own doctrinal approaches with those of rival mendicant Orders, their political and social commonalities outweighed their differences.[5] All three Orders arrived in the same generation of Spanish

---

[3] On native "counter-exploration," see David A. Chappell, *Double Ghosts: Oceanian Voyagers on Euro-American Ships* (Armonk, NY: M. E. Sharpe, 1997). Fromont, *Art of Conversion.*

[4] Dibble, "Nahuatlization," 225–33; Burkhart, *Slippery Earth*; Barry Sell, *Nahua Confraternities in Early Colonial Mexico* (Berkeley, CA: American Academy of Franciscan History, 2002); Tavárez, *Invisible War*; Lopes Don, *Bonfies of Culture.*

[5] The most important differences, in terms of native politics, were economic. See *Chapters 4 and 6.*

churchmen. They experienced the reformist campaigns for austerity and asceticism of the Observant movement as well as the rising influence of Northern Humanism. Mendicants shared a revivalist calling to renounce the material excesses of preceding generations and return to a life of poverty, evangelical preaching, and communion with their brethren.[6] This corporate organization of the mendicant Orders, marked by rotating offices and collective governance, resonated with indigenous elite. Indeed, the fundamental similarities among the Orders, combined with the appeal of the mendicant–pipiltin alliance among native rulers, drove a fierce competition among the mendicants over native territories.[7] And as their deployments to native communities expanded, the Orders' recruiting operations struggled to keep pace.

The scarcity of missionaries, relative to the rising native demand, made the mission enterprise rely heavily on indigenous social structures for its everyday operations. In the first decade after the founding of the mission enterprise in 1524, only a few dozen friars ministered to a population that numbered in the millions and that was extended across a vast territory. By 1544, 152 mendicants were staffing sixty-nine missions, roughly a 2:1 friar-mission ratio, while by 1576, the height of the mendicant enterprise, 809 friars staffed 203 missions, a 4:1 ratio.[8] Friars met their logistical challenges by organizing a peripatetic mission. They were constantly on the move, their entourage of mules and acolytes making their way along a circuit of towns and villages. Since missionaries visited each mission church only sporadically, it was the native church official who was omnipresent in the daily life of the mission. Native-language sources frequently refer to indigenous officials as *teopantlaca,* or "Church-people."[9] Mostly drawn from the native nobility, these officials were the guardians of the visible church: they kept watch over church property, heard last testaments, and policed the faith. As the local eyes and ears for the missionaries, the teopantlaca became an indigenous secular arm that

---

[6] The first Franciscans arrived in 1523, Dominicans arrived in 1526, and Augustinians arrived in 1532. Ricard, *Spiritual Conquest*, 139–54; Kubler, *Mexican Architecture*, vol. I, 1–21.

[7] A. C. Van Oss, *Church and Society in Spanish America* (Amsterdam: Aksant, 2003), 103–23.

[8] Accounts, Juan Alonso de Sosa (1544), AGI Contaduría 661, r. 3; Accounts, Melchor de Legaspi (1576), AGI Contaduría 677.

[9] Lockhart, *Nahuas,* 215–7; Other ethnicities had their own collective term. Mixtecs, for example, also referred to this group as the "church people," or *tay huahi ñuhu*: Terraciano, *Mixtecs,* 285.

meted out justice and wielded considerable political authority. The missionary–pipiltin alliance thus constructed the Mexican mission out of movement and rootedness, as unending mendicant circulations connected recovering native structures of power.

Three tools – the staff, the lash, and the trumpet – made the mission enterprise visible and present in the lives, habits, and power relations of indigenous communities. With the staff, rulers wielded the authority of their offices through pre-hispanic precedents. With the lash, subordinates punished transgressors, delinquents, and backsliders. And with the trumpet, musicians and choirs attracted neophytes with a blend of new and familiar sounds. By these means the "church-people" and missionaries perpetuated Mesoamerican patterns of sovereignty, subjugation, and deference, and they made the mission an indispensible force in colonial struggles to control native jurisdictions, resources, and people.

SOCIAL HIERARCHIES AND TERRITORIAL ORGANIZATION

Spaniards were nothing but relieved when they encountered the complex societies of Mesoamerica. Upon receiving one of Cortés' enthusiastic reports, Charles V gave thanks to God that Mexican natives had "more ability and capacity than the Indians of the other parts that until now have been seen, so that some profit will be made of them and they will be saved."[10] In the "tropics of empire," where Spaniards juxtaposed impressions of bounty and fecundity with derisive judgments of the barbarism and feebleness of native "Indians," the sedentary societies in the Mexican highlands offered a promise of both spiritual and material profit.[11] Missionaries recognized the order and wealth of native towns as indications of *policía*, their conception of a well-administered and productive republic. As they saw it, the same city-states that had bolstered the Spanish conquest could now, a decade later, generate converts and churches.[12] Nonetheless, this policía was still steeped in paganism. In the tropics of conversion, no matter how much promise natives showed, even the urbane denizens of Tenochtitlán required long-term missionary tutelage. Central Mexico thus stood out as a land of spiritual promise primarily because missionaries believed its well-ordered republics to be compatible

---

[10] Charles V to Hernán Cortés (1522), in Martínez, *Documentos cortesianos*, vol. I, 255.

[11] Gómez, *Tropics of Empire*, 48–53, 434; Cortés, First letter of relation (1519), *Cartas de relación*, 25–7.

[12] Fray Jacobo de Tastera to Charles V (1533), in *Cartas de Indias*, vol. I, 64.

with their objectives to intervene in indigenous society, indoctrinate it, and correct its ways.

Not all missionaries shared this optimism, however. The specter of the Caribbean haunted them even in the orderly cities and towns of Mexico. Fray Domingo de Betanzos, one of the first Dominicans in Mexico and a veteran of the Caribbean, considered the urban infrastructure of native cities and towns to be a mere façade for an incurable barbarism. In a letter to the Council of the Indies, Betanzos denounced the Indians of Mexico as brutes incapable of receiving Christianity. Betanzos' confrère Fray Tomás de Ortíz added that the Indians of Mexico "are more stupid than asses and refuse to better themselves in anything." The two Dominicans found themselves in agreement with Spanish settlers. In the recently-founded municipality of Compostela in Nueva Galicia, colonists declared that the "only way to prevent Indians from bestiality and robbery" was to "enslave them so that they may know God."[13] Since the Indians of Mexico were sure to die out like the Caribbean Indians, why shouldn't settlers be allowed to enslave them and profit from them?[14]

For most friars and royal officials, such cynicism fell in the face of the complex societies that surrounded them. In Mexico, Las Casas' argument that even a circle of huts in the Caribbean met Aristotelian definitions of *civitas* was unnecessary; it sufficed to simply point to the *urbs* – to the palaces and markets of Mesoamerican cities – to make the point.[15] In a series of letters to Charles V, mendicant missionaries and the Second Audiencia, the ruling body of reforming royal judges who replaced their corrupt predecessors, deemed indigenous society to be worthy of saving. The President of the Audiencia, Fray Sebastián Ramírez de Fuenleal, stated:

Not only are they capable in moral matters, but also in speculative ones, and many of them will surely be great Christians, as many [already] are. And if one is to judge peoples' [sic] understanding by exterior works, then they exceed the Spaniards: and provided that they remain alive until either they understand us or we

[13] Paticia Seed, "'Are These Not Also Men?': The Indians' Humanity and Capacity for Spanish Civilization." *Journal of Latin American Studies*, vol. 23, no. 3 (1993), 637, 644; Liss, *Mexico under Spain*, 87; Baudot, *Utopía e historia*, 117; Ayuntamiento of Compostela to Charles V (1533), in Paso y Troncoso, *Epistolario de Nueva España*, vol. III, 33.

[14] Carlos Sempat Assadourian, "La despoblación indígena en Perú y Nueva España durante el siglo XVI y la formación de la economía colonial." *Historia Mexicana*, vol. 38, no. 3 (1989), 425.

[15] Las Casas, *Apologética Historia Sumaria*, vol. I, 237–41, 261–79.

understand them, which will be very soon, their religion and human works will be of great admiration.[16]

In recognizing familiar social structures, friars like Fuenleal argued that Mesoamerican sedentary societies held out the promise of something as yet unseen in the New World: an established and stable system of native Christian government.

The socio-political outlook of sixteenth century missionaries was fundamentally hierarchical and corporatist. Like the conquistadors who first negotiated with native rulers during the wars of conquest, Spanish missionaries initially dealt with local authorities as they would potentates anywhere in Eurasia: as absolute sovereigns over a well-defined jurisdiction. In the violent conditions of the conquest and its aftermath such assumptions were "the only realistic way to proceed."[17] In terms of religion, as well, missionaries followed the contemporary assumptions that "the common people easily follow the lord, and prince, who guides them."[18] Mendicant perceptions of indigenous politics obeyed a logic similar to that of *cuius regio eius religio*, the unity of politics and confession that had marked recent Spanish history and would soon ravage Europe. Writing to Charles V in 1532, fray Martín de Valencia declared that the political order of the recently conquered territory would line up with the expectations of its new Spanish sovereign. "And since [each] land follows the customs of its prince," he wrote, "and being Your Majesty so Catholic, of whom Scripture states that Diod declared 'I have found the Baron,' then it must follow that all that is subjected to him would be Catholic."[19] Missionaries thus targeted local kings early in their spiritual campaign.[20] Fray Jacobo de Testera praised the "obedience" that the temporal lords commanded from their commoners. "What lords," he asked, "have ever been better served in the whole world than these?"[21] By the 1530s, the sight of indigenous commoners following their rulers to the baptismal font in their thousands seemed to vindicate these assumptions.[22]

Missionaries were even more impressed by the broader class of nobility that surrounded local kings. They viewed the indigenous nobility through the blinders of their own social context and experience. The indigenous nobility could easily be classed according to the Spanish political concept

---

[16] Fuenleal to Crown (1533), in Paso y Troncoso, *Epistolario*, vol. XV, 176.
[17] Lockhart, *Nahuas*, 31.   [18] Torquemada, *Monarquía Indiana*, vol. III, 45.
[19] *Cartas de Indias*, vol. I, 55.   [20] Torquemada, *Monarquía Indiana*, 45.
[21] Fray Jacobo de Tastera to Charles V (1533), in *Cartas de Indias*, vol. I, 64.
[22] Motolinía, *Memoriales*, 258.

of *señor natural*, natural lords who "by inherent nature of superior qualities, goodness, and virtue, and by birth of superior station, attain power legitimately and exercise dominion."[23] Missionaries believed indigenous nobility to be endogamous like the aristocracies of Europe; they recognized the nobility's right to rule over native commoners because they inspired "fear and obedience" and instinctively seemed to "know how to deal with them."[24] As in Europe there seemed to be little ambiguity in the distinction between lord and commoner in Mexico, and this was no small source of comfort.

To some degree the missionaries were not mistaken in their observations of indigenous class divisions. Indigenous nobles, or pipiltin, were indeed distinguished from *macehualtin* (commoners), *mayeques* (serfs), and *tlacotin* (slaves) primarily because they were exempt from obligatory labor or tribute payments. Studies of early colonial records suggest that the native nobility consisted of between four and eight percent of the total population.[25] Nobles were supported by stipends allocated by the tlatoani as well as rents and tributes paid by serfs residing on their lands. These privileges made the pipiltin appear to Europeans as an estate, a corporate body of "natural lords" who ruled by hereditary rights and "immemorial" customs. Spanish documents referred to these nobles as *principales,* or "headmen."[26] If Charles V was God's chosen baron, then the indigenous noblemen were the missionaries' chosen barons to carry out the work of building his empire in New Spain.

Local rulers were drawn from this class of nobles through a combination of inheritance, election, and ratification. While tlatoani rulership (*tlatocayotl*) often passed on within the same extended family, the class of pipiltin still had the right to choose their tlatoani from among the

---

[23] Robert Chamberlain, "The Concept of *Señor Natural* as Revealed by Castilian Law and Administrative Documents." *Hispanic American Historical Review*, vol. XIX, no. 2 (1939), 130–7; Alonso de Zorita, *Life and Labor in Ancient Mexico: The Brief and Summary Relation of the Lords of New Spain by Alonso de Zorita*, trans. and ed. Benjamin Keen (Norman, OK: University of Oklahoma Press, 1994), 104.

[24] Zorita, *Brief and Summary Relation*, 118.

[25] Marina Anguiano and Matilde Chapa, "Estratificación social en Tlaxcala durante el siglo xvi," in *La estratificación social en la Mesoamérica prehispánica*, eds. Pedro Carrasco and Johanna Broda (Mexico City: INAH, 1976), 126–35; Ursula Dyckerhoff and Hans J. Prem, "La estratificación social en Huexotzinco," in Carrasco and Broda, eds. *Estratificación social*, 165; Mercedes Olivera, *Pillis y macehuales: Las formaciones sociales y los modos de producción de Tecali del siglo XII al XVI* (Mexico City: INAH, 1978), 106–10.

[26] Zorita, *Brief and Summary Relation*, 88–122; Fuenleal, Parecer (1532), García Icazbalceta, *Colección de documentos*, 170.

brothers, sons, and cousins of the deceased ruler. The nobles thus retained the right to reject unqualified blood relatives of the tlatoani and select the most qualified candidate. Throughout the sixteenth century the pipiltin continued to exercise this right as electors (*vocales*).[27] Imperial rulers, first Aztec and later Spanish, "exercised the power of confirmation" and veto over the candidates elected by local pipiltin. Missionaries also intervened in local elections by manipulating factions and influencing electors.[28] In complex polities where equally-matched subunits had to maintain a balance of power, the pipiltin opted for a rotational model that allowed each subunit a turn in ruling over the city-state.[29]

For many friars, the process by which indigenous nobilities selected their rulers was a clear indicator of their sophistication. Audiencia President Fuenleal, for example, declared in 1533 that natives in Mexico had "a superior means of electing officials" and that it therefore would "not be prudent for them to know the bad [ways] of the Spaniards."[30] Observers admired that local ruling classes continued to elect their tlatoque and informed the Audiencia of their selection, just as they had previously done to Aztec imperial authorities. In 1535 the principales of Otumba informed the *oidores* (Audiencia judges) of their newly elected ruler upon the death of their ruler. Vasco de Quiroga, a judge on the Audiencia, recalled that when electors in Tlaxcala and Michoacán chose a more qualified relative of the deceased tlatoani in lieu of direct heirs, "They notified [us] with such harmony and order, and with such good reasoning, that it was hard to believe."[31] And the Franciscan chronicler, Fray Toribio de Benevente Motolinía, went so far as to imply that native processes of succession were superior to European customs of primogeniture:

For it is not a small harm to the Republic that by obligation a son should inherit the lordship from his father, whether he be good or bad, because the good one will preserve the republic and lordship, but the bad one will destroy it. In antiquity, in many places kings and lords were elected, and since they sought out a good king, they were ruled well.[32]

---

[27] Zorita, *Brief and Summary Relation*, 55–6; Lockhart, *Nahuas*, 32; Gibson, *Aztecs*, 176.

[28] Lockhart, *Nahuas*, 31, 33.

[29] Robert Haskett, "Indian Town Government in Colonial Cuernavaca: Persistence, Adaptation, and Change." *Hispanic American Historical Review*, vol. 67, no. 2 (1987), 203, 210; Gibson, *Tlaxcala*, 105–6.

[30] Paso y Troncoso, *Epistolario*, vol. XV, 164.

[31] Vasco de Quiroga, *Información en derecho*, ed. Carlos Herrejón (Mexico City: SEP, 1985), 86.

[32] Motolinía, *Memoriales*, 494.

In similar ways, mendicant missionaries praised indigenous courts and tribute-collection.[33] To their minds all this demonstrated the capacity – and the right – of the indigenous nobility to maintain its place and its privileges, albeit on the condition that they accepted Christianization. According to Fuenleal, indigenous rulers possessed a legitimate right as "*señores*," or lords, "who possess their lordship since time immemorial," whether it was passed on to them by rights of inheritance or by "other customs" like elections. Now, as subjects to the emperor, they deserved to retain their lordships and access to tributes, "especially those who did not resist the doctrine and faith, who indeed have sought to take on our beliefs and customs."[34]

Yet all was not as it seemed. Europeans assumed that the indigenous nobility was noble by virtue of birth. Not surprisingly, indigenous nobles who benefitted from this perception embraced it unreservedly, arguing in their petitions for recognition that their dynasties had been ruling over their jurisdictions "since time immemorial."[35] Such claims exaggerated both the exclusivity and the endogamy of native noble classes. For much of Aztec history, the nobility had not been as closed as it was at the time of the Spanish conquest. In the fifteenth century there was a degree of mobility and meritocracy in Aztec society, especially during the reign of Ahuitzotl (1486–1502). Commoners could advance into the ranks of the nobles through military or even commercial success; conversely, ne'er-do-well grandchildren of lords who sank low in wealth and reputation could become indistinguishable from commoners.[36] The ascension of Moctezuma II to the throne in 1502 abruptly ended this social mobility. Moctezuma restored and entrenched the nobility with genealogical tests, thereby blocking commoners from entering the circles of power.[37] Pipiltin claims, and missionaries' acceptance of them, further rigidified a society whose stratification was neither as ancient nor as divided as native nobles let on to believe. In local conflicts over land and labor between nobles and

---

[33] Motolinía, *Memoriales*, 490; Fuenleal, Parecer (1532), García Icazbalceta, *Colección de documentos*, 178.

[34] Fuenleal, Parecer (1532), García Icazbalceta *Colección de documentos*, 170.

[35] María Elena Martínez, *Genealogical Fictions: Limpieza de Sangre, Religion, and Gender in Colonial Mexico* (Stanford: Stanford University Press, 2009), 105–22.

[36] Frederic Hicks, "Pre-hispanic Background of Colonial Political and Economic Organization in Central Mexico," in *Supplement to the Handbook of Middle American Indians*, ed. Ronald Spores (Austin, TX: University of Texas Press, 1986), 33; Lockhart, *Nahuas*, 102, 110–12; Berdan, *Aztecs of Central Mexico*, 51–5; Smith, *Aztecs*, 142–3; Conrad and Demarest, *Religion and Empire*, 36–7, 82.

[37] Berdan, ibid.; Conrad and Demarest, *Religion and Empire*, 82.

commoners, friars often helped to further stratify native society. In Cuauhtinchán, for example, commoners declared that the *guardian* of their Franciscan monastery, Fray Diego de Estremera, supported a local nobleman who illegally seized their lands and reduced them to vassalage. Estremera allegedly lent his support directly from the pulpit.[38]

The mendicant–pipiltin alliance laid the groundwork for a broader alignment of indigenous governments with Spanish institutions. In the 1540s colonial authorities began to introduce Spanish-style municipal governments in indigenous polities. The highest office in an indigenous jurisdiction was no longer to be the tlatoani, but rather the holder of the office of governor, or *gobernador*. Indigenous nobles, however, simply reaffirmed their current tlatoani as their gobernador.[39] Viceregal appointments show that Spanish rulers followed indigenous precedent and confirmed local elections of gobernadores, on condition that they cooperated with the mission enterprise.[40] Spanish authorities also integrated indigenous leadership position into *cabildos*, or municipal councils. Ruling elites fared differently in these changes according to local circumstances: while most adapted and tended to hang on to power, the introduction of cabildo government sometimes undermined local dynasties.[41] For missionaries, however, this alignment of native hierarchies with their objectives opened the way for ever deeper interventions in indigenous lives: friars began to regulate marriage in the nobility, they could be found tipping conflicts over lands and inheritances in the favor of their allies, they swayed elections to get their candidates elected, and they interfered in jurisdictional disputes.[42]

Mendicant missionaries also saw enormous logistical advantages in indigenous territorial politics. The conquest had taught Spaniards that the

---

[38] Denunciation by macehualtin of Fray Diego de Estremera, in *Documentos sobre tierras y señoríos en Cuauhtinchan*, ed. Luís Reyes García (Mexico City: INAH, 1978), 209, 108–9.

[39] Gibson, *Aztecs*, 33, 63–76, 102–10.

[40] Viceregal appointment, Taliscula (1543), AGN Mercedes, vol. 2, exp. 410, f. 170r; Viceregal appointment, Tizantlán (1540), AGN Civil, vol. 1271, f. 195v; Viceregal appointment, Xipacoya (1550), AGN Civil, vol. 1271, f. 202r.

[41] Gibson, *Aztecs*, 167–9; Delfina López Sarrenlangue, *La nobleza indígena de Pátzcuaro en la época virreinal* (Mexico City: UNAM, 1965), 88; Menegus, *Del señorío indígena*, 93.

[42] Hildeberto Martínez, *Colección de documentos coloniales de Tepeaca* (Mexico City: INAH, 1984), 519; *Tecomatlan v. Yanhuitlán* (1584), AGI Escribanía de Cámara 162C, f. 364v.

building blocks of empire in Mesoamerica lay in its city-states, and now these local jurisdictions would also lay the foundation for mendicant missions.[43] Unlike encomiendas, which often wantonly divided native jurisdictions among encomenderos, the mendicant mission tended to base its territorial organization on the native city-state.[44] Thus, when missionaries selected an altepetl to serve as their headquarters in a given area, they made the jurisdiction a *doctrina* (lit. "a place where doctrine is taught"). At the core of the doctrina was the missionary headquarters, the doctrina-monastery complex, which consisted of a large church and wide churchyard for outdoor doctrinal instruction, and the monastery, the friars' residence. Monasteries included friars' cells, a library, communal kitchen, cloister, gardens, and often stables and a farm. Although there are notable exceptions, most native city-states that were chosen by missionaries to become doctrinas were also selected by Spanish civil authorities to become *cabeceras*, or "head-towns." Towns deemed by missionaries and their native allies to be less important then became *visitas*, or mission stations that the friars would occasionally visit. This hub-and-spoke system is clearly illustrated in *Fig. 3.1*, the *Relación de Cuzcatlán* of 1579.

Native city-states thus laid the foundation for the mission enterprise: it was there where missionaries and nobles sealed their alliances, punished resistance, gathered congregations, and raised churches. Yet indigenous territoriality, alluring though it was for its apparent convenience, in fact plunged Spaniards headlong into the thickets and unseen traps of indigenous micropatriotism. By deciding which city-states would become cabeceras and doctrinas, Spanish officials and missionaries were effectively picking winners in rivalries among city-states that they could barely fathom, and that often went back decades and even centuries. Moreover, altepeme numbered in the hundreds, had ambiguous boundaries and internal power structures, and had contested identities and histories. By recognizing some indigenous power centers by the secular status of cabecera and spiritual status as mission doctrina, it followed that outlying towns of (perceived) lesser standing would receive the dubious distinction of subject-town, or *sujeto*, in secular terms, and a visita in terms of the mission. Polities that gained recognition as cabeceras and doctrinas secured crucial control over tribute collection, land distribution, and Church institutions, while those that did not tended to lose much of their

---

[43] Smith, *Aztecs*, 153–4; Lockhart, *Nahuas*, 14–5, 28. Gibson, *Aztecs*, 34.
[44] Gibson, *Aztecs*, 63–5.

FIGURE 3.1 Territorial arrangement of the mission enterprise.
Anon. Indigenous painters, c. 1579, Relación geográfica de Cuzcatlán. Nettie Lee.
Benson Collection, University of Texas Libraries, University of Texas at Austin.

sovereignty. Based on pre-conquest precedents, the mission enterprise constituted the hierarchical power relations within jurisdictions: by attending mass, contributing to the sustenance of missionaries, building the doctrina church, and even by receiving sacraments from missionaries in the doctrina, visitas were seen to acknowledge their obedience to cabecera rulers.[45] In territorial disputes, native litigants clashed over whether sovereignty consisted of possessing the material manifestations of power – a church, prison, noble palace – or if it was relational, constituted through the visita's delivery of tributes, mass attendance, and participation in patron saint celebrations in the cabecera. Ultimately, both Spanish policies and indigenous practice affirmed that indigenous sovereignty was constructed through both material and relational elements.[46]

Initially, it was the rulers of the most salient polities – those who seemed to command the most deference and whose palaces and temples cast the longest shadows – who had the clearest advantage in attracting missionaries. After all, it was impossible for Spaniards, even the most studious of the *nahuatlato* (Náhuatl-speaking) friars, to look into the complex web of city-states and recognize all of them equally and simultaneously. Instead, they dealt first with what they perceived to be the most powerful city-states.[47] Not surprisingly, nearly all of the sixty-four doctrinas that were founded in the 1520s and 1530s had been major political, economic, and religious centers in the former Aztec and Tarascan empires. Franciscans established doctrinas in five of six sovereign prehispanic capitals in central Mexico (Tenochtitlán, Texcoco, Tzintzuntzán, and Tlaxcala); the sixth independent indigenous kingdom, Meztitlán, was among the first doctrinas to be founded by the Augustinians. Franciscans quickly established relations with the rulers of the foremost altepeme in central Mexico, including Huexotzingo, Chalco, Tepeapulco, Toluca, Tula, Cuernavaca, and Cuauhtitlán. By 1540 mendicant missionaries also founded doctrinas in eighteen former Aztec and Tarascan tribute-collecting centers and garrisons. They also established doctrinas in former

---

[45] Litigation between cabeceras and sujetos over autonomy and boundaries referred to visita participation in the mission as a clear indicator of subject status: *Tecomatlán v. Yanhuitlán* (1584), AGI Ecribanía de Cámara 162C, ff. 501r–2v; *Tepexpan v. Temascalapa* (1550), AGI Justicia 164, no. 2, f. 265r.

[46] This contrast, present in many cabecera/sujeto disputes, is clearly and eloquently contrasted in the clashing *interrogatorios* presented by Tlayacapa and Totolapa in 1571: AGI Justicia 176, no. 2.

[47] Lockhart, *Nahuas*, 14–5, 28; Gibson, *Aztecs*, 34.

pilgrimage sites like Cholula and Molango.[48] The Mesoamerican map of imperial, commercial, and cultural power thus provided the path of least resistance for the expansion of mendicant missions.

For native rulers, the goal was clear: they needed to secure doctrina status from missionaries in order to make the strongest case for gaining political recognition as cabeceras from Spaniards. Across central Mexico, the first wave of doctrina foundations overlooked dozens of jurisdictions, large and small, each with its own territorial ambitions, defensive postures, and local pride. At the same time, the collapse of imperial networks of tribute, alliance, and military deployments, which had in some ways contained rivalries among neighboring city-states, uncorked the forces of micropatriotism and particularism. Native rulers scrambled to secure support from friars for setting up doctrinas in their jurisdictions, and thereby gain recognition and autonomy.[49] In 1526 the rulers of Tepeapulco traveled eighty kilometers just to speak with the friars.[50] Tepeapulco was still subject to the former imperial capital of Texcoco, and it had long fallen in Texcoco's sphere of influence, but local rulers likely saw that the mission could serve as a means for asserting autonomy from their overlords. Their effort paid off, and soon other altepeme subject to Texcoco also mobilized to gain status as doctrinas and thereby separate from their former imperial overlords. Temascalapa, for example, ceased its tribute payments to Texcoco at the time of the conquest, the town's first step in an ongoing campaign to achieve sovereignty.[51] Inevitably, mission expansion drove forces of consolidation and separatism, and while missionaries and royal officials tended to emphasize their support for the concentration of power in recognized cabeceras, the necessity to deepen the mission's territorial coverage in fact favored those jurisdictions that wished to separate from cabeceras and former imperial powers.

The European-style hub-and-spoke arrangement of the mission, with doctrinas/cabeceras anchoring outlying visitas/sujetos, further exacerbated these indigenous territorial tensions. In contrast with Iberian towns and provinces, which showed a clear hierarchy between the urban nucleus and the outlying landscape, power tended to be more dispersed in pre-

---

[48] See Appendix.

[49] Motolinía, *Memoriales*, 290; Indians of *Tlayacapan v. Tototlapan* (1571), AGI Justicia, 176, no. 2.

[50] Relación geográfica, Tepeapulco (1581), in Fernando del Paso y Troncoso, ed., *Relaciones geográficas de México* (Mexico City: Cosmos, 1979), 302.

[51] Lockhart, *Nahuas*, 27. *Tepechpan v. Temascalapa* (1550), AGI Justicia, 164, no. 2, f. 252v.

conquest indigenous polities. Most altepeme were actually more like a federation of semi-autonomous subunits (*calpoltin* and *tlaxilacallis*) than a territory dominated by a single center of power.[52] Calpoltin preserved a balance of power in the altepetl by rotating positions of power in the altepetl among themselves. Spaniards ignored or overlooked these arrangements, and instead concentrated power in the calpolli with the most prominent or conveniently-located urban nucleus. In doing so, their chosen calpolli became the seat of the cabecera and the doctrina. Rulers of overlooked calpoltin would then seek to restore their influence and sovereignty by lobbying to become cabeceras and doctrinas themselves, or by forcing viceregal authorities and missionaries to recognize long-standing precedents of rotation. In Tlaxcala, for example, the rulers of two altepeme fought to restore a rotational system to their confederation after Spaniards had favored larger altepeme for two decades after the conquest.[53]

As much as missionaries made note of indigenous politics to advance their goals, native rulers observed the missionaries as well. In particular, native rulers manipulated the territorial rivalries among the mendicant Orders just as much as the missionaries manipulated indigenous politics. Ambitious rulers of overlooked jurisdictions were able to distance themselves from their native overlords by establishing ties with a different Order than the one based in their cabecera. Once they secured doctrina status from their new allies it was possible to secede from their cabecera. This was the pathway to political power for one ambitious ruler in the city-state of Amecameca named don Juan de Sandoval Tecuanxayacatzin, the ruler of the calpolli of Tlailotlacan. Amecameca was a composite altepetl, a federation of five calpoltin that shared power by rotation. The complexity of this polity lent itself to mutual intrigues among Spaniards and Indians alike: there was no clear ruler here nor was there an obvious cabecera.[54] When Franciscans first arrived in the area in 1525, they established themselves in a calpolli ruled by don Juan's sibling and fierce rival for power, don Tomás de San Martín Quetzalmazatzin.[55] Don Juan outflanked his brother by turning to the Franciscans' competitors, the Dominicans. For the Dominicans' part, Amecameca's position on the road that connected Mexico City with their mission field in Oaxaca, as well as its surrounding fertile plains, made it an appealing place to

---

[52] Lockhart, ibid., 14–58.
[53] Haskett, "Indian Town Government," 203, 210; Gibson, *Tlaxcala*, 105–6.
[54] Lockhart, *Nahuas*, 20, 24, 207.   [55] Chimalpáhin, *Ocho relaciones*, vol. II, 193.

establish a doctrina.[56] Accordingly Don Juan built a church and invited the Dominicans to come, which they accepted.[57] Similarly, in Tlaxcala, the secessionist altepetl of Quiahuiztlan broke away from its cabecera by offering the Dominicans an entry into a province where the Franciscans had held sway.[58] Both examples demonstrate the ways in which affiliation with a mendicant Order could have major implications for indigenous sovereignty.

The mission enterprise thus advanced rapidly on the terrain of native politics: first by legitimizing existing centers of power, and then by lending support to challengers. Mission expansion has long been presented as a purely European phenomenon, portraying missionaries as if they were pioneers plotting out areas where they could expand and consolidate their Orders' presence.[59] Yet missionaries only succeeded because their interests coincided with those of local rulers. Fierce competitions for territory raged within both indigenous and mendicant circles, driving the expansion of the mission. Above all, it advanced rapidly across central Mexico because native rulers, one by one, adopted the mission as a means of reconstructing political power in their communities in the wake of conquest, epidemics, and colonization.

ENFORCERS

The mission enterprise thrived in the realm of high Mesoamerican politics, but many questions remained regarding more quotidian questions of enforcement. Who would enforce the mission's imperatives among such an immense and dispersed population? How would a visible Church be built, and how would its exclusionary law be enforced? It remained, in

---

[56] Ricard, *Spiritual Conquest*, 70–1; Gerhard, *Guide*, 102–6; Elena Vázquez, *Distribución geográfica del Arzobispado de México, siglo XVI; Provincia de Chalco* (Mexico City: Biblioteca enciclopédica del Estado de México, 1968).

[57] Chimalpáhin, *Las ocho relaciones*, vol. II, 193–5; Kubler, *Mexican Architecture*. vol. II, 524–5; Mendieta, *Historia eclesiástica indiana*, vol. II, 303; Fray Antonio de Ciudad Real, *Tratado docto y curioso de las grandezas de la Nueva España*, eds. Josefina García Quintana and Víctor M. Castillo Farreras (Mexico City: UNAM, 1993), vol. II, 221–2; Peter Gerhard, "Congregaciones de indios en la Nueva España antes de 1570," *Historia Mexicana*, vol. 103 (1977), 356; Viceregal order to alcalde mayor de Chalco (1564), AGN Mercedes vol. 7, f. 299r–9v.

[58] James Lockhart, Frances Berdan, and Arthur J. O. Anderson, eds. and trans., *The Tlaxcalan Actas: A Compendium of the Records of the Cabildo de Tlaxcala (1545–1627)* (Salt Lake City, UT: University of Utah Press, 1986), 18, 98.

[59] Van Oss, *Church and Society*, 103–25; Vázquez Vázquez, *Distribución geográfica*.

effect, to make Christianity be seen, felt, and obeyed in the repeating patterns of daily life. In order to inculcate respect for the Church, the missionary–pipiltin alliance would have to police the mission enterprise among commoners, in rural hamlets, and even among the same nobles who were purportedly the missionaries' strongest allies.

Most friar-missionaries were firm believers in the redemptive potential of violence. As much as natives needed to be guided with "benignity and love," they also needed "pious punishment" to "stimulate" faith.[60] Fray Andrés de Olmos wrote in 1540 that, like children, natives would pay little heed to the missionaries' words unless they "felt a bit of the sting."[61] Only the fear of punishment would lend credence and power to the friars' demands: it corralled converts to mass, compelled the ambivalent to reject native rites, and ended the sin of concubinage.[62] Normally punishment fell to the secular arm. But friars contended that Mexico was an exceptional case because civil authorities were scarce, and the few that were available were so corrupt that they let crimes against the faith go unpunished. With this argument friars lobbied civil and papal authorities to grant them license to punish and incarcerate natives as they saw fit.[63] The future of the mission enterprise seemed to depend on the mendicants' control over the lash. Without it, one Franciscan stated, "there would be no more Christianity here than in Turkey."[64]

These efforts met with stiff resistance from Spanish civil and diocesan officials. After all, mendicant friars were not judges, neither in ecclesiastical nor civil law.[65] Spanish municipal authorities of México-Tenochtitlán in 1533 accused the Franciscans of whipping and beating the Indians, and worse, the friars sheared their hair (*"les trasquilaban"*) – the "greatest injury" that one could suffer in indigenous culture. Furthermore, they undermined royal justice by keeping prisons and stocks in their

---

[60] Cuevas, *Documentos*, 68–9.

[61] Andrés de Olmos to Archbishop Zumárraga (1540), in *Procesos de indios idólatras y hechiceros*, ed. Luís González Obregón (Mexico City: Archivo General de la Nación, 2002), 206.

[62] Cuevas, *Documentos*, ibid.; Obregón, ibid.; Fray Juan de Pimentel on applying corporal punishment (1562), AGI México, 368.

[63] Archbishop Zumárraga (1537), in Cuevas, *Documentos*, 68; Torquemada, *Monarquía indiana* vol. III, 281; Empress to Audiencia of Mexico (1532), in Paso y Troncoso, *Epistolario*, vol. III, 26.

[64] Miguel Navarro, *relación* (1569), in García Icazbalceta, *Códice Mendieta*, vol. I, 113.

[65] Jorge E. Traslosheros, *Iglesia, justicia, y sociedad en la Nueva España: La Audiencia del Arzobispado de México, 1528–1668* (Mexico City: Porrúa, 2004), 20–1.

doctrinas.[66] Temporal authorities likewise leveled damning accusations against a Dominican in the Zapotec highlands of Oaxaca who had allegedly burned four natives at the stake for idolatry – killing two and critically injuring the remainder – as well as jailing and flogging other natives as he willed, without trials.[67] Diocesan officials also denounced the friars, who were their chief intra-Church competitors in Mexico, for violating canon law by trying and punishing natives accused of idolatry.[68] The most infamous mendicant punishment was the inquisitorial execution of the native lord don Carlos Chichimecatecuhtli of Texcoco in 1539, a clear case of overstepping that moved Charles V to condemn the friars for their excessive punishment of a recent convert to Christianity.[69] A year later, Mexican bishops forbade friars from personally whipping natives or placing them in stocks or prisons, but they were allowed to apply "light coercion like that of a teacher over his student, or a master over his apprentice."[70] After initially defending their use of corporal punishment, by the 1560s the friars found themselves on the losing side of these battles. In 1564 the Franciscan Order officially banned all direct punishments, and in 1567 the viceroy ordered all mendicants to present their accusations against Indians to corregidores in lieu of punishing them themselves.[71]

More than the sight of friars on the hunt for idolaters, it was far more common for ecclesiastical investigations, punishments, and incarcerations to be carried out by local native officials. Even as they defended their right to inflict punishments, peripatetic friars like Fray Andrés de Olmos spoke in terms of *having* Indians lashed. After declaring a local ruler guilty of idolatry, for example, Olmos delegated the lash to his indigenous constable.[72] Indigenous officials assumed the exercise of day-to-day mission

---

[66] Ayuntamiento of Mexico to Charles V (1533), in Paso y Troncoso, *Epistolario*, vol. III, 84–5; Nuño de Guzmán to the Empress (1532), ibid., vol. II, 152–3.

[67] Audiencia commission, Zapotecas (1561), AGI Justicia, 279, no. 1, f. 2r.

[68] Traslosheros, *Iglesia, justicia, y sociedad*, 14–35; Archbishop Montúfar to Council of the Indies (1556), in Paso y Troncoso, *Epistolario*, vol. VIII, 75; Cathedral Chapter of Oaxaca on Dominican abuses (1562), AGI México, 368, no. 3.

[69] Royal Cédula (1540), in García Icazbalceta, *Zumárraga*, vol. IV, 172–3.

[70] Junta eclesiástica (1539), García Icazbalceta, *Zumárraga*, vol. III, 158–9.

[71] Miguel Navarro to Viceroy (1568), in *Cartas de religiosos (1539–1594)*, ed. Joaquín García Icazbalceta (Mexico City: Editorial Chávez Hayhoe, 1941), 55–6; Traslosheros, *Iglesia, justicia, y sociedad*, 24–31; Magnus Lundberg, *Unification and Conflict: The Church Politics of Alonso de Montúfar OP, Archbishop of Mexico, 1554–1572* (Uppsala: Swedish Institute of Missionary Research, 2002), 111–41.

[72] González Obregón, *Procesos*, 214–5.

discipline.[73] In Xochimilco, Franciscans instructed a native constable to "punish any rebel they find with twelve lashes or by putting them away in prison for a day."[74] Similarly, in doctrinas run by the diocesan clergy, priests delegated authority to local officials in open emulation of their mendicant counterparts.[75] Given the legal constraints on direct punishments as well as the logistical impossibility to monitor vast jurisdictions, missionaries passed the lash and prison keys over to native officials.

The friars found themselves on firmer legal ground in delegating the authority to punish to indigenous officials. The emperor himself had encouraged indirect rule in 1530, when he instructed Spanish officials to "examine the *policía*" of native communities and "keep [all] customs ... that are not contrary to our sacred religion."[76] Accordingly, Audiencia President Ramírez de Fuenleal first applied this concept to indigenous overseers in the markets of Mexico City. Over loud opposition, Fuenleal argued that indigenous *alguaciles* (officers) should be given full authority to punish minor offenders. The Crown approved Fuenleal's request and thus set an important precedent for the expansion of indigenous governance.[77]

The first generation of native constables who carried out punishments were niños de monasterio, veterans of the missionaries' early educational efforts as well as their violent campaigns of conversion. Through their work, Motolinía tells us, the *Ave María* and the *Our Father* echoed in remote villages and wilderness hermitages beyond the ambit of missionaries.[78] In 1550 Franciscan fray Rodrigo de la Cruz reported that he had deployed children of native elites to remote villages the frontier of Nueva Galicia (Jalisco) where "the fathers can only visit from time to time."[79] Soon these native acolytes passed from serving as proxy-preachers to

---

[73] Memorial, Fray Miguel Navarro (1569), in García Icazbalceta, *Códice Mendieta*, vol. I, 113; Mendicant provincials to Philip II (1561), *Cartas de Indias*, vol. I, 149; Mendicant provincials to Philip II (1564), in García Icazbalceta, *Códice Mendieta*, vol. I, 20.

[74] Relación, Fray Miguel Navarro (1569), in García Icazbalceta, *Códice Mendieta*, vol. I, 112.

[75] García Pimentel, *Descripción del arzobispado de México hecha en 1570 y otros documentos* (Mexico City, 1897), 62, 74–6, 89, 93, 97, 99, 143, 222.

[76] Royal cédula (1530), in Rodrigo de Aguiar y Acuña and Juan Francisco Montemayor y Córdoba de Cuenca, eds., *Sumarios de la recopilación general de las leyes de Indias Occidentales* [1677] (Mexico City: UNAM, Fondo de Cultura Económica, 1994), 4:4:60, p. 705.

[77] Fuenleal to Empress (1533), Paso y Troncoso, *Epistolario*, vol. XV, 164.

[78] Motolinía, *Memoriales*, 285; Fray Jacobo de Testera to Charles V (1533), in *Cartas de Indias*, vol. I, 64.

[79] Fray Rodrigo de la Cruz to Charles V (1550), in Cuevas, *Documentos*, 159–60.

proxy-enforcers. Many were students of the mission schools like San José de los Naturales in Mexico City, Santa Cruz de Tlatelolco and San Agustín in Tiripitío, institutions long recognized both for their audacious but failed projects of ordaining native clergy.[80] While racial restrictions prevented these mission schools from training native priests, missionaries nonetheless declared them to be "useful" in producing "judges, gobernadores, and officials of the republic."[81] Motolinía compared native students in Mexico favorably with the Moriscos of Spanish Granada, who "after so much time since their conversion" still had not even produced a set of reliable altar boys.[82] By contrast, thousands of students across central Mexico had career paths like Francisco, a niño de monasterio who served at the side of Fray Andrés de Olmos before taking a post as *nahuatlato* (interpreter) for the native ruler of Matatlán. The identities of such students remained tied to the friars: they were known to have been "raised" by them, a fact that evoked both respect and ridicule.[83]

This convergence of political and religious power was rooted in indigenous structures. Priestly and political leadership was deeply intertwined in pre-hispanic polities, with noble families simultaneously holding offices in both tecpan and teocalli. Young pipiltin served as acolytes and temple-keepers, assisting priests and tending flames.[84] The youths then advanced into civil-religious hierarchies. Similarly, native religious officials in the mission Church directed rituals in much the same way that their forbears had done in prehispanic temples. Missionaries like Motolinía attributed the mission's success to these precedents: just as assistants had once hauled firewood for their pagan shrines, they served the Church with

---

[80] Llaguno, *La personalidad jurídica*, 21; Martin Austin Nesvig, "The 'Indian Question' and the Case of Tlatelolco," in *Local Religion in Colonial Mexico*, Nesvig, ed. (Albuquerque: University of New Mexico Press, 2006), 63–85; Margarita Menegus and Rodolfo Aguirre, *Los indios, el sacerdocio, y la Universidad en Nueva España* (Mexico City: UNAM, 2006), 22–33.

[81] Martín de Valencia and Franciscans (1532), *Cartas de Indias*, vol. I, 56; Llaguno, *La personalidad jurídica*, 12; Joaquín García Icazbalceta, ed. *Códice Franciscano* (Mexico City: Editorial Chávez Hayhoe, 1941), 62.

[82] Motolinía, *Memoriales*, 285.

[83] The *tlatoani* of Matlatlán ridiculed Francisco for being "raised by the fathers." Testimony of Francisco, *nahuatlato* de Matlatlán (1540), in González Obregón, *Procesos*, 212. Don Carlos of Texcoco also challenged his nephew for believing what the friars had taught him: See González Obregón, *Proceso del cacique de Tezcoco*, 40–4.

[84] Pedro Carrasco, "The Civil-Religious Hierarchy in Mesoamerican Communities: Pre-Hispanic Background and Colonial Development." *American Anthropologist*, vol. 63, no. 3 (1961), 487–92; Lockhart, *Nahuas*, 40, 206; Motolinía, *Memoriales*, 149.

the same "fire of devotion."[85] In both cases, religious service dignified those who claimed the mantle of rule.[86]

The noble status of the teopantlaca – the "church people" who organized the native Church – can be seen in a hispanicized Nahuatl term employed in early missionary records. Inquisition and administrative records, first dated 1540, refer to the indigenous servants of the Church as *pilhuan*, a term that derives from the Nahua *tepilhuan*, meaning "someone's children." Thus, like the term for nobleman (*pilli*, "child"), *tepilhuan* loosely translates to the Spanish *hidalgo* – a child of noblemen – but it may also have a connotation of being the sons of the friars as well.[87] Inquisition trials detail the central role of these native Church constables in maintaining the Church, investigating accusations of idolatry, and punishing offenders. In Iguala, for example, two *"indios pilguanes de la santa iglesia"* named Domingo and Juan denounced their tlatoani for idolatry and concubinage.[88]

Soon the friars' former acolytes could be seen in communities bearing *varas de justicia*, the staffs of justice that indicated their civil authority to police religion. Known in Spanish records as *alguaciles* (constables), in native communities these officials were known as *topiles*, or staff-bearers.[89] These officials assisted in investigations against idolatry, ensured mass attendance, and carried out any punishments that missionaries required.[90] Initially these officials were responsible for both civil and ecclesiastical crimes, but missionaries lobbied hard to appoint constables focused exclusively on spiritual matters.[91] In 1550, Viceroy Mendoza appointed dozens of native constables to the newly-created office of *alguacil de la iglesia*, or church constable.[92] Church constables in the

---

[85] Motolinía, *Memoriales*, 149.

[86] Lockhart, *Nahuas*, 40; Carrasco, "Civil-Religious Hierarchy," 487–92.

[87] Alonso de Molina, *Vocabulario en lengua castellana/mexicana, mexicana/castellana* (Mexico City: Porrúa, 2004); Chimalpáhin, *Las ocho relaciones*, vol. II, 159, 232; Lockhart, *Nahuas*, 102; Carrasco, ibid.

[88] Inquisition trial of cacique of Iguala (1540), in González Obregón, *Procesos*, 201–3; See also Gerhard, *Guide*, 147; Kubler, *Mexican Architecture*, vol. II, 518; Grijalva, *Crónica*, 158.

[89] Molina translated *topil* as *alguazil*: ibid., 150. See also Lockhart, *Nahuas*, 43, 217; William B. Taylor, *Magistrates of the Sacred: Priests and Parishioners in Eighteenth-Century Mexico* (Stanford: Stanford University Press, 1996).

[90] Menegus, *Del señorío indígena*, 85.

[91] Manuel Pazos, "Los Misioneros Franciscanos de Méjico en el siglo XVI y su sistema penal respecto de los indios," *Archivo Ibero-Americano*, vol. XIII, no. 52 (1953), 416–8.

[92] Relación, Antonio de Mendoza (1550), in *Los virreyes españoles de América*, ed. Lewis Hanke (Madrid: Atlas, 1976), vol. I, 49–52; Menegus, *Del señorío indígena*, 84. The

sixteenth century tended to be indigenous nobles elected for one-year terms by their peers.[93] As was the case regarding tlatoanis and governadores, viceroys reserved the right to ratify or veto these appointments.[94]

An early viceregal appointment in 1550 illustrates the responsibilities of the alguacil de doctrina. Issued to don Antonio, a native nobleman in Jalapa (Veracruz), the appointment ratified his election by his fellow principales. The viceroy charged don Antonio with ensuring ecclesiastical justice in Jalapa, a recently founded Franciscan doctrina. Don Antonio was to assist the four resident friars in enforcing doctrinal requirements across a sprawling jurisdiction that included several large nearby towns as well as more sparsely populated regions to the north. Charged to obey the friars "in all matters related to doctrine and to the benefit of the natives' souls," he was to "prohibit and ensure that no drinking, sacrifices, nor other idolatries be practiced, nor any other offenses to our lord" during his patrols.[95] The viceroy also instructed him to ensure that everyone "heard the Christian doctrine, went to mass, and attended all other divine offices on the days and times that the friars of Xalapa designate." He had full discretion under royal law to punish transgressors as required.[96] By the 1570s, alguaciles de la iglesia like don Antonio could be found in indigenous governments at all levels and mission affiliations.[97] In densely

---

Mixtecs of Oaxaca called this same office the "church staffholder," or *tay tatnu huahi ñuhu*. Terraciano, *Mixtecs*, 286.

[93] Viceroy to alguaziles de doctrina, Suchicoatlán (1577), AGN Indios, vol. 1, exp. 137, f. 51r.

[94] Viceregal appointment of Antonio, Jalapa (1550), AGN Mercedes, tomo 3, exp. 197, f. 87v; Viceregal appointment of Esteban Cortés, principal, Jojutla (1591), AGN Indios, vol. 3, exp. 325, f. 75r.

[95] Kubler, *Mexican Architecture*, vol. II, 485–6; Gerhard, *Guide*, 376; Oroz, *Oroz Codex*, 257.

[96] Appointment of Antonio, ibid.

[97] García Pimentel, *Descripción del arzobispado*, 62, 74–6, 89, 93, 97, 99, 143, 222; Other viceregal appointments of alguaciles de doctrina: Xochimilco, 1558: Relación, Fray Miguel Navarro (1569) in García Icazbalceta, *Códice Mendieta*, vol. I, 111–2; Mexico City-San José de los Naturales, 1578: AGN Indiferente Virreinal, vol. 6063, exp. 14; Toluca, 1578, 1579, 1584, and 1585: AGN Hospital de Jesús, vol. 277, exp. 2, cuaderno primero, ff. 16r–20v; Mexico City-Capilla de San José de los Naturales, 1581: AGN General de Parte vol. 2, exp. 1085, f. 242r; Temascaltepec, 1582: AGN Indios vol. 2, exp. 216, f. 55v; Jojutla, 1591: AGN Indios vol. 3, exp. 325, f. 75r. The *tasación* (tribute reassement) of indigenous towns of 1575–1580 provides a valuable source the organization of indigenous governments. The *tasación* covers all of AGN Indios, vol. 1, and the office appears in entries for Tlancayula (Pánuco): exp. 100, f. 37v; Teozapotitlán: exp. 120, f. 44v; Malila (Sierra Norte de Meztitlán): exp. 122, f. 45r; Tecpatepec: exp. 129, f. 48r; Suchicoatlán: exp. 137, f. 51r; Cuatepec: exp. 139, f. 51v; Tlanchinoltepec (Sierra Norte de Metztitlán): exp.155, f. 57r; Oaxaca: exp. 170, f. 62v; Huamuxtitlán: exp. 182, f. 67r; Tlatlapanala: exp. 185, f. 67v;

populated cities and remote hamlets alike, the figure of the *topil* was essential to the task of enforcing adherence to the mission.

As native policing became more specialized, a new office emerged to coordinate and supervise church constables: that of the *fiscal*. Aptly called the "equivalent of cacique in spiritual matters," the fiscal oversaw investigations and directed *alguaciles* in their efforts to police idolatry and enforce Church attendance.[98] They were authorized to make arrests and deliver suspects to ecclesiastical authorities.[99] These officials became the missionaries' most important native interlocutors, for it was the fiscal who knew the religious life of the indigenous community, as well as how to "uncover the evils" of idolatry, bigamy, and indifference.[100] It has long been assumed that the office of fiscal was insignificant until the late sixteenth century, but records of ecclesiastical investigations reveal that *fiscales* were supervising native church constables as early as the late 1540s.[101] By the 1550s they could be found even in marginal areas like the Misteca and Western Michoacán.[102] Viceregal records note the excesses of fiscales like Juan de Gaytán in Indaparapeo, who took to the pulpit to forbid parishioners from listening to any priests other than the one for whom he worked. By viceregal decree, Gaytan was removed from his post.[103]

These church officials mobilized indigenous communities, especially those in outlying subject towns, to attend mass and indoctrination in the doctrina. Indigenous governments already had an entire infrastructure ready to assist them in the endeavor. Missionaries and constables relied on a network of ward-captains called "keepers of twenty" (*centepanpixque*)

Chalma (sujeto of Ocuila): exp. 186, f. 68r; Coatepec (sujeto of Jalapa): exp. 196, f. 72v; Cocula: exp. 197, f. 73r.

[98] Lockhart, *Nahuas*, 211; Taylor, *Magistrates of the Sacred*, 324–32.

[99] Appointment of Pablo Damián, *indio*, to assist in idolatry investigation (1564), AGN Mercedes, tomo 7, f. 331v.

[100] Bishops of Mexico to Audiencia (1565), in Cuevas, *Documentos*, 285; Appointment of diocesan fiscales in México-Tenochtitlán and Tlatelolco (1556), AGN Mercedes, tomo 4, f. 317r.

[101] Ricard, *Spiritual Conquest*, 97–9; Lockhart, *Nahuas*, 210–3; Trial of Juan, *indio* of Tula, for bigamy (1541, 1549), AGN Indiferente Virreinal, vol. 2529, exp. 1; Library of Congress, Krauss ms. 140, ff. 480v, 491r; Lundberg, *Unification and Conflict*, 127.

[102] Viceregal order to *alcalde mayor* of Oaxaca (1556), AGN General de Parte, vol. 1, exp. 49, f. 10r.

[103] Viceroy to Indians of Indaparapeo (1575), AGN Mercedes, tomo 4, f. 316v. The area had been evangelized by secular clergy, but that Dominican friars had recently taken over the nearby district of Huajuapan when this incident occurred: Gerhard, *Guide*, 130–1.

and "keepers of a hundred" (*macuiltecpanpixqui*), who then reported to barrio-officers called *tepixques* and *tequitlatos*.[104] These officials originally functioned as an indigenous "mode of governance" for tribute collection and rounding up laborers for public works, but now friars were "used this organization," a Franciscan report explained in 1569, "for everything that is related to doctrine and spiritual policing."[105] Officials kept track of those who failed to show up to mass, and if the truants lacked a credible reason the officials gave them twelve lashes before the assembled congregation. Franciscans were careful to note that officials lashed delinquents over their clothes, unlike the lashes that the same officials administered to civil offenders like those who failed to report for labor drafts. After these punishments the natives recited their prayers and heard mass.[106]

Mobilizing residents to attend mass was far more than an act of piety, for mass attendance was also a vital expression of political power and local sovereignty. Most crucially, mass attendance in the doctrina coincided with tribute collection cycles and aided labor drafts.[107] Moreover, civil power had long been reaffirmed in Mesoamerica through religious ritual. Examples of forced attendance of religious rites had abounded in the Aztec Empire, and rulers certainly must have recalled the more famous episodes like Ahuitzotl's temple dedication in 1487, when the emperor declared war on rulers who deigned to reject his invitation.[108] In this vein, in 1552 the rulers of Yanhuitlán ordered the rulers of their claimed sujeto, Tecomatlán, to be publically lashed for refusing to participate in celebrations of the patron saint's feast day.[109] The very act of participating in religious rituals reaffirmed the ties of obedience that bound the various jurisdictions and classes that comprised the city-state. This did not change after conversion to Christianity: indigenous rulers associated mass attendance with political obedience, and Spanish rulers, far from insisting on the best solution for indoctrination, were sympathetic to their native proxies. Ceding any

---

[104] Lockhart, *Nahuas*, 43; Gibson, *Aztecs*, 183; González Obregón, *Procesos*, 196.

[105] García Icazbalceta, *Códice Franciscano*, 70.

[106] García Icazbalceta, *Códice Franciscano*, 59, 70–4; García Pimentel, *Descripción del arzobispado*, 63, 92.

[107] García Icazbalceta, *Códice Mendieta*, vol. I, 86–8; García Icazbalceta, *Códice Franciscano*, 85, 116, 135. AGI Indiferente General 1529, f. 155v.

[108] Davies, *Aztecs*, 173–5.

[109] For their part, the natives of Tecomatlán contended that mass attendance did not constitute subjugation – an argument refuted by their indigenous opponents, friars, and royal justices at both the Audiencia and the Council of the Indies. *Tecomatlán v. Yanhuitlán* (1584), AGI Ecribanía de Cámara 162C, f. 388v.

ground to recalcitrant sujetos would only invite more protests, which in turn would unravel the fragile public order.[110]

The considerable distances between many subject towns and their doctrinas ensured a constant stream of petitions and complaints. For most people, the experience of the mission Church involved an arduous commute. Enforcing doctrinal discipline and mass attendance outside the principal centers, in the thousands of visitas where most indigenous neophytes in New Spain actually lived, required tremendous energies. Friars frequently complained of long mule-rides, drenching rainfalls, and treacherous passages across rivers as they sought to visit their native charges.[111] If the missionaries' visitation circuit was a lonely *vía crucis*, attending mass was a collective ordeal for the residents of outlying visitas. On most Sundays and feast days, constables rounded up visita residents and marched them to their doctrina churches. Their journeys were made on foot. The five hundred residents of the visita of Ecatzingo, including women and children, had to walk three leagues (16.5 km) to their Dominican doctrina in Chimalhuacan Chalco just to attend mass. In a petition for relief, they declared to the viceroy that these frequent journeys "placed their lives at risk."[112]

Although some of these commutes were unavoidable in sparsely populated areas, subject towns tended to be forced on these long marches to mass for reasons of politics. Residents of subject towns were not permitted to attend mass in doctrinas outside their jurisdictions. In 1566, for example, several visitas of Tenango sued their rulers and Dominican missionaries in order to shorten their marches to mass. The visitas declared that they were being forced to make grueling treks of between three and five leagues (15–20 km) to Tenango, simply because they were sujetos of that town, rather than to Totolapa, a Augustinian doctrina that was much closer to them. Rather than testing the journey himself, the

---

[110] Viceroy on mass attendance, Amilpaneca (1551), AGI Patronato 16, no. 2, r. 32, exp. 606; Viceroy to Tacubaya (1550), Library of Congress, Kraus ms. 140, f. 6v; *Atlatlauhca v. Tlayacapa* (1571), AGI Justicia, 176, no. 2.

[111] From the Franciscan monastery at Jalapa, for example, friars traveled eight leagues (forty-five kilometers) to their visita in the town of Ixhuacan. Fray Alonso Ponce traveled this route in 1589 by mule in one long day. Leaving early from Jalapa, he crossed three gorges, a major river, and five kilometers of difficult roads uphill until he reached Ixhuacan at night, drenched from hours of rain. Viceroy to Franciscans of Xalapa and natives of Ixguaca (1592), Indios vol. 6, exp. 308, f. 83r; Gerhard, *Guide*, 375–8; Ciudad Real, *Tratado docto y curioso*, vol. II, 387.

[112] Viceregal order to alcalde mayor, Chalco (1592), AGN Indios, vol. 6, exp. 249, f. 63r.

local Spanish *alcalde mayor* ordered to investigate the matter only interviewed the cabecera rulers, who dismissed the residents' complaints.[113]
Viceregal records abound with such desperate petitions: visitas reported
that friars stopped visiting them, compelling them to commute more
often; they also complained about the fines levied on pregnant women
for non-attendance that were lining the friars' pockets.[114] For their part,
Mexican bishops did attempt to regulate the distances traveled to mass,
and they exempted the young, the sick, the pregnant, and the elderly from
making these arduous journeys. In 1565, the Second Provincial Council
ruled that visitas could attend mass in their nearest doctrina without
regard to their jurisdictional affiliation.[115]

Yet because mass attendance held together the polities underlying the
colonial state, viceroys consistently sided with cabecera rulers in these
disputes.[116] The viceroyalty authorized local rulers to apply all force
necessary to ensure attendance.[117] The visitas were bound to their cabeceras, and as onerous as the distances were, that relationship was the best
guarantee that tributes would be collected, churches filled, and vices
combated. Residents of visitas marched on in the hope that their hamlets
would one day become doctrinas, and thereby end their commutes.

Even more challenging than ensuring collective attendance was catch-
ing individual truants who skipped mass. In Mexico City, dense urban
crowds provided ample opportunity for natives to escape their church
constables. On holy days of obligation in the 1570s and 1580s, church
constables working for the Chapel of San José de los Naturales tracked
delinquents to Spanish workshops and *pulquerías*, where they passed the
day with a holy water of their own. Others found refuge in rooms rented
on the rooftops of Spanish homes. "In the Spaniards' homes," the viceroy
wrote, "the Indians cannot be compelled to attend mass and catechesis,

---

[113] Depositions on Guaçoçongo mass attendance in Tenango (1566), UT Benson, WB
Stevens Collection, no. 890, f. 1r.

[114] Viceregal order, doctrina attendance in Tanchinol (1583), AGN Indios, vol. 2, exp. 653,
f. 150v.

[115] Llaguno, *La personalidad jurídica*, 181; García Pimentel, *Descripción del arzobispado*,
59, 85, 89, 135.

[116] Depositions on Guaçoçongo mass attendance (1566), UT Benson, WB Stevens Collection, no. 890, f. 1r.

[117] Ilamatlán, Veracruz: AGN Indios, vol. 6, exp. 1152, f. 316v; Tezontepec, Hidalgo: AGN
Indios vol. 6, 2a parte, exp. 193, f. 44r; Chimalhuacan: AGN Indios, vol. 6, 2a parte,
exp. 401, f. 90r.

nor are they punished for the sins that they commit in public."[118] The viceroy was obliged to authorize indigenous alguaciles to search for delinquents in Spanish houses and workshops.[119] This was urban flight from doctrine, alguaciles, and friars: instead of the hills, these natives escaped quite literally to the homes of their invaders.

The "church people" not only disciplined commoners; they also enforced the spirituality of their own elite class, the pipiltin. Native fiscales and alguaciles were at the front lines of policing high crimes against the faith like idolatry and bigamy. The apostolic Inquisition led by Fray Juan de Zumárraga in the 1530s relied extensively on the work of native constables, and in like manner viceregal authorities ordered them to report any leads to ecclesiastical prosecutors.[120] When rumors of idolatry in Texcoco reached Viceroy Mendoza in 1538, he instructed the gobernador of that jurisdiction to mobilize his alguaciles. This resulted in the arrest of the gobernador's own brother, don Carlos of Texcoco.[121]

Collaboration tested the strength of the mendicant–pipiltin alliance. Pragmatic though it was to ally with the friars, the pipiltin were pulled ever deeper into the missionaries' project of social and spiritual transformation. Missionaries took aim at two pillars of indigenous power deemed inimical with Christianity: elite kinship networks forged through polygamy, and elite patronage of native ritual practices. Missionaries sought to replace polygamous marriages, which were essential to sealing cross-regional elite networks, with monogamous conjugal unions.[122] By royal order all baptized Indians had to marry *in facie ecclesie* (before the Church) and renounce concubinage.[123] Mendicants urged husbands with multiple wives to select either their first or favorite wife and dispense with the others.[124] Indigenous annals record the beginning of this process as a

---

[118] License to *alguacil de doctrina*, Tlatelolco (1596), AGN Indios, vol. 6, exp. 1114, f. 305r.

[119] AGN Indiferente Virreinal, vol. 6063, exp. 14, ff. 1r–2r; Appointment of Miguel Francisco, Indian of the Chapel of San José (1581), AGN General de Parte, vol. 2, exp. 1085, f. 242r.

[120] González Obregón, *Procesos*, 99, 178, 196, 215; Viceregal order to *alguaciles* (1544), AGN Mercedes, vol. 2, exp. 578, f. 235v.

[121] Viceregal order to *gobernador* of Texcoco (1538), AGN Civil, vol. 1271, f. 173r.

[122] Motolinía, *Memoriales*, 278; Cline, "Spiritual Conquest Reexamined," 475; Josefina Muriel, *Las indias caciques de Corpus Christi* [1963] (Mexico City: UNAM, 2001), 27.

[123] Cline, "Spiritual Conquest Reexamined," 475.

[124] Ricard, *Spiritual Conquest*, 110–6; Cline, "Spiritual Conquest Reexamined," 476; AGN Indiferente Virreinal, vol. 2529, exp. 1.

significant event in the life of the community. One conflated the temple destructions in 1524 with alterations in family life: "and this was also when they took the mistresses from the houses of the lords."[125] Other annals simply stated, "Here marriage began."[126] Like matchmakers, missionaries intervened in each ruler's selection of a Christian bride from among their wives.[127]

Many nobles resisted these efforts. Censuses conducted in Tepoztlán (Morelos) in the 1530s show that indigenous rulers in three of the five towns surveyed admitted to their polygamy, apparently indifferent to any punishments that they could incur for their practices.[128] Meanwhile native constables in the nearby town of Ocuituco found local rulers were still marrying natives according to indigenous custom even ten years after receiving baptism.[129] Fiscales and alguaciles uncovered marriages in which native lords kept one wife according to indigenous custom and another according to the Christian one, as if they were hedging in this world as well as the next.[130] Some nobles warned that monogamy would undermine their status in indigenous society by rendering them indistinguishable from commoners who could not afford to maintain multiple wives. In 1539 don Carlos, heir to the rulership of Texcoco, upbraided his nephew, a niño de monasterio:

> It is not appropriate that we pay so much attention to what the friars preach to us ... they perform their duties and do all that they can not to have women. They disregard the things of this world, even women. So let the fathers do as they will ... it is their duty, *but it is not ours.*[131]

That same year, a native judge and former Franciscan student refused to renounce his wives and publicly questioned the friars' motives for

[125] Juan Manuel Pérez Zavallos and Luís Reyes García ed. and trans. *La fundación de San Luis Tlaxialtemalco, según los Títulos primordiales de San Gregorio Atlapulco (1519–1606)* (Mexico City: Delegación Xochimilco-Gobierno del Distrito Federal, 2003), 52.

[126] Pérez Zavallos and Reyes García, *La fundación*, 53; INAH, Anales antiguos de México, tomo 273, vol. II, f. 435; *Anales toltecas*: f. 235. The *Anales mexicanos* conflate the introduction of marriage with the destruction of the Temple of Azcapotzalco: f. 513.

[127] Motolinía, *Memoriales*, 277–8; Chimalpáhin, *Las ocho relaciones*, vol. II, 175.

[128] Cline, "Spiritual Conquest Reexamined," 475.

[129] Inquisition trial against Critobal and Martín, *indios principales* of Ocuituco (1539), in González Obregón, *Procesos*, 158.

[130] Trial of Juan, *indio* of Tula, for bigamy (1541 & 1549), AGN Indiferente Virreinal, vol. 2529, exp. 1; Trial of Francisco, *indio*, for bigamy (1538), in González Obregón, *Procesos*, 79–86; Library of Congress, Krauss ms. 140, ff. 480v, 491r.

[131] Denunciation of Francisco Maldonado (1539), in González Obregón, *Proceso inquisitorial del cacique de Texcoco*, 41. Emphasis is mine.

wanting to "know the sins of others."[132] In Inquisition evidence the pattern of resistance is clear: those who opposed the friars on matters of marriage also questioned their authority to intervene in native life. By maintaining vast kinship networks through polygamy, they were seeking to maintain a core ideal of what it meant to be a member of the pipiltin.[133]

The greatest threats to the mission enterprise thus seemed to be hiding in plain sight among the very nobles whom the friars had educated. A local ruler in Matatlán prevented residents from attending mass at the Franciscan doctrina of Hueytlalpan, and later admitted that he had kept concubines and performed native rites in secret.[134] Mendicants under the leadership of Archbishop Zumárraga decided to set an example: they took their most prominent prisoner, don Carlos of Texcoco, and had him burned alive in Mexico City. The friars warned other suspected idolaters that they, too, could end up tied to the pyre if they deceived them.[135] The *auto de fé* was remembered for centuries in indigenous annals.[136]

Missionaries, indigenous officials, and viceregal authorities agreed that fear was essential to lead the populace to virtue. After the initial "springtime" of missionary-native contact, one Franciscan wrote forebodingly, the newly converted – and especially nobles – now needed to "feel the bite of winter."[137] Attendance at mass also suffered in the absence of compulsion. In Cuauhtitlán, one of the first *doctrinas* founded in New Spain, native constables lapsed in prosecuting doctrinal delinquents in the 1590s, perhaps due to the disruptions of epidemics. When word reached the viceroy that masses were emptying out, he demanded that the jurisdiction deploy church constables to arrest the delinquents and set an example by lashing them in the market.[138] For without the staff and the lash to ensure religious adherence, the crowds in church patios would thin

---

[132] Trial of Marcos and Francisco, *indios* (1539), in González Obregón, *Procesos*, 110–2.

[133] González Obregón ibid.; Lopes Don, *Bonfires of Culture: Franciscans, Indigenous Leaders, and Inquisition in Early Mexico, 1524–1540* (Norman, OK: University of Oklahoma Press, 2010), 159.

[134] Trial, ruler of Matatlán (1540), González Obregón, *Procesos*, 205–15.

[135] Trial of Martín, *indio* of Coyoacán (1539), AGN Inquisición vol. 36, ff. 224r–5bis; Obregón, ed. ibid., 15, 106, 113, 171, 207; AGN Inquisición, vol. 1, exp. 6, f. 6v.

[136] Indigenous annals mention the execution. INAH, Anales antiguos de México, tomo 273, vol. II, f. 513; Eustaquio Celestino Solís and Luis Reyes García, eds. *Anales de Tecamachalco: 1398–1590* (Mexico City: Fondo de Cultura Económica, 1992), 27; Pérez Zavallos and Reyes García, *La fundación*, 57; Chimalpáhin, *Las ocho relaciones*, vol. II, 198–9.

[137] Trial of ruler of Matatlán (1540), González, ed., *Procesos*, ibid., 206–7.

[138] Viceregal order, Cuauhtitlán (1595), AGN Indios, vol. 6, exp. 937, f. 253r; Viceroy to *gobernador*, Cuauhtitlán (1593), AGN Indios, vol. 6, exp. 431, f. 113v.

and the proscribed rites would edge back into native life. Unless, that is, the friars found the proper lure.

THE CHOIR

Missionaries and the "church people" not only had the tools of indigenous enforcement at their disposal; their "softly spoken magic spells" of music and theater also enticed neophytes to the Church.[139] Music mollified the harshness of ecclesiastical trials, the long treks to mass, the sting of the lash, and the humiliation of the stock. It echoed in the great stone monasteries and in makeshift *jacales* (straw huts), in doctrinas and their most distant visitas; it reached where painters, sculptors, and even missionaries did not go. Native singers and musicians who performed liturgical and festive music in the churches were known as *cantores y trompeteros* (choir-members and musicians), and they became a permanent fixture in nearly every church. Like indigenous church officials and constables, musicians also formed part of the pipiltin. Native music in the mission church simultaneously indicated success and autonomy: missionaries pointed to it as evidence of their triumph, while each community held it to be an expression of their autonomous religious life.

Missionaries hoped to appeal to the indigenous multitudes through music. This was not unusual for sixteenth-century Spanish ecclesiastics, who also put on lavish displays to awe their flocks in Iberia.[140] Fray Pedro de Gante, one of the earliest Franciscans in Mexico, noted that "all of their adorations to their gods consisted of singing and dancing before them." Accordingly he began to draw on his sequestered students' knowledge to compose "some solemn verses about the Law of God and his faith" according to native poetics and rhythms.[141] The missionaries' use of music reflected their low opinion of commoners, who, according to Archbishop Zumárraga, were "weak by nature and forgetful of interior things."[142] External stimuli were necessary to cultivate the faith of the masses. "More than through [the friars'] sermons," Zumárraga commented, "the Indians convert through music."[143]

---

[139] Quote from Roger Waters, "Breathe (Reprise)," 1973.
[140] Robert Stevenson, *Spanish Cathedral Music in the Golden Age* (Berkeley: University of California Press, 1961).
[141] Pedro de Gante to Philip II, García Icazbalceta, *Códice Franciscano*, 223–4.
[142] García Icazbalceta, *Códice Franciscano*, 58.
[143] Zumárraga to Charles V (1540), in Cuevas, *Documentos*, 99.

Like native church constables, cantores y trompeteros were veterans of mission schools. In the first years of the mission, six hundred children were taught to sing, make instruments, and compose music in the patio of Fray Pedro de Gante's school at San José de los Naturales in Mexico City.[144] This set the pattern for mission schools in towns across Mexico, where students with musical talent were taught by native instructors known as *maestros de capilla*.[145] Meanwhile, elite students at schools for superior instruction such as Santiago Tlatelolco and Tiripitío in Michoacán translated and adapted indigenous poetic forms to Christian hymns and chants.[146] Such was the case of one cantor named Bernardo, who stated that he had studied Latin and Spanish at Tlatelolco and went on to serve at the Franciscan monastery in Cuernavaca.[147] By the 1580s, cantores and trompeteros could be found in nearly every corner of New Spain, serving in masses and heralding the arrival of missionaries and dignitaries. The indefatigable Fray Alonso Ponce, a Franciscan traveller who traversed much of New Spain in the 1570s, found boisterous welcomes from town musicians regardless of the time of day or the size of the town.[148]

Missionaries marveled at the indigenous mastery of liturgical singing and instrumental music. Fray Pedro de Gante boasted that some of his singers might even qualify for the choir of the royal chapel.[149] His praise was not gratuitous. Native singers mastered the two major forms of melodic liturgies, *canto llano* and *canto de órgano*. *Canto llano* referred to *a capella* Gregorian chants; *canto de órgano* however, was polyphonic and employed unequal time measures.[150] Missionaries trumpeted native mastery of these forms as evidence that a living Church had emerged in New Spain and that the native population could perform on par with Europeans.[151]

Yet if natives seemed to be reaching for the heavens with their singing, other Spanish observers were convinced that their instrumental music was tugging them back into the pits of pagan sensuality. Indigenous musicians

---

[144] Pedro de Gante to Charles V (1532), *Cartas de Indias*, vol. I, 32–3.

[145] García Pimentel, *Descripción del arzobispado*, 62, 99.

[146] Lourdes Turrent, *La conquista musical de México* (Mexico City: Fondo de Cultura Económica, 1993), 132–8; Diego de Baselenque, *Los agustinos, aquellos misioneros hacendados*, ed. Heriberto García Moreno (Mexico City: Conaculta, 1998), 101.

[147] Testimony of Bernardo, *indio cantor* (1591), AGN Tierras, vol. 1979, exp. 4, f. 139r.

[148] Ciudad Real, *Tratado docto y curioso*.

[149] Jacobo de Tastera to Charles V (1533), *Cartas de Indias*, vol. I, 66; Pedro de Gante to Charles V (1532), ibid., 52.

[150] Turrent, *Conquista musical*, 37, 201.

[151] Motolinía, *Memoriales*, 340; García Icazbalceta, *Códice Franciscano*, 58.

quickly learned to play and produce a vast array of European instruments: trumpets, sackbuts, cornets, bugles, flageolets, *jabelas* or Moorish cane flutes, rebecs, various types of flutes, and *vihuelas de arco* (an early guitar also known as *viola de gamba*). To these they added the *atabales* (kettle drums), conch shells, and whistles of their own traditions.[152] Wind instruments and percussion marked the vital moments in the Church liturgy.[153] While friars approved of these adaptations since they stood in for non-existent bells and organs, other Spaniards found it to be an unholy cacophony. The mendicants' diocesan rivals at the First Provincial Council of 1555 banned all instrumental music because it conjured "corporal reminiscences" that recalled paganism, and in 1546, the viceroyalty warned that anyone found performing indigenous songs and dances without missionary oversight would receive a hundred lashes.[154] Mexican bishops also denounced *voladores*, practitioners of a pre-hispanic fertility ritual that involved suspending several men from a pole to the sound of flutes.[155] Skeptics like Fray Diego Durán considered the dances and songs that indigenous congregations used to honor their local saints perilously similar to the ones they had sung to honor their gods.[156]

Nonetheless, Spanish suspicions did not halt the rising importance of cantores and trompeteros. Through their performances native communities assumed control over Christian rituals, and elites deployed these musicians to accentuate their status. In doctrinas, native rulers drew on their local tributes to finance the largest musical ensembles possible. In Zacatlán, a mid-sized altepetl north of Tlaxcala, twenty-four cantores and trompeteros were listed on the payroll in 1578 – enough to stage lavish rituals and processions.[157] In visitas, smaller populations and resource bases limited the size of choirs, but even the smallest church could boast of at least six cantores. In these outlying missions, cantores were responsible for leading the local populace in prayers at matins and vespers in the absence of missionaries.[158] Tribute records from the 1570s are a

---

[152] Motolinía, *Memoriales*, 340–2; García Icazbalceta, *Códice franciscano*, 65; Mendieta, *Historia eclesiástica indiana*, vol. II, 76; Ricard, *Spiritual Conquest*, 177.

[153] Focher, *Manual del bautismo*, 32.

[154] Lorenzana, *Concilios*, 140; Turrent, *Conquista Musical*, 131; Lota M. Spell, "Music in the Cathedral of Mexico in the Sixteenth Century." *Hispanic American Historical Review*, vol. 26, no. 3 (1946), 303.

[155] O'Gorman, "Una ordenanza," 189.   [156] Turrent, *Conquista musical*, 169.

[157] Report of public official salaries, Zacatlán (1579), AGN Indios, vol. 1, exp. 171, f. 62v.

[158] A viceregal regulation of cantores serving at the Franciscan monastery of Cholula in 1561 set the limit there at 16 cantores, at a salary of 2 pesos per year. AGN Mercedes,

testament to this: Axtaquemecan, a visita of the Franciscan monastery of Otumba, reported six cantores, while the Augustinian visita at Chalma, subject to the monastery at Ocuilan, counted on eight cantores.[159] While large ensembles of cantores and trompeteros helped to magnify the profile of the cabecera, visitas had to deploy their cantores to cabeceras during major festivals as a sign of deference.[160]

The prominence of cantores had roots in pre-hispanic religious institutions. Prior to the Spanish conquest, temples housed ritual specialists who formed part of the ruling pipiltin elite. These temple singers, known as the *teotlamacazque*, were directed by a *tlapixcatzin*, which one Franciscan chronicler equated to a *chantre*, a cathedral choir director. These officiates led rituals in honor of the rising Sun, observances at sunset, and vigils at night.[161] Bishop Fuenleal noted in 1532 that they were "held in high esteem" because they composed and sang "of all that has passed, what is happening at present, and what they believe."[162] The *teotlamacazque* were exempt from tributes and maintained this status after the conquest by receiving lands, goods, and services like other native office-holders and rulers.[163] After the conquest, colonial authorities maintained the native temple officiates' economic privileges and political status. In the first decades of the mission enterprise, indigenous cantores received payments in lands, goods, and services like other native office-holders and rulers. In Cuauhtinchán, for example, cantores received 200 *brazas* of land in 1563.[164] Unlike other indigenous offices, however, cantores were not elected; instead they were selected by missionaries and often went on to serve in other positions of civil government.[165]

Privilege only fuelled conspicuous displays of the cantores' status. At the monastery of Tiripitío, cantores "took great care in the adornment of their persons," wearing fine scarlet gowns with the finest linen surplices.

---

vol. 6, f. 342v; AGN Indios, vol. 1, exp. 171, f. 62v. García Icazbalceta, *Códice Franciscano*, 71; Mendieta, *Historia eclesiástica indiana*, vol. II, 76.

[159] Internal tribute assessment, Axtaquemecan (1579), AGN Indios, vol. 1, exp. 190, f. 70r; Report of public official salaries, Chalma (1579), AGN Indios, vol. 1, exp. 186, f. 68r.

[160] Viceroy to alcalde mayor, Azcapotzalco (1582), AGN Indios, vol. 2, exp. 220, f. 56v.

[161] Torquemada, *Monarquía indiana*, vol. II, 178–9, 226–7; Mendieta, *Historia eclesiástica indiana*, vol. I, 263–4.

[162] Fuenleal to Charles V (1532), in *Colección de documentos inéditos relativos al descubrimiento*, vol. XIII, 254–5.

[163] ibid.

[164] Viceroy to *indios cantores*, Cuauhtinchan (1563), AGN Mercedes, tomo 6, f. 311v.

[165] Testimony, Juan Bautista, *indio principal*, Tequistengo (1591), AGN Tierras, vol. 1979, exp. 4, f. 143r; Turrent, *Conquista musical*, 166–70.

"To see them in that gown was like seeing a whole choir of illustrious canons," an Augustinian friar quipped.[166] Spanish officials looked with growing concern on the increasing power of cantores: they had no onerous governing responsibilities, did not pay tributes, and had inherited the dignities of their office from pagan predecessors. Finally, in 1561, Philip II ordered his authorities to curb the "excesses, superfluity ... and great costs" of the cantores. The king minced no words, declaring that they had learned only to be "loafers" (*holgazanes*) during their schooling in the monasteries. Once they left the cloisters, they were free from taxation, leaving them with time to "get to know all the ladies in town, destroying married women and maidens, and committing other vices related to the idleness in which they were raised." The "Prudent King" concluded: "By means of their trumpets," cantores directly threatened both local and royal authority.[167]

Such decrees were powerless against the rising influence of this office because cantores provided spiritual leadership. This was especially the case in visitas where the lack of regular contact with missionaries left a vacuum of spiritual authority. In the visita of Sant Miguel, for example, five hundred Otomís received doctrinal instruction from their native choir-master (*maestro de capilla*), who also led the congregation in singing daily prayers. Their missionary, a diocesan priest stationed just five kilometers away in the doctrina of Hueyhueytoca, only managed to visit them about once a month. For his part, the priest was not particularly worried about the spiritual care of his flock: "During the time when I do not go there, the *maestro de capilla* is in charge, and he gathers the children for catechesis ... and [leads] the cantores to sing the Hours of Our Lady every day."[168] Cantores showed leadership especially in deaths and burials. Since logistics made it nearly impossible to summon a priest to give last rites to the dying or bury the dead, cantores and fiscales were authorized to administer sacraments in cases of "urgent need" when unbaptized children or adults were on the verge of death.[169] They also heard the testaments of the dying and presided over burials.[170]

The cantores' spiritual services nonetheless came at a price. Following the example of Spanish diocesan priests, cantores charged residents for

---

[166] Baselenque, *Los agustinos*, 99–100.
[167] Real Cédula (1561), Genaro García, *Documentos inéditos ó muy raros para la historia de México* (Mexico City: Librería de la viuda de Bouret, 1907), 141–2.
[168] García Pimentel, *Descripción del arzobispado*, 263.
[169] García Icazbalceta, *Códice Franciscano*, 71–2; Llaguno, *La personalidad jurídica*, 278.
[170] Lockhart, *Nahuas*, 215.

attending to their spiritual needs.[171] Cantores might have enjoyed social prestige and lavish clothing, but their economic standing was in fact quite precarious. In the 1560s their salaries were set at just two pesos per year – a meager sum that, Mexican bishops correctly predicted in 1565, would lead them to look for sustenance outside of their towns. Local governments found themselves increasingly unable to pay their cantores even these small salaries as tributes declined with the population. In 1591, for example, the cantores of Tepexoxuma declared in a petition to the viceroy that they had not been paid for eighteen years.[172] Low salaries, and even worse unpaid ones, the Mexican bishops warned, would only "cause the dead to suffer at their burials for not having anyone to aid them with *responsos* (responses for the dead)." Their final warning was a testament to how essential the cantores had become: if the problem was not solved "the entire divine cult, or nearly all of it, shall cease."[173] The very same drum-beating pagans thus were, at the same time, indispensible pillars of native faith.

Falling tributes eventually made it impossible for many native governments to maintain large ensembles of cantores. Consequently native singers and musicians became free agents, selling their musical and spiritual talents that they learned in the missions. It became custom for dying natives to leave a half-peso to cantores in their wills, and consequently funerals became "their best business."[174] As the Mexican bishops had predicted, roving bands of cantores and trompeteros peddled their musical talents to any grieving widow or celebrating congregation that was willing to pay. In 1576, Juan de Meza, the secular priest at the doctrina of Tempoal in the Huasteca region (Northern Veracruz), complained to the viceroy that he had "trained several Indians that serve in the church" as cantores. "But having achieved some skill, they now go out to other towns ... like vagabonds in detriment to the Lord and his holy service." The priest argued that he did pay his cantores, but this was likely the one or two-peso salary that inspired so much "vagabondage" in the first place.[175]

---

[171] Viceroy to alcaldes, Taxco (1579), AGN General de Parte vol. 2, exp. 123, f. 26v.
[172] Viceroy to alcalde mayor, Izucar (1591), AGN Indios, vol. 6, 2a parte, exp. 642, f. 145r; Viceroy to officials, Tenayuca (1591), AGN Indios, vol. 6, 2a parte, exp. 182, f. 42r; Relación, *cantores* of Tlalnepantla (1580), AGN General de Parte, vol. 2, exp. 965, f. 207v.
[173] Petition to Real Audiencia, Mexican Bishops (1565), in Cuevas, *Documentos*, 282.
[174] Lockhart, *Nahuas*, 538.
[175] Viceregal order on *cantores*, Tempoal (1576), AGN General de Parte, vol. 1, exp. 1253, f. 235v.

CONCLUSION

In his ethnohistory of indigenous Mexico, James Lockhart has argued
that native–Spanish interactions could be best understood as "double
mistaken identity": an encounter in which "each side perceived a certain
phenomenon in similar but far from identical ways, often without having
any notion of the divergent perceptions of the other side."[176] By this
telling, two sides moved in parallel, allowing decades to pass before they
connected. The story of the missionary–pipiltin alliance, however, reveals
a much quicker adjustment, as well as more pointed mutual perceptions
than the theory allows. It points to an encounter characterized not by
haughty navel-gazing, but rather by mutual awareness and adaptation to
new circumstances. The mission emerged from what I. C. Campbell, in his
analysis of European–Polynesian encounters of the eighteenth century,
called a "culture of culture-contact."[177] Natives and missionaries took
full advantage of each other's rivalries, and each side saw the usefulness of
adapting church needs to indigenous governmental structures, often over
the protests of their own internal critics. And each intended to see the
church and altepetl exalted with music that, by virtue of its very hybridity,
at first must have sounded rather foreign to both sides. The incongruences
and conflicts were many: native nobles were uneasy – to put it mildly –
that their fellow noblemen and kin policed their private lives, and friars
fretted that native songs might debase the faith with paganism. But in the
main the opportunities for both sides outweighed the apprehensions. As a
result the mission correlated elements from both cultures and made them
anew. To borrow Cécile Fromont's description of missions in the early
modern Kongo, the mission was a "constitutive force": it joined structures of native power and missionary Christianity into an edifice that, by
all appearances, seemed to be unshakeable.[178]

Like the runaway *cantores* of Tempoal, the mission enterprise had
taken a life of its own in indigenous communities by the second half of
the sixteenth century. Having begun under the close monitoring of friars,
the mission's day-to-day authority, enforcement, and ritual celebrations
passed to indigenous hands. It became an indispensable institution in the
urgent tasks of rebuilding communities and consolidating power.

[176] Lockhart, "Nahua Concepts," 467–8; Lockhart, *Nahuas*, 45.
[177] I. C. Campbell, "The Culture of Culture-Contact: Refractions from Polynesia." *Journal
of World History*, vol. 14, no. 1 (2003), 63–86.
[178] Fromont, *Art of Conversion*.

Indigenous communities no longer divided over whether they should collaborate with the mission enterprise, as they had in the 1520s and 1530s, for having seen and felt the powers of the staff, lash, and trumpet, they began to fight to control it for themselves. Doctrina status, more than outright resistance, became the most viable pathway to local autonomy within the constraints of colonialism. Any aspirant to power in the indigenous world would aspire to control and draw legitimacy from the mission. Or for talented individuals who could sing or play the *viola da gamba*, the role of the cantor provided another potential pathway to individual autonomy. Across New Spain, indigenous communities – from proud altepeme to commoners in distant visitas sore from long treks to mass – learned from the example of their cabecera rulers and struggled to make the mission their own. The sanctification of native leadership, the flows of tributes laborers, marches to mass, accusations and trials of "idolaters," and financing of musicians – amid countless other everyday gestures and exchanges – made the mission enterprise the "order of things" in the native town, at once "an edifice of command and a condition of being."[179] As we shall see in the next chapter, however, commitments to this edifice came at considerable cost, the burden of which would only get heavier as populations declined.

---

[179] Jean and John Comaroff, *Of Revelation and Revolution: Christianity, Colonialism, and Consciousness in South Africa* (Chicago: University of Chicago Press, 1991), vol. I, 18.

4

Paying for Thebaid

The Colonial Economy of a Mendicant Paradise

INTRODUCTION

After long days of struggling with garbled translations and confused questions on doctrine, friars at the Augustinian monastery of Actopan would gather to pray in their *sala de profundis* beneath this mural (*Fig. 4.1*). The painting depicts them not as the apostolic preachers that they were but as the ascetic hermits that they wished to be. In this imagined world we find the black-robed friars following the paths of spiritual perfection: they meditate in caves, study doctrine, farm the land, fast, and piously flagellate themselves. The surrounding landscape clearly evokes Mexico. The desert-like crags and vegetation equate the environs of Actopan with Thebaid, the desert province in Egypt where early Christians once sought solitude and poverty. Like the desert hermits – and in emulation of Jesus – the friars in this Mexican desert are at the mercy of the wilderness. The friars confront the temptations and evils of this world, manifested here in the form of the devil, the hunchbacked horned *tameme* (native porter) who is stalking the land. Nevertheless, the friars' grace and humility have tamed this wilderness, as the lions, coyotes, and snakes have lost their ferocity. The Augustinians' message is clear: through their grace, labor, and poverty, they have redeemed a desert of paganism and turned it into an American Thebaid.[1]

---

[1] Escobar, *Americana Thebaida*; Antonio Rubial García, "*Hortus eremitarum*: Las pinturas de tebaidas en los claustros agustinos," *Anales del Instituto de Investigaciones Estéticas*, no. 92 (2008), 85–105; Martín Olmedo Muñoz, "La visión del mundo agustino en Meztitlán: Ideales y virtudes en tres pinturas murales," *Anales del Instituto de Investiga-ciones Estéticas*, no. 94 (2009), 27–58; Rubial García, "Tebaidas en el paraíso: Los

FIGURE 4.1 Detail of Tebaida by indigenous painters, late sixteenth century.
Anon. Indigenous painters, Sala de Profundis, Convento de San Nicolás de Tolentino,
Actopan, Hidalgo. Photo by Manuel Cerón

The Thebaid mural at Actopan is one of half a dozen eremitic paintings
in monasteries across Mexico. These idylls perfectly encapsulate the
contradictions of their mission. In Europe, mendicants had long struggled
to balance the life of the hermit and that of the apostle. Their vows bound
them to live according to the rules of their Order, the goals of which were
to build an ascetic spiritual community dedicated to spiritual perfection. This life of inner spiritual improvement, however, tensely coexisted
with the need to teach and provide spiritual comfort in society at large.[2]
In America, these competing vocations were even harder to reconcile.

---

ermitaños de la Nueva España," *Historia Mexicana*, vol. 44, no. 3 (1995), 378–9; Jeanette
Favrot Peterson, *The Paradise Garden Murals of Malinalco: Utopia and Empire in
Sixteenth-Century Mexico* (Austin, TX: University of Texas press, 1993), 165; Rubial
García, "La insulana, un ideal eremético medieval en Nueva España," *Estudios de historia
novohispana* vol. VI (1978), 39–46; Jacques Le Goff, *Lo maravilloso y lo cotidiano en el
occidente medieval* (Barcelona: Gedisa, 1994), 25–39; Felipe Castro Gutiérrez, "Ereme-
tismo y mundanidad en *La Americana Thebaida* de Fray Matías de Escobar," *Estudios de
Historia Novohispana*, vol. 9, no. 9 (1987), 157–67.

[2] Giorgio Agamben, *The Highest Poverty: Monastic Rules and Form-of-Life* (Stanford:
Stanford University Press, 2013).

By committing themselves to missionary work overseas, mendicants took on the burdens of a life of service that outweighed their asceticism. The post-conquest politics of Mexico also required them to mediate in a place of great suffering between colonizers and colonized. Inevitably this gave rise to thorny questions. How could they support themselves where there was no prior church presence and few pious donors? How were they to maintain their probity in a place where they wielded considerable worldly power? Many friars, it is true, embraced their temporal power in the native world – indeed, more than a few clamored to gain even more of it.[3] But ascetic ideals also tugged at their consciences, urging them to renounce comfort, power, and prestige. The Thebaid painting at Actopan functioned as a daily reminder of these spiritual ideals at the core of their identity.[4]

Disdain for the trappings of this world was, in fact, the very reason why mendicants had come to Mexico. For colonists and royal officials in Spain who were profoundly influenced by ascetic Observant movements in the mendicant Orders, the begging friar seemed suited to the demands of the New World. The mendicants' ascetic vows and communal life seemed untainted by the rampant clerical corruption in Europe, they seemed to require few resources to sustain them, and their humility could set an example for new converts.[5]

Mendicants claimed that their selflessness allowed them to focus entirely on improving native communities. Indeed friars introduced new crops, expanded cattle and sheep husbandry, developed silk industries, and instructed indigenous artisans in European arts.[6] They also designed large-scale irrigation systems like Fray Francisco de Tembleque's aqueduct in Cempoala, a gargantuan structure that was over forty kilometers in length and reached a height of forty meters at its tallest point.[7] Mendicants, their apologists, and even anti-clerical historians of the Liberal tradition held up these projects as evidence of a program of development.

---

[3] Georges Baudot, *La pugna francsicana por México* (Mexico City: Conaculta, 1990).

[4] Rubial García, "La insulana"; Rubial García, *La hermana pobreza*, 114–8; Rubial García, "*Hortus eremitarum*," 82.

[5] Cortés, Fourth Letter of Relation (1524), *Cartas de Relación*, 256–8; Mendieta, *Historia ecclesiástica Indiana*, vol. I, 314–17; Mendieta to Francisco de Bustamante (1562), in García Icazbalceta, *Cartas de religiosos*, 12.

[6] See Woodrow Borah, *Silk-Raising in Colonial Mexico* (Berkeley: University of California Press, 1943); and Kubler, *Mexican Architecture*, 187–229.

[7] Luís Ortíz Macedo, *La historia del arquitecto mexicano, siglos XVI–XX* (Mexico City: Editorial Proyección, 2004), 30.

Historical scholarship on the mission economy has rarely strayed beyond this focus on missionaries' temporal contributions to native economies.[8] Neither have mendicant building programs and farming schemes been studied for their nuances and conflicts. In Tepeaca, for example, Spanish petitioners denounced Franciscan friars in 1583 for claiming exclusive control over irrigation systems, which they diverted solely to their gardens to the alleged detriment of local inhabitants.[9]

Returning to the Thebaid painting at Actopan, we find the shortcomings of mendicant claims regarding economic improvement. For if we examine its production, instead of its message, we find evidence of a mission economy based not on development of native economies but dependence upon them. The mural, after all, was painted by indigenous artists who drew their salaries from community funds, which were based on tribute revenues and obligatory donations. Moreover, natives wove the coarse tunics that friars wore while meditating on this image, they produced the food that they consumed, and built the walls upon which the friars could project – through the natives' mediating hands – their ascetic ideals. Local arrangements between friars and indigenous rulers made all of these economic activities possible. In this sense, the Thebaid painting is an indicator of mendicant dependency on native communities. Even the friars' pious dreams of poverty carried a dear price for the natives compelled to underwrite them.

Beyond its aqueducts, churches, and murals, there was a darker, more parasitic side to the mission economy. Friars demanded a constant flow of goods, services, and payments from macehualtin (commoners) for their "sustenance," and native rulers – themselves exempt from such taxes – generally cooperated. Friars refused to designate the native taxes and corvée labor that supported them by name, preferring instead to refer to them as pious donations. These "alms," Franciscan Jerónimo de Mendieta admitted, were the friars' "primary resource."[10] This alchemical transmutation of terms may have eased consciences. But far from their ascetic self-image of begging for their livelihood, reality was far more prosaic: missionaries simply gained access to the same indigenous taxation systems that benefitted Spanish encomenderos and

---

[8] Ricard, *Spiritual Conquest*, 135–55; Kubler, *Mexican Architecture*, vol. I, chap. 5; Van Oss, *Church and Society*, 188–97; Mendieta, *Historia eclesiástica indiana*, vol. II, 419–21; Baselenque, *Los agustinos*, 183–5.

[9] Hildeberto Martínez, *Documentos coloniales de Tepeaca*, 193.

[10] Jerónimo de Mendieta (1567), in García Icazbalceta, *Códice Mendieta*, vol. I, 83.

settlers – the very colonists whom they routinely excoriated for their exploitation of native peoples.

This dependence on native tribute-payers did not come without a cost to the friars' consciences as well as to their ascetic reputation, which was the basis of their political legitimacy. Mendicant identity and legitimacy, after all, hinged upon the presumption that native economic support was voluntary.[11] The economy of obligatory donations brought missionaries uneasily close to the sins of greed and gluttony, and the close presence of native servants called their celibacy and propriety into question. As beneficiaries of the richest economy in the New World, equal only to Peru, missionaries in Mexico risked breaking their vows, and their actions made them vulnerable to critics who questioned their rule.

PATRONS AND TRIBUTARIES

Missionaries referred to financial support for their mission as *sustento,* or "sustenance." The term conveniently conjured up the image of almsgiving, yet securing funding of any kind was difficult in the frontier society of New Spain. Postconquest Mexico lacked the revenues that supported the Church in Europe. Indigenous peoples were generally excluded from paying tithes, and in any case this tax financed the diocesan clergy, the mendicants' chief competitors in Mexico.[12] Friars considered investing in property, but this did not become a substantial source of income until the later in the century. They also experimented with holding encomiendas, as well as the possibility of seizing lands once held by Aztec priesthoods. All these initiatives were short-lived: the New Laws prohibited ecclesiastical encomiendas, and Aztec "temple lands" (*teopantlalli*) proved to be too ambiguous in indigenous law to justify a wholesale transfer of properties to mendicants.[13]

---

[11] Cortés, Fourth Letter of Relation (1524), in *Cartas de Relación,* 256–8; Mendieta, *Historia eclesiástica indiana,* vol. I, 315–17; Mendieta to Bustamante (1562) in García Icazbalceta, *Códice Mendieta,* 12.

[12] Indigenous peoples only paid tithes on Spanish-origin products, known as the "three things": wheat, cattle, and silk. John F. Schwaller, *The Origins of Church Wealth in Mexico: Ecclesiastical Revenues and Church Finances, 1523–1600* (Albuquerque: University of New Mexico Press, 1985), 22.

[13] Zumárraga to Charles V (1536), Cuevas, *Documentos,* 58–9; Zumárraga to Juan de Samano (1537), *Cartas de Indias,* vol. I, 167; AGN Mercedes, tomo 2, exp. 759, f. 331r; Grijalva, *Crónica,* 149. Alfonso García Gallo, ed., *Cedulario Indiano,* (Madrid: Ediciones Cultura Hispánica, 1945) vol. I, 199; Nicolás de Witte (1554), in Cuevas, *Documentos,* 224.

Missionaries found a workable solution in their alliances with native rulers, with whom they cobbled together a system of patronage that combined imperial imperatives with indigenous systems of tax collection. The Crown granted missionaries rights to a share of royal and encomienda revenues, while indigenous authorities provided them with the actual goods and services in these grants through locally-negotiated agreements.

In theory, responsibility for missionary sustenance lay entirely with the kings of Spain. When Pope Alexander VI granted Spain dominion over the New World, he did so on condition that the Spanish kings serve as patrons of the Church in all newly conquered territories. Spanish officials exacted payments of tribute and service from conquered populations as a sign of recognition of the Castilian Crown's supremacy.[14] In order to comply with the Alexandrine Bulls, the Crown was obliged to apply a portion of the profits of colonization to the costs of evangelization.[15] The Crown assumed the transportation costs of all missionaries who traveled to the New World, and its metropolitan and colonial treasuries paid for wine and oil needed for mass. Crown officials also funded bells for all new churches.[16] Officials also assisted missions in poor areas where local tributes could not provide for missionaries.[17] In 1564, for example, four hungry Augustinians in Zacualpa received such support after they informed the viceroy of the meager provisions they were receiving from the local population.[18] In most cases, however, direct royal funding dissipated not long after missionaries stepped ashore in Veracruz. Friars

---

[14] Pinelo, *Recopilación*, 2:1:1 and 6:5:1.

[15] Juan de Solórzano y Pereira, *Política indiana*, 5 vols. (Madrid: Ediciones Atlas, 1972), 318; José Miranda, *El tributo en Nueva España durante el siglo XVI* (Mexico City: El Colegio de México, 1952), 144–6.

[16] Subventions for wine, lamp oil, and bells can be found in the accounts of royal treasurers for this period, in AGI Contaduría, legs. 661–97. These grants sometimes included funding for chalices. On subventions for transport, see Pedro Borges Moran, *El envío de misioneros a América durante la época española* (Salamanca: Universidad Pontificia de Salamanca, 1977), 68–9; Antonio Rubial García, *El convento agustino y la sociedad novohispana: 1533–1630* (Mexico City: Universidad Nacional Autónoma de México, 1989), 172–6.

[17] Viceroy to Augustinians, Mixquic (1560), AGN Mercedes, vol. 84, f. 87r; Rubial García, *Convento*, 175.

[18] Viceregal response to Augustinian petition (1563), AGN Mercedes, vol. 7, f. 59r; Gerhard, *Guide*, 93.

even had to implore the Crown to fund their medicine purchases on account of their high cost in the Indies.[19]

In indigenous towns assigned to encomenderos, royal obligations devolved to grantees. Encomiendas, which were awarded to conquistadors and their immediate descendants (and in a handful cases, to indigenous royal descendants), granted encomenderos rights to native tributes and labor within a demarcated area. As a manifestation of the papal donation on a local scale, encomenderos accessed indigenous resources on condition that they supported missionary efforts.[20] Viceregal records are replete with injunctions that encomenderos donate funds for wine and candles, wool for the friars' clothing, pigs for their farms, and support for their travel.[21] A handful of pious encomenderos are noted in mendicant chronicles, such as don Juan de Alvarado, who sponsored an Augustinian school for indigenous boys at his encomienda in Tiripitío.[22] By the 1550s, viceregal officials ordered encomenderos to pay one hundred pesos and fifty fanegas of corn per year to each missionary in their jurisdictions in addition to extraordinary expenses such as church construction.[23]

Despite these legal obligations, Spanish beneficiaries often reneged on their spiritual obligations. Hernán Cortés' own heir, for example, failed to provide funding for Dominicans on the volatile and impoverished Southern Oaxacan frontier, who were facing "extreme hunger ... because with the food that the Indians give them they barely get by."[24] Many encomenderos and royal officials simply evaded their obligations to pay missionary salaries and fund churches, and pocketed the portions of tribute earmarked for the mission.[25] Indigenous residents in Tepapayuca denounced this peculation in 1550 as effectively a double levy: with their encomendero having pocketed tribute revenue intended for their

---

[19] Francisco de Soto to Council of the Indies (1550), AGI Indiferente General, 1093.

[20] Silvio Zavala, *La encomienda indiana* (Mexico City: Porrúa, 1973), chaps. 2–5; Gibson, *Aztecs*, 58–60.

[21] Viceroy to Dominicans of Tehuantepec and Xalapa (1554), AGN Mercedes, vol. 4, f. 138r; Viceroy to Bernardino Vasquez de Tapia (1558), AGN Mercedes, vol. 84, exp. 113, f. 43v.

[22] Baselenque, *Los agustinos*, 67, 84.

[23] Rubial García, *Convento*, 176. Viceroy to encomendero of Coyoacán (1551), Silvio Zavala, *Libros de asientos de la gobernación de la Nueva España (periodo del virrey don Luís de Velasco, 1550–1552* (Mexico City: Archivo General de la Nación, 1982), 256; Viceroy to Marqués del Valle (1552), NL, Ayer Collection, ms. 1121, f. 168r; Viceroy to encomenderos of Ocuila (1552), NL, Ayer Collection, ms. 1121, f. 30v.

[24] Viceroy to Marqués del Valle (1558), AGN Mercedes, vol. 84, exp. 99, f. 39r.

[25] García Gallo, *Cedulario Indiano*, vol. II, 219, 245; Viceregal order, Chieguautla (1565), AGN Mercedes, vol. 8, f. 93v; AGN Mercedes, vol. 8, f. 226v.

Franciscan missionaries, they were forced to raise the missionaries' funds all over again.[26]

As the failures of patronage forced local actors to directly fund mission efforts by levying new taxes, royal officials and theologians gravely warned of the corrosive spiritual effects that direct taxation would have on the apostolic mission. In 1533, Charles V expressed concern that if missionaries collected tithes from neophytes, natives might not recognize the missionaries' "love and charity," and instead see only "self-interest."[27] He forbade encomenderos, royal officials, and churchmen from collecting tithes from natives. Instead, he instructed his officials to quietly increase tributes and services by the amount that missionaries needed. The tithe, in effect, was to be hidden among tribute and labor arrangements, "in such a way that [natives] would only understand this as a general tribute that they had to pay."[28] In theory, then, the Crown retained its role as patron by dedicating a portion of local tributes to the Church.[29] In reality, mission funding was an outcome of local negotiations, the result of *ad hoc* agreements.[30] Most of these payments and services went unrecorded between the 1520s and 1550s. From the point of view of royal officials, this unreported revenue and labor constituted a "hidden exaction" on native society, invisible to Spanish authorities.[31] This would only come to be seen as a problem when the Crown decided to extract even more tributes from indigenous communities in the second half of the century.

Royal patronage was therefore little more than a legal fiction in the everyday life of indigenous doctrinas. It was a sleight-of-hand that saved the royal treasury millions of pesos, since local arrangements obviated the need to pay for daily functions directly from royal coffers. Far beyond the gaze of royal tax officials or the reach of royal orders, missionaries and local authorities funded the mission largely on their own through obligatory "donations." Jerónimo Valderrama, the *visitador* (inspector-general)

---

[26] Viceroy to Tepapayuca (1580), AGN General de Parte, vol. 2, exp. 860, f. 181r. Oaxtepec natives experienced a similar problem with Cortés' *marquesado*: Viceroy to Cristobal de Arellano, AGN Mercedes, vol. 8, f. 167r.

[27] Miranda, *El tributo*, 14.   [28] ibid.

[29] Coyoacán, 1558: AGN Mercedes, vol. 84, exp. 113, f. 43v; Tepapayuca, 1580: General vol. 2, exp. 860, f. 181r; Cuetzala, 1591: AGN Indios, vol. 3, exp. 476, f. 110r; Zacapoaxtla,1591: AGN Indios, 3, exp. 483, f. 112r; Tacuba, 1590: AGN Indios, vol. 4, exp. 842, f. 228v.

[30] Gibson, *Aztecs*, 196; Horn, *Postconquest Coyoacan*, 90.

[31] Library of Congress, Krauss ms. 140, f. 487v; Antonio de Mendoza, *relación* (1550), in Hanke, *Los virreyes*, vol. I, 39; Miranda, *El tributo*, 25; Gibson, *Aztecs*, 197.

who reformed native tributes between 1563 and 1565, saw this gulf between imperial ideology and local reality firsthand when he visited the construction sites of the immense doctrina monasteries: "His Majesty has issued an order by which churches are to be built, and this is to be performed at His Majesty's cost ... [it] is not supposed to be heaped upon the Indians, as has been done thus far, to their tremendous detriment."[32] At the local level, such charitable donations were indistinguishable from other taxes. When a secessionist sujeto sought to reduce the political implications of their "almsgiving" to the doctrina monastery in their cabecera by arguing that they did so "only out of charity," Augustinians in the doctrina revealed their material interests when they testified against the sujeto and declared the alms to be an obligatory exaction that proved their subordinate status.[33] Throughout New Spain, friars of all three Orders miraculously turned taxes into alms, all while claiming that the whole exercise was teaching natives a vital lesson in Christian charity.[34]

While the tribute systems that supported the missionaries were complex and varied from region to region, all of them reflected the social hierarchies of native societies. The tributary relationship marked a gaping socioeconomic chasm, for despite some grey areas and ambiguities between wealthy commoners and the lower rungs of the nobility, indigenous societies were divided between the vast majority that had to render tributes and a small minority that lived off of them. Tributes were "the basis of social stratification" in central Mexico.[35] Commoners, or macehualtin, were expected to fulfill two kinds of contributions: tribute payments and labor levies at long and short-term intervals, and additional payments or services on demand. In exchange, commoners received the right to work a plot in usufruct on land belonging either to the commune (*calpolli*) or a local lord.[36] Nobles were distinguished from commoners by

---

[32] France V. Scholes and Eleanor B. Adams, eds., *Cartas del licenciado Jerónimo Valderrama y otros documentos sobre su visita al gobierno de Nueva España, 1563–1565* (Mexico City: Porrúa, 1961), 199.

[33] *Tlayacapa v. Totolapa* (1571), AGI Justicia, 176, no. 2.

[34] García Icazbalceta, *Códice Mendieta*, vol. I, 83.

[35] Smith, "Role of Social Stratification," 74.

[36] Hicks, "Prehispanic Background," 38–53; Lockhart, *Nahuas*, ibid., 96; Olivera, *Pillis y macehuales*, 84. A viceregal order in 1549 to don Antonio, *gobernador* of Ocuituco, affirmed that all tribute-paying macehuales were to receive access to a plot of land: LC, Krauss ms. 140, ff. 27v–9r.

virtue of the fact that they were exempt from draft labor and commanded commoners' labor. Nobles did have to pay tributes based on the extent of their landholdings, but since they controlled the labor of commoners working on their lands, they "had the means to obtain tribute" that they paid to their rulers. In effect, while commoners worked with their hands to meet their tribute requirements, nobles received tributes from their dependents and siphoned off a share of the proceeds for their overlords.[37]

Indigenous tributes and services can be divided into two revenue streams, one flowing outward and the other inward. The outward stream of goods and services flowed to imperial authorities, first Aztec and later Spanish, in recognition of their suzerainty. In exchange, subject polities received imperial recognition of their autonomy. Most secular Spanish beneficiaries drew from this outflowing tribute stream, which consisted of tribute goods, liquid currency (such as cacao), and unpaid labor for households and sites of economic production like farms and mines. An example of this prehispanic tribute system can be seen in the payment schedule for Hernán Cortés' encomiendas. The towns of Cuernavaca, Yautepec, and Tepoztlán each made payments at eighty and hundred-day intervals. Moreover, every two weeks they paid Cortés' estates in perishable items, which the three communities paid on a rotational basis.[38]

The second, internal stream channeled resources and labor to local rulers, nobles, and religious institutions.[39] Missionaries drew their sustenance – far more than they needed – from this inflowing stream. Like native rulers, nobles, and temple priests before the conquest, missionaries received scheduled payments in bulk goods and specie, as well as daily domestic services such as housekeeping, cooking, and gardening, and artisanal products. Communities consistently provided beneficiaries with "personal services" according to a rotating schedule, and friars often employed unpaid obligatory labor for purposes other than mere sustenance: commoners could be found building their wheat mills and stables,

---

[37] Hicks, "Prehispanic Background," 50; Smith, *Aztecs*, 143–8; Lockhart, *Nahuas*, 94–5, 106–7; Hildeberto Martínez, *Tepeaca en el siglo XVI: Tenencia de la tierra y organización de un señorío* (Mexico City: CIESAS, 1984), 92–5. Mixtecs in Oaxaca had a similar social structure: Terraciano, *Mixtecs*, 131–40.

[38] Hodge, "Political Organization," 30. Haskett, "Indian Town Government," 211; Miranda, *El tributo*, 24–7.

[39] Smith, "Role of Social Stratification," 74; Zorita, *Brief and Summary Relation*, 104–5; Don Pedro de Sureo, *tasación* of Xochimilco (1548), LC Krauss ms. 140, ff. 5r–20v; Smith, *Aztecs*, 155–6.

picking cotton, cultivating fields, working textile looms, or cutting fire-wood for the friars' profit.[40] Friars also had communal property at their disposal, like the two ponies owned by the altepetl of Cuauhtinchan that local Franciscans rode on their treks out to visitas.[41] These transfers of goods and services were not donations; they were customary internal taxes that the missionaries appropriated with the approval of local officials.

Tribute payments consisted of a broad array of goods and services. A household could be expected to provide foodstuffs like corn, local resources like wood or stone, and finished products like cloths or *huipiles* (cotton blouses) every sixty to eighty days. In addition, commoners also provided turkeys, salt, and tomatoes – and for Spaniards, fodder – at shorter intervals.[42] Commoners also had to meet a variety of labor requirements, which rotated from household to household. Wards (cal-poltin) had to deploy labor in special projects like building temples and repairing aqueducts, and they had to work both common or seigniorial lands at appointed times during the year. They also provided what came to be known as "personal services" (*servicios personales*): daily house-hold labor, gardening, and wood-cutting for lords, rulers, and missionar-ies.[43] Tributes were the currency of political power in the native city-state, for the tlatoani redistributed a sizeable portion of his collected tributes to noblemen in exchange for their administrative services, temples and priesthoods, and to commoners performing draft labor.[44] The very pay-ment of tribute and provisioning of labor, both before and after the conquest, was therefore a sign of subjecthood.[45]

Royal officials began to monitor missionary access to tributes and labor in the mid-1540s. These investigations provide the earliest detailed

[40] Audiencia investigation on Augustinians, Ocuituco (1560), AGI Justicia 205, no. 3; Real Audiencia to natives of Agueguecingo (1584), AGN Tierras, vol. 3002, exp. 20, f. 1r–v; Audiencia trial, Tlaquiltenango (1583–1595), AGN Tierras, vol. 1979, exp. 4, ff. 129v, 147v, 151r, 158v, 161r, 164v; Viceroy to alcalde Mayor, Pánuco (1589), AGN Indios vol. 4, exp. 74, f. 22v.

[41] Ordenanzas de Cuauhtinchan (1559), in Reyes García, *Documentos sobre tierras y señoríos en Cuauhtinchan*, 209.

[42] Gibson, *Aztecs*, 197–8; Miranda, *El tributo*, 27–31, 34–6; Horn, *Postconquest Coyoacan*, 95.

[43] Lockhart, *Nahuas*, 17, 96; Gibson, *Aztecs*, 44, 221–3; Miranda, *El tributo*, 35–6.

[44] Hicks, "Prehispanic Background," 46, 49–51; Terraciano, *Mixtecs*.

[45] *Tecomatlán v. Yanhuitlán* (1584), AGI Escribanía de Cámara 162C; *Nepopo and other sujetos v. Totolapa* (1556), AGI Justicia, 156, no. 1; *Tepechpan v. Temascalapa* (1550), AGI Justicia, 164, no. 2.

evidence of the ad hoc agreements between missionaries and native rulers. A record from an investigation in to tributes in Coyoacán in 1551 by Audiencia judge (*oidor*) Antonio Rodríguez de Quesada reveals the mission to be thoroughly integrated into the internal tribute system of the altepetl. Quesada based his report on depositions from the principales (ruling nobles) of Coyoacán.[46] Out of 4,084 tributaries in the jurisdiction, at any given time 374 tributaries (9 percent of the total) were employed continuously in the service of the friars.[47] The indigenous government also channeled 1,224 pesos per year to the Dominican doctrina, of which 499 pesos directly supported the two friars in residence. The missionaries' portion was only slightly less than the indigenous government's share of the total revenue, which amounted to 1,257 pesos per year. The indigenous gobernador received 216 pesos per year, roughly the same that the community paid each individual priest. Only 597 pesos remained for other community expenses, and half of that amount covered indemnities incurred by the local government in civil lawsuits. The ledger thus clearly shows that the burden of the mission in this jurisdiction equaled that of the native ruling elite, with each consuming forty percent of revenues. The community, meanwhile, was left with just half of the remainder.[48]

The principales itemized the specific payments and services that macehualtin in Coyoacán provided to the Dominicans. Every day, fifty-nine commoners served the missionaries. They swept, cooked, tended the gardens, hauled provisions, served as a doorkeepers, and rounded up children for indoctrination. Others cared for the sick in the monastery patio and gathered townsfolk for mass and prayer. The Dominicans even had their own tax collector: every two days, a commoner made the rounds to gather one-and-a-half *fanegas* of corn (almost four bushels) and one hundred eggs from every barrio in Coyoacán. Such collections were commonplace. In Tlaquiltenango, a Spanish resident complained, "Whenever the Franciscans lacked anything, someone would go ringing a little bell around the town in search of it."[49] In Coyoacán, once the corn and eggs were delivered, women assigned to the kitchen made tortillas "for the boys in the monastery," though we can assume that the friars ate

[46] Emma Pérez Rocha, *El tributo en Coyoacán en el siglo XVI* (Mexico City: INAH, 2008), 53–4.

[47] ibid., 58–9.   [48] ibid., 108.

[49] Juan de Boga, Spanish *vecino* of Oaxtepec (1591), AGN Tierras, vol. 1979, exp. 4, f. 241v.

them as well.[50] The production of hundreds of tortillas consumed untold hours of female labor. Investigators at the Augustinian doctrina of Ocuituco, for example, found that friars were receiving two hundred tortillas, an unspecified amount of fruit, a hen, and two loads of firewood every day, all year round.[51]

The Dominicans of Coyoacán also took full advantage of their access to the *coatequitl*, or drafts of unpaid obligatory labor by commoners. In 1551, 268 skilled artisans and workers were found building the friars' residence, which included a garden and an outdoor refectory. Fifty-five carpenters and two masons cut lumber and labored at the monastery, while six master-craftsmen oversaw the operations. The friars even rented out tribute labor to local Spaniards when they did not require all the labor to which they were entitled. In one case, the Dominicans rented ten of their allocated commoners to Juan de Castañeda, a local Spanish resident who needed construction work, for ten pesos. The Dominicans then used the proceeds from the transaction to purchase wagons.[52]

Mendicants were not above selling the goods that they received as tribute payments. In Coyoacán, every day eighty tributaries were sent to the forested hillsides to the west of the altepetl to cut and haul eighty *cargas* (loads) of firewood – about fifty pounds per person.[53] An additional twelve laborers were assigned to collect charcoal. Once the firewood and charcoal arrived at the monastery, ten commoners were tasked with hauling it to México-Tenochtitlán to sell it there.[54] Later investigations revealed that the friars bartered the firewood and charcoal for wine, lamps, tools, and locks, and in one case, the services of a visiting barber from the city.[55] Such profiteering was not uncommon. Dominicans at Yanhuitlán in Oaxaca exploited unpaid labor to produce candles, hats, and bolts of cloth which they sold for profit, while Augustinians in Ocuituco used prisoners arrested for drunkenness to produce cloth and

---

[50] Pedro Carrasco and Jesús Monjarás-Ruiz, eds., *Colección de documentos sobre Coyoacán*, 2 vols. (Mexico City: INAH, 1976), vol. 1, 88–91.

[51] Rubial García, *Convento*, 184–5; Roulet, *L'evangelisation*, 152.

[52] Carrasco and Monajarás-Ruiz, *Colección*, ibid.

[53] Ross Hassig, *Trade, Tribute, and Transportation: The Sixteenth-Century Political Economy in the Valley of Mexico* (Norman, OK: University of Oklahoma Press, 1985), 192.

[54] The oxen for the carts generated yet another line on the tribute list: four commoners were tasked with guarding the oxen, while ten others had to collect feed for the animals.

[55] Horn, *Postconquest Coyoacan*, 83.

bundle raw wool from their sheep farm, which were tended by tribute laborers.[56] As for oidor Quesada in Coyoacán, it appears that the judge lost little sleep over this. Although he reduced tributes to the town's native rulers, he left the Dominicans' share of local tributes untouched.[57]

In 1555, Viceroy Luís de Velasco witnessed this tribute economy first-hand in the town of Ucareo, an Augustinian doctrina on the road between Mexico City and Michoacán.[58] Velasco found a town at the service of the friars: four fishermen provided them with fish on demand, artisans produced goods at their request, and other local inhabitants delivered food. Typical of these tribute arrangements, these payments were unregulated. The viceroy intervened by enumerating the exact contributions required, specifying that the natives were to provide two hens and forty tortillas to the friars each day.[59] The viceroy also insisted that friars paid the towns-people for all the goods that they consumed, including basket-weavers for *petates* (straw mats), tailors for sheets and clothing, shoemakers for their *alpargatas* (espadrilles), and gardeners for tending their crops. Prior to the viceroy's visit, none of these laborers had received compensation.[60]

Contrary to claims that they received donations of goods and labor from a wellspring of native charity, mendicants sustained themselves, often opulently, by drawing upon native systems of taxation and forced labor. Commoners underwrote their daily existence and monumental aspirations. Their enrichment from native society called into question their reputation as impoverished servants of the Faith. Unbeknownst to the friars, who in 1550 were confidently building their missions on the backs of macehualtin across New Spain, this contradiction would soon expose them to attack from their Spanish rivals, as well as from the very commoners whose labor they took for granted.

REFORMS AND PROTESTS

After mid-century, the *laissez faire* approach that allowed missionaries and native rulers to organize their own internal tribute systems gave

---

[56] Alonso Caballero to Jerónimo Valderrama (1563), in Scholes and Adams, *Cartas del licenciado Jerónimo Valderrama*, 297; Audiencia investigation on Augustinians, Ocui-tuco (1560), AGI Justicia, 205, no. 3.

[57] Carrasco and Monajarás-Ruiz, *Colección*, 54.   [58] Gerhard, *Guide*, 320.

[59] Viceregal order on sustenance, Ucareo (1555), AGN Mercedes, vol. 4, f. 264r.

[60] ibid.

way to far stricter control.[61] In 1550 the Crown signaled its intentions to change tribute collection in its instructions to the incoming viceroy Luís de Velasco: he was to standardize all tribute burdens so that the natives did not pay more than they owe.[62] A series of similar royal orders followed over the next years. Friars and natives were prohibited from using unpaid tribute labor, per capita burdens were to be reduced, and friars were to receive a yearly stipend from Spanish authorities, not natives, to pay for goods and services.[63]

Two objectives guided the new directives. The first was to adjust tribute burdens to demographic changes. After the 1545–1547 *hueyco-colixtli* epidemic claimed a third of the native population, commoners were meeting their multiple tribute obligations with great difficulty. The per capita burden therefore needed to be reduced or at least consolidated to as few payments as possible. At the same time, however, the cash-strapped Crown had the contradictory goal of increasing its own revenues. In order to meet both objectives, the royal officials targeted encomenderos, missionaries, internal tribute systems, and above all, they sharply reduced the number of indigenous nobles who could enjoy tax exemptions.[64]

Given that native tributes were the foundation of wealth in sixteenth century New Spain, the drastic changes proposed in royal reforms sparked bitter disputes. Reform efforts were led by three successive *visitadores,* inspector-generals appointed by the king. Visitadores had broad powers to investigate malfeasance at all levels of the colonial bureaucracy, including the friars, tlatoque, corregidores, encomenderos, and even viceroys. Each visitador amplified the struggle to control native resources. The first, Diego Ramírez, proposed only modest changes to missionary funding, primarily by regularizing tribute schedules and by ordering missionaries to pay for services.[65] Ramírez gave priority to easing native tax burdens over the Crown's objective of raising funds, and he clearly laid blame on encomenderos for the natives' plight. Such was the visitador's reputation

---

[61] Margarita Menegus, "La destrucción del señorío indígena y la formación de la república de indios en la Nueva España," in *El sistema colonial en la América Española,* ed. Heraclio Bonilla (Madrid: Crítica, 1991), 32–4.

[62] Vasco de Puga, *Cedulario de la Nueva España* (Mexico City: Condumex, 1985), f. 135; Miranda, *El tributo,* 111–7; Menegus, "La destrucción," 33; Scholes and Adams, *Cartas del licenciado Jerónimo Valderrama,* 13–4.

[63] Miranda, *El tributo,* 110–37; García Gallo, *Cedulario Indiano,* vol. II, 245.

[64] Miranda, ibid.

[65] Diego Ramírez, tribute assessment of Pahuatlán (1555), in Paso y Troncoso, *Epistolario,* vol. VIII, 232.

for reducing tributes that when encomenderos heard that he was approaching, they attempted to pre-empt him by announcing tribute reductions before he arrived. The result was a visitation that provided relief to indigenous towns at the expense of encomenderos and the Crown.[66] But in rather suspicious timing, Ramírez died before he could complete his investigations. At the cabildo (municipal council) of Mexico City, colonists could not contain their joy at Ramírez's demise: in their annals, they memorialized the judge's untimely death.[67]

After Ramírez's demise, the brief reprieve for friars and native nobles ended abruptly. Thereafter the Crown was determined to swell its coffers. In 1561, a new visitador, Vasco de Puga, laid blame squarely on native nobles and their missionary allies for the Crown's falling tributes. Puga accused friars and native rulers of failing to report all of their tribute-paying commoners to royal investigators, thereby robbing the Crown of revenue. But Philip II's greatest champion was the third visitador, Jerónimo de Valderrama, whose aggressive style won him few friends in Mexico. Friars and native rulers denounced him as a diabolical bureaucrat determined to undermine them.[68] Arriving in 1563, he denounced internal tribute and labor arrangements in native polities as a "fraud" to the royal treasury.[69] In Xochimilco, for example, Valderrama found that the Franciscans were assessing and collecting tributes on their own authority. When native officers raised objections, the Franciscans simply removed them from their posts. At the Council of the Indies in Spain, an official glossed Valderrama's report in the margin: *tasan los frailes* – "friars are assessing tributes."[70] So settled were they in their own New World "empire," Valderrama grumbled in a letter to the king, that friars "cared about as much for the king of Spain's treasury as they did for that of the Turk."[71]

Valderrama increased royal revenues by eliminating internal tributes: gone were unpaid personal services, payments in goods at varying times, and daily offerings of food. Instead, indigenous rulers and missionaries

---

[66] Miranda, *El tributo*, 131–2; Walter V. Scholes, *The Diego Ramírez Visita* (Columbia: University of Missouri Press, 1946); Bernardo García Martínez, *Los pueblos de la sierra: El poder y el espacio entre los indios del norte de Puebla hasta 1700* (Mexico City: El Colegio de México, 1987), 87–91, 193.

[67] García Martínez, *Los pueblos de la sierra*, ibid.

[68] Miranda, *El tributo*, 133–7; Zavala, *Libros*, 130–3.

[69] Valderrama to Philip II (1564), in Scholes and Adams *Cartas del licenciado Jerónimo Valderrama*, 46, 57–9, 92–4; 9–15.

[70] ibid., 196–7.   [71] ibid., 180–1.

would now draw fixed salaries from the same stream of revenue that flowed to the Crown. Most controversially, Valderrama increased the number of natives required to pay tributes to include minor nobles and their dependents. For example *mayeques,* tenants on nobles' lands, were no longer exempt from paying tributes to the Crown. Valderrama himself interviewed many of these serfs, who wasted no time in declaring that they would gladly pay tribute in return for a plot of land.[72] At one stroke Valderrama eliminated the currency of indigenous power, which for centuries had consisted of collecting and redistributing labor, offerings of food, banquets for dignitaries, and tribute goods. While we might choose not to lament the passing of such an onerous tribute system, Bernardo García Martínez cautions us not to see native rulers in the same light as some "*junior manirroto,*" a spendthrift scion of the contemporary Mexican elite. Valderrama sought to replace this complex Mesoamerican system of taxation with a far simpler colonial hierarchy that envisioned native rulers only as salaried collaborators.[73]

Valderrama's reforms substantially altered missionary funding. All services, short-term provisions, and tributes were reduced to a single yearly payment fixed at one peso and a half fanega (a little over one bushel) of corn per payer.[74] No unpaid services or provisioning was allowed; instead, missionaries received salaries drawn from a community fund known as *sobras de tributos*, or surplus tribute after the Crown extracted its share of local revenue. Viceregal legislation required sobras to be locked into a *caja de comunidad*, a community chest with three locks. Keys for each lock were then distributed to three local officials, generally the gobernador, cleric, and corregidor, who were to oversee all deposits and payments from the community chest.[75] In an early record of a *caja de comunidad* in 1553, the royal judge Santillán, who visited Coyoacán to investigate local tributes, ordered the local native alcalde and fiscal to report with their keys to open the chest for him.[76] A record from the town of Acatlán details the new tributary and accounting procedures. In 1564, royal officials set the total local tribute at 1,216 pesos and 511 fanegas (roughly 1,260 bushels) of corn; of that amount,

[72] Menegus, "La destrucción," 36–7.

[73] García Martínez, *Los pueblos de la sierra*, 192–4; Menegus, "La destrucción," 38.

[74] Miranda, *El tributo*, 14–17, 138.

[75] Haskett, "Indian Town Government," 213; Ordenanzas de Cuauhtinchan (1559), in Reyes García, *Documentos sobre tierras y señoríos en Cuauhtinchan*, 193.

[76] *Oidor* Santillán to officials of Coyoacán (1553), Carrasco and Monjarás-Ruíz, *Colección*, vol. I, 159–60.

the Crown was to receive 1,024 pesos and all of the corn. 191 pesos remained as sobras, which funded the salaries of missionaries and native officials.[77] Valderrama boasted to Philip II of the great quantity of pesos saved for the Crown: "All these increases in royal rents and decreased burdens for the tribute-payers, before were consumed in the eating and drinking of Indian principales, and in what the friars spent."[78]

In practice, of course, Valderrama's reforms did not so drastically alter native taxation. Local governments, friars, and viceregal authorities combined elements of Valderrama's reforms with earlier procedures. An example of this can be seen in a viceregal directive on taxation issued to the native government of Tetiquipac (Oaxaca) in 1561. For the sustenance of four Dominican friars, the viceroy ordered the town to release funds from their sobras according to customary short- and long-term cycles. Natives were to provide each missionary with three hundred pesos, fifty fanegas of wheat, seventy fanegas of corn every year, and twenty-five pesos every month. But the viceroy expressly forbade natives from giving "anything else" to the missionaries, and he stressed that all funds were to proceed from sobras alone.[79] Viceregal orders also instructed native communities to record payments with a *carta de pago* (receipt) to serve as proof that both sides had met their obligations.[80]

This emphasis on legal procedure in the mid-century tribute reforms allowed native communities to assert their rights. While the reforms stripped native governments of much of their fiscal autonomy, the very fact that they reaffirmed the Crown and viceroyalty as ultimate arbiters in matters of taxation allowed natives to vent their grievances over the heads of their local rulers and missionaries. Indeed, some indigenous governments embraced the reforms to the point of refusing to support

---

[77] Tribute assessment (*tasación*), Acatlán (1564), AGN Mercedes, vol. 7, f. 321v; Miranda, *El tributo*, 14; García Martínez, *Los pueblos de la sierra*, 103–4.

[78] Miranda, *El tributo*, 136, 139.

[79] Viceregal provision, Tetiquipa (1561), AGN Mercedes, tomo 6, f. 341v. Viceregal provision, Ocuituco (1563) AGN Mercedes, vol. 7, f. 185r; Viceregal provision, Huexotzingo (1563), AGN Mercedes, vol. 7, f. 213v; Tribute assessment, Tepeaca (1579), in Martínez, *Documentos coloniales de Tepeaca*, 143.

[80] Few *cartas de pago* survive for these early transactions, but one example from Misantla lists as signatories the *corregidor*, the indigenous *cabildo* and *principales*, commoners, and the local vicar. All parties at the signing acknowledged that the priest had received all of the corn, fish, and vegetables that he required, as well as feed for his horse, and that he had paid the proper price for these goods. He had also paid servants two *tomines* per week for personal services. *Carta de pago*, Cleric of Miçantla (1575), AGN Indiferente Virreinal, vol. 5657, exp. 75, ff. 1r–2v.

missionaries until the new procedures were put into place.[81] In one case, a group of Augustinians was left starving because the viceregal order that authorized their provisioning had accidentally caught fire, and the indigenous community was refusing to supply them with food until they received another order.[82]

Despite the shortcomings of royal officials in enforcing the new policies, indigenous communities came to expect order and regularity in the collection of their tribute. When missionaries overcharged them, natives demanded justice from viceregal authorities, denouncing the "disquiet and anxiety" caused by unpredictable and sudden demands for goods and services. These sentiments rarely surfaced in earlier ad hoc arrangements.[83] For example don Gonzalo, gobernador of Guytlacotla on the Pacific coast of Guerrero, complained that "every macehual is aggrieved" for having to making sure that their priest was properly provisioned whenever he visited. He asked the viceroy to clarify their exact obligations. The viceroy obliged by ordering don Gonzalo to provide a hen and fifty tortillas every day "and nothing more."[84] In Chiegautla (near Tula), natives appealed to the legal principles of the tribute reforms in order to end the double taxation that they paid to support local Franciscans. They called upon the viceroy to compel their encomendero to meet his obligation of paying one hundred fanegas of corn and fifty fanegas of wheat per year to the missionaries.[85] In other cases, commoners denounced friars and clerics for demanding unpaid services for their own profit.[86]

[81] Viceregal order, Cuytertenique (1556), AGN Mercedes, vol. 4, parte 2, f. 372v; Viceregal order, Cuitzeo (1563), AGN Mercedes, vol. 7, f. 151r. Viceregal order, Cuitzeo (1563), AGN Mercedes, vol. 7, f. 152r; Viceregal order, Chachalintla and Tuzapa (1575) AGN General de Parte, vol. 1, exp. 137, f. 27r.

[82] Viceregal order, Chapulhuacan Maquiesuchil (1576), AGN General, vol. 1, exp. 1155, f. 218v.

[83] Viceregal order, Corregidor de Chietla (1583), AGN Indios, vol. 2, exp. 402, f. 96v.

[84] Viceregal order, natives of Guytlacotla (1558), AGN Mercedes, vol. 84, exp. 190, f. 67v.

[85] Viceregal order, Chieguautla (1565), AGN Mercedes, vol. 8, f. 93v.

[86] Viceregal order, Xilotepec (1566), AGN Mercedes, vol. 8, f. 251r; Viceregal order, Tenango (1563), AGN Mercedes, vol. 84, f. 100r; Amparo, Sabinan (1563), AGN Mercedes, tomo 6, f. 481v; Viceregal order, Tepequaquilco (1563), AGN Mercedes, vol. 7, f. 185v; Viceregal order, Zapotitlán (1587), AGN Indiferente Virreinal, vol. 562, exp. 34, ff. 1r–3v; Viceregal order, San Juan Epatlán (1580), AGN General de Parte, vol. 2, exp. 865, f. 182v; Viceregal order, Tututepec y Nopala (1583), AGN Indios, vol. 2, exp. 491, f. 115r; Audiencia trial, Tlaquiltenango (1583–1595), AGN Tierras, vol. 1979, exp. 4, ff. 129v, 147v, 151r, 158v, 161r, 164v; Viceregal order, Pánuco (1589), AGN Indios, vol. 4, exp. 74, f. 22v.

Artisans also began to seek fair pay in their transactions with friars. In Tlatelolco, ten indigenous painters denounced the Franciscans for forcing them to produce retables for monasteries throughout New Spain. For ten years they labored without pay. When some painters failed to report to work on holy days of obligation, they were punished so harshly that one of their older *maestros* nearly died from the lashings he received. The painters declared that if they did not find relief they would flee: "Since God made us free, we want to be paid for our work."[87] Cantores felt much the same way when missionaries failed to pay them for their services.[88] Such was the case of one don Jerónimo Feliciano, a former choir singer whose voice so charmed the Augustinians at Axacuba that they forced him to perform on several occasions without compensation.[89] Under the new policies on tributes and labor, even praising God in hymns now carried a price in Mexico, and don Jerónimo knew enough of the law to demand compensation.

Even though the tribute reforms sought to restrict missionaries' and native rulers' demands on commoners, they were still no match against depopulation and exploitation. Indeed, for poor jurisdictions that continued to see numbers decline, the sobra reform proved to be as inflexible as earlier tribute arrangements. The problem lay in the fact that the new reforms levied a head tax on each tribute-payer but also set fixed amounts allocated to the Crown and the Church. As populations fell, payments to the Church consumed an ever-greater share of tributes, reaching as much as two thirds of surpluses in some towns after the devastating epidemics of the 1570s and 1580s.[90] Communities reached their breaking

---

[87] Painters of Tlatelolco, denunciation of Franciscans (1605), AGN Bienes Nacionales, vol. 732c, exp. 1.

[88] Viceregal order, Tenayuca (1591), AGN Indios, vol. 6, 2a parte, exp. 182, f. 42r; Cantores of Tlalnepantla, (1580), AGN General de Parte, vol. 2, exp. 965, f. 207v; Viceregal order, Alcalde Mayor de Izucar (1591), AGN Indios, vol. 6, 2a parte, exp. 642, f. 145r; Viceroy to alcalde mayor of San Ildefonso, AGN Indios, vol. 5, exp. 970, f. 319v; Viceregal order, Sicoaque (1576), AGN General de Parte, vol. 1, exp. 678, f. 136r.

[89] Viceregal order, alcalde mayor de Hueypoxtla (1591), AGN Indios, vol. 3, exp. 813, f. 193v.

[90] Cases in which missionaries consumed one third of local *sobras*: Quetzala (doctrina), 1591: AGN Indios, vol. 3, exp. 476, f. 110r; Atzingo (doctrina), 1591: AGN Indios, vol. 3, exp. 610, f. 146v. Half of local *sobras* – San Bernardo and San Sebastián (sujetos of Huejutla), 1579: AGN General de Parte, vol. 2, exp. 210, f. 63r; Chiautla, 1575: AGN General de Parte, vol. 1, exp. 103, f. 21r. Two thirds of *sobras* – Sujetos of Tacuba, 1590: AGN Indios, vol. 4, exp. 842, f. 228v. In 1592, Viceroy Luís de Velasco II forbade

point when missionaries loaded additional demands on native laborers. In 1584, the commoners of Ahuehuetzingo, a sujeto of Chietla, protested unpaid labor levies for Augustinian friars. "For the friars' own benefit," the petitioners declared, the friars were deploying native officials to force them to cut wood in a forest on the slopes of the Cocopetlayuca Volcano, so that the friars might build new stables. The commoners knew their rights: "We are not obligated to give them these Indians ... [and in any case] the friars already have a church, a house, and everything else, with stone roofs, as well as a perfectly good stable."[91] If they did not receive relief soon, the petitioners warned, this illegal exploitation "will be the cause of the total destruction of the natives."[92] Demographic figures for the Chietla region in those years lend a chilling evidence to back their arguments: between 1571 and 1592, the number of tributaries fell from 906 to 553, a decline of 39 percent.[93]

Native rulers and missionaries responded to these protests with threats and intimidation. In Chiauhtla, a desolate jurisdiction south of Puebla, the leaders of eight sujetos denounced their cabecera rulers and Augustinian friars for demanding labor far in excess of the requirements stipulated in their tribute assessment.[94] In that agreement, the sujetos were only required to provide four percent of their able-bodied laborers to work at standard wages in the nearby mines of Tlauzinco.[95] Nonetheless, local indigenous rulers, missionaries, and the Spanish alcalde mayor continued to make extra demands on the sujetos. Seven female corn-grinders served the Spanish alcalde mayor and the native gobernador; to add insult to injury, the women had to carry the ingredients on their backs over 1.5 leagues (4.5 km). Eight commoners, meanwhile, had to herd the Augustinians' flocks of goats and sheep. And the list went on: two alguaciles served the alcalde mayor; five men served each week as *tamemes* (carriers) and messengers; another five burned lime and delivered it to the

---

Augustinians from consuming more than half of the *sobras* in Chiutepeque: AGN Indios, vol. 6, exp. 189, f. 47v.
[91] Real Audiencia to natives of Agueguecingo (1584), AGN Tierras, vol. 3002, exp. 20, f. 1r–v.
[92] AGN Tierras, vol. 3002, exp. 20, f. 1r.
[93] By 1626, only 165 tributaries remained, down from 1,718 in 1548. Gerhard, *Guide*, 110–1.
[94] Sujetos of Chiauhtla, denunciation of Augustinians (1591), AGN Tierras, vol. 2913, exp. 10, ff. 243r–9v.
[95] AGN Tierras, vol. 2913, exp. 10, ff. 244r, 246r.

Augustinians (who most likely resold it since their church was complete); other natives hauled a hundred loads of fodder for the friars' horses. For all of this the commoners received no compensation.[96]

After receiving the commoners' petition to address these abuses, the viceroy issued a sweeping rebuke to the native rulers and Augustinians and ordered them to cease their illegal exactions. Yet without enforcement, the injunction alone was useless in the face of local intimidation: the protestors were too afraid to present the viceroy's order to their rulers and missionaries. "There is no one here who dares to confront the alcalde mayor or the prior of the monastery with this," they explained.[97] Finally, when a local Spanish mining official volunteered to present the viceroy's verdict on behalf of the commoners, the Augustinian prior – one of the parties obligated to receive and acknowledge the order – simply refused to appear.[98] Shortly thereafter, native cabecera authorities arrested all the indigenous leaders in the protesting sujetos, and they harassed the commoners until they returned to work for the Augustinians and lords. As the grim pace of depopulation only compounded the burden borne by survivors, the protests against illegal abuses in Chiauhtla fell silent, at least in the viceregal record.[99]

It is impossible, of course, to know how many aggrieved macehuales grudgingly bore these burdens when faced with intimidation, instead of protesting them like the macehualtin of Chiauhtla. Archives record the occasional protest, but not the innumerable daily compromises, both large and small, that commoners made in order to simply farm their *milpas* in peace. Despite attempts to regulate the economic relationship between missionaries and indigenous communities, reports of abuses continued to surface over the next two centuries.[100] Yet this economic system not only weighed heavily on the backs of the macehualtin; it also threatened the spirits of its ecclesiastical beneficiaries.

---

[96] Viceregal order, Alcalde Mayor de Chiauhtla (1590), AGN Tierras, vol. 2913, exp. 10, f. 246r.

[97] ibid., f. 245r.   [98] ibid., f. 246v.

[99] ibid., ff. 243r, 247r–8v. The number of tributaries in Chiautla declined from an estimated 6,000 in the 1540s to 3,800 in 1554, 2,816 in 1571, 2,348 in 1588, to 1,050 in 1610. Gerhard, *Guide*, 108–9.

[100] Silvio Zavala, ed., *Fuentes para la historia del trabajo en la Nueva España* (Mexico City: Centro de Estudios Históricos del Movimiento Obrero Mexicano, 1980), vol. VI, 114; Robert S. Haskett, "'Not a Pastor, but a Wolf:' Indigenous-Clergy Relations in Early Cuernavaca and Taxco," *The Americas*, vol. 50, no. 3 (1994), 293–336.

LOSING THEBAID

G. – In a land where greed reigns, is there any place for wisdom?
Mesa. – The more valuable and powerful of the two has triumphed.

Cervantes de Salazar, *Diálogos*[101]

The year was 1540, and Alonso Ortiz de Zúñiga and his wife had just
arrived in Mexico City after a long journey from their encomienda in
Cuynmantlán, a town in the mountainous Sierra Alta far to the North.
On the way they had stopped to rest at the Augustinian monastery at
Molango, where they claimed to witness a rather unspiritual conquest of
native towns by the friars.[102] Upon arriving in Mexico City, Ortíz and his
wife hastened to see Diego Velázquez, the *provisor* (diocesan prosecutor)
of the Archdiocese, to unburden their consciences.[103] Their testimony
struck at the greatest fears of the missionaries in New Spain: that the
lucre, power, and temptations of the friars' mission might unravel their
vows to forswear the temporal world.

Ortíz depicted an Augustinian Order that was as corrupt as any
other group of Spanish colonists, as they too exploited natives, traded
in slaves, and abused women. He alleged that the friars in the Sierra
Alta were extorting exorbitant amounts of labor and tribute from local
communities, obliging towns over rugged mountain passes ten leagues
(55 km) away to deliver hens and *mantas* (tribute-blankets) on daily
and weekly cycles. The friars ensured compliance by abusing the children of native lords from those towns, whom they held sequestered at
their mission school in Molango. He also claimed that the Augustinians
were also using local *tamemes* (human carriers) to haul their belongings "anywhere they wished" at little to no notice.[104] The friars also

---

[101] "Gutiérrez: En tierra donde la codicia impera, ¿queda acaso algún lugar para la sabi-
duría? Mesa: Venció la que vale y puede más." Francisco Cervantes de Salazar, *México
en 1554 y túmulo imperial* ed. Edmundo O'Gorman (Mexico City: Porrúa, 2000), 21.

[102] Cuymantlán (modern-day Acuimantla, Northern Hidalgo), a sujeto of Tlanchinolticpac,
was split from its cabecera by the Second Audiencia in 1534, which awarded the town as
an encomienda to Alonso Ortiz de Zúñiga. The town later reverted to sujeto status under
Tlanchinolticpac. Gerhard, *Guide*, 185, 187.

[103] Auto against Fray Juan de San Martín (1540), AGN Indiferente Virreinal, vol. 5678,
exp. 37.

[104] AGN Indiferente Virreinal, vol. 5678, exp. 37, f. 2 r–v.

owned an indigenous slave who worked in their kitchen, a fact that struck Ortíz as suspect.[105]

Ortíz's most serious allegations, however, concerned the behavior of one Augustinian in particular, Fray Juan de San Martín. Ortíz informed the provisor that while his entourage stayed in Molango Fray Juan had propositioned one of his female slaves in the monastery garden.[106] According to Ortíz this incident was not the first: a year earlier at Ortíz's encomienda in Cuynmatlán, Fray Juan had raped Catalina, an African slave belonging to Ortíz. "He took her at night by force," he declared, "[and] had carnal relations with her." Fray Juan also allegedly attempted to rape an indigenous *naboria* (indentured laborer) in the same town. Fray Juan had given her a *crucecita*, a "little Cross," in his attempt to convince her. Ortíz was left speechless "that this friar would set such a bad example among the Indians." In this remote town where evangelization had only commenced a year earlier, he declared, "the Indians have been left scandalized."[107]

Augustinians, of course, told a very different tale of their first years in the Sierra Alta. They preferred not to acknowledge the privileges that supported them in their daily contacts with laborers in their kitchens, dining halls, and gardens, and they muted all suggestions of impropriety that these contacts gave rise to. Instead, they imagined themselves cleansing their souls in their American Thebaid. Yet the eremitic desert of their dreams was in reality a colonial frontier, a place where they wielded such temporal power that their decisions affected thousands of native lives, a place where they could live off the largesse of native tributes and unpaid labor and enjoy the privilege of writing it all off as pious donations. All missionaries faced the same reckoning that the distance between Thebaid and Mexico was indeed vast, nearly insurmountable. At that point each missionary, like Albert Memmi's tortured colonizers, faced a choice to either accept the colonial reality or resist it.[108] In the rugged Sierra Alta of Meztitlán this diverging path was particularly stark.

Mendicant chronicles and paintings focused on the missionaries' efforts to bridge the gulf between Mexico and Thebaid. The principal

---

[105] AGN Indiferente Virreinal, vol. 5678, exp. 37, ff. 2v–3r. Alonso Ortíz de Zúñiga was accused of widespread abuses in his encomiendas during Diego Ramírez's investigations in 1554. Paso y Troncoso, *Epistolario*, vol. VII, 203–7.

[106] AGN Indiferente Virreinal, vol. 5678, exp. 37, f. 2r.

[107] AGN Indiferente Virreinal, vol. 5678, exp. 37, f. 1r.

[108] Albert Memmi, *The Colonizer and the Colonized*, trans. Howard Greenfield (Boston, MA: Beacon Books, 1991 [1957]).

chronicler of the Augustinians in Mexico, Fray Juan de Grijalva, attributed the rapid evangelization of the Sierra Norte to the power of worldly denial. In the crags of Meztitlán, he wrote, the Augustinians waged a spiritual battle against the Devil, who had fled there from the conquered cities and valleys of central Mexico.[109] In Grijalva's telling, the victory over idolatry in the Sierra was the work of a humble friar named Fray Antonio de la Roa, a "monster of holiness" whose asceticism inspired both "admiration and astonishment."[110] In Spain, De la Roa's spiritual discipline had consisted of self-mortification, fasting, prayer, and contemplation. As if to sacrifice his life of spiritual perfection in a safe European cloister, he answered the call to join the New World mission in Mexico, where he despaired that his "search for solitude and tranquility of the soul" was rapidly ceding ground to the work of preaching.[111] Such conflicts typified the "double life" of all mendicant missionaries, who struggled to balance worldly engagement with interior contemplation.[112]

De la Roa resolved this conflict by turning his asceticism into his evangelical message. The mission became, for him, an affirmation of his denial of this world. When he made long journeys on foot, he wore his Augustinian habit so that the coarse wool would constantly scratch him "to tame his body with its harshness." He never slept horizontally and he went hungry every day.[113] De la Roa turned his mortification, which in normal conditions was to be practiced in the privacy in a cell or cave, into a public spectacle. He had his indigenous disciples beat him fiercely "as if he were their enemy," and when he traveled to outlying towns, they would tug him about so witnesses could contemplate "the way of bitterness" before stripping him of his habit, beating him in public, and lashing him until "his blood would burst out." Before one sermon at the monastery of Molango, he explained the torments of Hell by walking over hot coals in the churchyard. He then had his assistants pour scalding water over him.[114] This public war against his own flesh, the chronicler Grijalva states, kept his mission labors from corrupting the "work of his spirit."[115]

It is instructive that Fray Juan de San Martín, the all-too-mundane friar who allegedly lived by the flesh, coincided in Molango with Fray Antonio

[109] Grijalva, *Crónica*, 79, 174–5.   [110] ibid., 75.   [111] ibid., 216–7.
[112] Focher, *Itinerario*, 30–2; Steven E. Turley, *Franciscan Spirituality and Mission in New Spain, 1524–1599: Conflict Beneath the Sycamore Tress (Luke 19:1–10)* (Farnham: Ashgate, 2014), 57–81, 122.
[113] Grijalva, *Crónica*, 218.   [114] ibid., 221–2.   [115] ibid., 223–4.

de la Roa, the friar who sought his refuge from the flesh in pain and self-disfigurement. Each embodied an extreme of the mission. Fray Juan de San Martín is an example of mendicant accommodation with – and in his case flagrant abuse of – the colonial society of which his mission formed part. Fray Antonio de la Roa, who feared that the life of the missionary would corrupt his spirit, needed acolytes to beat him into obedience. Mendicant missionaries in New Spain navigated between these two extremes. Their work challenged the Orders' special role in the Church as vehicles of spiritual perfection. After all, Thomas Aquinas had written: "The religious state [in holy orders] is an exercise or discipline by which one reaches perfection of charity, [and for this reason] it is necessary for one to detach his heart from all mundane things."[116]

Yet colonial Mexico offered anything but detachment from mundane things. The post-conquest order gave friars power as administrators and as judges, even if this was not stipulated by law; it involved them in political struggles that tempted them to battle for pride and reputation; it entitled them to access native wealth and labor; and it provided an embarrassment of food for their table. All this threatened the integrity of mendicant vows. Archbishop Montúfar expressed the opinion of many Spanish critics when he accused friars of grasping for "supreme command and lordship" over the Indians and reducing them to "personal servitude under the guise of indoctrinating them."[117] Occasionally victims of abuse also bravely came forward like Francisca, a slave who accused a friar of twice demanding sex from her as a personal *limosna* (donation).[118] Even Archbishop Fray Juan de Zumárraga, no enemy of the friars, despaired that he had to expel several mendicant missionaries from New Spain, without providing further details.[119] Years later, this consummate apologist for the Orders confessed that New Spain had become "the sewer, latrine and receptacle of all bad clerics and friars." The once hopeful bishop proclaimed Mexico a "great Babylon."[120]

The friars' own internal legislation indicates that they were aware of the ways in which their temporal power and privileges could undermine

---

[116] Daniel Ulloa, *Los predicadores divididos* (Mexico City: El Colegio de México, 1985), 151.

[117] Montúfar to the Council of the Indies (1555), in Paso y Troncoso *Epistolario*, vol. VIII, 42–3.

[118] Testimony, Francisca de Baldivieso (1540), AGN Indiferente Virreinal, vol. 5678, exp. 37, ff. 5v, 7v.

[119] Zumárraga to Charles V (1540), in Cuevas, *Documentos*, 103–4.

[120] Zumárraga to Tello de Sandoval (1547), in Cuevas, *Documentos*, 103–4, 125–7.

their apostolic mission and unravel their vows.[121] Dominicans fretted that the wealth of the colony could "sully the friars with uncontrollable greed."[122] In 1564, Augustinians meeting at Acolmán denounced their confrères for demanding bribes of money and goods. Accepting such "donations" threatened their vows of poverty.[123] Dominicans also regulated the friars' economic activity: they restricted their use of horses, forbade them from demanding gratuities, sought to limit the number of their servants, and banned them from shopping in *tianguis* (native marketplaces). In one telling clause, the Dominican leadership reminded the friars that they had to pay all their indigenous workers for their labor.[124]

The internal legislation of the mendicant Orders also addressed infractions of the vow of celibacy. Most of these provisions sought to maximize collective supervision over friars. To prevent friars from sneaking out of their monasteries at night, Dominicans at their Chapter of 1541 ordered that every monastery should have only two outside doors, each with a double lock.[125] Friars were to only travel in pairs and were never to find themselves alone in the monastery.[126] Other clauses identified the confessional as a place particularly prone to sexual violence, while a disciplinary guide declared that fixing one's gaze on women while traveling outside the monastery constituted a *gravis culpa*.[127] A clause from the Dominican Chapter of 1568 showed how economic relations with indigenous communities threatened both poverty and chastity: "No women are to enter our convents, not even in the gardens."[128] The prohibition addresses the dangerous proximity of servants to the friars' living quarters, which is evinced as well by Ortíz's testimony of the abuses that took place in the gardens of Molango.

CONCLUSION

Having left their monasteries in Spain, mendicants found themselves flung among a foreign people whom they ruled, ministered to, and depended upon. De la Roa and others quickly saw that their new vocation consisted not only of spreading the Gospel, but also of establishing worldly relations with indigenous communities that could undermine their vows.

---

[121] Roulet, *L'évangélisation*, 171–4.   [122] Ulloa, *Predicadores divididos*, 151.
[123] Rubial García, *Convento*, 185.
[124] Ulloa, *Predicadores divididos*, 166, 169, 177, 153, 162, 170, 173, 183, 180, 187.
[125] ibid., 157; AGN Indiferente Virreinal, vol. 5768, exp. 37, ff. 5r–v, 7v.   [126] ibid., 162.
[127] ibid., 166, 181, 207.   [128] ibid., 178.

For this reason mendicants plastered their monastery walls with images of a paradise that they were losing to the daily sins of power, dependence, exploitation, and temptation. Others dreamed of escaping. The Augustinians Fray Antonio de la Roa and Fray Juan Bautista Moya fantasized living out their days as hermits in caves like the anchorites of Thebaid.[129] Franciscans, meanwhile, seriously considered a project to create a hermit province for themselves in the deserts of northern New Spain, far from missions and natives.[130]

Missionary dependence on tribute gave the mendicants' opponents ample reason to doubt their integrity. And as de la Roa's harrowing acts of asceticism attest, mendicants felt uneasy about their engagement with this colonial world. These doubts lingered on in the many institutional efforts to preserve vows of poverty, both within Orders as well as in the bishops' decrees of the Third Mexican Council. But in public, of course, missionaries continued to argue that native labor and tributes were alms rather than forced contributions. Crown officials agreed that the mendicant missions should continue to be financed through tribute while hoping that natives would somehow conclude that their conversion had come free of charge. Instead, indigenous communities knew how much labor they provided, how many goods they donated, and how much specie they paid to maintain their missionaries. Mexico was no Thebaid, and indigenous people were not blank slates. Instead, the landscape was populated with communities that did not always hold back from raising protests against the worldly excesses of their spiritual fathers.

---

[129] Rubial García, *Convento*, 86.
[130] Rubial García, "La insulana," 39–46; Rubial García, *Hermana pobreza*, 101–46; Turley, *Franciscan Mission*, 86–9.

5

Building in the Shadow of Death

Monastery Construction and the Politics of Community Reconstitution

Around the year 1550, an indigenous *tlacuilo* (a painter–scribe–historian) in Tepechpan, a small altepetl north of Mexico City, narrated the tumultuous events of his lifetime. In the image below (*Fig. 5.1*), we can see an excerpt of the tlacuilo's contribution to the town's annals, the *Tira de Tepechpan*, which depicts a sequence of events from 1545 to 1549. On the left, beneath the glyph for the year 1545, the tlacuilo paints a dangling corpse, its arms crossed and eyes shut, with blood spurting from the nose and mouth. Here the tlacuilo is telling us of the 1545 *hueycocolixtli*, the "great sickness" that killed at least a third of the population, according to conservative estimates. Among the victims was Tepechpan's ruler, the crowned figure wrapped in funeral cloth above the year glyph.

To the right of the ruler, the tlacuilo tells quite a different story for the year 1549. Here he paints a stone church atop what appears to be a prehispanic temple platform, with a fine gothic portal and bell tower. The glyph marks the construction of a new stone church.[1] The contrast here, between mass death and monumental construction, is jarring. In the stark visual language of Mexican codices, the tlacuilo seems to be telling us that

---

[1] See Lori Boornazian Diel, *The Tira de Tepechpan: Negotiating Place under Aztec and Spanish Rule* (Austin, TX: University of Texas Press, 2008), 17, 86–7, and 91. In 1552, an indigenous witness named Luís Quiab declared to a Spanish judge that the teocalli of Tepechpan was "next to the church." *Tepechpan v. Temascalapa* (1552), AGI Justicia, leg. 164, no. 2, f. 261r.

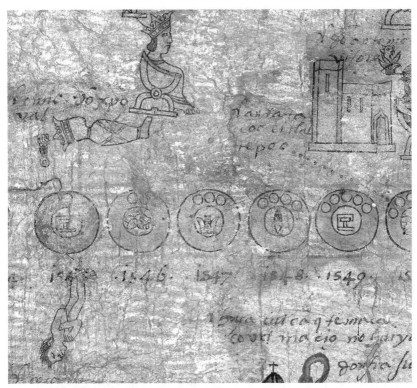

FIGURE 5.1 Excerpt from the *Tira de Tepechpan*, years 1545–1549.
Anon. Indigenous tlacuilos, c. 1550. Bibliothèque Nationale de France (BNF), Manuscrits
Mexicains, nos. 13–14. By permission of the BNF

despite losing much of its population, Tepechpan still persisted in a
building program that was as costly as it was ambitious.

As in Tepechpan, so it was throughout central Mexico: from the Río
Pánuco in the north to Oaxaca in the south, indigenous communities of
different ethnicities and varying economic circumstances replaced their
churches of thatch and wood with stone churches and monasteries.
Laborers covered their mass graves and then dug open quarries; they
razed forests, hauled lumber, and burned lime; they assembled scaffolds
and raised immense walls of stone; they set delicately carved limestone
into gothic arches that soared high into the heavens. Between the 1530s
and 1580s, in the wake of demographic catastrophe, indigenous communities built 251 large church-and-monastery complexes. Many of these
structures still loom today over provincial cities, bustling country towns,
and sparsely populated villages. As if defying their dire circumstances,

FIGURE 5.2 *Doctrina* monastery, Yanhuitlán (Oaxaca), atop the platform
of a former teocalli.
Photo by Author

indigenous communities built some of the largest edifices ever raised in
colonial Mexico – in the shadow of mass death.[2]

These Mexican church–monastery complexes (*Fig. 5.2*) present the
most tangible evidence of the sixteenth-century mission enterprise and
the political and social relations that comprised it. The largest of these
structures, numbering at least sixty, are distinguishable by their single-
nave churches crowned with merlons, their attached monasteries, and
their vast *atrios*, or enclosed churchyards. Rising to heights of between
eighteen and twenty-five meters, the churches stand out as hulking, windowless masses of stone and dark-red volcanic *tezontle*. Adjoining them
are equally impressive monasteries that served as the friars' residence and

---

[2] Kubler classified these constructions into three groups according to size and artistic
ornamentation. The largest structures had high "vaults or richly decorated wooden
ceilings" and "elaborate conventual layouts in two stories with ... vaulted walks." Next
were "medium size, well-built churches" with "two-storied conventual buildings."
Churches in these two categories had vaults as high as 24 meters and ranged from 40 to
60 meters in length. Finally, Kubler mentions "small edifices of permanent construction,"
in which adjoining convents were often incomplete. Kubler underrates many of the
structures listed, including the large Dominican monastery at Coyoacán, which took
considerable time to build and still overshadows surrounding modern structures, or the
Franciscan monastery at Erongarícuaro, a stone structure that boasts skilled stonework – a
sign of community investment. Out of a total of 87 structures listed, 59 structures rank in
the first two categories. See Kubler, *Mexican Architecture*, vol. I, 24–7, and vol. II, 274.

headquarters. On façades, elegant colonnades, and along cloister walls, stone carvings and fresco paintings exquisitely combine biblical scenes with Mesoamerican motifs, the result of an astonishing dynamism between Euro-Christian and indigenous imaginaries.[3] Surrounding the church and monastery, the shady atrio laid out on the scale of a town plaza attests to the multitudes that once received doctrinal instruction and participated in Christian rites – outdoors and in front of the temple, as their forebears had done in front of their *teocallis* (temples).[4]

Apart from their large scale, these complexes stood out from other colonial churches in two key ways. First, since they served as logistical and liturgical hubs in the mendicants' mission system, these structures were ostentatious markers of doctrina status. Second, in terms of indigenous politics, these complexes served as the core of political and religious life in local polities, and as such they confirmed the preeminence of all the communities that housed them over surrounding sujetos. Given the elevated status that these monasteries conferred on the towns that built them, I refer to these complexes as doctrina monasteries.[5] This monumental mission architecture went on to influence subsequent mission fields, most notably in the Philippines.[6]

Because these voluminous and mysterious structures rose in the first decades of colonization, the travelers and scholars who have stumbled upon them have long assumed that their walls had quite a story to tell. Successive generations have combed these structures in their completed form, parsing their façades, mural paintings, and architectural layouts for clues about the cultural encounters between natives and Europeans. Most studies have traced these elements back to their origins, to Medieval and Renaissance Europe or to pre-conquest Mesoamerica.[7] Early scholars saw

---

[3] See Gruzinski, *Conquest of Mexico*; Peterson, *Paradise Garden Murals*.

[4] Jaime Lara, *City, Temple, Stage: Eschatological Architecture and Liturgical Theatrics in New Spain* (Notre Dame: University of Notre Dame Press, 2004); and Samuel Y. Edgerton, *Theaters of Conversion: Religious Architecture and Indian Artisans in Colonial Mexico* (Albuquerque, NM: University of New Mexico Press, 2001).

[5] These structures are frequently referred to by their misnomer, "fortress monasteries," the remnant of a now-debunked argument that these structures served a defensive function. George Kubler, "Mexican Urbanism in the Sixteenth Century," *The Art Bulletin* (1942), 160–71.

[6] Pedro G. Galende, *Angels in Stone: Augustinian Churches in the Philippines* (Manila: San Agustín Museum, 1996).

[7] Carolyn Dean and Dana Leibsohn, "Hybridity and Its Discontents: Considering Visual Culture in Colonial Spanish America," *Colonial Latin American Review*, vol. 12, no. 1 (1995), 5.

the large scale and widespread diffusion of these monasteries as indices of the completeness of the Spanish conquest. George Kubler's classic study, for example, attributed the rapid emergence of stone complexes to the friars' "remarkable feats of moral persuasion," which apparently sufficed to make entire communities move stone and lumber for two decades.[8] Subsequent architectural studies have been subtler, tracing the circulation and reach of European styles, architects, technologies, and iconography.[9] Meanwhile, over the past several decades *indigenistas* have issued their riposte to studies of European expansion: for them, the presence of indigenous elements – from the overall spatial layout of the complexes down to the detail of an indigenous town-glyph tucked away in a cloister in Cuauhtinchán – serve as tangible evidence of native agency. A structure that at first seems to be easily identifiable as European thus becomes, on closer examination, also a product of Mesoamerica: a "reassembly" of the indigenous temple in a Christian form.[10] What scholars once took for a symbol of conquest has effectively transmuted into a sign of indigenous endurance – into a new teocalli.

While the visible evidence etched into these walls has yielded telling discoveries, the social production of these edifices – the very *processes* involved in their construction – are far less visible to the naked eye, and

[8] Kubler, *Mexican Architecture*, vol. I, 30; Kubler, "Mexican Urbanism," ibid.; Van Oss, *Church and Society*, 103–25. See also Valerie Fraser, *The Architecture of Conquest: Building the Viceroyalty of Peru, 1535–1635* (Cambridge: Cambridge University Press, 1990).

[9] Miguel Ángel Fernández, *La Jerusalén indiana. Los conventos-fortaleza mexicanos del siglo XVI* (Mexico: Smurfit, 1992); Luís Javier Cuesta Hernández, *Arquitectura del Renacimiento en Nueva España* (Mexico City: Universidad Iberoamericana, 2009); Lara, *City, Temple, Stage.*

[10] Jaime Lara employs the term "reassembly" in his monumental work on mission architecture and raises an important question: "Should we more accurately speak of the process [or temple destruction/church construction] as one of reuse or recycling?" *City, Temple, Stage*, 7. See also: Escalante Gonzalbo, "El patrocinio," 215–35; Clara Bargellini, "Representations of Conversion: Sixteenth-Century Architecture in New Spain," in *The Word Made Image: Religion, Art, and Architecture in Spain and Spanish America, 1500–1600*, ed. Jonathan Brown (Boston: Isabella Stewart Gardner Museum, 1998), 97–8; Constantino Reyes-Valerio, *Arte indocristiano* (Mexico City: INAH, 2000); Edgerton, *Theaters of Conversion*; Peterson, *Paradise Garden Murals*; Wake, *Framing*; Christian Duverger, *Agua y fuego: Arte sacro indígena de México en el siglo XVI* (Mexico City: Santander Serfín, 2003); Carlos Chanfón Olmos, *Historia de la arquitectura y el urbanismo mexicanos* (Mexico City: Fondo de Cultura Económica, 1997).

therefore remain largely neglected.[11] As in the Tepechpan tlacuilo's painted narrative, in most histories the large stone church simply appears *ex nihilo*. It only serves as evidence in its completed, visible form; it is significant only when finished. Yet here the Tepechpan tlacuilo, a historian in his own right, has left us with a silence so great it raises a question. Returning to the tlacuilo's painting, note the void between mass death in 1545 and the completion of the stone church in 1549. Those unmarked years were undoubtedly full of both grieving and hauling heavy loads, of rebuilding lives and laying stone upon stone into the thick walls of naves and cloisters. What motivated these communities to undertake the great and costly endeavor of stone church construction at such a dire moment?

In the history of the region as a whole, the same silence hangs over the years between the mid-century demographic crisis and the completion of the doctrina monastery complexes not long thereafter. This is even more important because archival records demonstrate that this gap was not one of decades, as had been previously assumed, but of years – just as it is portrayed in the *Tira de Tepechpan*. Previous mission scholarship had tracked building campaigns solely in published mendicant sources and concluded that monastery construction peaked in the 1570s. However, having scoured viceregal records held at the Archivo General de la Nación in Mexico City and the Archivo General de Indias in Seville – account ledgers, building licenses, procurement orders, and labor mobilization decrees – I have found that monastery construction campaigns in central Mexico actually peaked two decades earlier, in the 1550s, as shown in *Figure 5.3*.[12]

Thus, the pattern of monastery construction throughout central Mexico is similar to the rapid (but as yet unexplained) turnaround in the tlacuilo's painting: after losing at least a third of their population, precisely when one might assume that building activity would stall or even cease, 119 towns instead commenced or continued building.[13]

---

[11] Dean and Leibsohn note the lack of social production in studies of hybrid colonial art: "Hybridity and Its Discontents," 5. See also Henri Lefebvre, *The Production of Space* (Cambridge: Blackwell, 1991), 14–18, 26–30.

[12] Archival data for figures and charts is drawn from: AGN Mercedes, General de Parte, Indios, Civil, and Tierras; and AGI Contaduría, Escribanía, México, Real Patronato, and Justicia. See Appendix.

[13] Kubler, for example, drew his data from published primary sources, which showed a peak in construction in the 1570s with about 62 active projects. He also argued that different mendicant constructions peaked in different decades: Augustinians, inattentive to the post-*cocolixtli* crisis, peaked in the 1550s, while Franciscans and Dominicans adjusted to circumstances and peaked in the 1570s. My archival data overturns these

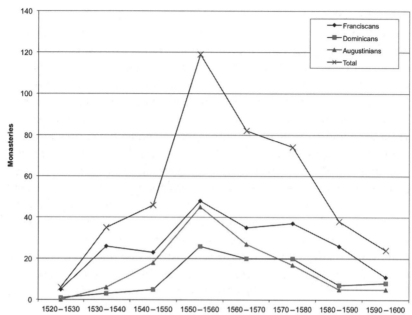

FIGURE 5.3 *Doctrina* monasteries under construction in Central Mexico.
Source: AGN, AGI. See Appendix 2

In turn each one of these projects affected dozens of outlying *sujetos*, or subject-towns. An endeavor of such magnitude, on the heels of catastrophe, evinces a region-wide movement that must be understood in socio-political terms. Why did hundreds of indigenous communities mobilize vast amounts of human labor, tributes, and natural resources to build on such an enormous scale? What impetus – what political and social forces – drove them to participate in these building campaigns?

To explore these questions, this chapter examines the social and political contingencies that were involved in the production of these immense structures. Mendicant expansion and rivalry, as mission scholarship has long noted, presented a demand for missionary infrastructure, but each newly founded doctrina depended on the imperatives of local politics.[14] When placed in their immediate context, the construction campaigns are inextricable from native rulers' efforts to reconstitute their polities during

figures: construction peaked in the 1550s at 122 projects (instead of 55), and construction projects for all Orders peaked in that decade. *Mexican Architecture*, ibid., vol. I, 65.

[14] Ricard, *Spiritual Conquest*; Van Oss, *Church and Society*; Kubler, *Mexican Architecture*; Duverger, *Agua y fuego*.

the volatile years after the *hueycocolixtli*. As depopulation intensified territorial conflicts and strained local hierarchies, monastery construction served as a conspicuous means to reassert power over lands and people. Like a chameleon – or a *nahual*, the shape-shifting sorcerers of Mesoamerican religions – the doctrina monastery constantly shifted its attributes: at one moment it functioned as a colonial mission, at the next, it rematerialized as a teocalli. While these structures bolstered Spanish claims to sovereignty over New Spain and established an infrastructure for missionaries, they also reasserted local indigenous claims to sovereignty in ways uncannily similar in practice to pre-conquest Mesoamerican teocallis. Yet, precisely due to this political importance in both indigenous and Spanish colonial contexts, these structures were also battlegrounds in struggles over lands and labor. Far from being the products of a community-wide consensus, as scholars have generally assumed, these costly projects involved constant negotiation, contestation, and resistance. In the shadow of death, each stone laid into these vast structures both reflected and remade a fragile and contested social order.

HUEYCOCOLIXTLI

The principal catalyst behind the accelerated monastery building campaigns was the far-reaching demographic catastrophe that swept Mexico in the 1540s. The calamity, especially the social and political disruptions that it caused, made the construction of the doctrina monasteries seem urgent and necessary to indigenous rulers. In the spring of 1545, a devastating epidemic, known as the *hueycocolixtli* or "great sickness," struck several indigenous towns surrounding Mexico City and over the next months spread across the length and breadth of central Mexico.[15] This was the second of three major step-like crashes in the sixteenth-century indigenous population of New Spain. The epidemic cut apart ruling native hierarchies, it decimated families, and it reduced rural populations to such an extent that the countryside – the once densely-populated lands so vividly portrayed in conquistadors' reports – now appeared to Spaniards to be irregularly settled, even fallow.[16]

---

[15] Domingo de Betanzos to Dominican *procuradores* (1545), in García Icazbalceta, *Colección de documentos*, vol. II, 200–1.
[16] Slicher Van Bath, "The Calculation of the Population," 67–95; Whitmore, *Disease*; Livi-Bacci, *Conquest*, 135.

Indigenous and Spanish histories note the same symptoms and social effects: the onset of fever followed by blood flowing from the orifices, the indiscriminate way that the disease struck lords and commoners alike, and the cruel indignity of mass burials.[17] The symptoms suggest that the illness was *typhus exanthematicus*, pneumonic plague, which spread as a virgin soil epidemic.[18] Although some Spaniards also fell ill, typhus was generally endemic to Western Europeans – potentially fatal, but not catastrophically so for society at large. Thus Spanish colonists went relatively unscathed while millions of indigenous people died.[19] A passage from the *Anales de Tecamachalco* conveys the horrific reach and suddenness of the catastrophe:

1545. In this year occurred the *hueycocolixtli*. Blood came out of people's mouths, their noses, and through their teeth. It came here during planting season, in May. The mortality was terrifying; at the beginning of the epidemic they would bury ten, then fifteen, twenty, thirty, forty in one day. And many children died over the course of a year until the sickness was over. Then the nobles [*pipiltin*] died, the one who was *hueyteuctli* [great lord], and other lords.[20]

Nothing – not prayers to gods old or new, nor medicinal remedies – could stop the dying.[21] For almost two years the disease raged, straining communities' abilities to produce food and care for the sick. Famine soon followed. The escalating mortality quickly overwhelmed communities' abilities to bury the dead. In Coixtlahuaca, according to an eyewitness, between thirty and forty people were perishing each day, faster than the survivors could dig open graves. "It is unbelievable how many people have died and still die every day," wrote Fray Domingo de Betanzos at the height of the epidemic. At least a thousand were dying every day in Tlaxcala; in Cholula "one day there were nine hundred bodies, but generally [the number of dead] is four, five, six and seven hundred every day."[22] The corpses were so many in Chalco, the indigenous historian

---

[17] Prem, "Disease Outbreaks," 34; Noble David Cook, *Born to Die: Disease and New World Conquest, 1492–1650* (Cambridge: Cambridge University Press, 1998), 100–3; Diel, *Tira de Tepechpan*; Dibble, *Codex en Cruz*; Pérez Zavallos and Reyes García *La fundación*, 58; INAH, Colección Antigua, tomo 273, vol. II: *Anales Mexicanos no. 1*, 433; *Anales de Tlatelolco y Mexico, no. 1*, p. 610; Anales de Quecholac (1519–1642), 949; *Anales de Tepeaca*, 401.

[18] Prem, ibid.; Cook, *Born to Die*, 100–3.

[19] Cook, *Born to Die*, 100; Sahagún, *Florentine Codex*, vol. I, 99.

[20] Celestino Solís and Reyes García, *Anales de Tecamachalco*, 70.

[21] Gruzinski, *Conquest of Mexico*, 80–1; Terraciano, *Mixtecs*, 362.

[22] Betanzos to Dominican *procuradores* (1545), in García Icazbalceta, *Colección de documentos*, vol. II, 200–1.

Domingo Chimalpáhin wrote, that dogs and coyotes were devouring them before they could be buried.[23]

With great alarm, missionaries and royal officials sought to quantify the losses and warned that the indigenous population was in danger of disappearing like that of the Caribbean. Spanish observers conveyed the magnitude of the catastrophe with biblical figures. Archbishop Zumárraga estimated the population loss at a third, Fray Bernardino de Sahagún at half, and Fray Toribio de Benevente Motolinía placed the losses as high as two thirds. Betanzos, meanwhile, estimated that "not a tenth remains of the population that there was here twenty years ago."[24] These contemporary estimates do not differ greatly from those of modern historical demographers. After the "Berkeley School" historians Cook and Borah projected mid-century losses at a staggering 80 percent, subsequent revisionists lowered estimated losses to a "moderate" 62.5 percent and a "mild" 31.5 percent.[25] Thus even the most conservative estimates point to a demographic catastrophe.[26] In 1554, Motolinía stated the only certainty: "many, many people are missing."[27]

By the time the survivors covered the last mass graves in 1547, the *hueycocolixtli* had already begun to transform the social and political landscape of central Mexico. For contemporary observers this was a watershed moment after which "the land remained very depleted of people," the point when "these kingdoms began their diminution and fall to ruin."[28] Disease and death had moved unevenly across the land, altering rural patterns of settlement, reshuffling territorial arrangements among rival polities, and destabilizing local hierarchies. Mesoamerican local states tended to integrate agricultural and urban settlement more evenly than the European *urbs*. Outside the complexes of stone buildings that housed the temple, ruler's palace, and market, indigenous towns seamlessly blended into a landscape dotted with hamlets among *milpas*

---

[23] Chimalpáhin, *Las ocho relaciones*, vol. II, 202–3.

[24] Zumárraga to Prince Philip (1547), in Cuevas, *Documentos*, 143; Torquemada, *Monarquía indiana*, 643; Sahagún, *Florentine Codex*, vol. 1, 99; Motolinía to Charles V (1555), in García Icazbalceta, *Colección de documentos*, vol. I, 264; Bernardo de Albuquerque to the Indies Council (1554), in Cuevas, ibid., 181.

[25] Whitmore, *Disease*, 118–19.

[26] McCaa, "Spanish and Nahuatl Views," 417–19, 423.

[27] Motolinía to Charles V (1555), in García Icazbalceta, *Colección de documentos*, vol. I, 264.

[28] Sahagún, *Florentine Codex*, vol. 1, 99; Torquemada, *Monarquía indiana*, 13, 615; Terraciano, *Mixtecs*, 362.

(corn plots) and terraces.[29] After the *hueycocolixtli* this landscape lay devastated. Indigenous and Spanish authorities noted that famished refugees were fleeing decimated communities and roaming the countryside. Once-proud towns that had boasted their own ruling lineages and ancient histories were reduced to a few dozen homes, while former cabeceras like Teteoc near Chimalhuacan, or Yucanuma in Oaxaca, disappeared entirely from the tribute lists. The landscape, once "full of people," was now eerily "empty." Hillside terracing, another sign of dense population and labor-intensive agriculture, ceased as survivors moved down to valley floors to cultivate in abandoned fields. Crop failures and famines only further destabilized community economies.[30]

The colonial relations between Spanish and indigenous communities only magnified these disruptions. In a letter to Prince Philip in 1547, Archbishop Zumárraga wrote that communities that had already been struggling to feed themselves under onerous Spanish demands were now stretched beyond capacity. With tribute and labor schedules still fixed according to the pre-*hueycocolixtli* populations, the survivors bore an increasingly heavy burden. When a royal commissioner inquired into the tributes paid by the town of Azoyú (Guerrero), for example, the inhabitants bluntly stated, "the tribute was too heavy because many people have died."[31] Spanish colonists were not immune to the deepening economic crisis that resulted, for major construction projects like Archbishop Zumárraga's cathedral in Mexico City stalled. Zumárraga declared that the emergency made reducing tribute and labor burdens an imperative, even for his cathedral. To rely on native labor in such grim circumstances, he confessed, would be rather like adding "Indian blood to the mortar mixture" for the cathedral walls.[32] Ironically, however, as he penned

---

[29] Bernal García and García Zambrano, "El altepetl colonial," 33, 74–6; Olivera, *Pillis y macehuales*, 133.

[30] Motolinía to Charles V (1555), Icazbalceta, *Colección de documentos*, vol. I, 264; Terraciano, *Mixtecs*, 362; Acuña, *Relaciones geográficas*, vol. 2, 144; Francisco del Paso y Troncoso ed., *Papeles de Nueva España* (Madrid, 1905), vol. VI, 46, 67, vol. V, 49, 100, vol. IV, 80, 59, vol. VI, 278, 57, 245, 315; Gerhard, "Congregaciones de indios," 354–6; Fray Domingo de la Anunciación (1554), Cuevas, *Documentos*, 241; Gerhard, *Guide*, 105; Paso y Troncoso, *Relaciones geográficas*, 67–9; Lockhart et al., *Tlaxcalan Actas*, 43; Martínez Baracs, *Un gobierno de indios*, 204; Sahagún, *Florentine Codex*, vol. 1, 99.

[31] Zumárraga to Prince Philip (1547), in Cuevas, *Documentos*, 141; Woodrow Borah and S. F. Cook, *The Population of Central Mexico in 1548: An Analysis of the Suma de Visitas de Pueblos* (Berkeley: University of California Press, 1960), 12, 21; Francisco del Paso y Troncoso, ed. *Suma de visitas* (Madrid, 1905), 49.

[32] Cuevas, *Documentos*, 141.

those very lines, the survivors were mixing mortar for structures of unprecedented size in their own communities: the doctrina monasteries.

BUILDING A NEW TEOCALLI

> It is no surprise that today there are already a thousand churches [in New Spain], because every priest, every neighborhood, and every native ruler wanted a church of their own to build.
>
> Fray Toribio de Benevente Motolinía[33]

It would be entirely reasonable to assume that while indigenous communities strained to recover, feed themselves, and work for Spaniards in the aftermath of the *hueycocolixtli*, they would have avoided building edifices whose design had no precedent in Mesoamerica. Construction projects depended on the availability of obligatory commoner labor, and the loss of a third of the population entailed an equivalent reduction of the available labor pool. Yet build they did. In Tepechpan, the *hueycocolixtli* had devastated the community: testimonies in 1550 reported that famished survivors were fleeing, missionaries could barely be fed, and in light of their predicament local rulers were seeking to reduce their tributes to Spaniards. Even so, the construction of the local church continued. Indeed the local rulers sued their resisting sujetos, taking their case all the way to the Council of the Indies in Seville in order to compel them to provide labor for church construction.[34] Similar stories abound across the rest of New Spain. In the wake of the *hueycocolixtli*, more than eighty communities across New Spain *initiated* these costly building campaigns after the *hueycocolixtli* while other projects already underway proceeded apace. As can be seen below in *Figure 5.4*, in the 1540s, forty-six monasteries were under construction, of which thirty-eight were new projects initiated in that decade. At least seven of those projects were begun during or after the *hueycocolixtli*.[35] In the 1550s this number soared to 119 projects. Of these, seventy-seven projects – sixty-five percent of the total – were new projects begun in that decade. In 1550 alone, just three years after the *hueycocolixtli* abated, Viceroy Velasco approved twenty proposals for

---

[33] Motolinía, *Memoriales*, 296.
[34] Civil suit, *Tepechpan v. Temascalapa*, over cabecera rights (Preliminary sentence, 1551), AGI Justicia, leg. 164, no. 2, ff. 328v–30r.
[35] Account ledgers (1540–1550), AGI Contaduría, leg. 661.

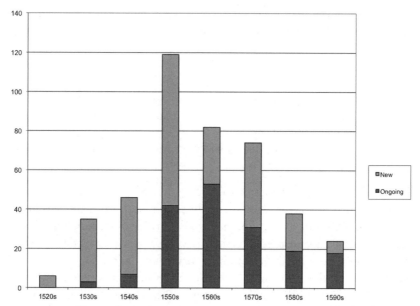

FIGURE 5.4 New and ongoing monastery construction projects by decade.
Source: AGN, AGI. See Appendix 2

new monasteries.[36] All this activity amounted to a colossal marshaling of human energies, a unique movement that, for three decades, defied the grim realities of demographic crisis.

Only a handful of scholars have addressed the relation between mid-century monastery construction and demographic crisis. George Kubler, and later Adrian Van Oss, posited that construction campaigns redoubled due to an allegedly robust demographic recovery – a claim that historical demography has negated entirely.[37] More recently, Eleanor Wake has argued that an "ecstatic" indigenous religiosity in the wake of the *huey-cocolixtli* drove these construction campaigns. Wake holds that the construction campaign can be reduced to one overarching motive: "ritual and image as the basis of religious expression." According to this view, having suffered demographic losses, indigenous populations concurred that they needed new ritual centers in order to maintain their "traditional native

[36] Viceregal license for Augustinian monasteries (1550), AGN Mercedes, tomo 3, tomo 135, f. 61v; Viceregal license for Franciscan monasteries, Teutalco, Xalacingo, and Tepexique (1550), AGN Mercedes, vol. 3, exp. 150, f. 65r; Viceregal license for Augustinian monastery, Guango (1550), AGN Civil, vol. 1271, f. 205r.

[37] Kubler, *Mexican Architecture*, 23–4, 30, 36–8, 60–7; Van Oss, *Church and Society*, 137.

religious practices."[38] Wake describes sixteenth-century native religiosity as a nearly unaltered form of prehispanic Mesoamerican spirituality, and defines native religion exclusively in terms of ritual and cosmovision. The implication is that religion was impervious to demographic crises, contested territorial arrangements, rigid social stratification, and the ever-starker asymmetry of colonial power relations. Consequently, the doctrina monastery was a manifestation of a deep and unchanging native spirituality, not of the colonial world around it.[39] This argument, however, separates indigenous spirituality from material factors and historical contingency. Yet politics and spirituality were in fact always deeply intertwined, even entangled, in indigenous communities, and the spiritual and ritual elements of doctrina monasteries were susceptible to political calculations, material interests, and power plays.[40] Raising a teocalli or a doctrina monastery was a grand act of world-making in the broadest sense: at once it established a new spiritual home, and it reconstituted and empowered the political and economic networks that were connected to it. It materialized the sacred and sacralized worldly power, and in so doing it asserted the endurance of the community.[41]

Although the demographic crisis was not a propitious time to build on a grand scale, its disruptions also made obvious the need to inscribe power relations into stone. The mid-century crisis had sown chaos into an already turbulent indigenous political world: it intensified territorial struggles that the fall of the Aztec Empire had unleashed nearly three decades earlier, and it destabilized brittle social hierarchies. The cellular organization of indigenous politics, by which city-states (altepeme) consisted of semi-autonomous statelets (calpoltin) with ambitions and interests of their own, provided local communities with some flexibility to adapt to crises. But it also opened the way for factionalism and territorial fragmentation. Altepeme and calpoltin weakened by war or depopulation could join to form regional powers, but ambitious subunits that survived the crisis could just as easily opt to seek greater control over their own

---

[38] Wake, *Framing*, 86–9.   [39] Wake, *Framing*, 58.

[40] For a nuanced analysis of how Mesoamerican ritual spaces interacted with the changing politics of the mission enterprise, see Laura Ledesma Gallegos, *Génesis de la arquitectura mendicante del siglo XVI en el plan de las Amilpas y las Cañadas de Morelos* (Mexico City: INAH, 2012); and Solari, *Maya Ideologies*. See also García Martínez, *Los pueblos de la Sierra*, 94; Terraciano, *Mixtecs*, 287–93; Federico Fernández Christlieb and Pedro Sergio Urquijo Torres, "Los espacios del pueblo de indios tras el proceso de Congregación, 1550–1625," *Investigaciones Geográficas*, no. 60 (2006), 145–58.

[41] Davíd Carrasco, *Religions of Mesoamerica* (Long Grove, IL: Waveland Press, 1990), 20.

resources and labor either by asserting their power within the confederation, or by simply seceding from it. Thus, there was an inherent tension in Mesoamerican politics that was marked by "contrary tendencies of formation and separation."[42] The doctrina monasteries were the results of this tension.

The *hueycocolixtli* crisis of the late 1540s only exacerbated these centripetal and centrifugal forces, due to the uneven manner in which the epidemic had brought down some sub-units while sparing others. Not surprisingly, this opened up new opportunities for rulers in surviving subunits to seize power at their rivals' expense.[43] They did so by erecting churches. In Amecameca, for example, a long-running power-struggle between two sibling noblemen who ruled over rival subunits came to an end after one of the brothers died during the *hueycocolixtli*. The surviving brother, Don Juan de Sandoval, proceeded to concentrate local power around his subunit by building an immense Dominican monastery. In so doing, Don Juan subjected his deceased brother's calpolli to his new cabecera, the head-town of the reconstituted polity that emerged around his new doctrina monastery.[44] Similarly, across the devastated landscape of post-*hueycocolixtli* Mexico, local hierarchies harnessed the rebuilding efforts of the survivors and asserted their control over lands, tributes, and commoners' labor. They did what they had always done during crises: they remade Mesoamerica by maintaining, splitting, and fusing polities. Church construction, like temple construction before the conquest, was both a tool and a principal expression of the contrary forces that reconstructed local native states.

The struggles to assert local sovereignty are plainly visible in a variety of works commissioned by indigenous rulers in the mid-sixteenth century. Recent studies of cartography, painted manuscripts, *lienzos* ("cloths" depicting royal lineages or territorial claims), and native histories have revealed efforts of their patrons – mostly local rulers – to retell the histories of their communities in a way that was advantageous to them. Even while they drew upon their own visual and symbolic systems, native tlacuilos also appropriated European styles of perspective and Roman script. These hybrid manuscripts recounted the sacred foundation of the

[42] Lockhart, *Nahuas*, 14–15, 27–8, 54. Schroeder, *Chimalpahin*, 119–53; Terraciano, *Mixtecs*, 347–8; Martínez Baracs, *Convivencia y utopia*, 56; Horn, *Postconquest Coyoacan*, 21–3.

[43] Lockhart, *Nahuas*; Schroeder, *Chimalpahin*, 119–53; Terraciano, *Mixtecs*, 347–8; Martínez Baracs, *Convivencia y utopia*, 56; Horn, *Postconquest Coyoacan*, 21–3.

[44] Chimalpáhin, *Las ocho relaciones*, vol. II, 203–5.

altepetl, documented the chain of lineages that ruled over it and its constituent subunits, and delineated the territorial limits of the polity.[45] The *Tira de Tepechpan*, the painted annals that opened this chapter, is a prime example of this effort to retell and reframe history in order to strengthen the altepetl and its rulers against internal and external threats.[46] Similarly, in Cuauhtinchan, a nobleman named don Alonso de Castañeda commissioned the monumental *Historia Tolteca-Chichimeca*, which exalted the sacred origins of his altepetl, and used this ancient prestige to legitimize claims over disputed lands with the neighboring rival altepetl of Tepeaca. At the same time, the *Historia* also reveals ongoing ethnic disputes within Cuauhtinchan, as don Alonso advocated for his marginalized Nahuas against the Pinome that held sway over the polity.[47] Across central Mexico, native tlacuilos reframed the past in order to stake their claims over space and power, and ultimately have leverage over an uncertain future.[48] While the painted manuscripts of the tlacuilos drew boundaries around land claims and traced ancient lineages, the stone church also served to reaffirm a sense of place, history, and socio-political order in the central Mexican local state.[49]

Local rulers did not hesitate to sponsor native painters and sculptors, who inscribed their historical narratives onto monastery walls, façades, fountains, and vaults.[50] In Cuauhtinchan, during the same years when the *Historia Tolteca-Chichimeca* was written, native painters decorated the friars' cloister with the symbols of their altepetl: the eagle, the jaguar, and the sacred red cave central to their origin myth (see *Figure 5.5* below).[51]

---

[45] Boone, *Stories in Red and Black*, 128, 239–41; Elizabeth Hill Boone, "Pictorial Documents and Visual Thinking in Postconquest Mexico," in *Native Traditions in the Postconquest World*, ed. Elizabeth Hill Boone and Tom Cummins (Washington, DC: Dumbarton Oaks, 1998), 181–93; Bas van Doesburg, "The Lienzo of Tlapiltepec: The Royal Historiography of the Coixtlahuaca City-State," in *The Lienzo of Tlapiltepec: A Painted History from the Northern Mixteca*, ed. Arni Brownstone (Norman, OK: University of Oklahoma Press, 2015), 35–73.

[46] See Diel, *Tira de Tepechpan*, Introduction.

[47] Carrasco and Sessions, *Cave, City, and Eagle's Nest*; Escalante Gonzalbo, "El patrocinio," 224; Reyes García, *Documentos sobre tierras y señoríos en Cuauhtinchán*, 102; Luís Reyes García, *Cuauhtinchán del siglo XII al XVI: formación y desarrollo histórico de un señorío prehispánico* (Wiesbaden: Steiner, 1977), 7; Leibsohn, *Script and Glyph*, 21–2.

[48] Boone, *Stories in Red and Black*, 128; Leibsohn, ibid.

[49] Bargellini, "Representations of Conversion," 96; Escalante Gonzalbo, "El patrocinio," ibid.

[50] Peterson, *Paradise Garden Murals*; Reyes Valerio, *Arte Indocristiano*; Bargellini, "Representations of Conversion," 96.

[51] Escalante Gonzalbo, "El patrocinio," 229–31.

FIGURE 5.5 Jaguar and eagle place-glyphs alongside Annunciation of the Virgin. Anon. indigenous painters, Doctrina monastery cloister, Cuauhtinchan (Puebla), c. 1550s. Photo by Author

Thus, while some Spanish missionaries contentedly let themselves believe that by building "glorious churches ... the Indians forgot the things of the past and the flower of their gentility," indigenous communities appropriated this architecture for their own ends and made it embody their own sacred histories.[52]

The new stone church filled the void left by the destroyed teocalli and took its place in the enduring grids of indigenous political power, spirituality, and identities. In many cases the overlay was literal. Tlaxcalan cabildo records, for example, simply refer to churches as teocallis.[53] Communities throughout New Spain, urged on by iconoclastic friars, built doctrina monasteries atop the platforms of their former teocallis or used the masonry of their temples to build churches.[54] Friars reveled in the material destruction of the teocalli, but for natives the very stones, sacred location, and power of the teocalli was invested in the new stone church. Indigenous histories depict the teocalli as the sacred site upon which the community was founded, the place where wandering peoples found their corner of the earth where they could settle and honor their gods, the node between heaven and earth that linked the community to the otherworld and to the ancestral past.[55] Yet the teocalli, and the stone church that replaced it, also mirrored the social order of this world. It

[52] Grijalva, *Crónica*, 172–3.
[53] Lockhart et al., *Tlaxcalan Actas*, 90, 123–4; see also Chanfón Olmos, *Historia de la arquitectura*, 22, 26.
[54] Wake, *Framing*, 115; Lockhart et al., ibid.
[55] Carrasco, *City of Sacrifice*, 65–8; Carrasco, *Religions*, 20–3, 70–7; Diel, *Tira de Tepechpan*, 67–71, 91.

embodied the material interests of its patrons. Indigenous nobles and priests had legitimized and reaffirmed their authority by deploying commoner labor to adorn and maintain the teocalli, and the structure proudly proclaimed the altepetl's autonomy and territorial integrity to neighbors and imperial powers.[56] Long into the colonial period, the memory of a town's teocalli served as evidence of ancient autonomy in legal battles over jurisdiction.[57] Such memories were buttressed by emerging Christian temples. Rising in place of the teocalli, the new stone church absorbed its spiritual and political powers, and in so doing, it made a strong argument that the history, territorial integrity, and social order of the community would endure.

Striking evidence of this association of church and teocalli can be seen in indigenous visual representations. Scholars of indigenous art have traced a transition in manuscript painting in which the stone church emerged as a symbol of the pueblo itself in manuscript painting, accompanying and sometimes replacing indigenous hill-glyph symbols.[58] In the *Mapa de Cuauhtinchan*, a history-cartography of Cuauhtinchan produced in the mid-sixteenth century, the core of the altepetl consists of a hill-glyph symbol, the prehispanic teocalli, and a symbol of the new doctrina monastery, with its cavernous church and atrio.[59] Symbols of churches also bolstered the claims to power of ruling lineages. In the images below, two local rulers, their status indicated by reed mats, are seated beside local churches to indicate their patronage. In *Figure 5.6*, from the Mixtec *ñuu* (indigenous polity) of Zacotepec in Oaxaca, a married couple of two hereditary rulers (*yuhuitayu*) are shown on their reed mats between a stone church, which sits atop a sacred platform, and a "palace/temple." *Figure 5.7*, meanwhile, depicts the ruler of Misquiahuala facing a church that he sponsored.[60] In both images,

[56] Lockhart, *Nahuas*, 15–17, 421.

[57] See, for example, witness testimonies in favor of Temascalapa's claims against Tepechpan (1561): AGI Justicia, leg. 164, no. 2, ff. 405r, 407v.

[58] Dana Leibsohn, "Colony and Cartography: Shifting Signs on Indigenous Maps of New Spain," in Claire Farago, ed., *Reframing the Renaissance: Visual Culture in Europe and Latin America, 1450–1650* (New Haven: Yale University Press, 1995), 67–80; Wake, *Framing*, 120; Boone, *Stories in Red and Black*, 138; Ethelia Ruíz Medrano, "En el cerro y la iglesia: La figura cosmológica atl-tépetl-oztotl," in *Relaciones: Estudios de historia y sociedad*, vol. XXII, no. 86 (2001), 162–3; Mundy, *Mapping*, 68–9, 171; Fernández Christlieb and Urquijo Torres, "Los espacios," 154.

[59] Carrasco and Sessions, *Cave, City, and Eagle's Nest*.

[60] Terraciano, *Mixtecs*, 105, 287; Relación Geográfica de Misquiahuala, Hidalgo. UT-Benson library; van Doesburg, "Lienzo of Tlapiltepec," 38–9, 60–1.

FIGURE 5.6 Detail of *Lienzo de Zacatepec*.
Anon. Indigenous painters, sixteenth century Biblioteca Nacional de Antropología e Historia (BNAH). Reproduction authorized by the Instituto Nacional de Arqueología e Historia

FIGURE 5.7 Detail of Relación Geográfica de Atengo.
Anon. Indigenous painters, c. 1579. Nettie Lee Benson Collection, University of Texas Libraries, University of Texas at Austin

the church symbolizes both the polity's territorial integrity as well as its internal hierarchies.

These associations had immediate, worldly implications, for the church assumed the temporal roles of the teocalli in everyday governance and the reordering of space. In pre-Hispanic urbanism, the teocalli had formed part of a ceremonial center of stone structures that included a tianquiztli (market) and tecpan (ruler's house or seat of government). Religion, worldly power, and commerce converged in the same space, providing a stage on which political and religious relations were confirmed.[61] On religious holidays, commoners and subject towns delivered tribute and attended religious ceremonies. In the decades that followed the conquest, a new urban space adapted these Mesoamerican political, commercial, and religious functions to the European plaza, market, and church. At the center of this nucleus was the doctrina monastery. The complex reaffirmed the preeminence of the subunit that hosted it over outlying towns and villages, and their subservience was repeatedly reaffirmed by their obligatory tribute deliveries and mass attendance performed at the doctrina monastery site. Thus the stone church restored the indigenous *urbs* – the political-religious center – within a Spanish colonial context. Like the teocalli, the church anchored the local indigenous state, binding together its elite networks, ties of subservience and cooperation, flows of

[61] Lockhart, *Nahuas*, 15–17, 421.

tributes and labor, and the rituals that reaffirmed elite privilege.[62] These socio-political functions of the new teocalli were more urgently needed than ever in the aftermath of the 1540s demographic crisis.

As heir to the teocalli, the doctrina monastery helped indigenous polities regroup populations and shore-up community lands. In Cuauhtinchan, for example, a handful of families of three minority ethnic groups who were seeking land were grouped together as a subunit with usufruct rights, and their integration into the community and its laws was enacted by building a modest thatch church and receiving the indoctrination of the Franciscan *guardián* of the doctrina, Fray Antonio Santo.[63] Throughout New Spain, depopulation made land vulnerable to seizure, and it complicated power structures and missionary logistics. In Tlaxcala, for example, the cabildo ordered the construction of three doctrina monasteries specifically in depopulated areas where lands were at risk of occupation by Spanish ranchers.[64] Across New Spain, indigenous leaders sought to gather "fleeing" Indians and "reduce" them to their local rule.[65] In the Sierra Norte of Puebla, refugees from the depopulated tropical lowlands fled upslope to Xuxupango, where they were "congregated" around that town's church.[66] These indigenous efforts coincided with the Spanish colonial policies of *congregación*, which sought to relocate and "reduce" outlying populations in peripheral areas to European-style towns arranged along a grid with a stone church at its center. Spanish intentions behind these policies were to physically "congregate" dispersed native populations into the more regulated space of the *pueblo de indios*, where their everyday life could be ordered according to Christian principles.[67] The most sweeping application of this policy took place in Peru in the 1570s under Viceroy Toledo.[68] In Mexico, however, widespread resettlement programs would not be effective until the congregación campaigns of the 1590s and the first decade of the seventeenth century. Instead, while midcentury congregación policies did lead to the setting of

---

[62] Garcia Martínez, *Los pueblos de la Sierra*, 94.
[63] Reyes García, *Documentos sobre tierras y señoríos en Cuauhtinchan*, 102.
[64] Bernal García and García Zambrano, "El altepetl colonial," 33, 74–6; Martínez Baracs, *Convivencia y utopia*, 216; Christlieb and Torres, ibid., 148.
[65] López Caballero, *Los títulos primordiales*, 145, 157; Viceregal congregación order, Tequecastlan (1563), AGN Mercedes, tomo 6, f. 416r; Congregación order, Turicado (1555), AGN Mercedes, tomo 4, f. 269r.
[66] García Martínez, *Los pueblos de la Sierra*, 113–14.
[67] See Hanks, *Converting Words*, 60–3.
[68] See Jeremy Ravi Mumford, *Vertical Empire: The General Resettlement of Indians in the Colonial Andes* (Durham: Duke University Press, 2012), 46–51.

trazas – rectilinear streets centered around a town's main church and plaza – resettlement efforts turned out to be piecemeal, locally contingent, and often ineffectual, especially when they met with stiff resistance.[69]

Doctrina monasteries served more to concentrate power more than people. This, too, reflected Mesoamerican social organization. Since power was on conspicuous display wherever rulers and nobles resided, local rulers prioritized concentrating the elite, not commoners, in the new urban nuclei that developed around the stone church.[70] This is clearly visible in the municipal records of Tlaxcala. In 1560, Tlaxcalan nobles openly resisted Spanish orders to resettle rural commoners precisely because outlying lands needed to be worked, occupied, and defended from usurpers. Instead, the noblemen in the local government decided to recruit exclusively among nobles to resettle in nuclei concentrated around the new churches:

The lords of the cabildo said, 'Let the established noblemen be the ones who are [to] be assembled, since they are somewhat well-to-do and prosperous, so that they can build their houses and enclosures ... at first only the established nobles be congregated and then the commoners only gradually.'[71]

Tribute records tell a similar story. Nobles were concentrated in cabeceras where stone churches and cabildos were located, while commoners remained in more dispersed settlements near their fields.[72] A similar pattern emerged in Yanhuitlán, Oaxaca, where urban nucleation around the colossal Dominican monastery still reflected a prehispanic pattern of settlement more than a European one.[73] Even in areas where subunits relocated wholesale to a new urban nucleus, the constituent cellular

---

[69] Christlieb and Torres, ibid., 148; Viceregal congregación order, Molango (1555), AGN Mercedes, vol. 4, f. 160r; Francisco del Paso y Troncoso, ed., *Descripción del Arzobispado* (Madrid, 1905), vol. III, 118–19; Viceregal congregación order, Chalco and Tlalmanalco (1558), AGN Mercedes, vol. 84, exp. 135, f. 50r.

[70] Matthew Restall, Lisa Sousa, and Kevin Terraciano, eds. *Mesoamerican Voices: Native-Language Writings from Colonial Mexico, Oaxaca, Yucatán and Guatemala* (New York: Cambridge University Press, 2005), 75–7; Lockhart, *Nahuas*, 44; Gerhard, "Congregaciones de indios," 350–1; Zavala, *Libros*, 315–17, 349; García Martínez, *Los pueblos de la Sierra*, 151, 155.

[71] Lockhart, *Nahuas*, 123–4; Constantino Medina Luna ed. *Libro de los guardianes y gobernadores de Cuauhtinchan (1519–1640)* (Mexico City: CIESAS, 1995), 49.

[72] Anguiano and Chapa, "Estratificación social en Tlaxcala," 126–35; Mercedes Olivera, "El despotismo tributario en la región de Cuauhtinchan-Tepeaca," in Carrasco and Broda, eds., *Estratificación social*, 198–9.

[73] Alessia Frassani, "El centro monumental de Yanhuitlán y su arquitectura: un proceso histórico y ritual," *Desacatos*, 42 (2013), 145–60.

calpoltin continued as distinct subunits that retained their semi-autonomy. With ruling nobles ensconced in the ceremonial center that clustered around the new doctrina monastery, the cellular organization of the indigenous polity persisted.[74] Whether rulers responded to the crises by relocating subunits or by concentrating the nobility, the new stone monastery served as their focal point for consolidating political power.

Even while the church emerged as a new teocalli in indigenous communities, native rulers never lost sight of the enormous political prestige these structures carried in Spanish colonial politics. They were keenly aware that a doctrina monastery complex with resident friars had the power to change Spanish officials' perceptions of their jurisdictions. The monastery served as conspicuous proof of an altepetl's political and economic viability as a cabecera – the highest status to which an indigenous polity could aspire. Cabecera status provided ample autonomy to local rulers. No other indigenous polity was ranked above it. In political terms, the cabecera coordinated labor drafts for the benefit of native elites and Spaniards alike, and it regulated and exploited natural resources within its jurisdiction. Doctrina status provided the clearest pathway to cabecera status. To obtain doctrina status, local rulers needed mendicant support and a viable plan to build a monastery. This was the case for jurisdictions in encomiendas as well as those under royal jurisdiction.[75] In this way, doctrina monasteries were integral to indigenous struggles for autonomy, and often predominance over nearby towns, within the Spanish colonial system.

At once a colonial mission and a new teocalli, the doctrina monastery was a bicultural structure that fused the symbols and networks of the Spanish Empire with those of the Mesoamerican local state. For this reason, it was the hotly-disputed prize in the indigenous territorial struggles that intensified after the *hueycocolixtli*. As the opposing centrifugal and centripetal forces continued to tug at indigenous polities, building a church furthered all territorial ambitions in this period: it aided some rulers to reassert their domination over their neighbors, helped others secede from their neighbors, and moved still others to join in confederation.[76] Let us briefly examine how monasteries furthered each of these three contrary forces in indigenous politics after the *hueycocolixtli*.

---

[74] Restall, Sousa, and Terraciano, *Mesoamerican Voices*, 75; Lockhart, *Nahuas*, 45; Chimalpáhin, *Las ocho relaciones*, vol. II, 213–17.

[75] Horn, *Postconquest Coyoacan*, 31–4.

[76] García Martínez, *Los pueblos de la Sierra*, 124, 130, 215.

First, for polities that enjoyed political pre-eminence over surrounding jurisdictions before and after the Spanish conquest, raising a monastery made a strong argument about the antiquity and inviolability of these territories and their ruling lineages. Such was the case of former imperial capitals like Texcoco and Tzintzuntzán, independent kingdoms like Meztitlán and Tlaxcala, former Aztec garrisons like Tepeaca and Tlapa, religious sites like Molango, and provincial trading centers like Izúcar. Nearly all of the seventy-two doctrinas established before 1540 had been prehispanic power centers. Yet these large jurisdictions were not the only polities that built monasteries to maintain power. In smaller jurisdictions that claimed authority over surrounding towns, doctrina monasteries also strengthened territorial claims. In Tepechpan, whose tlacuilo opened this chapter, a new stone church proclaimed altepetl sovereignty over its subunits. In fact the construction campaign provoked a protracted dispute between Tepechpan and an unruly sujeto, Temascalapa. In a clear effort to secede from Tepechpan, Temascalapa had refused to provide its laborers for Tepechpan's church, leaving Tepechpan without haulers of lumber in the wake of the *hueycocolixtli*. This led to a protracted trial between the two towns. Tepechpan eventually won the dispute, securing a legal injunction from royal officials compelling Temascalapa to provide laborers to help build Tepechpan's church. By securing Temascalapa's laborers for the construction of its church, Tepechpan not only brought a costly project closer to completion; it also reaffirmed its dominance over Temascalapa and prevented the fragmentation of its jurisdiction.[77]

Similar legal disputes arose from church constructions in Yanhuitlán and Totolapan in those years, as cabecera rulers sought to draw upon the labor of outlying towns whose historical ties to them were ambiguous.[78] Such disputes did not revolve around tangibles – the stone church or boundaries – as much as the social ties of obligation, for all parties saw the deployment of labor for church construction as a primary acknowledgement of political subservience. In this way, for polities that sought to maintain dominance over outlying towns or that saw an opportunity to expand, the doctrina monastery – and especially the political and economic processes of its production – served to bolster their jurisdictional claims.

---

[77] Diel, *Tira de Tepechpan*, 91.
[78] *Indios of Tecomatlan v. rulers of Yanhuitlán* (1584), AGI Escribanía de Cámara leg. 162C; *Indios of Atlatlauhca and Tlayacapa v. indios of Totolapa* (1571), AGI Justicia leg. 176, no. 2.

Although doctrina monasteries could bolster efforts to establish claims over jurisdictions, most mid-century projects empowered precisely the opposite forces – those of separatism. Most of the eighty polities that began construction of doctrina monasteries after the *hueycocolixtli* did so in order to separate from a dominant power. These were mid-sized or small local states that had been subjected to stronger regional altepeme where missionaries had first established themselves in the first two decades after the conquest.[79] Lacking a large doctrina monastery of their own, these jurisdictions were rather oversized visitas whose subservient status did not reflect their size, their history, or their rulers' ambitions. Rulers of these jurisdictions begrudged their rivals' doctrina status, not to mention the fact that they had to lead their townsfolk to their competitors' monasteries for mass and tribute collection. The rulers of the overlooked altepetl of Cuauhtinchan, for example, bemoaned the fact that their proud altepetl was treated "as if we were a sujeto."[80] In these jurisdictions, church construction asserted the altepetl's viability as a future doctrina and cabecera. Not solely for spiritual reasons did local rulers travel far to the Franciscans' chapter meetings to lobby friars in the hopes that they might establish doctrinas in their polities.[81] This rush to establish doctrinas is clearly visible below in *Figure 5.8*, which shows that foundations of mendicant doctrinas peaked in the 1550s, at the same time as monastery construction.

The post-*hueycocolixtli* boom in monastery construction can therefore be credited to intensifying separatist ambitions. As societies recovered from the devastation, ambitious rulers pursued separatism as a strategy to control local resources and populations. Across dozens of jurisdictions, much of the sweat and labor expended in raising walls and hauling stone formed part of a region-wide fragmentation of indigenous jurisdictions. In Tepeaca, a former regional power in the Aztec Empire, four altepeme, each with its own proud history and ruling lineage, managed to secede by raising monasteries. Having been passed over by missionaries in the first decades of Spanish rule, one by one Tecamachalco, Tecali, Quecholac, and Acatzingo secured mendicant support and raised monasteries during and after the *hueycocolixtli* crisis in the late 1540s.[82] Meanwhile

---

[79] Lockhart, *Nahuas*, 14–15.
[80] García Icazbalceta, *Cartas de religiosos*, 69–70. Viceregal order on Ecatzingo and Chalco (1591), AGN Indios vol. 6, exp. 249, f. 63r.
[81] Motolinía, *Memoriales*, 290.
[82] Gerhard, *Guide*, 278–81; Celestino Solís and Reyes García, *Anales de Tecamachalco*, 64–77; *Anales de Tecamachalco y Quecholac (1520–1558)* and *Anales de Quecholac*,

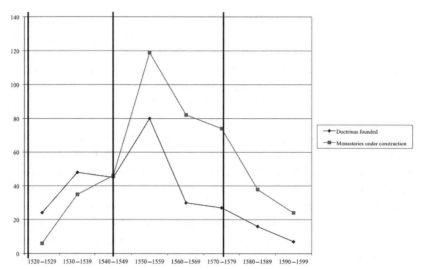

FIGURE 5.8 Foundations of mendicant *doctrinas* and monasteries under construction.
See Appendices 1 and 2

Huexotzingo, a large prehispanic lordship and early Franciscan doctrina, saw its former dependencies of Calpan, Acapetlahuacan, and its former enemy, Huaquechula, achieve doctrina status between 1545 and 1550.[83] Since church construction became a primary means of secession, it is therefore no surprise that construction campaigns in upstart jurisdictions triggered litigation. Totolapa, for example, fought hard to prevent new Augustinian doctrinas in Tlayacapan (1554) and Atlatlahuca (1570s) from seceding as fully independent cabeceras.[84] In the end, two decades of transatlantic legal battles could not thwart the autonomy that a completed monastery so concretely expressed.

INAH, Anales antiguos de México, vol. 273, tomo II, 911, 949; AGN Mercedes, vol. 2, exp. 426, f. 179r; Kubler, *Mexican Architecture*. vol. II, 470; Paso y Troncoso, *Suma de visitas*, 206; Hildeberto Martínez, *Tepeaca en el siglo XVI*, 135.

[83] Hanns Prem, ed., *Matrícula de Huexotzingo: Ms. Mex. 387 der Bibliothèque Nationale Paris* (Graz: Akadem, 1974); Gerhard, *Guide*, 56, 328–9; AGN Mercedes, 2, exp. 427, f. 179v; Paso y Troncoso, *Suma de visitas*, no. 260; AGN Mercedes, tomo 3, exp. 256, f. 123r; Paso y Troncoso *Epistolario*, vol. IV, 138; Torquemada, *Monarquía indiana*, vol. I, 315–22.

[84] AGN Mercedes, tomo 4, exp. 145, f. 42r; AGI Justicia, 156; Gerhard, *Guide*, 96; Grijalva, *Crónica*, 66.

Finally, in addition to concentrating and fragmenting territorial power, doctrina monastery construction could also amalgamate separate polities. Mesoamerica abounded in complex polities where multiple nuclei ruled through a careful balance of power. This was often the case of polities with significant ethnic divisions. In these cases Spaniards could not perceive any clear dominant unit or cabecera. Since these jurisdictions lacked an obvious power center, friars and nobles negotiated accords to build their doctrina monastery at a neutral site. The rulers of the constituent towns would then collectively manage altepetl affairs in a cabildo next to the new monastery. The most salient example of the neutral-ground monastery was the city of Tlaxcala, which lay at the intersection of the four altepeme that constituted this province.[85] Monasteries in Actopan, Ixmiquilpan, and Tepexi del Río served a similar function.[86] Neutral-ground monasteries could also join divided ethnicities into a shared government. A prime example of this is the Franciscan monastery in Tlalnepantla – a toponym meaning "middle ground" in Nahuatl – which reconciled Otomís and Nahuas. Similarly, a Dominican monastery on neutral ground sealed a power-sharing arrangement between opposing Chalca and Tlatelolca groups in Tenango-Tepopula.[87] In these cases, monastery constructions elevated the status of the overall jurisdiction while maintaining the distinctions of the constituent parts. Yet not all efforts to build on neutral ground succeeded: a Franciscan monastery built between Otlaxpan and Tepexí del Río failed to attract the residents of either town, who persistently refused to relocate. As a doctrina without a settlement, Spanish documents referred to both towns when discussing the church that lay between them.[88]

Whether they helped maintain, divide, or amalgamate indigenous jurisdictions, these structures reasserted the intangible powers of the altepetl: its history, identity, and ritual. At the same time, they bolstered claims over the tangible markers of power – control over lands, labor, and territory. The heft of these structures is a testament to the urgency to set such assertions into stone in a time of instability. These ambitions

---

[85] Gerhard, *Guide*, 326.

[86] Gerhard, *Guide*, 45, 155–6, 333–4; García Icazbalceta, *Códice franciscano*, 15; Birgitta Leander, ed., *Códice de Otlazpan* (Mexico City: INAH, 1967), 74; Church construction agreement between Xipicoya and Talicapa (1551), in Zavala, *Libros*, 325.

[87] Gerhard, *Guide*, 249; AGN, Bienes Nacionales, tomo 775, exp. 14, no. 2; LOC Krauss ms. 140, ff. 24v, 31v–2v, 110v–11v, 118r–v, 420; AGN Mercedes, vol. 6, ff. 378r; Schroeder, *Chimalpahin*, 103–6.

[88] Leander, *Códice de Otlazpan*, 74; Account ledger (1558), AGI Contaduría, leg. 664.

corresponded seamlessly with those of the friar-missionaries, whose own territorial ambitions and rivalries motivated them to encourage these vast projects.[89] Royal officials could only warily look on as indigenous rulers and friars agreed to "build big, build solid, and build fast."[90] Driven by crisis and rivalry, for three decades the campaigns proceeded on a grand scale.

Nonetheless, having examined how local efforts to remake local polities drove these campaigns, an account of motive is only part of this story. For behind the ambitions of native rulers and mendicants, behind the mission church's shape-shifting into a new teocalli, there is also a contested social history of labor and class that remains deeply embedded in the walls of every doctrina monastery.

It is to that tale that we now turn.

HAULERS AND BUILDERS

Splendor reposes on oft-repeated gestures of carpenters and stevedores.
Henri Lefebvre[91]

I can swear to you, as a Christian, that there is not one stone [in these walls] that did not require a thousand Indians pulling it to get it here.
Franciscan friar to Royal Investigator, 1564.[92]

The monastery construction site set the power relations and cultural hybridization of mid-sixteenth century Mexico into stone and mortar. Draft laborers and itinerant skilled artisans resided in busy makeshift camps shrouded in smoke that smelled of corn and wood-fire. Building sites hummed with activity: haulers of stone and timber sang work shanties as they brought in their heavy loads on their backs, stone-cutters hammered away, carpenters cut beams, acrid clouds of lime and dust swirled about, ropes and pulleys on scaffolds creaked. High above, masons set finished stones into massive walls and soaring vaults. Throughout the

---

[89] Van Oss, *Church and Society*, 116–17.
[90] Damián Bayón, "The Architecture and Art of Colonial Spanish America," in *The Cambridge History of Latin America*, ed., Lesley Bethel (Cambridge: Cambridge University Press, 1984) vol. II, 714.
[91] Lefebvre, *Production of Space*, 77.
[92] Valderrama to Philip II (1564), in Scholes and Adams *Cartas del licenciado Jerónimo Valderrama*, 58.

site, *mandones* – native overseers – barked out their orders. Observing the scene, a friar, himself a newcomer to construction, conversed and shared the general plan with visiting inspectors sent by a nervous viceroy to keep an eye on these costly enterprises. At most sites, this scene – this tangle of languages, techniques, tired bodies and frustrations – unfolded within ten years of the *hueycocolixtli*. What mobilized commoners to toil day after day without compensation in these long-term projects?

On the rare occasions that scholars have addressed this question, most treat the doctrina monastery as if it were a force of nature, the result of a relatively seamless fusion between timeless Mesoamerican customs and missionary zeal. The production of these monasteries tends to fall by the wayside, leaving only an assumption that thousands of laborers toiled in each project solely out of unquestioned tradition or loyalty to local rulers. Once the friars tapped into the immemorial Mesoamerican customs of working without compensation, so the thinking goes, these vast edifices sprouted like so many mushrooms across the Mexican *altiplano*.[93] However, the largely unexamined archival records of these building campaigns challenge such assumptions. Petitions, court battles, and reports of labor strife all indicate that mobilizing the vast resources and labor forces called upon to raise a doctrina monastery required complex negotiations both within and outside the polity. Diverse workforces needed to be coordinated; good stone had to be dug up, cut and hauled over large distances. If limestone was available nearby, it had to be heated and processed to make mortar and plaster; otherwise the community needed to pay dearly for it elsewhere. The same applied to lumber, essential in all stages of construction, which had to be cut and hauled from forests that were rapidly diminishing. New building techniques, too, had to be transmitted by Spanish or indigenous tradesmen in a society that had no prior experience building immense cavernous structures with high walls and stone ceilings.[94]

The high cost of these projects, in terms of labor-hours and tribute, stretched political negotiations to the maximum. To mobilize multitudes of commoners, indigenous rulers had to carefully negotiate territorial rivalries and strained class divisions within their polities. Yet the potential reward was substantial: in the majority of cases where native states successfully coordinated mobilizations of labor and resources, the

---

[93] Ricard, *Spiritual Conquest*, 77–8, 170–1; Kubler, *Mexican Architecture*, vol. I, 136–8, 144–5; Van Oss, *Church and Society*, 105–8.
[94] Motolinía, *Memoriales*, 347; Kubler, ibid.

completed project proved the local state's viability. Each stone delivered and each beam raised by commoners under the command of local rulers consolidated ties of subordination and deference. To contribute to the raising of a teocalli, be it for Emperor Ahuitzotl in the 1480s or for the altepetl of Tepechpan in the 1540s – as Luís Quiab, a fifty-five year old native witness of pre-conquest Mexico, declared in 1550 – also raised a Mesoamerican political structure.[95] Thus the very means of producing a monastery was therefore a political end in itself, whose meaning was known to ruler and laborer alike.

The first challenge for native rulers and friars in raising doctrina monasteries was the shortage of trained architects and artisans in New Spain. Local communities drew upon a fledgling colonial network of specialists. Trained architects were few and far between, and consequently many friars became "handymen in mendicant habits" by designing and overseeing projects.[96] Across Mexico, indigenous elders and annalists recalled the names of these friars who, in consultation with indigenous nobles, "set the *traza* [design]" and "laid the foundation" for these structures.[97] The widespread improvisation in those early years led to numerous structural failures.[98] Later in the century, a handful of Spanish artisans migrated to Mexico. Most notable of these was Claudio de Arciniega, who left a Mannerist mark on several projects, and Francisco Becerra, a mason who hired out his architectural knowledge in a dozen monastery projects.[99] Becerra had a checkered record: hired by the rulers of Tepoztlán in 1580 to design a gothic vault above their altar, he chose instead to run off with their eighty-peso deposit before work was completed. Becerra eventually surfaced in Quito where, not long thereafter, he designed a vast Dominican monastery that still stands today.[100]

[95] Testimony, Luís Quiab (1550), in *Temascalapa v. Tepechpan* (1550–1564): AGI Justicia, leg. 164, no. 2, f. 261r.

[96] Kubler, *Mexican Architecture*. I, 127–30; Ortíz Macedo, *Historia del arquitecto mexicano*, 30.

[97] Audiencia trial, Tlaquiltenango monastery (1591), AGN Tierras, vol. 1979, exp. 4, f. 143v; Church construction agreement between Xipicoya and Talicapa (1551), in Zavala, *Libros*, 325.

[98] Cuernavaca principals to Viceroy (1565), AGN Mercedes, vol. 8, f. 5v; Construction request by Zacatlán principales (1565), AGN Mercedes, vol. 8, f. 131r; Monastery investigation order, Ucareo (1563), AGN Mercedes, vol. 7, f. 73r; Monastery investigation, Gayangareo (1565), AGN Mercedes, vol. 8, f. 92v.

[99] Cuesta Hernández, *Arquitectura del Renacimiento*, 57–38, 97–135.

[100] Tepoztlán claim against Francisco Becerra (1580), AGN General de Parte vol. 2, exp. 520, f. 102v; AGN General de Parte, vol. 2, exp. 631, f. 127v; Kubler, *Mexican Architecture*, vol. I, 123–4.

Indigenous nobles and friars also contracted the labor of itinerant indigenous specialists, including sculptors, painters, and carpenters.[101] Many of these tradesmen combined native artisanship with European train... acquired at mission schools like San José de los Naturales in México-Tenochtitlán and Tiripitío in Michoacán.[102] In 1576, native masons (*tezonzonques*) working on the Dominican monastery at Coixtlahuaca denounced local nobles for pocketing their wages.[103] Their accusations were similar to those of other artisans in other parts of New Spain. Indigenous master masons (*maestros*) in Michoacán, for example, gained such fame for their church construction that Spanish colonists hired them for their projects. Yet because the masons were *indios*, Spaniards underpaid these *maestros* as if they were mere bricklayers (*albañiles*). According to the chronicler Fray Matías de Escobar, this led native masons to "hide" their talents since their low pay would never equal the quality of their finest work.[104]

While the friar-architects, Tenochtitlán-trained carpenters, and Spanish tradesmen were essential to monastery building programs, it was the multitudes of commoners who produced these monasteries through a decade of hauling and building. The roads of mid-sixteenth century Mexico swelled with teams of macehualtin hauling immense stones, tree trunks, and baskets of lime over long distances. In order to procure the vast resources required for these projects, communities were compelled to go outside their jurisdictions for quarries, lime-pits, and forests.[105] The indigenous rulers of Acolmán, for example, deployed their commoners in 1576 to the woodlands above Texcoco to cut lumber for an enormous

---

[101] Eustaquio Celestino, Armando Valencia, and Constantino Medina Lima, eds. *Actas de Cabildo de Tlaxcala, 1547–1567* (Mexico City: AGN, 1985), 310; Escalante Gonzalbo, "El patrocinio," ibid.

[102] Reyes Valerio, *Arte indocristiano*; Peterson, *Paradise Garden Murals*.

[103] Tezonzonques' claim against Coixtlahuaca (1576), AGN General de Parte, vol. 1, exp. 580, f. 120r.

[104] "...hoy hay grades maestros ... y más hubiera, si los españoles les pagaran como a maestros [españoles], sino que como son indios, por muy insignes que sean los reputan por oficiales y albañiles, y así ellos ocultan lo que saben, porque no experimentan la paga de lo que obran." Escobar, *Americana Thebaida*, 140–1. See also Reyes Valerio, *Arte indocristiano*, 301–5; Peterson, *Paradise Garden Murals*, 21.

[105] Burgoa, *Geográfica descripción*, 291. The long distances that communities traveled to access resources for construction is clearly visible viceregal licenses issued to authorize the procurement of lumber, stone, and lime outside community boundaries. A brief sample follows: License to Cuauhtinchan to use Santiago Tecali quarry (1579), AGN General, vol. 2, exp. 131, f. 28r; License to México-Tenochtitlán to use Cuitláhuac quarry (1543), AGN Mercedes, tomo 2, exp. 356, f. 145v; License to Zacapu to use Puruandiro quarry (1590), AGN General de Parte, vol. 2, exp. 1232, f. 265r; License to cut wood, Teotihuacán (1565), AGN Mercedes, vol. 8, f. 217v.

retablo (altarpiece) in their newly finished church: this required eight beams and one hundred planks for the scaffolds, and 155-foot beams for the *retablo* itself. The commoners hauled this lumber on their backs over a distance of at least forty kilometers.[106] Motolinía vividly described an analogous scene in Mexico City:

> They bring in all the materials on their backs; [while] they drag the beams and great stones with halters. And since they lacked ingenuity but had great numbers of people, if a stone or beam required one hundred men [to carry it], four hundred carried it. And it is their custom that, while they transport these materials, and since they are so many, they go chanting and heaving...[107]

For Motolinía, it was Mexico's wealth in population, combined with its ample forests and quarries, which produced these edifices. "[The Indians] are a rich people," he wrote, "because everyone works."[108] Despite severe population losses, indigenous communities mobilized sufficient numbers of laborers to haul stone and lumber, make lime and adobe, cut wood and stone, and raise walls and vaults.

The draft that mobilized these multitudes of commoners was known as the coatequitl, which formed part of the internal tribute systems discussed in *Chapter 4*. Local rulers had long mobilized this draft for public works projects like temple construction. The coatequitl was the linchpin of indigenous politics, for it reaffirmed the internal hierarchies of class and territoriality within the polity. In a similar fashion, the coatequitl also reaffirmed the cellular and rotational organization of the local indigenous state. Each subunit was responsible for providing a constant stream of macehualtin to perform specialized tasks in communal projects.[109] A rare record from Tlatelolco provides a vivid example of the functioning of the coatequitl. Describing the labor arrangements for building a *tecpan* (ruler's palace), the nineteen subunits of Tlatelolco stipulate their respective tasks: Tequipehuqui and Nepantla shall build a great hall "with sixteen or seventeen colonnades and fifty-six *varas* in length"; Cuauhtlalpan and Tecalca shall install pipes for potable water; Cuauhtepec and

---

[106] Licence to Acolmán to cut wood in Texcoco *monte* (1576), AGN General de Parte, vol. 1, exp. 1294, f. 242v.

[107] Motolinía, *Memoriales*, 142.   [108] Motolinía, *Memoriales*, 355.

[109] Lockhart, *Nahuas*, 96; Gibson, *Aztecs*, 222; Olivera, *Pillis y macehuales*, 162–73; Vicenta Cortés Alonso, ed., *Pintura del gobernador, alcaldes, y regidores de México, "Código Osuna"* (Madrid: Ministerio de Educación y Ciencia, 1993), ff. 7/469r, 14/476r–25/487v, and 37/499–39/501v.

Tepetlalca shall "provide food for everyone else."[110] The division of labor thus required careful coordination based on each sub-unit's natural resources and workforce specializations. Such arrangements were memorialized and passed on in oral histories precisely because of their political significance. In Cuernavaca's heavily forested sujeto of Quaxomulco, for example, elders declared in a primordial title narrative that their ancestors' coatequitl obligations consisted of providing lumber and carpenters for the doctrina monastery in their cabecera. This labor and provision of resources, they claimed, was provided in exchange for recognition of local lands and boundaries.[111] Sixteenth-century tribute rolls in Tlaxcala and Huexotzingo tell a similar story, carefully noting the numbers of stone-cutters, masons, lumberjacks, carpenters, and painters in each sub-unit. An entry for the sub-unit of Santa Bárbara Tamazolco, for example, reads "all are lumbermen," suggesting that this subunit specialized in processing lumber from a nearby forest, while in nearby Santa María Texcalac there were four lumbermen (*tlaxinque*) and nineteen stone-cutters (*texinque*).[112]

This rotating cellular system allowed for thousands of laborers at a time to mobilize in large-scale projects that required significant coordination and specialized tasks. Coatequitl laborers were organized into groups of twenty. To build a monastery in Tula, for example, indigenous rulers, friars, and viceregal officials concurred that each of the polity's three sujetos would continuously provide twenty commoners per day until construction was completed. A similar agreement for building the Dominican monastery in Nexapa detailed exact coatequitl requirements for eighteen sujetos, ranging from three to twenty workmen per sujeto. Each subunit was to consistently provide the number of workmen stipulated in the order: "Xaltepeque can give eight Indians," the document reads, while "Tonacayotepeque is to provide twelve Indians," Petlacaltepeque six Indians, Tlalpaltepeque twenty Indians, and so on.[113]

---

[110] Justino Fernández and Hugo Leicht, "Códice del Tecpan de Santiago Tlatelolco (1576–1581)." *Investigaciones históricas*, vol. I, no. II (1939), 260–1.

[111] López Caballero, *Los títulos primordiales*, 168, 171; Robert S. Haskett, *Visions of Paradise: Primordial Titles and Mesoamerican History in Cuernavaca* (Norman, OK: Oklahoma University Press, 2005), 257.

[112] Dyckerhoff and Prem, "La estratificación social en Huexotzinco," 165; Marina Anguiano, "División del trabajo en Tlaxcala a mediados del siglo XVI," in *Padrones de Tlaxcala del siglo XVI y padrón de nobles de Ocotelolco*, ed., Teresa Rojas Rabiela (Mexico City: CIESAS, 1987), 28–38.

[113] Zavala, *Libros*, 332; Labor for Nexapa Monastery (1558), AGN Mercedes, tomo 84, exp. 52, f. 24v.

Within each calpolli subunit the coatequitl was a shared, rotating burden. At the level of the street or several patios of homes, a ward captain known as the *centecpanpixqui* (keeper of twenty) was placed in charge of twenty households and was supposed to "converse with" laborers regarding drafts, according to the *Ordenanzas of Cuauhtinchan*. In turn, a superior captain known as *macuiltecpanpixqui*, or "keeper of one hundred," gathered five of these groups of twenty. In turn, these groups of a hundred would then receive instructions from a *tepixqui*, or "keeper of the people" directly associated with the community project. According to records from the Puebla-Tlaxcala region, these neighborhood captains were elders who were *tlatinimi*, or those who "knew well" the households and groups of twenty in their subunits.[114] This cellular and rotational system of mobilizing commoner labor provided for considerable flexibility since these units of twenty, forty, or a hundred households could be grouped into multiple cells according to the needs and scale of each task.

For commoners, coatequitl draft labor for large monastery construction projects was a long-term burden that joined many other tribute and labor commitments. The immense Dominican monastery at Yanhuitlán in Oaxaca, shown in *Figure 5.2*, consumed the unpaid labor of six thousand commoners who toiled in ten rotational shifts. In other words, on any given day six hundred men were working at the monastery construction site. According to laborers working at the site, every tribute-payer was spending ten weeks every year providing their unpaid labor to raising this behemoth: "four weeks for building the church, two weeks to remove stone from the quarry, two weeks to make lime, one week in the forests to cut lumber, and another week to haul lime back to the monastery." This, in addition to sixteen weeks spent working on friars' and caciques' lands, as well as tribute payments, was leaving the commoners "without any time to work their own plots." Given that this construction campaign dragged on for twenty-five years, all while their population declined, the commoners must have felt as if their labors would never end.[115]

The plight of Yanhuitlán's commoners raises a vital question regarding the social production of doctrina monasteries. Given that coatequitl labor

---

[114] Lockhart, *Nahuas*, 43; Luís Reyes García, "Ordenanzas para el gobierno de Cuauhtinchan, 1559," *Estudios de Cultural Náhuatl*, vol. 10 (1972), 285; Anguiano, "División del trabajo," 26–7; Terraciano, *Mixtecs*, 39, 49; Olivera, *Pillis y macehuales*, 173–8.

[115] Burgoa, *Geográfica descripción*, 291–2; Alonso Caballero, vecino de Yanhuitlán (1563), AGI México 2564.

forces juggled multiple tribute and labor burdens that only increased as their numbers diminished, on what terms did they participate in these campaigns? What motivated sub-units and commoners to toil in these projects?

Perhaps due to the scarcity of sources, it has become something of a commonplace to assume that commoners willingly accepted these burdens out of deference to immemorial tradition. Christian Duverger, for example, has argued that indigenous populations "spontaneously provided part of the collective labor that was laid out in their ancient laws."[116] Since pre-Hispanic times, so the argument goes, indigenous commoners had been providing their labor for temple construction voluntarily and enthusiastically, out of a unanimous sense of community pride that they shared with their rulers. In this vein, too, James Lockhart has argued that monastery construction was driven by a sense of altepetl pride that transcended class divisions.[117] Others, meanwhile, have argued that coatequitl was in fact not labor at all, but instead was the result of a "compulsion for ritualized labor" that formed part of an unaltered Mesoamerican tradition. In effect, indigenous commoners labored solely out of a need to maintain Mesoamerican ritual cycles in their daily lives.[118] Tellingly, these arguments align with the defensive claims of mendicant authors, who countered their critics by insisting that indigenous laborers only offered their labor with delight.[119] The underlying assumption is that commoners toiled away simply because this was the order of things.

A closer look at the socio-political context of the coatequitl reveals a labor system that was rooted not in tradition but in the give-and-take of everyday politics. In the sujeto of San Juan Teotihuacán, for example, commoners protested plans to turn their visita into an Augustinian doctrina, in spite of the higher political status that this would give to this proud and ancient jurisdiction, because this would entail a long building campaign for an Order known for its architectural largesse. Indeed, commoners needed only to look next-door to Acolmán, where construction on a costly Augustinian complex dragged on for decades.[120]

---

[116] Duverger, *Agua y fuego*, 80–1; See also Roberto Meli Piralla, *Los conventos mexicanos del siglo XVI: Construcción ingeniería estructural y conservación* (Mexico City: Porrúa, 2011), 58; Chanfón Olmos, *Historia de la arquitectura*, vol. 1, 139; Kubler, *Mexican Architecture*, 136–9.

[117] Lockhart, *Nahuas*, 55.   [118] Wake, *Framing*, 92.

[119] Wake, *Framing*, 88–93; Duverger, *Agua y fuego*; Chanfón Olmos, *Historia de la arquitectura*, vol. 1, 139; Meli, *Los conventos mexicanos*, 58.

[120] Rubial García, *Convento*, 204.

Like the *teotihuacanos*, communities throughout central Mexico
weighed the costs and benefits of monastery construction. Their petitions, protests, and internal records attest that labor drafts for monastery
construction functioned as a social contract in terms of both the class
structure and territorial makeup of the polity: it reciprocally bound
commoners to local rulers, and sujetos to cabeceras. Coatequitl draft
labor was unpaid, but it was by no means free. At its core there was a
transaction that was directly linked to the individual commoner's right to
farm plots of land for subsistence. Coatequitl labor gave commoners –
who were generally landless – the right to cultivate a plot in usufruct from
the calpolli subunit.[121] In Cuauhtinchan, for example, an indigenous land
record lays out a nobles' perspective of the sociopolitical order: "Only
tlatoanis hold lands, in their lands they rule, in their lands they favor the
commoners" – that is, the ruling nobles in altepeme and calpoltin provided commoners with access to lands in exchange for their participation
in the coatequitl. In addition, there are indications that the coatequitl also
included an expectation that workers would be fed in exchange for their
labors. "At most," the Franciscan Fray Jerónimo de Alcalá wrote, "they
would be fed in the monasteries where they worked and built."[122] Indigenous communities frequently made their protests known when Spanish
and indigenous rulers violated local agreements exchanging land for
tributes and labor.[123] More than a timeless ritual, then, the coatequitl
was based on a reciprocal, if unequal, exchange of labor for land access.
Despite the asymmetry in power relations between commoners and nobles
(and, for that matter, between commoners and Spaniards in general),
these understandings were not lost upon those who had to perform this
grueling labor.

A similar transaction characterized the coatequitl in territorial politics.
For sujetos, participation in church construction campaigns reaffirmed
not only their subservience to the cabecera but also their local boundaries
and hierarchies of power. In exchange for benefiting from their labor,
altepetl and Spanish authorities recognized local rulers of the sujetos and

---

[121] Lockhart, *Nahuas*, 96–7; Martínez, *Tepeaca en el siglo XVI*, 161–3, 176–8; Horn, *Postconquest Coyoacan*, 91.

[122] Fray Pablo Beaumont, *Crónica de Michoacán* (Mexico City: Talleres Gráficos de la Nación, 1932), vol. II, 105.

[123] Cortés Alonso, *Pintura del gobernador*, f. 7/469r; Reyes García, *Cómo te confundes?*, 34; Lockhart, *Nahuas*; Leander, *Códice de Otlazpan*, 31; Hildeberto Martínez, *Los pueblos de la Sierra*, 176–84.

confirmed their boundaries.[124] This territorial arrangement is evident in indigenous cartography, in which the internal power relations in native polities were represented by church glyphs, with large symbols for cabeceras and near-identical smaller ones for sujetos.[125] Reciprocal understandings in power relations, which predate the conquest, are evident in primordial title narratives compiled over a century after the church building campaigns. A number of sujetos in Cuernavaca, for instance, declared that their macehual ancestors had contributed labor and building materials for the construction of the Franciscan monastery in their cabecera in exchange for confirmation of their lands and ruling lineages by altepetl rulers and Spanish authorities. "Because we helped make the [*cabecera*] church of Cuernavaca," the authors of one primordial title in San Juan Chiamilpa wrote, "we received our land grant ... and our boundaries were measured."[126] In a way quite reminiscent of preconquest politics, "by trumpeting their willing and voluntary support of the cabecera's church," Robert Haskett writes, "[the sujetos] are asserting their own autonomy."[127] Just as coatequitl labor reaffirmed an individual commoner's right to land, so the labor of the *tequitl* – the sujeto squad of draft labor – also reaffirmed sujeto rights to lands and resources.

Yet while the coatequitl was an expression of commoner and sujeto rights and obligations, it was also social contract that dangled on the thinnest of threads. Dependent as it was on demographic stability and competing with other tribute and labor burdens, the political and economic model of the coatequitl was set on a downward spiral over the course of the sixteenth century. The overall decline and periodic step-like crashes of population only increased the per capita burden every time the inflexible demands of church construction rotated back to sub-units and barrios. With fewer and fewer hands available, the burden of coatequitl began to infringe upon the time that commoners needed to sustain themselves on their own plots. In these circumstances, indigenous commoners and sujetos did not resign themselves to the increasing workload out of an unquestioning devotion to their altepetl or to their "rituals." Instead, some towns resisted coatequitl drafts in ever-greater numbers after the 1550s.[128] In Jantetelco, for instance, four hundred commoners in the

---

[124] Lockhart, *Nahuas.*   [125] Mundy, *Mapping New Spain*, 120–32.

[126] Haskett, *Visions of Paradise*, 208–10, 264–5; López Caballero, *Los títulos primordiales*, 144–5; Gruzinski, *Conquest of Mexico*, 115–16; Wood, *Transcending Conquest.*

[127] Haskett, ibid., 257.

[128] Lockhart, *Nahuas*, 96; Hicks, "Prehispanic Background," 35–54.

cabecera and sujetos were slated for labor drafts to build a Dominican monastery in the 1570s; when this already meager number was severely cut by epidemics two decades later, the sujetos simply withdrew their surviving laborers from the yet-unfinished church.[129] Meanwhile the commoners at Yanhuitlán, whose labors we saw above, were so hard pressed that they demanded a reprieve in order to feed themselves. In their depositions, the commoners directly faulted the friars and local rulers for their opulent architecture, which had a detrimental effect on the commoners' household economies.[130] In other cases, commoners simply withdrew their labor. Construction campaigns collapsed amid macehual protests in Tlapa, Calimaya, and Pahuatlán, where four forlorn Augustinians reported in 1579 that commoners had left their cells thinly covered with thatch, and the adobe church was disintegrating before their eyes.[131] In the end, feeding one's family was a far more important ritual than building a monastery.

Dissident sujetos also resisted coatequitl drafts for monasteries. Sujeto labor for cabecera church construction and repair was a pillar of cabecera political authority. As in pre-Hispanic society, labor drafts for the construction and maintenance of temples defined the relations between dominant and subject states. Sujetos petitioned viceregal authorities for assistance when they believed that cabecera rulers were unduly exploiting the coatequitl to their detriment, while others chose to provoke a crisis by refusing to send their laborers.[132] In 1565, for example, commoners in Tlayacapan openly revolted against native officials from Totolapan who were attempting to reduce their town to sujeto status in light of the fact that they had been compelled to help build Totolapan's monastery. Stone-throwing macehualtin forced cabecera officials to seek refuge in Tlayacapan's monastery, passing a nervous night while the crowd outside in the

---

[129] Viceroy to Corregidor of Jantetelco on church construction (1591), Indios vol. 5, exp. 157, f. 113v; Viceroy to Corregidor of Cuernavaca on church construction (1591), Indios vol. 5, exp. 966, f. 319r; Kubler, *Mexican Architecture*, vol. II, 512.

[130] María Teresa Pita Moreda, *Los predicadores novohispanos del siglo XVI* (Salamanca: Editorial San Esteban, 1992), 249.

[131] García Icazbalceta, *Códice franciscano*, 15; Agustín de Vetancurt, *Teatro Mexicano*, 4 vols. (Mexico City: Porrúa, 1960) vol. IV, 4, 70; Paso y Troncoso, *Papeles de Nueva España* vol. VII, 280–1; Viceregal order to Atlimapaque (1576), AGN General de Parte vol. I, exp. 726, f. 141v.

[132] Order compeling sujeto labor for Mizantla monastery (1579), AGN General de Parte, vol. 2, exp. 407, f. 84v; Order compeling Analco, sujeto of Xochimilco (1576), AGN General de Parte, vol. I, exp. 604, f. 124r; Gibson, *Aztecs*, 120; Lockhart, *Nahuas*, 209–10.

atrio pelted the walls. The commoners of Tlayacapan had never desired to haul stone and lumber for their rivals in Totolapan, and now they violently resisted efforts to transform their grudging labor into long-term political subjugation.[133]

When faced with such resistance, native rulers in cabeceras had no choice but to petition the viceroy for assistance in compelling dissident commoners and sujetos – or "rebellious Indians," as frustrated rulers in Tepetotutla called them – to compel them to return to work.[134] As reports of these conflicts reached the viceregal chancellery, the resulting investigations tended to side with the local rulers and the friars over the commoners. A well-documented case in Tepeapulco in 1575 provides a dramatic example. There, the sujetos and the cabecera collided over the cabecera's right to use sujeto labor to build a second doctrina monastery in their jurisdiction in the town of Apam. Apam, however, was only a sujeto, not the cabecera. In a series of petitions sent to Viceroy Martín Enríquez, five sujetos of Tepeapulco argued that their cabecera rulers had violated a basic principle of coatequitl labor: sujetos had to provide draft labor for the cabecera, they argued, but not for other sujetos.[135] After all, it was the cabecera of Tepeapulco that guaranteed access to local lands in exchange for coatequitl labor, not Apam. Moreover, this was especially grievous, since they already had other obligations. The sujetos declared that they were also providing labor for Spaniards in Mexico City (some seventy kilometers away), for the still-unfinished Franciscan doctrina monastery in Tepeapulco, and they had to "supply the *mesón*" (inn) in the cabecera with provisions. All this, they declared, left them with little time to feed themselves, let alone trek twenty kilometers miles to build yet another monastery in Apam. "We have few people and cannot give any more [labor] for anything else," declared the natives of Tlatecaguan, conveying a sense of exasperation that still leaps off the document some four centuries later.[136]

Expressing concern, the viceroy ordered an investigation by the local corregidor. Most importantly, the viceroy wanted to know why one

---

[133] Atlatlauhcan and *Tlayacapan v. Totolapan* (1565), AGI Justicia, leg. 176, no. 2.

[134] Order compeling sujeto labor for Tepetotutla monastery (1575), AGN General de Parte, vol. 1, exp. 28, f. 5v; Gerhard, *Guide*, 300–6.

[135] Viceroy to Corregidor of Tepeapulco (1571), AGN General de Parte, vol. 1, f. 38r; Viceroy to Corregidor of Tepeapulco (1575), AGN General de Parte, vol. 1, exp. 216, f. 44v.

[136] AGN General de Parte, vol. 1, exp. 216, f. 44v; AGN General de Parte, vol. 1, exp. 191, f. 38r.

sujeto of Tepeapulco, Apam, was being privileged over the others.[137] In this, history might have provided some guidance: prior to the conquest, Apam had played a prominent role as the site of an important garrison that guarded the Triple Alliance's hostile mountain frontier with its arch-enemy, Tlaxcala.[138] Demography likely was also a factor, since Apam had twice as many people as the nearest contender among Tepeapulco's sujetos. When a third major *cocolixtli* epidemic decimated the population of Tepeapulco in 1575, Apam emerged relatively unscathed and soon rose to prominence in the area. By the mid-seventeenth century, in fact, Tepeapulco would be demoted to visita status to Apam, which became the doctrina in this jurisdiction.[139] For Viceroy Enríquez, there were two options. He could back the sujetos' argument that coatequitl labor was solely intended for the cabecera, or he could back the nobles of Tepeapulco and Apam. Echoing the corregidor's report, the viceroy ordered the sujetos of Tepeapulco "to assist the said church of Apamon a rotational basis." The viceroy not only declined the sujetos' petition to spare them this extra labor; he also negated their arguments and reinforced the authority of local rulers. Nevertheless, he softened the blow by appealing to the reciprocal understandings that undergirded the coatequitl: in the future the residents of Apam, he stated, would be obligated to respond in kind for the assistance that they were receiving from these poorer sujetos. In this way, the viceroy attempted to reestablish reciprocity in a tense situation where the aggrieved sujetos only saw exploitation.[140]

Throughout New Spain, monastery construction proceeded for a time despite population losses, based on a basic political bargain inside each indigenous polity. In hundreds of major construction projects, sub-units and commoners contributed their labor to the temple-monastery in their altepetl as a way to strengthen a broader indigenous polity that, in turn, would protect and legitimize their jurisdictions and rights to access land. The proliferation of doctrina monasteries is evidence of the functioning of these reciprocal understandings. But as seen in the resistance that broke out in Tepeapulco, Tepechpan, Tlayacapan, Tlapa, and other jurisdictions, when a church construction project appeared to violate this social contract, the monastery project itself was in danger. For while commoners

---

[137] Viceroy to Corregidor of Tepeapulco (1575), AGN General de Parte, vol. 1, exp. 191, f. 38r.

[138] Gerhard, *Guide*, 52–3; Pedro Carrasco, *Tenochca Empire*, 152; Gibson, *Aztecs*, 18.

[139] Paso y Troncoso, *Descripción del Arzobispado*, 84–6; Gerhard, *Guide*, 53.

[140] Viceregal order (1575), AGN General de Parte, vol. 1, exp. 315, f. 67v.

mobilized labor for projects in their political sphere according to reciprocal understandings, without reciprocity all else was but labor, to be best remunerated with a wage.

CONCLUSION

We built it, not the Spaniards.

The elders of Sultepeque, seventeenth century[141]

In the second decade of the seventeenth century, the Augustinian chronicler Fray Juan de Grijalva looked back sixty years to what already seemed to be an heroic age. Even in the aftermath of the great *hueycocolixtli* of 1545, he wrote, enough indigenous hands had nonetheless remained "to show the greatness and generosity of their souls." Through their labor, the kingdom of New Spain abounded in "proud edifices, so strong, so great, so beautiful and so architecturally perfect that [they] have left us with nothing more to desire." By his time, the wealth of New Spain rested on its minerals, but Grijalva waxed nostalgic for the depleted riches of the missionary. To him, the great sixteenth-century monasteries were "witnesses for posterity to the opulence of the kingdom and to the great number of Indians that there once was." What the indigenous population in New Spain had accomplished in the 1550s and 1560s, he implied, could not be repeated; the seventeenth century indigenous and mendicant inheritors of these buildings were left to admire what this earlier generation had accomplished and defend what remained.[142]

As the result of a colossal human enterprise, the doctrina monasteries of Mexico are the most tangible record of indigenous responses to the series of tragedies that they experienced in the sixteenth century. The production of churches in the shadow of death, in that space of time so starkly portrayed on the *Tira de Tepechpan*, was fraught with conflict and struggle, but once the structure was built and completed it stood as visible evidence of local political sovereignty – evidence as important for indigenous communities as it was for Spaniards who saw it as tangible proof that Christianity had indeed laid roots in Mexico. So powerful was it that dissident sujetos and commoners knew that the most effective resistance to their overlords consisted in erecting a church of their own.

---

[141] Primordial title of Sultepeque, in López Caballero, *Los títulos primordiales*, 305.
[142] Grijalva, *Crónica*, 160.

Territorial disputes, age-old rivalries, and class struggles between nobles and commoners are embedded in these great edifices. They embodied the efforts to rebuild in a disastrously transformative time – efforts that often proved more fragile than the stone and mortar of their hulking walls.

Over time, however, complex memories of conflicts over church construction faded, and the monastery fully assumed its role as a symbol of unity and consensus. While Grijalva wistfully looked back at this heroic time, the indigenous communities that inherited these structures embraced them as proof of their own legitimacy and vitality. In the seventeenth and eighteenth centuries, as elders retold their community histories, church construction served as a foundational story and as a justification of local ruling lineages.[143] In one primordial title narrative, a nobleman reminds future generations that the destiny of their community would be forever intertwined with that of the church that he had raised: "I, Don Pedro de Santiago Maxixcatzin, vecino of Quatepec, state that the Franciscan fathers baptized me and my brother Don Juan Mecatlal, and they were the ones who founded the church of San Miguel; and we built it, not the Spaniards. And so, my children, I entrust you to care for all of the belongings of the church: the surplice, banner, chalice, [and] bell; all are belongings of Quatepec of San Miguel."[144] For them, as for the tlacuilo of Tepechpan, the sixteenth-century church embodied their community, powerfully asserting its vitality and endurance.

---

[143] Códice municipal de Cuernavaca, in López Caballero, *Los títulos primordiales*, 179.
[144] ibid., 305.

PART III

A FRAYING FABRIC

6

The Burning Church

Native and Spanish Wars Over the Mission Enterprise

Tlazazalca, June 23, 1560. On the vigil of the feast of Saint John, the midsummer night of bonfires in Europe, indigenous Tarascans and Augustinian friars gathered to prepare their festivities in this isolated town in the western highlands of Michoacán. In the atrio that surrounded the wood and thatch structure that served as their church and monastery, they arranged flowers, boughs of pine, and aromatic herbs for the festivities. Yet the celebrants could not mask their frayed nerves, for Tlazazalca was a town divided. A jurisdictional dispute between Augustinians and diocesan priests over possession of this doctrina had descended from legal squabbles to open threats of violence, and the town split into pro-Augustinian and pro-diocesan factions. Shortly after sundown, the worst fears of the Augustinian party came to fruition. Two secular priests, a diocesan deacon, and an armed indigenous fiscal led a contingent of supporters into the Augustinian churchyard, demanding that the friars cancel the procession and leave town since they lacked diocesan approval to preach or reside there. Arguments broke out. Above the fracas, a senior Augustinian friar swore that nothing would stop their procession the following day. The diocesan priests and their indigenous fiscal destroyed the celebrants' decorations, and returned to the secular priest's church on the other side of the village. To mark their triumph, the bells of the secular church rang out.

The evening assault on the Augustinian doctrina was but a prelude of what was to come. Later that night, around one in the morning, a group of horsemen rode into town and set fire to the Augustinian church. The structure burst into flames, driving four friars and the local corregidor out in their nightshirts. Fray Alonso de la Veracruz, one of the foremost intellectuals of New Spain, was among those who barely escaped with their lives. Sacred images, crosses, and books were lost. The Augustinian mission, hastily built to lay claim to Tlazazalca in this turf war, was reduced to ashes.[1]

The burning church at Tlazazalca was but one of a series of clashes over doctrinas in the second half of the sixteenth century. The episode is an indicator of how powerful the mission enterprise had become in New Spain, but also of how quickly the mission Church was becoming an apple of discord. By the 1550s, the mission had become the linchpin of a colonial system that bound together local indigenous and Spanish imperial sovereignty. Its infrastructure had become an indispensible fixture in indigenous communities, with doctrina monasteries dotting the landscape and buttressing over two hundred altepeme. Mendicant Orders, for their part, saw their emerging visible Church as an unqualified success. Spaniards and native rulers alike relied on this infrastructure to gain legitimacy in – and access to – each other's worlds. The very indispensability of the mission, however, made it a target. Those in indigenous communities and the colonial Church who did not reap the benefits of the native-mendicant alliance coveted the mission's sources of power: its bicultural networks, its legitimizing religious ideology, and its connections to the wealth of tributes, labor, and donations. Native commoners, whose declining numbers increased the per capita burdens of their socage, built unauthorized chapels in bids to win autonomy and thereby shelter themselves from abuse. Spanish secular priests, long the plucky and outnumbered rivals of the mendicant friars, courted dissident native factions to carve new parishes for themselves out of overextended mendicant jurisdictions. And all the while, native governments and their allied friars resisted these incursions with legal briefs and petitions to the Audiencia to preserve their hard-won polities. Like the teocallis of pre-conquest Mesoamerica, the mission churches became contested symbols of sovereignty and territoriality. And just as temples had burned to mark a conquest, so the mission Church, too, began to burn.

In mendicant chronicles and classic mission historiography, the 1560s marked an abrupt turn from euphoria to malaise. Friar-chroniclers wove a tale of lamentation, speaking of a paradise lost to internecine conflicts,

---

[1] Alberto Carrillo Cázares has published a full transcription of the legal dispute in Tlazazalca, in *Vasco de Quiroga: La pasión por el derecho* (Zamora, Michoacán: El Colegio de Michoacán, 2003), vol. I. For testimonies that serve as the basis for this description, see 135–7.

widespread demoralization, and cynical political contests.[2] These were not mere exaggerations. After the mid-sixteenth century, Spanish politics and culture shifted from the humanism of the early decades of the reign of Charles V to the steelier Counter-Reformation politics of Philip II. In Mexico, mendicant missions that had been so favored by Cortés and the Crown faced overlapping crises of understaffing, stalling expansion, and a rapid loss of political hegemony. Most importantly, the secular clergy – the diocesan Church – took advantage of this conjuncture and began to wrest doctrinas from mendicants. Historians refer to this process, by which the diocesan Church sought to bring about an end to mendicant ascendancy, as secularization.[3] Mendicants and secular clergymen battled each other to control indigenous cabeceras and sujetos in their litigation and correspondence, by allying with native factions, and as in Tlazazalca, occasionally though physical violence. Distracted by these turf wars, missionaries lost sight of their original concern for their charges, to the detriment of natives. "For the Indians," Stafford Poole has eloquently written, "it meant being reduced to the status of pawns in a tawdry game of power politics."[4] In effect, natives were hapless victims of the intrigues and rivalries of Spanish clergymen.

Yet this "tawdry game" was not limited to Spaniards, for native hands also set this Church ablaze. Because it took on the political and social attributes of teocallis, the mission church was all too important for communities to allow themselves to be manipulated. Doctrina churches were also battlegrounds in indigenous struggles over a diminishing supply of natural and human resources in the second half of the sixteenth century. Native rulers sought to preserve their jurisdictions and their hold on power, while marginalized commoners and sujetos sought to gain some control over their land, labor, and tributes by seceding from their rulers' jurisdictions. These struggles marked the terrain and influenced the outcomes of Spanish ecclesiastical disputes, for dissidents and rivals within native polities and the Spanish diocesan Church shared common cause in undermining local native-mendicant alliances. Amid these parallel wars for control over the mission Church, the cracks in its hegemony over indigenous central Mexico became visible to all.

---

[2] Mendieta, *Historia eclesiástica indiana*, vol. II, 249.

[3] Burkhart, *Slippery Earth*, 4; Ricard, *Spiritual Conquest*, 2–4; John Leddy Phelan, *The Millenial Kingdom of the Franciscans in the New World* (Berkeley: University of California Press, 1970); Gómez Canedo, *Evangelización*, 210.

[4] Stafford Poole, *Pedro Moya de Contreras: Catholic Reform and Royal Power in New Spain, 1571–1591* (Berkeley: University of California Press, 1987), 86.

TURF WARS

Spanish observers viewed the violence in Tlazazalca as part of a broader internecine conflict within the mission that was spiraling out of control. That a struggle to control an isolated frontier doctrina would escalate to violence only heightened their concern and embarrassment, for although the surrounding area of Tlazazalca had ample lands for ranching, this was not exactly the jewel in the missionaries' crown. Both groups coveted Tlazazalca and sought to own it at each other's expense. Secular clerics had resided in the town for a decade, but they were barely able to fulfill their pastoral duties – indigenous witnesses suspected that they were too busy managing their ranches. In search of a more dependable missionary presence, local noblemen sealed an alliance with the Augustinians and secured the viceroy's approval for their doctrina. The secular clergy, however, refused to surrender their jurisdiction, and the local priest, the diocesan cabildo, and Bishop Vasco de Quiroga of Michoacán, retained lawyers and gathered auxiliaries to fight for their cause. While the case made the rounds through Spanish courts, native constables working for the diocesan clergy jailed the indigenous gobernador until he repudiated his support for the Augustinians. After setting fire to the Augustinian monastery, the secular priest placed the Augustinian prior in chains, tied him up in a hammock, and had native *tamemes* haul the weeping friar over the sierras to Valladolid (present-day Morelia). The priest then sealed his victory with a final insult: he ordered indigenous supporters of the Augustinians to dig up the bodies of relatives interred in the atrio of the former Augustinian mission and rebury them in the graveyard of his parish church. Even the dead had to obey the diocesan clergy in Tlazazalca.[5]

Turf wars like that of Tlazazalca brought disrepute on missionaries, both mendicant and diocesan. No missionary group held a monopoly on sacramental sabotage, manipulations of native parishioners, or litigiousness and rumor-mongering. In Oaxaca, where mendicant-secular battles were particularly intense, Dominicans mobilized indigenous parishioners in Justlavaca, a visita of their doctrina in Taxquiaco, to boycott a parish priest assigned to minister in that town. When the diocesan priest refused to give up his new post, a Dominican friar from Taxquiaco entered his church, seized its sacred ornaments, and made away on horseback as the

---

[5] Carrillo Cázares, *La pasión por el derecho*, vol. I, 135–7.

screaming priest chased him on foot.[6] Dominicans in Taxquiaco also led natives to destroy another rival church in their doctrina.[7] In the Diocese of Michoacán, where Tlazazalca was located, diocesan clergymen toppled baptismal fonts and sent Franciscan friars fleeing from their monastery in Pátzcuaro, while in Necotlán Augustinian friars chased a secular priest out of town.[8] In Tula, meanwhile, a group of natives led by a Franciscan friar set fire to a hospital that the Archdiocese of Mexico had founded in this Franciscan doctrina.[9] In Calimaya, a Franciscan defied diocesan orders to desist from destroying a parish church so that his Order could build a large doctrina monastery in an area claimed by the diocese.[10] Chronicles, viceregal records, court trials, and letters detail these territorial struggles fought out in the form of petty sacrileges, thefts, vandalisms, brawls, insults, inquisitorial denunciations, and prolonged legal proceedings.[11] In ways great and small, churchmen and royal officials turned on each other with an intensity that threatened to undermine their standing in indigenous communities.

Each dispute was a battleground in an intensifying turf war over a sedentary indigenous zone that was running out of room for so many competing missionaries. The three mendicant orders had long competed for territory, but their rivalries paled in comparison with the conflicts between the mendicants and diocesan priests. Friars and priests clashed due to their opposing views of how the New World Church ultimately should be organized. Yet the ferocity of these struggles had as much to do with what they had in common. Mendicants and diocesan clergymen shared the same Iberian preferences to reside in sedentary settlements and cooler climate zones. Most friars and priests aspired to settle in densely populated towns where indigenous people lived "in *policía*," in recognizable and ordered towns as opposed to sparse populations, and if possible, in healthy, cool climes. Competing missionaries accused their rivals of laziness for preferring a comfortable doctrina in central Mexico rather than coping with mosquitos and heat in the lowlands, or hostile

---

[6] Diocese of Oaxaca against Dominicans (1562), AGI México, 368, no. 3.

[7] Diocese of Oaxaca against Dominicans (1562), AGI México, 368.

[8] María Justina Sarabia Viejo, *Don Luís de Velasco virrey de la Nueva España 1550–1564* (Seville: CSIC, 1978), 186.

[9] Deposition on Franciscans in Tula (1558), AGI México, 2606.

[10] Lundberg, *Unification and Conflict*, 124, 129; Sarabia Viejo, *Don Luís de Velasco*, 185.

[11] Lundberg, ibid..; Poole, *Moya de Contreras*; Valderrama to Philip II (1564), in Scholes and Adams, *Cartas del licenciado Jerónimo Valderrama*, 121.

chichimecas on New Spain's frontiers.[12] Priests and friars coveted the same diminishing supply of viable sedentary highland towns in the second half of the sixteenth century.[13]

As they battled for control of native towns, mendicants and seculars presented their opposing visions of the mission enterprise. Mendicants argued that the papal privileges granted to them earlier in the sixteenth century had given them extraordinary powers that were, as Stafford Poole writes, "outside the regular administrative machinery of the Catholic church."[14] Because they were exempt from episcopal oversight, they could establish and run missions at their discretion.[15] In addition, friars in jurisdictions like Tlazazalca claimed that they were uniquely suited for mission work, in contrast to secular competitors who were only interested in enriching themselves.[16] Indeed, one Franciscan went so far as to ask the king to render all New Spain into an immense classroom under exclusive tutelage of the mendicant orders.[17] For their part, secular clergymen saw mendicant claims as proof of their rivals' conceit. Seculars read the mendicants' papal privileges more as a temporary assignment than as a permanent concession. In their eyes, friars were supposed to secure footholds for Christianity where the Church had no presence and then, having prepared the ground for a future diocesan parish, they were to release their doctrinas to diocesan clerics and move on to new frontiers.[18]

Diocesan campaigns against the mendicants were emboldened by the politics of secularization that swept through the Spanish Empire and Church in the 1550s. The monarchical transition from Charles V to his son Philip II signaled a dramatic shift in royal favor from the mendicant Orders to diocesan clerics and bishops. More broadly, this change in royal policy reflected the decrees of the Council of Trent, which reduced

---

[12] Luís de Anguis to Philip II (1561), Cuevas, *Documentos*, 261. Toribio de Santiago, principal, Tlaquiltenango, AGN Tierras, vol. 1979, exp. 4, f. 252r; Don Francisco Sánchez, principal, Tlaquiltenango, AGN ibid., f. 252r; Juan de Boga, vecino, Oaxtepec, AGN ibid., f. 241r; Diego de Mercado, vecino, México, AGN ibid., ff. 116r, 118r.

[13] Van Oss, *Church and Society*, 103–23.   [14] Poole, *Moya de Contreras*, 67.

[15] Mendicant privileges were founded on the brief *Exponi nobis fecisti* (the "*Omnímoda*") issued by Adrian VI in 1522, and the bull *Alias felicis* by Paul III in 1535. Josef Metzler, ed., *America Pontificia Primi Saeculi Evangelizationis 1493–1592*, 2 vols. (Vatican: Libreria Editrice Vaticana, 1991), vol. I, 160–2 and 306–8.

[16] Carrillo Cázares, *La pasión por el derecho*, vol. I, 501.

[17] Mendieta to Philip II (1565), García Icazbalceta, *Códice franciscano*, 35; Mendieta to Francisco de Bustamante (1562), Icazbalceta, ibid., 15–28.

[18] Poole, *Moya de Contreras*, 71.

the power of the mendicant Orders.[19] These political shifts animated diocesan campaigns to remove the mendicants from their pastoral duties and send them back to their cloisters or onward to new frontiers.[20] In 1555, secular clergymen sought to engineer the transfer of doctrinas from mendicants to seculars at the First Provincial Council; ten years later, Mexican bishops drew upon the secularizing policies of the Council of Trent at the Second Provincial Council; and in 1574, they mobilized yet again after royal ordinances ordered mendicants to submit to diocesan oversight. Whereas the mendicants had once expanded into new territories with little more than a viceroy's nod and local indigenous support, diocesan clergymen and royal officials now challenged their every move and exploited their mishaps. Hence the rhetoric heated up, altercations got physical, and each side began to seek the wholesale expulsion of the other from central Mexico.[21]

The secular challenge could not have come at a more inopportune time for the mendicants. Mendicants had enthusiastically accepted the invitations of indigenous rulers to establish doctrinas in their polities in the 1540s and 1550s, only to face a severe staffing shortage as a result. In 1554, Viceroy Velasco reported that the Dominicans had founded more doctrinas than their numbers and training allowed. Out of one hundred and eighty friars serving in New Spain, half were novices; of those serving in the field, "only a few speak [local] languages."[22] Meanwhile Franciscans struggled with retention. Newly arrived recruits to replace an aging generation of veterans were instead returning to Spain. So many had left Mexico, in fact, that in 1564 the Crown decreed that all missionaries were to spend at least ten years in the field before they

---

[19] Ybot León, *La Iglesia*, 623–39; Morales, ibid., 34–63; Margarita Menegus, Francisco Morales, and Oscar Mazín, *La secularización de las doctrinas de indios en la Nueva España: La pugna entre las dos iglesias* (Mexico City: UNAM, 2010) 34–63, 82–114.

[20] Paso y Troncoso, *Epistolario*, vol. VII, 312; Lundberg, *Unification and Conflict*, 145–7; Poole, *Moya de Contreras* (1583) *Cartas de Indias*, vol. I, 235–6.

[21] Lundberg, *Unification and Conflict*, 117, 121, 134–7 145–7; Bishops to Royal Audiencia (1565) Cuevas, *Documentos*, 279–86, 312; Reynerio Lebroc, "Proyección tridentina en América," *Missionalia Hispánica*, vol. 26 (1969), 129–307; Poole, *Moya de Contreras*, 80–1; Archbishop of Mexico to Indies Council (1574), Paso y Troncoso, *Epistolario*, vol. XI, 213–21; Llaguno, *La personalidad jurídica*, 14–22; Traslosheros, *Iglesia, justicia, y sociedad*, 15–20; Ybot León, *La iglesia*, 623–39; Moya de Contreras (1583), *Cartas de Indias*, vol. I, 235–6; Fray Pedro Xuarez de Escobar to Philip II (1579), Cuevas, *Documentos*, 312; Luís de Anguis to Philip II (1561), Cuevas, ibid., 256, 260.

[22] Velasco to Philip II (1554), Cuevas, *Documentos*, 187.

could return to Spain.[23] By 1577, this failure in generational replacement led the Franciscan provincial, Fray Miguel Navarro, to inform Viceroy Enríquez that they would need a hundred new recruits from Spain in order to maintain all of their doctrinas – and at the very least, they needed fifty more just to "limp along."[24] No assistance came. Navarro therefore had to make the difficult decision to abandon eight Franciscan doctrinas. The Franciscans did not "flee from their labor," he explained to the viceroy, "but they could not fulfill their duty nor finish their work in so many areas."[25] Navarro begrudgingly handed over the doctrinas to his Order's competitors: Augustinians, Dominicans, and most embarrassingly, the diocesan clergy.[26]

As the mendicants faltered, diocesan clergymen smelled blood. In a series of offensives, clergymen attempted to capture entire doctrinas or carve out neglected visita jurisdictions as new secular parishes for themselves.[27] Clergymen often began their efforts by showing up unannounced to preach in a mendicant town, shocking residents who had grown accustomed to their ambulatory and mostly absent friars.[28] The diocesan priests would then demand donations and labor from indigenous communities, and order the community to build residences and churches. In Cuzcatlán, natives denounced a priest for showing up and demanding a hundred pesos on the spot. "For this," angry petitioners wrote, "the natives are much harmed because they do not have the means to pay salaries or feed the priest, [and in any case] the doctrine of the friars has been sufficient for them."[29] Priests then set up farms, cattle ranches, and mills in their

---

[23] Miguel Navarro to Viceroy Enríquez (1577), in García Icazbalceta, *Cartas de religiosos*, 54; Viceroy Enríquez to Philip II (1572), *Cartas de indias*, vol. I, 280; Borges Morán, *El envío de misioneros*, 206.

[24] Miguel Navarro (1577), García Icazbalceta, *Cartas de religiosos*, 60–1.

[25] Navarro to Viceroy (1568), García Icazbalceta, *Cartas de religiosos*, 59–60.

[26] ibid., 59. The abandoned doctrinas were Xalatzingo, Hueytlalpan, and Tlatlauquitepec (both to Diocese of Tlaxcala), San Juan Iztaquimaxtitlán and Tepexic de la Seda (to Dominicans), Tehuacán and Chietla (to Augustinians), Teutitlán (transferred to Diocese of Oaxaca). Enríquez to Philip II (1572), *Cartas de indias*, vol. I, 280–1. Mendieta (1574), Cuevas, *Documentos*, 298.

[27] For example, secular clergymen in Oaxaca sought to seize various mendicant doctrinas in 1556. AGN Mercedes, tomo 4, f. 315r.

[28] Indigenous petition to keep Augustinian visitations (1563), AGN Mercedes, vol. 7, f. 37v. Mendicant rivals also targeted each other's jurisdictions in a similar fashion: Audiencia *autos* on Tlaquiltenango doctrina (1573–1574) AGN ibid., ff. 6r–7v. Other attempted seizures of missions include: Viceregal amparo for Atoyaque (1563), AGN Mercedes, vol. 7, f. 82r; Viceregal amparo for Sevinan (1563), AGN Mercedes, tomo 6, f. 481v.

[29] Viceregal amparo to Cuzcatlán (1563), AGN Mercedes, vol. 7, f. 63r.

new parishes. In Pánuco, natives denounced their parish priest for running a store, compelling them to work on his ranches, and sending his mares and mules to pasture in their cornfields.[30] In some cases, priests were more like carpetbaggers, bringing their relatives to set up businesses and benefit from local labor drafts.[31]

Mendicants responded to diocesan efforts by asserting their legal possession of doctrinas. In 1559, for example, Franciscans in Tlaxcala performed "ceremonies of possession" to protect several visita churches that secular clergymen were attempting to seize. Calling on a notary and indigenous rulers to serve as witnesses, they laid claim to the buildings by encircling the edifices, driving crosses into church floors, and ringing bells. Following protocol, the indigenous witnesses declared that "they did not contradict" the Franciscans' legal possession.[32] Mendicants clearly resented having to cede what had cost them so much effort. "How," Fray Pedro de Xuárez asked King Philip II in 1579, after "founding many monasteries" and adorning them with "bells, images and retablos, and organs ... could Your Majesty could allow us to be dispossessed of all this?" Seculars did not deserve to inherit what they themselves had built with "our own tremendous sweat and labor."[33] Such arguments, along with threats to abandon all their missions, invariably convinced the king to reverse plans to expel the friars from their doctrinas. Radical policies of comprehensive secularization thus gave way to piecemeal modifications.[34]

The conflict between mendicants and seculars may not have produced an abrupt change in missionary authority, but it did destabilize the alliances forged between mendicants and indigenous nobles. In Tlazazalca, for example, the indigenous gobernador grew tired of clerical battles. At the trial that followed the destruction of the Augustinian church in his town, he requested that an entirely different Order – not the seculars, nor the Augustinians – should assume pastoral duties in his doctrina.[35] His wish had little effect. In a record dated 1582, two sujetos

---

[30] Accusation against Fabián de la Peña (1595), AGN Bienes Nacionales, vol. 687, exp. 2.

[31] Viceroy to Corregidor of Chichicapa (1589), AGN Indios, vol. 4, exp. 3, f. 1v; Viceroy to Corregidor of Teziutlán (1591), AGN Indios, vol. 5, exp. 190, f. 121v.

[32] BNM Fondo Franciscano, caja 57, exp. 1158, ff. 349v–351r; On legal affirmations of "precarious possessions," see Brian P. Owensby, *Empire of Law and Indian Justice in Colonial Mexico* (Stanford: Stanford University Press, 2008), 90–103.

[33] Pedro de Xuárez to Philip II (1579), Cuevas, *Documentos*, 310; Alonso de la Veracruz (1570), AGI México 282.

[34] Ybot León, *La Iglesia*, 629.   [35] Carrillo Cázares, *La pasión por el derecho*, vol. I, 411.

of Tlazazalca reported that they had been called to help build a new church for the seculars who triumphed there twenty years earlier.[36] Like a burnt teocalli on a list of conquests by the Triple Alliance, the burning of the mendicant doctrina marked the conquest of the Augustinians by their diocesan rivals. The Augustinians never returned to their former mission in Tlazazalca.

With their defamatory sermons, embarrassing brawls at church doorways, interminable lawsuits, and vandalism, Spaniards cringed at the missionaries' turf wars and fretted over the bad example that they set for neophytes. What would become of native Christianity if clerical squabbles contaminated it? Such concerns were nonetheless irrelevant. It was impossible to limit these conflicts to the Spanish world, for the fracas in the mission Church was inseparable from disputes that were sweeping through the indigenous world.

SEIZING THE NEW *TEOCALLI*

In 1561 the native ruler of Azcapotzalco, Don Hernando de Molina, informed King Philip II that indigenous people would not sit idly by while clerics exchanged blows over doctrinas. "Should Indians," he asked, "never dare to speak with their king, prince, or emperor?" The answer was clear: "On the contrary, we must dare so that nobody ever suspects that we are spineless, and even though we might hold a little timidity in our souls, we must drive it out, for Fortune favors the bold and rejects the fearful."[37]

Secularization disputes had far-reaching temporal and spiritual consequences for indigenous communities. For natives the transfer of their doctrina from one group of missionaries to another generally took place without their consent, and it involuntarily committed them to learning an entirely different doctrinal approach. Even more destabilizing, however, were the political effects of this change in affiliation, for it altered one of the primary sources of political cohesion in native jurisdictions. Like the colonial legal system, the mission enterprise had become central to native political authority. Changes in affiliation altered the balance of power within native communities, fueled factionalism, and increased the likelihood of territorial fragmentation. Throughout central Mexico, indigenous rulers, factions in sujetos, and commoners argued that their

---

[36] Viceregal exemption, Cuario (1582), AGN Indios, vol. 2, exp. 38, f. 9v.
[37] Don Hernando Molina to Philip II (1561), Paso y Troncoso, *Epistolario*, vol. XVI, 214.

investments of labor, resources, and tributes made them interested parties in all decisions regarding their doctrinas.[38] Like Don Hernando de Molina, they demanded to be included in decisions that were made in inaccessible chambers of power far from their villages.

Indigenous efforts to sway mission politics came in many forms: natives went to court, reached out to sympathetic Spanish officials, marched in the streets, and even abandoned their towns to protest changes in the mission enterprise. On most occasions communities mobilized to defend their original mission alliances forged with mendicants, although in a few exceptional cases towns also defended popular secular priests. In Cuauhtinchán, for example, indigenous rulers protested the handover of their jurisdiction from Franciscan to Dominican control in 1554 by boycotting their newly installed missionaries. The native fiscal performed what was effectively an indigenous *cessatio a divinis*: he removed sacred ornaments from the church, laborers stopped tending the friars' gardens, and rulers halted deliveries of eggs and tortillas. Although the protests drew ire from the viceroy, Cuauhtinchán's resistance secured the Franciscans' return.[39] In Teotihuacán, meanwhile, indigenous officials in 1557 resisted Augustinian attempts to take control of their Franciscan visita church. When local rulers refused to receive the Augustinians, the friars returned with civil and diocesan officials who proceeded to lash the recalcitrant leaders in public. What followed was a display of indigenous power: the residents abandoned Teotihuacán, leaving the Augustinians without a population to feed them. A crowd of four hundred *teotihuacanos* then marched fifty kilometers to the viceregal palace in Mexico City, where they demanded that the viceroy restore their visita to the Franciscans. The viceroy conceded to the *teotihuacanos'* demands.[40]

Mendicants interpreted this indigenous activism not as a defense of local sovereignty but rather as a demonstration of indigenous loyalty and devotion to their Orders. In his *Historia eclesiástica indiana*, Fray Gerónimo de Mendieta depicted the mobilizations in Teotihuacán and Cuauhtinchán as evidence of native devotion to the Franciscans. After the Franciscans left Cuauhtinchán, Mendieta claimed, local rulers lamented

---

[38] *Franciscans v. Dominicans, Tlaquiltenango* (1590) AGN Tierras, vol. 1979, exp. 4, ff. 3r, 49r; Menegus et al., *La secularización*, 82–8.

[39] Escalante Gonzalbo, "El patrocinio," 226; Mendieta, *Historia eclesiástica indiana*, vol. I, 505–19. Viceroy Velasco issued two compliance orders in 1554 and 1556: AGN Mercedes, vol. 4, f. 44r & 294v.

[40] Mendieta, *Historia eclesiástica indiana*, vol. I, 521–6.

that "although they have left us and looked down upon us, we cannot leave them." Similar paternalism can be found in indigenous sources: petitioners and chroniclers routinely spoke of the "love" that they received from the "fathers," who "protected and consoled" them.[41] "We revere the friars as fathers," the lords of Mexico, Tacuba, and Texcoco wrote, "who have raised, taught, and indoctrinated us, taking us out of the inferno of our errors."[42] In 1591, an indigenous *regidor* (municipal officer) defended the Franciscans in their protracted battle with the Dominicans over the possession of the doctrina in his town of Tlaquiltenango: "the Franciscan friars have been [our] solace since the beginning of the conversion of [our] parents and grandparents."[43] Another stated that the Franciscans "raised the Indians and [the Indians] were their children."[44] When doctrinas changed hands, indigenous residents were known to tearfully cling to the departing missionaries' garments in a futile effort to make them stay.[45]

Taken at face value, such statements suggest that indigenous communities remained fervently loyal to friars even when they had to abandon them.[46] It is impossible to distinguish sincerity from the boilerplate. Yet underlying these pro-mendicant narratives – with their tropes of native innocence, love, and suffering – indigenous sources also mention the central importance of mutual familiarity between villagers and missionaries. Given that alliances with mendicants were central in the reconstruction of indigenous polities, natives associated any change in religious affiliation with the breakdown of the polity itself. Petitioners backed missionaries they knew, spoke with, and trusted. Decades of visitations, baptisms, and involvement in local politics, economic relations, and church construction tied missionaries to indigenous communities in ways that went beyond doctrinal matters. In 1563, the natives of Cuzcatlán (Eastern Puebla) protested the arrival of a secular priest on the grounds that the Franciscans had already helped to "populate" their town – a

[41] Mendieta, *Historia eclesiástica indiana*, vol. I, 509.
[42] Indigenous rulers of Mexico, Texcoco, and Tacuba to Philip II (1583), AGI Mexico 286.
[43] Pablo de Sant Francisco, regidor de Tetelpan (1591), AGN Tierras, vol. 1979, exp. 4, f. 150r.
[44] Toribio de Santiago, cantor, Tlaquiltenango (1591), AGN Tierras, vol. 1979, exp. 4, f. 249v.
[45] Antonio de Sevilla, vecino, Cuernavaca (1591), AGN Tierras, vol. 1979, exp. 4, f. 154v.
[46] Menegus et al., *La secularización*, 82–7.

reference to the congregation of dispersed groups around their visita church.[47] That same year, the Mixtec town of Tlacotepeque (Western Oaxaca), which had been a Dominican visita for twenty years, repelled an attempt to secularize their jurisdiction by securing a viceregal injunction in their favor.[48]

History and habit weighed heavily on local preferences for missionaries. The bonds of familiarity, communication, and predictable economic arrangements bolstered the status quo, and for this reason indigenous rulers in cabeceras tended profess their undying support for the original missionary group that founded their doctrina. A completed stone church served as physical proof of this bond; it anchored the polity and protected it against the many threats that struck from all angles in the sixteenth century. The very "sweat, industriousness, and care of a large number of Indians" in building their churches, one native witness declared in Tlaquiltenango, proved the strength of their alliance with Franciscans; like mortar in the church walls, their community labor sealed an enduring, even eternal relationship.[49] "With our help," stated the gobernador of Cuernavaca, don Toribio de San Martín Cortés, "[the Franciscans] founded the church and monastery" – and that collective investment, intended in this case for the Franciscans, was not to be transfered to any other missionaries.[50]

Language was a vital part of these bonds of loyalty. As diocesan clergymen began to take over doctrinas and visitas, the replacements were often deficient in local native languages, and even worse, they often demonstrated little interest in improving communications. Sermons, confessions, sacraments, and day-to-day negotiations became onerous and awkward. In the Audiencia investigations into the burning of the church in Tlazazalca, numerous witnesses roundly criticized the secular clergy for not making an effort to learn Tarascan. Many natives in Tlazazalca backed the Augustinians, who had at least taken the time to study their language.[51] In Tizayuca, an area that had been initially visited by Franciscans but which passed to secular control, Otomí petitioners won a viceregal injunction to allow Franciscans to continue to visit them and

---

[47] Viceroy to Cuzcatlán (1563), AGN Mercedes, vol. 7, f. 63r.
[48] Viceregal order on Justlavaca Dominicans (1563), AGN Mercedes, vol. 7, f. 69r.
[49] Toribio Velázquez, principal de Tetilpan (1591), AGN Tierras, vol. 1979, exp. 4, f. 147r.
[50] Toribio de San Martín Cortés to Philip II (1590), AGN Tierras, vol. 1979, exp. 4, f. 39r.
[51] Carrillo Cázares, *La pasión por el derecho*, vol. I, 486. Residents of Huexotzingo also denounced a secular priest for his lack of Náhuatl: See Menegus et al., *La secularización*, 82.

preach in their native tongue, a minority language that Spaniards counted among the hardest in Mexico, "because the priest there does not know it."[52] Occasionally secular priests overcame their reputation for linguistic laziness: the inhabitants of one secular *doctrina* in the Mixteca petitioned to keep a secular priest "because he speaks the Mixtec language very well, so that we understand him and he understands us, and we are very happy and satisfied with him."[53]

Economic relations between indigenous communities and missionaries also shaped native preferences. Natives evaluated and compared the economic systems of the various mendicant Orders and diocesan clergymen in light of their own efforts to grapple with declining populations. In general, communities preferred to have predictable economic arrangements with missionaries, with steady and rotating burdens. That said, indigenous communities rarely reached the kind of broad consensus on these matters that they claimed in their petitions. Their differences are particularly evident in litigation over doctrina affiliation in this period. In Tlaquiltenango, a doctrina that was the subject of a decades-long lawsuit between Franciscans and Dominicans, residents of all statuses and classes differed over the material burdens and benefits of both Orders. While Franciscans renounced property and profiteering, the Dominicans invested in haciendas and engaged in commerce, even selling their cotton and cacao in the local tianguiz.[54] Indigenous trial witnesses weighed the two Orders' contrasting economic models in terms of their burden on labor and tribute demands, and their divergences are telling. On the one hand, witnesses acknowledged that the Franciscan vow of ascetic poverty was comprehensive: friars simply depended entirely upon "donations" from the community. The Franciscans' native allies argued that this extreme vow of poverty made the "yoke" – the burden of sustaining the friars – "far lighter" than that of the Dominicans, who channeled their share of native repartimiento

---

[52] Viceregal order on Tizayuca Franciscans (1563), AGN Mercedes, vol. 7, f. 150v.

[53] Petition, Caciques of Paltlanala, Tzilacayvapa, and Tlalpantzinco (1582), AGN Indiferente Virreinal vol. 2414, exp. 45. By 1582, a diocesan report stated that 65 percent of secular priests spoke at least one indigenous language. John F. Schwaller, *The Church and Clergy in Sixteenth-Century Mexico* (Albuquerque: University of New Mexico Press, 1987), 98.

[54] Toribio Velázquez, principal, Tetilpan (1590), AGN Tierras, vol. 1979, exp. 4, f. 147v; Pablo de Sant Francisco, regidor, Tetilpan, ibid., f. 151r; Tomás de San Nicolás, alguacil mayor, Yztla, ibid., f. 152v; Antonio de Sevilla, native of Jojutla, ibid., f. 154v; Juan de la Camara, principal of Metlán, ibid., f. 161v.

labor to their haciendas for profit.[55] In a similar way, indigenous rulers in México-Tenochtitlán also praised the Franciscans for being "people without economic interests."[56] More surprising, however, were the responses of native witnesses who rejected this argument. The Dominicans' defenders in Tlaquiltenengo argued that since Dominicans owned property and profited from their investments in cattle, cacao, and cotton, they were more self-sustaining. In the long run, they declared, this meant that Dominicans relied less on community funds and forced donations than the Franciscans.[57] In the words of an indigenous commoner, the Dominicans "always paid for whatever food they asked for, as well as for labor whenever they were served." Several witnesses added that the Dominicans even paid out of pocket for Spanish masons who oversaw building a gothic vault in the church, an event rare enough that it warranted a special mention in their depositions.[58] The evidence of these differing opinions are an apt reminder that indigenous communities were not as unified as they or their friars claimed, and that their differences went beyond micropatriotic or factional reasons.

Despite their differing economic approaches, all mendicants nonetheless shared a similar corporate structure of shared governance and pooled resources. Far different was the diocesan clergyman, who arrived alone to his newly-assigned doctrina. His installation as *doctrinero* (missionary) heralded a new set of economic relations. For native communities assigned to support a diocesan priest, the transition sowed uncertainty and unpredictability. Although hosting secular priests could serve local rulers' ambitions to upgrade their jurisdictions to full cabecera status, the economic burden of sustaining a secular priest exceeded their obligations as visitas to mendicant doctrinas, which distributed the burden of sustenance among more communities. Now they alone would have to serve a priest who was all too often bent on profiteering. The rulers of Cuautlaucan, a

---

[55] Toribio Velázquez, principal de Tetilpan, AGN Tierras, vol. 1979, exp. 4, f. 147v; Juan Palencia on behalf of natives of Cuernavaca and Tlaquiltenango (1590), ibid., f. 55r; Juan de Boga, Spanish vecino of Oaxtepec, ibid., f. 241v.

[56] Native lords of Mexico to the King (1584), AGI México, 286.

[57] Augustinians in Ocuituco made a similar argument regarding the proceeds of their wheat mills and sheep-farms, which they operated using native *repartimiento* labor. *Fiscal Maldonado v. Augustinians of Ocuituco* (1560), AGI Justicia, 205, no. 3.

[58] Miguel de Galizia, principal, AGN Tierras, vol. 1979, exp. 4, f. 237r; Francisco Cortés, principal, Yztla, AGN Tierras, vol. 1979, exp. 4, f. 240r; Miguel Toribiano, principal, AGN Tierras, vol. 1979, exp. 4, f. 243v; Martín de las Navas, commoner, AGN Tierras, vol. 1979, exp. 4, f. 255r.

small Augustinian visita near Puebla, asked the viceroy in 1563 to prevent secular priests from settling among them since they could not support them.[59] In Atoyac, a Franciscan doctrina near Sayula (Southwest Jalisco), indigenous petitioners complained that a secular priest had appeared in town and demanded a one-hundred peso salary that went far beyond the town's capacity. "The friars' doctrine is enough for [us]."[60] Similar complaints flooded the viceregal chancery in the second half of the sixteenth century: priests ordered natives to pay them salaries even though they had already been paid from royal coffers, forced them to weave thread out of cotton grown on a priest's farm, and made exorbitant demands for food. In such cases indigenous towns were keen to ask the viceroy to "clarify" the obligations that they owed their new resident missionaries.[61]

A series of denunciations brought before the Audiencia by the nobles of Teutitlán provide an example of the troubles that could befall a town when compelled to change its affiliation. In this doctrina in the arid region of northeastern Oaxaca, a diocesan priest arrived in 1567, replacing the Franciscans who had ministered to the local population for decades. According to the petitioners, the town had been "very happy" with the Franciscans because they always "gave them doctrine with all love and care."[62] Yet when the Franciscan staffing crisis struck in the late 1560s, Teutitlán was one of several dozen poor and marginalized doctrinas slated for closure. Unable to staff Teutitlán any longer, in 1567 the Franciscans transferred the doctrina to the Diocese of Oaxaca.[63] What followed, the plaintiffs claimed, was a series of abuses that ranged from mere neglect to profiteering and outright criminality at the hands of their cleric, Diego Carrillo. After five years in the village, Carrillo had still not learned Mazateca, the local language, and consequently natives were dying without confession. Carrillo also failed to attend to requests to perform last rites to the mortally ill. An indigenous noblewoman who lived "just a harquebus shot away from him," for example, died without the succor of the sacrament. Though generally absent, Carrillo always

---

[59] Petition to retain Augustinians, Cuautlatlaucan (1563), AGN Mercedes, vol. 7, f. 37v.

[60] Viceregal amparo for Atoyaque (1563), AGN Mercedes, vol. 7, f. 82r.

[61] Viceroy to Atlatlauca (1563), AGN Mercedes, vol. 7, f. 57v; Viceroy to Spanish authorities, Tututepec (1583), AGN Indios, vol. 2, exp. 491, f. 115r; Viceroy to Tenango (1563), AGN Mercedes, vol. 84, f. 100r; Viceroy to Papalutla (1563) AGN Mercedes, vol. 7, f. 216v.

[62] *Indios of Teutitlán v. Diego Carrillo* (1583), AGN Civil, vol. 890, exp. 11, f. 2r.

[63] Friars visited in the late 1530s; by 1559 Teutitlán was a *doctrina*. AGN Mercedes, 84, f. 81.

managed to return for religious fiestas to collect obligatory donations. If these shortcomings were not bad enough, the nobles also brought forward allegations of sexual abuse and murder. They declared that Carrillo kept a mistress in town, raped young women in the confessional, and enlisted his alguaciles de doctrina to bring women to his home. When a commoner named María Quaumisquitl fought off his sexual assault, Carrillo had her arrested and sheared her hair in public. Even worse, Carrillo and an unnamed accomplice kidnapped, raped, and beat a woman named Angelina and left her for dead.[64] These crimes led the nobles to seek the advice of a lawyer, who urged them to press their case in the Audiencia. Carrillo, however, had the full backing of his diocese, and the Audiencia ordered that he remain in his position "despite the abovementioned accusations."[65]

Given the problems that arose when a new missionary group arrived with poor linguistic skills, unfamiliar economic demands, and inexperience with local inhabitants, indigenous rulers tended to cling to their original alliances. There were very strong territorial reasons for doing so. An unwritten principle shared by indigenous and Spanish authorities associated the religious unity of a doctrina with the political unity of a cabecera. There was no room for differing doctrinal affiliations within an indigenous polity; each jurisdiction was supposed to be under the exclusive authority of a single missionary group. A Spanish lawyer in the Tlaquiltenango dispute succinctly expressed this principle: "sujetos do not have different ministers from their cabecera because in having them, dissensions generally arise."[66] Thus, when Franciscans abandoned a doctrina in Tlatlauquitepec (Northern Puebla) in the 1570s, they released the town to secular clerics because some of the sujetos were already secular parishes. In this way they hoped that the cabecera and its sujetos would "form one body and be in peace" and would avoid becoming divided "into bands and parties."[67] This principle combined missionary affiliation with territorial jurisdiction in a way similar to confessionalization in sixteenth-century Germany after the Peace of Augsburg: whereas Catholic and Lutheran princes organized territory according to the principle of *cuius regio, eius religio* ("whose kingdom, his religion"), indigenous rulers organized territory according to 'whose doctrina, his affiliation.'[68]

---

[64] AGN Civil, vol. 890, exp. 11, ff. 4r–5r.   [65] AGN Civil, vol. 890, exp. 11, ff. 7r, 16r.

[66] Juan Palencia (1590), AGN Tierras, vol. 1979, exp. 4, ff. 55r, 61r.

[67] Miguel Navarro to Viceroy (1578), García Icazbalceta, *Cartas de religiosos*, 60.

[68] Geoffrey Parker, *The Thirty Years War* (London: Routledge, 1984), 17.

In this vein Don Toribio de San Martín Cortés, the ruler of Cuernavaca whose sprawling jurisdiction nearly splintered in 1591, avowed that the Franciscan Order was *la única fuerza* – "the only force" – that bound together his territory.[69]

Certainly there was a religious element to this emphasis on conformity. Even the slightest variations in doctrinal instruction, indigenous rulers feared, would give secessionist *sujetos* the opportunity to manipulate them to their advantage. This was only made worse by the fact that competing missionary groups openly denigrated the spiritual practices of their competitors. In Tlazazalca, secular clergymen led their indigenous supporters through town chanting that their Augustinian competitors were *luteranos*, or Lutherans – a low-handed insult to the Augustinian Order, of which Martin Luther had once been a member.[70] Elite indigenous and Spanish observers alike understood that the differences between the Orders and secular clergy amounted to minor differences in practice, not faith, but they doubted that commoners could perceive these subtleties, especially when the disputes were so politically charged. "Because they are Indians," an indigenous principal of Tetelpan disparagingly declared in the Tlaquiltenango trial in 1591, "many will believe that that what [the Dominicans] teach them is different from that which the Franciscan friars have taught them." The confusion of doctrines could only lead to "disturbances" among the commoners, pro-Franciscan indigenous witnesses warned, which would lead to "dissensions, agitations, and passions" with grave consequences for the body-politic. At stake in these doctrinal disputes were the very functions of indigenous governance: the execution of justice, the collection of tributes, and the administration of labor levies.[71] For this reason, indigenous rulers and mendicant friars clung to their mutual alliances, praised each other's loyalty, and spoke of their bond as a lasting, even "indissoluble" contract – until, that is, missionaries decided that staffing troubles no longer allowed it to be so.[72]

Beneath their florid professions of undying devotion, unswerving loyalty, and everlasting bonds, native petitioners ultimately sought missionary alliances that provided them with a means of managing uncertainty.

[69] Governor and alcaldes of Cuernavaca (1591), AGN Tierras, vol. 1979, exp. 4, f. 46r.
[70] Carrillo Cázares, *La pasión por el derecho*, vol. I, 133.
[71] Toribio Velázquez, principal (1591), AGN Tierras, vol. 1979, exp. 4, f. 147v. Pablo de Sant Francisco, regidor, AGN Tierras, vol. 1979, exp. 4, ff. 149v–150r; Juan Bautista, principal, AGN Tierras, vol. 1979, exp. 4, f. 144v; Antonio de Sevilla, AGN Tierras, vol. 1979, exp. 4, f. 155r.
[72] Joan de Palencia, lawyer for Franciscans (1590), AGN Tierras, vol. 1979, exp. 4, f. 50r.

Indigenous polities relied on the stability that came with missionaries who were familiar to them, spoke their language, were predictable in their use of funds, and advocated on behalf of the community when necessary. While indigenous activism and intervention in the Spanish turf wars sought to turn colonial politics to their advantage, local rulers also looked nervously inward at their own factional divides. The supposed internal unanimity of *el pueblo* and *los naturales* (the town and natives), so prevalent in their petitions, testimonies, and chronicles, was increasingly elusive in the late sixteenth century missions. Unanimity was a fiction. Contrary to all their efforts, the internal disputes that native rulers tried to suppress were beginning to connect with the widening Spanish turf wars over the mission enterprise – and in some flashpoints, natives battled fiercely for control of the Church.

REBEL CHURCHES AND ORNAMENT RAIDERS

On August 12, 1591, the natives of Telhuacán, a sujeto of Atzcapotzalco (Northwest Valley of Mexico), received a troubling command from Mexico City. By order of the viceroy in his capacity as vice-patron of the Church in New Spain, they were to demolish the stone church that they had dedicated to San Juan Bautista, their patron saint, which they had been building for over a year with their own sweat and donations. The viceregal command came at the request of rulers in the cabecera of Azcapotzalco, who declared the inhabitants of Telhuacán to be "rebel Indians." The petitioners argued that the natives of Telhuacán were building their church "in order not to recognize their cabecera," in complete disregard of orders from their superiors.[73] The rulers of Azcapotzalco had good reason to suspect Telhuacán's motives: over the previous decade, the natives had shown the telltale signs of secession. First they withdrew from coatequitl labor rotations for the construction of Azcapotzalco's doctrina monastery, and they ceased sending laborers for their rotation in the Dominicans' kitchen. They then stopped attending doctrinal instruction in the cabecera, and they refused to send their cantores to the cabecera on feast days.[74] Finally, they began building a stone church without

[73] The viceroy issued two orders in 1591 affirming his authority to regulate church construction: AGN Indios, vol. 3, exp. 896, f. 218v; AGN Indios, vol. 6, 2a parte, exp. 37, f. 11r.

[74] Viceroy to Alcalde Mayor of Azcapotzalco (1582), AGN Indios, vol. 2, exp. 220, f. 56v. The sujetos protested rotational labor arrangements in 1583: AGN Indios, vol. 2, exp. 393, f. 94v. In response, the viceroy restated the order: AGN Indios, vol. 2,

permission. This was the final act of defiance for cabecera rulers. As soon
as the new church was completed, they argued, the structure would be
able to house a competing missionary group, thereby fortifying Telhuacán's alleged separatist project. Alarmed at the political danger of this
new church, the viceroy issued his demolition order. Remarkably, in this
viceroyalty ostensibly founded on spiritual imperatives, colonial politics
construed the unlicensed building of a visita chapel into an act of rebellion
that threatened to undermine the very political order that made the
mission enterprise possible.

Such was the mission's importance that, in dozens of jurisdictions like
Telhuacán, the Church had become a principal battlefield in the fragmentation of indigenous polities. At the same time that mendicant power
slipped in the face of secular challenges, indigenous cabeceras – some of
whom had only recently ceased being sujetos after raising doctrina monasteries themselves – began to face challenges from secessionist sujetos.
Sujetos that bemoaned paying tribute to their cabeceras, attending mass
at a distant doctrina monastery, and expending their sweat and treasure
for doctrina monasteries saw a solution in building a doctrina monastery
of their own. Their ambitions in the last third of the sixteenth century
resembled earlier processes of territorial "formation and separation" that
had underwritten the most dramatic phases of mendicant expansion.[75]
Centuries of associating the teocalli with sovereignty, and decades of
experience of colonial mission politics suggested that the pathway to
independence led through the stone church. Accordingly, sujetos throughout New Spain acquired sacred ornaments and erected church buildings,
core emblems of indigenous autonomy.[76]

Unlike the large separatist altepeme that had become cabeceras in mid-
century, separatist sujetos like Telhuacán tended to have far smaller
populations and tributary bases. More often than not, economic motives
drove their efforts. Ever-greater numbers of sujetos fought to obtain
cabecera status in the 1560s, unleashing a new wave of territorial fragmentation.[77] Decades of extending and strengthening church institutions
in indigenous communities meant that any aspiring subject town with the
capacity to build a respectable stone church and support a cleric – regular

exp. 468, f. 111v. See also Kubler, *Mexican Architecture*, 525; Gibson, *Aztecs*, 39–40,
   46–7, 189; Gerhard, *Guide*, 248–9.
[75] Lockhart, *Nahuas*; Gibson, *Aztecs*; Menegus et al., *La secularización*.
[76] Gibson, *Aztecs*, 54, 111–12, 121; Lockhart, *Nahuas*, 26, 53–5, 209; Terraciano, *Mixtecs*,
   121–30.
[77] García Martínez, *Los pueblos de la sierra*, 210, 215.

or secular – could reasonably attempt to upgrade their temporal status. Secularization, however, altered the dynamic, for while mendicants had been prime beneficiaries of seceding sujetos in previous decades, by the 1560s they were too understaffed and embattled by secular clergy to take advantage of this latest cycle of fragmentation.

Sujeto churches like that of Telhuacán carried a potentially dangerous contradiction between their roles in their communities and in the mission enterprise. In religious terms, sujetos tended to be mission visitas: modest, small churches where visiting missionaries could say mass, administer the sacraments, and impart the basic tenets of Christian doctrine. In large jurisdictions where the doctrina monastery was more than a day's journey away, sujetos often built visita churches that included sleeping quarters for visiting missionaries. Such was the case of Irechuato, a sujeto that petitioned the viceroy for permission to build a visita with a residence for their Augustinian missionaries, since this town lay a grueling five leagues (27.5 km) from their doctrina in Ucareo.[78] These visita churches began as wood or thatch structures, but over time they were to be converted into permanent stone structures. When a visita decided to switch to stone construction, it mobilized local labor as would an indigenous calpolli: collectively, though on a far smaller scale than for larger and more complex doctrina monasteries. Yet these modest churches served a similar political function as the behemoth structures in the doctrinas. For rural villages and town barrios, these stone churches "contributed to the honor of a community at the most local level."[79]

Yet while visita churches in sujetos focused and strengthened local religiosity, cabecera authorities often suspected that a more sinister factionalism lay behind their spiritual façades. Although no law explicitly linked doctrina status to the autonomous political powers of the cabecera, indigenous rulers actively sought to prevent any churches from rivaling the pre-eminence of the doctrina church in size or status. In Irechuato, for example, pressure from cabecera rulers was sufficient to prevent construction from proceeding, for the visita's proposed church never resurfaced in the records.[80] This association of unauthorized church construction with sovereignty was just as real for secessionists as it was for rulers. In 1591, a dissident indigenous principal in the Mixe town of Nova (Nobaá,

---

[78] The project had the support of three former priors of the monastery at Ucareo. Viceroy to Corregidor of Ucareo (1563), AGN Mercedes, vol. 7, f. 73r.

[79] Gibson, *Aztecs*, 121.   [80] Gerhard, *Guide*, 320.

Southern Oaxaca) led his partisans to "divide their town" by building a new church "just two gunshots away" from their former cabecera. At the behest of concerned local rulers, the viceroy ordered the Spanish alcalde mayor to punish this "troublesome Indian" and his henchmen.[81] Other rulers acted to pre-empt factionalism. The indigenous gobernador in Amecameca, don Juan de Sandoval, had several visita churches burned to the ground in order to guarantee the pre-eminence of the newly-completed doctrina monastery in his cabecera. Tellingly, he counted on the support of Dominican friars in destroying these places of Christian worship.[82]

To reduce the potential for territorial conflicts, viceroys attempted to regulate sujeto church construction by establishing an approval process that involved native rulers and local Spanish officials. Sujetos were responsible for petitioning the viceroy for permission to build local churches, and upon receiving requests, the viceroy ordered local officials to investigate the sujetos' true intentions.[83] In 1575, rulers in the town of Iztaczoquitlán (Veracruz) declared in a petition to Viceroy Enríquez that they needed to build a small church where they could "bury their dead and gather to learn the Christian doctrine." The viceroy ordered the local Spanish corregidor in Zozocolco to investigate the need for the edifice, available local resources, and the design and scale of the proposed structure.[84] In Mexico City, the viceroy appointed Antonio Valeriano, gobernador of the indigenous cabildo of the city's *parcialidad* of San Juan Tenochtitlán, to investigate a native petition from a sujeto of Ixtacalco to rebuild an *ermita*, a small chapel. The sujeto justified the request by stating that their present *ermita* was "in ruins and about to fall." Responding to the viceroy's request to investigate the sujeto's political ambitions, resources, and needs, Valeriano confirmed that it was indeed necessary "to renovate and repair the *ermita*...where the old and young gather to pray." The gobernador specifically referred to the viceroy's political concern: "I have verified that they are not doing this to secede"

---

[81] Viceroy to alcalde mayor of San Ildefonso (1591), AGN Indios, vol. 6, 2a parte, exp. 64, f. 15r.

[82] Gibson, *Aztecs*, 54; Viceroy to alcalde mayor of Chalco (1564), AGN Mercedes, vol. 7, f. 299r.

[83] Viceroy to corregidor of Tepeji (1591), AGN Indios, vol. 5, exp. 899, f. 302v.

[84] Viceroy to corregidor of Tonatico (1575) AGN General de Parte, vol. 1, exp. 281, f. 55r. Remoteness and population collapse mark the history of this area. According to Gerhard, several towns disappeared in this area. Gerhard, *Guide*, 221–2, 389.

from Tenochtitlán.[85] Having met these tests, sujetos like Ixtacalco could build their visita churches.[86]

Lavish churches in sujetos threatened cabecera rule precisely because they were prizes in the intensifying rivalries that plagued the Spanish missionaries. Franciscans and Dominicans vied for twenty years to wrest control of Tlaquiltenango, a sprawling mission doctrina that had fallen to the latter order after the Franciscans abandoned the doctrina during their staffing crisis in 1567. This transfer set into motion a series of struggles over the doctrina that wound up dividing and fragmenting one of the largest cabeceras in sixteenth-century New Spain, that of Cuernavaca. Located at the far southern reaches of Cuernavaca's sprawling territory, Tlaquiltenango was a political anomaly. Although it was a doctrina due to its distance from Cuernavaca (about fifty kilometers away), in political terms it remained a sujeto. Tlaquiltenango was thus subordinate, still part of a vast jurisdiction that predated the conquest, but in religious terms it was effectively independent.[87] This peculiar status split the town's leaders into two factions: on one side, separatists saw their independent doctrina as their path to full sovereignty, and on the other, Franciscan loyalists strove to maintain political ties to Cuernavaca that went back a full century.

When the Franciscans abandoned Tlaquiltenango in 1572, separatists seized their opportunity to sever their ties to Cuernavaca. After evaluating their options, they invited the Dominican Order to take over the doctrina. This immediately set off a crisis in Cuernavaca, where the lifetime native gobernador, Don Toribio de San Martín Cortés, sent his protests to the viceroy. It was essential, he declared in several depositions, that the Franciscans preserve the unity of his jurisdiction. His pro-Franciscan

---

[85] Viceregal investigation on *ermita* in Iztacalco (1589), AGN Indios, vol. 4, exp. 29, f. 8r.

[86] In 1591 the cabecera government of Tecamachalco approved a request from its sujeto of Aztatecho, four leagues (22 km) away. Cabecera rulers acknowledged that the natives there were "disconsolate," lacking even a proper place where they could bury their dead. Viceroy to alcalde mayor of Tepeaca (1591), AGN Indios, vol. 5, exp. 881, f. 296v.

[87] At the time of the Spanish conquest, Tlaquiltenango was an altepetl that was subordinate to the "conquest state" of Cuauhnauhuac, or Cuernavaca, the dominant altepetl in the region. Tlaquiltenango paid tribute to Cuernavaca and many of its elites were likely intermarried with those of Cuernavaca. When Cuernavaca was integrated into Hernán Cortés' *marquesado*, Cuernavaca's pre-eminence in its jurisdiction only increased. Consequently, Tlaquiltenango's status suffered another blow when the Spaniards relegated it to sujeto status. Robert S. Haskett, *Indigenous Rulers: An Ethnohistory of Town Government in Colonial Cuernavaca* (Albuquerque, NM: University of New Mexico Press, 1991), 9–13; Deposition, Gobernador and alcaldes of Cuernavaca (1591), AGN Tierras, vol. 1979, exp. 4, f. 46r.

allies in Tlaquiltenango concurred. Only the return of the Franciscans would restore the "concord and conformity" that had once existed "between the Indians of the ... cabecera and those of the town, which no longer exists today because it is administered by a different order."[88] Franciscans, meanwhile, were divided over whether they should have abandoned Tlaquiltenango in the first place, and many urged their Order to return to the doctrina. Some Franciscans even reached out to their former parishioners by illegally entering the doctrina and preaching in secret to their sympathizers.[89] When Dominicans refused to leave, the Franciscans sued the Dominicans. In court the Franciscans echoed don Toribio's political line of argument. If the Dominicans were allowed to remain, the Franciscans' lawyer warned, "the Indians of Tlaquiltenango shall pretend to be a cabecera and they will not subject themselves [to Cuernavaca] so easily."[90] The politics of the mission thus effectively created a situation in which underground missionaries preached a forbidden, crypto-Franciscan teaching in this Dominican jurisdiction.

Against accusations that their very presence in Tlaquiltenango was politically divisive, Dominicans countered that upon taking possession of the doctrina they had sworn that the town would "not separate from Cuernavaca."[91] Yet such statements were mere formalities. Although indigenous witnesses for the Dominicans consistently denied that they were motivated by political concerns, their lawyer confirmed his opponents' suspicions when he declared: "this town of Tlaquiltenango is a cabecera in its own right ... and [the Indians] of Cuernavaca have no subjection over them."[92] Tlaquiltenango withdrew all the customary signs of "obedience" to Cuernavaca: they roughed up and ejected tax collectors sent by the cabecera, denied entry to its justices, began electing their own town officials, refused to send laborers as part of Cuernavaca's repartimiento obligations to the Taxco mines, and they stopped sending their musicians to Cuernavaca on feast days.[93] This only intensified the

---

[88] Juan Ximénez, principal of Tlaquiltenango (1591), AGN Tierras, vol. 1979, exp. 4, f. 190r.

[89] Depositions by Juan Palencia (1590), AGN Tierras, vol. 1979, exp. 4, ff. 55r, 61r.

[90] Autos de la Audiencia y Reales Provisiones (1573–1574), AGN Tierras, vol. 1979, exp. 4, ff. 6r–7v.

[91] Auto (1574), AGN Tierras, vol. 1979, exp. 4, f. 6v.

[92] Auto (1591), AGN Tierras, vol. 1979, exp. 4, f. 14r.

[93] On labor levies see Robert S. Haskett, "'Our Suffering with the Taxco Tribute': Involuntary Mine Labor and Indigenous Society in Central New Spain," *The Hispanic American Historical Review*, vol. 71, no. 3 (August, 1991), 447–75; Francisco de Bustos, principal, Tlaquiltenango, AGN Tierras, vol. 1979, exp. 4, f. 158r; Francisco Cortés, principal,

factional disputes among local elites, which soon devolved into corrupt gambits. In the sujeto of Yztla, for example, pro-Franciscan nobles intimidated a pro-Dominican principal into signing their petitions.[94]

The turf war of Tlaquiltenango ultimately was resolved in the Dominicans' favor in 1591, over the loud protests and threats of the gobernador of Cuernavaca, don Toribio de San Martín Cortés. The result effectively dismembered his vast jurisdiction, just as he had predicted. Tlaquiltenango's confirmation as a Dominican doctrina soon led to its recognition as a cabecera. For the first time in more than a century, Tlaquiltenango was now fully autonomous.[95] That same year, perhaps buoyed by Tlaquiltenango's recent success, other large sujetos in Cuernavaca's jurisdiction followed suit by appearing before the viceroy to ask for "resident friars." In 1592, the principales of two sujetos, Santa María Asunción and San Lorenzo, declared that the gobernador of Cuernavaca had imprisoned four local leaders and threatened others "with all the harm that is possible." The viceroy defended the aggrieved parties, but he also forbade the creation of any new doctrinas in the area.[96] The secessionists of Tlaquiltenango reduced the chances, at least in the short term, for other sujetos to follow its lead.

While mendicant competition opened an opportunity for sujetos like Tlaquiltenango to secede from their cabeceras, the diocesan clergy also fueled indigenous separatism in their attempts to wrest doctrina and visita churches from mendicants. Cabecera rulers and their mendicant allies accused priests of fomenting internal dissent. Fray Alonso de Escalona expressed widely held mendicant opinion when he warned the Audiencia not to allow bishops and their secular clerics into indigenous jurisdictions because they only joined "rebellious, ambitious, and agitating" Indians who "worked to remove sujetos from cabeceras."[97] Similarly, Viceroy

Zinahuatlan, and Agustín Xuárez, indio, Tanchimilco (1590), ibid., ff. 175v and 184v. Cristobal del Castillo, vecino, ibid., f. 194v; Toribio de San Martín Cortés (1590), ibid., f. 63r; Bernardo, cantor (1590), ibid., f. 140r.

94 Francisco Cortés, principal, Yztla, AGN Tierras, vol. 1979, exp. 4, f. 240r–v; Tomás de San Nicolás, alguacil mayor, Yztla, ibid., f. 152v.

95 I am grateful to Robert Haskett for sharing his translation of Náhuatl annals of Tlaquiltenango, referred to as *huehuetlatolli*, which form part of a lawsuit between Tlaquiltenango and neighboring Jojutla over their cabecera status, dated 1712. AGN Hospital de Jesús, leg. 115, exp. 37; Haskett, *Indigenous Rulers*, 13, 15.

96 Viceregal order to protect native petitioners in Cuernavaca (1592), AGN Indios, vol. 6, exp. 141, f. 35r.

97 Alonso de Escalona to Real Audiencia (1570), García Icazbalceta, *Cartas de religiosos*, 93.

Enríquez cited the bizarre case of a secular cleric named Juan Troyano, who allegedly provoked the "competition between cabeceras and sujetos" in Chalco. According to denunciations brought before the viceroy, Troyano "disturbed" the Indians of Chalco by encouraging sujeto factions to stop attending mass in their Dominican doctrina. Enríquez identified this as one of the first steps by which "sujetos begin to extract themselves from their cabeceras."[98] Another dispute four years later demonstrates that the dangers of transferring sujetos to secular clerics extended beyond doctrine to economics. In a petition to the viceroy, the indigenous rulers of the cabecera of Quecholac (Central Puebla), a Franciscan visita, reported that a secular cleric appointed to their sujeto of Tlacotepec was impeding their tribute collection and labor mobilizations. In so doing, they argued, the cleric was encouraging the natives of the sujeto to rebel against Quecholac, which ultimately affected their ability to supply repartimiento labor to Spanish farms. The cleric further subverted their civil authority by erecting a stock and a prison.[99] In his rebuttal, the priest accused cabecera rulers of supporting a dissident faction within his parish that sought to undermine his own authority by attending mass in Franciscan-run Quecholac instead of his church.[100] The viceroy ruled in favor the indigenous cabecera government's allegations against the Spanish priest, but this apparently did not end the troubles between the two parties: in 1585, the same priest declared that the cabecera rulers had suspended the provisioning of wine and wax for the divine office in Tlacotepec.[101]

While many indigenous disputes revolved around the construction and possession of Church edifices, however, they were not the sole markers of local sovereignty. The spiritual and political power of the mission also rested in the objects that were indispensable in its rituals. Indigenous towns invested great sums of communal funds in church ornaments: retables, tapestries, chalices, monstrances, altarcloths, and surplices.

---

[98] Investigation on Juan Troyano (1569), AGI México 98; Viceroy Enríquez to Philip II (1572), *Cartas de Indias*, vol. I, 287.

[99] Viceregal order to maintain sujeto-cabecera relations, Quecholac (1576), AGN General de Parte, vol. 1, exp. 522, f. 110r; Viceregal order banning civil punishments by secular priests (1576), AGN General de Parte, vol. 1, exp. 540, ff. 113v–14r.

[100] Viceroy to alcalde mayor, Tepeaca (1576), AGN General de Parte, vol. 1, exp. 523, f. 110v.

[101] A petition by Christoval de Rivera in 1585 declares that the gobernador and alcaldes withheld the wax and wine. According to Gerhard, the visita had become a secular parish in 1570: AGN Indiferente Virreinal, vol. 3684, exp. 14; Gerhard, *Guide*, 279.

Indigenous towns took great pride in their provision of these items, for along with the edifices that housed them, they became symbols of the community. Thus when doctrinas or visitas were transferred to new missionary groups, indigenous communities made sure that the ornaments they had purchased remained in the possession of the community. Natives frequently complained that outgoing missionaries removed these items as they left, like the diocesan priest who made off with the silver chalice of Mezontla after the town denied his demands for twenty unpaid servants.[102]

In the heat of territorial conflicts, indigenous factions found that their rivals' church ornaments were easy targets. Religious ornaments were vital accouterments in the performance of political deference in indigenous polities. On major feast days, for example, sujetos carried their church ornaments to the doctrina monastery as expressions of their political and spiritual obedience. When conflicts erupted, competing factions raided their rivals' churches and stole their holy images and statues, trumpets and sackbuts, chalices, and ivories.[103] These raids effectively denied a town of its ability to observe mass, thereby rendering it ineligible as a doctrina center. In 1590 the inhabitants of Atzomba, a disputed area in arid Zapotitlán (Southeast Puebla), reported that raiders from nearby Acapetec "entered ... and forcibly took the ornaments from the church, and even carried away our trumpets." A former semi-autonomous state before the Spanish conquest, Atzomba claimed to be a cabecera, but Acatepec was rising in importance in the area. Acatepec's raid signaled its regional ascendance, for a few years later the aggrieved residents of Atzomba were compelled to move to Acatepec in a general reordering of indigenous settlement known as civil congregation.[104] Similarly, two sujetos of Epatlán (Southern Puebla) were the prime suspects in an assault on their cabecera church. Intruders carried away an image of Saint John, the cabecera's patron saint, and they beat an elderly nobleman who ran to save the sacred objects that guaranteed his community's sovereignty.[105]

[102] Viceroy to Alcalde Mayor, Tehuacán (1583), AGN Indios, vol. 2, exp. 658, f. 152r. Inventory, secular priest of Tepeacuilco in 1563: AGN Bienes Nacionales, tomo 775, exp. 13. Dominicans in Tlaquiltenango denied removing sacred ornaments upon exiting: AGN Tierras, vol. 1979, exp. 4, ff. 17r–26v.

[103] Viceroy to alcaldes and officials, Tlapalcatepec (1580), AGN General de Parte, vol. 2, exp. 427, f. 87v.

[104] Viceroy to Alcalde Mayor, Tehuacán (1590), AGN Indios, vol. 4, exp. 693, f. 196r; Gerhard, *Guide*, 262–3.

[105] Viceroy to Corregidor, Epatlán (1591), AGN Indios, vol. 5, exp. 930, f. 308r.

Amid the ongoing struggles for sovereignty in post-conquest Mexico, those who held power – especially those indigenous rulers who presided over cabeceras – nervously sought to preserve the power that they had become accustomed to draw from the mission enterprise. They asserted their claims to sovereignty over land and people by upholding the pre-eminence of the churches they had raised at such great cost, and conversely, by preventing the construction and recognition of churches in jurisdictions that they claimed. It is telling that cabecera rulers, missionaries, and royal officials concurred that churches occasionally needed to be destroyed in order to preserve the political order – and indeed the colonial Church itself.

Yet hopes for some measure of local sovereignty were hard to extinguish. In Telhuacán, the visita church whose destruction opened this section, locals simply delayed their implementation of the viceroy's order and waited for political winds to shift. They did not have to wait for long. When a new viceroy arrived just a year later, they asked him to suspend his predecessor's demolition order and grant a license to build their church. They justified this as an act of respect for their dead. "It is fair and just," they wrote, "that the site where they are interred be kept sacred so that [locals] ... can help [the dead] with their spiritual aid." They also requested permission to celebrate the feast day of their patron, Saint John the Baptist, "because the community enjoys it, fulfilling their devotion." Moved by these arguments, the viceroy reversed his predecessor's order and allowed them to build a modest church on condition that they recognize their cabecera in Azcapotzalco.[106] The compromise appears to have worked. Telhuacán never became a cabecera, but its natives recovered their spiritual communion in an age when turf wars politicized sujeto churches like theirs as potential sites of subversion.

CONCLUSION

Indigenous doctrinas were just as much the pawns of native politics as they were of Spanish churchmen. The torch-bearing secular priests of Tlazazalca, the petitioning natives in Teutitlán, the weeping Franciscans at Tlaquiltenango, and the protesting natives of Teotihuacán all came from spheres that we could easily classify as Spanish and indigenous, and we could just as easily separate their interests into the same categories.

[106] Viceroy to San Juan Telhuacán (1592), AGN Indios, vol. 6, exp. 310, f. 84r.

Yet doing so obscures the extent to which these interests were intercon-
nected. The mission enterprise catered to the aspirations of missionaries
and natives alike. For the former, it offered a means to seal the destiny of
their Orders and their own clerical careers, and for the latter, it helped
them mend a political and social order that was continually threatened by
depopulation and exploitation. This is why the mission Church provoked
such passions.

These battles to control the mission Church only intensified as political
and economic crises further reduced indigenous communities in the
second half of the sixteenth century. As their numbers declined and their
taxation and labor burdens rose, inhabitants of sujetos sought greater
control over labor and resources by seceding from their cabeceras. If
aspirants to cabecera and doctrina status had once been proud former
kingdoms, cities, and tribute-collection centers, now it was the turn of
neglected villages and hamlets that, tired of laboring for others, struck
out to rule themselves. And just as their cabeceras had done, aggrieved
communities in the second half of the century built churches and invited
missionaries to reside among them as a means of asserting independence
from their native overlords.

Yet much had changed by the 1570s. Whereas indigenous fragmentation had provided mendicants with ample opportunities to expand their
enterprise at mid-century, administrative and political troubles hindered
their ability to expand in pace with seceding sujetos. The new candidates
for doctrina status were smaller and poorer, and therefore far less capable
of sustaining monasteries and friars. This process of fragmentation undermined the ascendance that the mission enterprise had once enjoyed in
New Spain. Embattled and underfunded, it was ill prepared to meet the
challenge of the demographic catastrophe to come.

7

Hecatomb

We have no permanent residence in this world, as we are in it only as guests
and pilgrims,
en route in search of our Eternal City.

Dominican General Chapter, *1540*[1]

In 1576, an indigenous annals-keeper in México-Tenochtitlán marked the
passing year with a skull. Below it, he noted the indigenous calendar year
and added this grim notice: "In this year of Seven-House, the terrible
plague called *cocolixtli* invaded. It sacrificed nearly everyone, and because
of this the dead, both old and young, were buried in huge pits."[2] The
disease had struck abruptly, and as in previous epidemics, it mercilessly
killed nearly every native it infected while it spared Spaniards.[3] During the
onset of an unusually heavy monsoon in April 1576, indigenous people in
the Valley of Mexico suddenly fell ill with fevers, extreme thirst, head-
aches, and a weakening pulse, followed by jaundice and restlessness so
intense that they could not stand any blankets or clothes on their skin.

[1] Cited in Javier Gómez Martínez, *Fortalezas mendicantes* (Mexico City: Universidad
Iberoamericana, 1997), 100.
[2] Anales de Tlatelolco y México, no. 1 (1519–1633), BNAH, Anales antiguos de México,
tomo 273, vol. II, 603.
[3] Rodolfo Acuña-Soto, David W. Stahle, Matthew D. Therrell, Tichard D. Griffin and
Malcolm K. Cleaveland, "When Half of the Population Died: The Epidemic of Hemorrhagic Fevers of 1576 in Mexico," *FEMS Microbiology Letters*, no. 240 (2004), 1–3;
Prem, "Disease Outbreaks," 39.

Pustules soon covered their bodies, dysentery set in, and blood flowed from their orifices. Within five days they were dead.[4]

Over the next three years the cocolixtli surged each rainy season, reaching every corner of New Spain from Maya communities in the southern Yucatán Peninsula to frontier missions in Sonora.[5] Census data point to a mortality of biblical proportions. In Tepeapulco, the total number of tributaries dropped from 6,700 in 1570 to 2,512 in 1588, while the ancient altepetl of Tepeaca reported a decline from 25,300 tributaries in 1570 to 11,500 in 1600. Friars estimated losses in Cholula and Tlaxcala at forty thousand each, and four hundred thousand in the Valley of Mexico. Reports from indigenous towns reported losses of half, two-thirds, and even nine-tenths of their populations.[6] While some friars gravely attributed their plight to divine punishment for the sins of paganism, most natives blamed secular factors like disease and overwork, which interacted with one another in ways that were barely fathomable.[7] Indigenous informants for a *relación geográfica* in Oaxaca grimly noted that this was the third catastrophe since the conquest in which "the Indians have died off."[8]

Like the prior epidemics of 1521 and 1545, the epidemic of 1576 set into motion profound transformations in central Mexico. For longtime Spanish residents, post-cocolixtli Mexico was nearly unrecognizable, a hollowed-out land where "a great multitude of Indians is missing," in the words of the Augustinian theologian Fray Alonso de la Veracruz.[9] "So many people died that year," the Franciscan chronicler Juan de Torquemada wrote, that afterwards it was hard to believe "that this [was] the

---

[4] Anales de Tlatelolco y México, BNAH, ibid.; Mendieta, *Historia eclesiástica indiana*, vol. II, 197–8; Acuña-Soto et al., "When Half of the Population Died," ibid.; Acuña-Soto et al., "Megadrought and Megadeath in 16th-Century Mexico," *Emerging Infectious Diseases*, vol. 8, no. 4 (2002), 360–2; Prem, ibid.

[5] Cook, *Born to Die*, 121; Acuña-Soto et al., "When Half the Population Died," ibid.

[6] Gerhard, *Guide*, 53, 280; Prem, "Disease Outbreaks," 42. In the Valley of Mexico, over a quarter of the population is believed to have perished: Gibson, *Aztecs*, 138; Borah and Cook, *Population of Central Mexico in 1548*, 52. For the Pánuco and Valles regions in northeastern New Spain, estimates based on tributes show losses of 76 percent and 96 percent respectively: Acuña-Soto et al., "When Half the Population Died," 3. See also Fray Rodrigo de Segura to Philip II (1578), AGI México, 284; Fray Pedro de Oroz to Philip II (1576), AGI México, 283; Juan de la Cueba to Philip II (1576), AGI México, 100.

[7] Barry L. Isaac, "Witnesses to Demographic Catastrophe: Indigenous Testimony in the Relaciones Geográficas of 1577–1586 for Central Mexico," *Ethnohistory* vol. 62, no. 2 (2015), 309–31.

[8] Isaac, "Witnesses to Demographic Catastrophe," 313; Acuña, *Relaciones*, vol. 1, 288.

[9] Fray Alonso de la Veracruz to Philip II (1577), AGI México, 283.

same country that Don Fernando Cortés and his comrades had conquered." After the epidemic, he added, it would take multiple witnesses
of pre-1576 Mexico to convince recent arrivals from Spain that their
descriptions of a crowded land were not the stuff of legend.[10] And the
cocolixtli of 1576 was only the beginning. Over the following twenty
years, six more epidemics swept across New Spain, coming in waves
and then abating, only to strike again before communities had time to
recover.[11] Corn shortages in 1587 in the Valley of Mexico led to starvation, which opened the way for deadly fevers; epidemics moved from
central Mexico to the Mixtec region of Oaxaca, as well as Michoacán,
Jalisco, and Sinaloa from 1588 to 1592; and a host of diseases, believed to
be measles, mumps, and smallpox, capped off this devastating century of
mortality between 1595 and 1597.[12] All told, census data show that
between 1575 and 1595 the indigenous population in New Spain declined
by as much as 60 percent, or from roughly 3.3 million to 1.3 million.[13] As
in previous crises, during these disasters labor and tribute demands continued to burden grieving survivors.

This late-century hecatomb cut down the post-conquest world that
natives and missionaries had built together. Though most missions and
larger indigenous communities survived, the catastrophic losses triggered
far-reaching crises that ultimately transformed economy and society in
New Spain, including the mission enterprise. New Spain underwent a
decade of depression in the 1580s, followed by stagnation in the 1590s.
Mines in Zacatecas, Guanajuato and Pachuca saw their profits fall, and

---

[10] Torquemada, *Monarquía Indiana*, vol. I, 642.

[11] Cook, *Born to Die*, 121. On the need to consider social and economic factors in
mortality, see Livi-Bacci, "Depopulation," 199–232.

[12] Prem, "Disease Outbreaks," 42–3; Mendieta, *Historia eclesiástica indiana*, vol. II, 197–8;
Three viceregal orders responded to indigenous petitions from this region to readjust
repartimientos: Viceroy to Alcalde Mayor of Ávalos (1589), AGN Indios, vol. 4,
exp. 126, f. 39r; Viceroy to Alcalde Mayor of Ávalos (1592), AGN Indios, vol. 6,
exp. 211, f. 54v. Viceregal exemption from mine labor for Acámbaro (1592), AGN
Indios, vol. 6, 2a parte, exp. 366, f. 82r; Antonio de Tello, *Crónica miscelánea de la
santa provincia de Xalisco* (Mexico City: Porrúa, 1997), 699; Viceroy to Alcalde Mayor
of Teposcolula (1591), AGN Indios, vol. 5, exp. 698, f. 259r; Gerhard, *Guide*, 23; Daniel
T. Reff, "Contact Shock in Northwestern New Spain, 1518–1764," in *Disease and
Demography in the Americas*, ed. John W. Verano and Douglas H. Ubelaker (Washington DC: Smithsonian Institution Press, 1992), 268.

[13] Van Bath, "The Calculation of the Population," 67–95; Whitmore, *Disease*, 118–9;
Gerhard, *Guide*, 53, 280; Isaac, "Witnesses to Demographic Catastrophe," 313; Elsa
Malvido, "La epidemiología, una propuesta para explicar la despoblación americana,"
Revista de Indias, vol. 63, no. 227 (2003), 65–78; Acuña-Soto et al., "When Half the
Population Died," 3.

a general malaise regarding New Spain's prospects overtook Spanish colonists, many of whom emigrated to the new and promising frontiers then opening up in the Philippines.[14] And in indigenous towns across the countryside, officials redistributed lands vacated by the dead, work in quarries fell silent, and families groaned under tribute and labor demands that grew more burdensome with each death.[15] The provincials of the three mendicant Orders summed up the disaster in a letter of protest against excessive repartimiento demands: "so much poverty simply cannot pay such exorbitant tributes."[16]

Because the mission economy still depended largely on the mass mobilization of tribute labor, depopulation dealt it a severe blow. Mendicant friars in 1588 warned that given the fact that New Spain's entire economy rested on diminishing numbers of tribute-payers, the kingdom could suffer the same desolation that beset the Caribbean islands unless authorities addressed the excesses of forced labor.[17] Moreover, although missions had been resistant to depopulation in earlier decades because they had served as a means of recovery, the mid-century mission model had become unsustainable. Reduced populations could barely sustain the mission Church, let alone build behemoth churches. Indigenous towns petitioned the viceroy with a clear message: there were simply not enough bodies to meet inflexible quotas. One by one, the diminution of native towns brought about the mission's unraveling, a fact plainly visible in viceregal records: expansion grounded to a halt, monumental construction faced the unyielding gravity of the circumstances, and an enterprise that had once been at the vanguard of indigenous politics became a defensive institution with insufficient resources. Having risen through the work of millions to remake Mesoamerica in the wake of earlier disasters, this third demographic catastrophe marked the end of the post-conquest period in which indigenous communities reconstituted themselves around new mendicant missions. Henceforth, communities with mendicant missions would defend what their ancestors and first friars had accomplished.

---

[14] Schwaller, *Origins of Church Wealth*, 153–61, 174; P. J. Bakewell, *Silver Mining and Society in Colonial Mexico: Zacatecas, 1546–1700* (Cambridge, 1971), 227–30; Archbishop-Viceroy Moya de Contreras to Philip II (1577) AGI México, 336A; Moya de Contreras to Philip II (1581), AGI México, 336A.

[15] Paso y Troncoso, *Relaciones geográficas*, 30; Xochimilco land report (1581), AGN General de Parte, vol. 2, exp. 1145, f. 252r.

[16] Mendicant provincials to Philip II (1595), AGI México, 290.

[17] Fray Pedro de Pavia to Philip II (1588), AGI México, 288.

THE LATE-CENTURY CRISIS

Indigenous petitions for relief arrived at the viceregal chancellery as one disease after another swept across New Spain in the last decades of the century. Each plea, sent by local rulers and sometimes missionaries advocating on their behalf, reveals not only the immediate tragedy of these losses but also the failing mechanisms of local tribute economies.[18] During an outbreak of typhoid in 1592, for example, principales in Ajijic, on Lake Chapala in present-day Jalisco, denounced diocesan clerics in Guadalajara for forcing them to provide thirteen laborers for cathedral construction and a Jesuit hacienda nearby. "One hundred people have already perished, and every day more get ill," the viceregal summary of their petition reads, "and they are no longer able to send the number that [the Spanish clerics] demand," adding that they could only pay tributes by selling the clothes off their backs.[19] Likewise, the indigenous government of Xochimilco (20 km south of Mexico-Tenochtitlán) informed the viceregal administration in 1590 that it could not longer provide royal officials with free canoe transportation, a service that they had been able to provide for over forty years "because then there were many people." Disease, emigration, and "other calamities" forced them to ask for a reduction in services, since the town had other obligations, such as the construction of the cathedral in Mexico City. The viceregal administration denied the request.[20] Such denials of relief often had dire consequences. In Chilapa (Guerrero), survivors of the 1576–1578 epidemic were subjected to corporal punishment, fines, and imprisonment by their corregidor for working their own plots of land – their primary source of sustenance – in lieu of repartimiento labor for Spaniards.[21]

As native economies struggled to recover from these latest catastrophes, the demands of the mission pushed some local tribute systems

---

[18] Petition, Fray Juan de Córdoba (no date), AGI México, 96; Instructions to Fray Estevan de Alzua by Tenango (1593), AGI México, 113; Mendicant provincials to Philip II (1595), AGI México, 290.

[19] Viceroy to Alcalde Mayor, Ávalos (1592), AGN Indios, vol. 6, exp. 211, f. 54v. According to Gerhard, the number of tributaries in Sayula, of which Ajijic formed part, declined from 5,800 in 1569 to 3,500 in 1597: Gerhard, *Guide*, 241.Three years earlier nearby Cocula protested the same levy for the same reasons: Viceroy to Alcalde Mayor, Ávalos (1589), AGN Indios, vol. 4, exp. 126, f. 39r.

[20] Viceroy to Xochimilco (1590), AGN Indios, vol. 4, exp. 290, f. 97v, Petition, indios of Izúcar (1582), AGI México, 106.

[21] Viceroy to Chilapa (1580), AGN General de Parte, vol. 2, exp. 1284, f. 273r; Viceroy to Alcalde Mayor of Texcoco (1590), AGN Indios, vol. 4, exp. 325, f. 108r.

close to their breaking point.[22] In the small sujeto of Totoltepec near Tacuba (Western Distrito Federal), native petitioners reported in 1590 that Franciscan missionaries who visited them were consuming sixty-six percent of their tributes for their food and housing needs. This vastly exceeded the target that viceregal officials had set for the economic impact of missionaries on local economies a generation earlier, which was twenty-five percent.[23] In Acolmán, local rulers in 1581 sought a viceregal injunction to reduce the number of friars stationed there "due to the recent mortality [which resulted] in the notable diminution and reduction" of the local population.[24] The crisis also bankrupted towns that had undertaken grand projects just years before. In Tulancingo, a recently-completed *retablo* graced the doctrina of monastery in 1580, but the three artisans hired on credit to paint it were left unpaid for their work after the mortalities forced the local government to default on the nine thousand pesos that they were due.[25]

In many cases, demands from missionaries for indigenous labor proved to be as inflexible as those of other Spaniards. Like Spanish owners of *obrajes* (textile mills) and haciendas, as well as many indigenous rulers, missionaries often turned a blind eye to the reality of population losses out of convenience. In 1580, the indigenous government and commoners of Etla (Oaxaca) declared that they could no longer simultaneously supply thirty repartimiento laborers for Antequera (Oaxaca City) and the demands of their own Dominican monastery, which left the survivors "with no time to work on their own crops." The viceroy authorized a revision of repartimiento labor demands, but retained the town's labor drafts for the essential labor destined to monasteries.[26] Similarly, the natives of Puctlán, a small sujeto of Otumba (near Teotihuacán), asked to reduce the number of coatequitl laborers for their doctrina monastery from seven to three, in light of the fact that the cocolixtli had reduced their number of available tributaries from thirty-nine to twenty-seven. This reduction of more than half was now "the most that they could give"

[22] Viceroy to friars in Tlalnalapa (1583), AGN Indios, vol. 2, exp. 1007, f. 231v.

[23] Viceroy to Totoltepeque (1590), AGN Indios, vol. 4, exp. 842, f. 228v.

[24] Gerhard's data for encomiendas show a 52 percent decline, in *Guide*, 314. Viceroy to Acolmán (1581), AGN General de Parte, vol. 2, exp. 1174, f. 257v.

[25] Viceroy to Tulancingo (1580), AGN General de Parte, vol. 2, exp. 902, f. 190v.

[26] Viceroy to Alcalde Mayor, Antequera (1580), AGN General de Parte, vol. 2, exp. 624, f. 126v. See also Livi-Bacci, *Conquest*.

to the monastery since they also had to meet repartimiento obligations at Spanish-owned wheat fields, all while they also attempted to feed themselves.[27]

The burden of supporting the mission enterprise weighed the heaviest in the poorest jurisdictions at the margins of the sedentary heartland of central Mexico. Native petitions to the viceroy described haunting scenes redolent of the writings of Juan Rulfo: In these depopulated areas, church construction always progressed slowly; meager offerings of food motivated missionaries to seek better appointments elsewhere (or, for holier souls, served as a path of spiritual perfection); and half-finished structures seemed to be on the verge of collapse. Such was the predicament of the inhabitants and friars of Tepexi de la Seda in the aftermath of the cocolixtli. Poor soils and limited resources had always made the mission enterprise in Tepexi a struggle. Even before the cocolixtli, the town had been relying on viceregal handouts to purchase tools and building materials to build its church.[28] In a series of petitions, native rulers reported that they could no longer support the four resident friars and their frequent guests who stopped at this doctrina along the busy route between Oaxaca and Mexico City.[29] "Due to the pestilence and mortality, and the great hunger and labor that the natives suffer," a principal named Pedro Jiménez stated, "building on the church has ceased."[30] Wood was rotting in the ceiling and the walls were beginning to crumble, and the friars were forced to reside in "some vile little cells" in the ruined thatched remains of what had been a school "where boys were once taught to read and sing."[31] Local inhabitants, meanwhile, had to focus on finding food for their families and left the mission to its fate.[32] Food was so scarce, one principal declared, that the only donations that the natives could offer the Dominicans was "a little bit of chile and pumpkin seeds (*pepitas*), which they sometimes give when they go to confession."[33]

---

[27] Viceroy on labor in Puctla (1583), AGN Indios, vol. 2, exp. 489, f. 114v. In Otumba over half of the population perished in the 1576–1578 cocolixtli. Gerhard, *Guide*, 208.

[28] Petition, Tepexi de la Seda, AGN Tierras, vol. 2723, exp. 28, ff. 308–13r.

[29] Pedro Jimenez, principal (1579), AGN Tierras, vol. 2723, exp. 28, ff. 311r–311v; Luís de San Francisco, principal (1579), ibid., ff. 310v–11r; Martín de la Cruz, principal (1579), ibid., f. 311v.

[30] Luis de San Francisco, principal (1579), AGN Tierras, vol. 2723, exp. 28, f. 311r.

[31] Martín de la Cruz, principal (1579), AGN Tierras, vol. 2723, exp. 28, f. 311v, Tepexi petition (1579), ibid., f. 309r; Luís de San Francisco, indio principal (1579), ibid., f. 310v; Alonso de Sanctiago, principal (1579), AGN, ibid., f. 310r.

[32] Alonso de Santiago, principal (1579), AGN Tierras, vol. 2723, exp. 28, f. 310r.

[33] Martín de la Cruz, principal (1579), AGN Tierras, vol. 2723, exp. 28, f. 311v.

Their inability to provide the friars with better nourishment, the petitioners lamented, had brought "shame" upon them all.[34] "No friar wants to come to this town," principal Martín de la Cruz stated, "and those who are here have not come willingly." Their requested aid apparently never arrived, for thirteen years later the town once again petitioned the viceroy to assist their doctrina. Now "the church and monastery is falling down," the summary of their petition states, "[and] there is no decent place where mass can be said, nor a decent place for the friars, since the ceilings of their cells have been under construction for many years now."[35]

As in Tepejí de la Seda, epidemics and their resulting economic crises halted church construction in towns throughout New Spain. In 1591, the residents of Caquamilpa informed the viceroy that, in the midst of an ongoing epidemic, repartimiento levies were requiring them to consistently dedicate over a third of their available tributaries – seventy laborers out of a total of two hundred – to the ongoing construction of a church, monastery, and *casas reales* in Totolapa, their cabecera. Able-bodied survivors were being compelled, often by force, to work in the cabecera instead of working on their own plots to grow food for their families. So great were these difficulties that thirty residents had already emigrated from the town in order to feed themselves. The petitioners sought a reduction of their repartimiento from seventy to twenty workers for the duration of the illness. In a routine response, the viceroy instructed the local corregidor to investigate the total number laborers that the cabecera's project required, whether sujetos received payment for their labor, the demographic impact of the illness, and the time remaining for the monastery's completion.[36] Even this formulaic questionnaire reveals an awareness of the mounting challenges facing monastery construction during the late-century depopulation crisis: increasingly, viceregal officials saw mendicant construction projects as obstacles to efforts to forestall famine. Consequently the time to completion for major projects dragged on ever longer as Spanish and indigenous authorities balanced church construction and repartimiento obligations with the urgent task of disaster recovery.

---

[34] Joan Baptista, principal (1579), AGN Tierras, vol. 2723, exp. 28, f. 312r.

[35] Martín de la Cruz, principal (1579), AGN Tierras, vol. 2723, exp. 28, f. 311v; Viceregal order to investigate monastery construction, Tepexi (1592), AGN Indios, vol. 6, 2a parte, exp. 639, f. 144r.

[36] Viceroy to Caquamilpa (1591), AGN Indios, vol. 3, exp. 635, f. 151v.

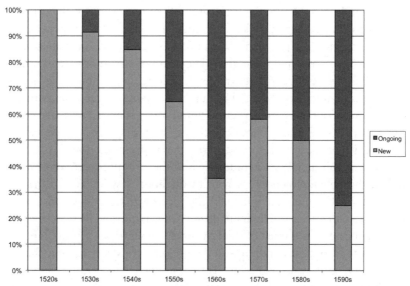

FIGURE 7.1 Proportion of new and ongoing monastery construction projects by decade.
Source: AGN, AGI. See Appendix 2

The petition from Caquamilpa illustrates the challenge facing church construction projects during the late-century depopulation crisis: with ever fewer hands available, the task of supporting the mission impeded the more urgent mission of feeding one's family. As a result, church construction across New Spain declined by 68 percent between 1570 and 1600.[37] During the same period, the native population declined by roughly 50–60 percent. *Figure 7.1*, above, shows that by the 1590s, 60 percent of all monastery construction projects consisted of repair work and ongoing projects from previous decades. Kubler and Van Oss attributed this decline in doctrina foundations and church construction to the "oversaturation" of missionary Orders in New Spain, arguing that mendicants simply ran out of jurisdictions.[38] Yet, as we saw in *Chapter 6*, the central Mexican highlands by no means suffered a shortage of indigenous sujetos that were eager to separate from their cabeceras. The unflagging indigenous pursuit of autonomy, which had fueled mendicant expansion, remained unchanged and still coincided with the equally

[37] See Appendix 2.
[38] Kubler, *Mexican Architecture*, vol. I, 66–7; Van Oss, *Church and Society*, 116–18.

powerful mendicant ambitions to found new monasteries. What was lacking in this late-century crisis was not the political will to create doctrinas, but the labor sufficient enough to buoy a mendicant doctrina with all its material demands. Mendicants initially hoped that the crisis would pass quickly. Fray Jerónimo de Mendieta, for example, expressed his hope that the Franciscan order would transcend the difficult political moment and found new monasteries in the future.[39] Amid the far-reaching effects of mass mortality, however, such ambitions steadily diminished. Foundations of new doctrinas and church construction halted because the third round of epidemics brought local populations below the critical threshold of local populations necessary to sustain a mission enterprise that had been calibrated to a far larger population.

For towns once capable of consistently fielding dozens or hundreds of laborers, as well as for their ambitious mendicant missionaries, the time had come to recalibrate. At the Dominican General Chapter in 1583, friars voted to conclude construction as quickly as possible to avoid "burdening the Indians with excessive costs." For their part, Franciscans had already acknowledged that large cabeceras were having difficulty in finishing large projects. They stressed that future constructions should be of "moderate" size, as opposed to the far grander scale of mid-century complexes like Cholula.[40] Fray Gerónimo de Mendieta still held out hope that his Order could continue to expand under increasingly dire circumstances, but stressed that friars in new establishments needed to use the small "but pleasant" monastery at San Juan Teotihuacán as a model.[41] Diminishing populations and tributes had forced the mendicant mission enterprise to scale down.

Mendicant downsizing did not convince royal authorities, however. By the 1590s, the viceregal chancellery effectively ceased granting licenses for new mendicant doctrinas. Indeed, only one license for a new monastery foundation appears in the viceregal orderbooks: for the cabecera of San Juan Ecatzingo, which had been a reluctant visita of the distant doctrina of Chimalhuacan Chalco for six decades. Viceregal permission to build the church only came after the community had proven that it had sufficient funds and labor at its disposal to finance construction and maintain

[39] García Icazbaceta, *Códice Mendieta*, vol. I, 79–80; Fray Miguel Navarro to Viceroy Enríquez (1577), García Icazbalceta, *Cartas de religiosos*, 60–1.

[40] Ulloa, *Predicadores divididos*, 186; García Icazbalceta, ibid.

[41] Miguel Navarro to Viceroy Enríquez (1577), in García Icazbalceta, *Cartas de religiosos*, 60–1.

four Dominican friars. As the last mendicant doctrina foundation in the sixteenth century, Ecatzingo was a lone exception in the 1590s.[42]

ACTS OF GOD

Viceregal records in the 1580s and 1590s reveal a telling shift in monastery construction campaigns in indigenous towns. After several decades of receiving requests to issue licenses for new construction, the viceregal chancellery now had to respond to requests that overwhelmingly dealt with problems of shoring up a crumbling mission infrastructure. This is not to say that structures had not failed in earlier decades; indeed, the improvisational and transcultural building campaigns of mid-century also produced their share of miscalculations and embarrassing collapses.[43] But after the 1576 cocolixtli, new constructions gave way to repairing failing walls and aging edifices. Stone walls crashed to the ground, wooden ceilings rotted and collapsed, and thatched roofs leaked, leaving residents with "no place to gather to hear mass and receive the sacraments," as dozens of native petitions stated.[44] Lightning strikes also set fire to churches and monasteries. In Tamazula, one group of petitioners lamented, tragedy struck on All Saints Day, 1580.[45] Petitioners generally

---

[42] Viceregal investigatation order, Ecatzingo (1592), AGN Indios, vol. 6, exp. 249, f. 63r. Dominicans established the *doctrina* around 1600: Gerhard, *Guide*, 104.

[43] Two early examples of ruined monasteries: Viceregal outlay, 300 pesos, Chiautla (1563), AGN Mercedes, vol. 7, f. 70r; Viceregal outlay, 300 pesos, Miçantla (1565), AGN Mercedes, vol. 8, f. 42r.

[44] The petitions are summarized in viceregal orders to Spanish officials to investigate local claims. Viceroy to Alcalde Mayor, Hueytlalpan (1580), AGN General de Parte, vol. 2, exp. 627, f. 127r; Viceregal license to repair church roof, Tiquicho (1580), AGN General de Parte, vol. 2, exp. 734, f. 151v; Viceroy to Corregidor, Tlaxcocuatitla (1590), AGN Indios, vol. 4, exp. 744, f. 206v; Viceroy to Corregidor, Teutitlan (1591), AGN Indios, vol. 3, exp. 432, f. 100v; Viceregal license to cut 500 beams, Pahuatlán (1591), AGN Indios, vol. 5, exp. 231, f. 131r; Viceroy to Corregidor, Tazuntla (1580), AGN General de Parte, vol. 2, exp. 648, f. 131v; Viceroy to Alcalde Mayor on church, Etla (1580), AGN General de Parte, vol. 2, exp. 632, f. 128r; Viceroy to Corregidor, Silacayoapan (1580), AGN General de Parte, vol. 2, exp. 549, f. 111v; Viceroy to Corregidor, Zimatlan (1580), AGN General de Parte, vol. 2, exp. 1351, f. 284r; Viceroy to Corregidor, Zoquitlán (1583), AGN Indios, vol. 2, exp. 492, f. 115v; Viceregal labor exemption, Yatzi (1592), AGN Indios, vol. 6, 2a parte, exp. 502, f. 110r; Viceroy on church repairs, San Lucas (1592), AGN Indios, vol. 6, exp. 128, f. 31v.

[45] Lightning struck Tamazula twice, in 1580 and 1594: AGN General de Parte, vol. 2, exp. 781, f. 162v; AGN Indios, vol. 6, exp. 920, f. 247r. A fire caused by a lightning strike destroyed the ceilings and ornaments at Amecameca in 1591: AGN Indios, vol. 6, 2a parte, exp. 120, f. 29r.

requested financial assistance and exemptions from obligatory labor to carry out their repairs. In the late-century crisis, however, collapsing arches and lightning strikes were not mere accidents; they were also "acts of God" – extraordinary failures that, in the political context of New Spain, also presented an opportunity for relief.

Indigenous petitioners deftly turned their news of tragedy into a case for broader programs of recovery. With a well-phrased petition, lightning strikes and rotting beams could turn out to be a blessing for struggling communities. In the political culture of the viceroyalty, failing structures provided struggling indigenous communities with a convenient pretext for rallying their communities and earning a respite from the existential threats posed by exorbitant labor demands and unrelenting diseases. Native rulers and petitioners were fully aware of the ideological underpinnings of viceregal policy, which in times of labor shortages pressured viceroys to prioritize labor for the evangelical mission over temporal needs like mining or ranching. A sensible request to repair a church or support missionaries could therefore win temporary exemptions from more onerous labors.[46] In 1591, a fortuitous bolt of lightning in 1591 set fire to Amecameca's monastery ceiling and destroyed its ornaments. The disaster prompted local inhabitants to secure a viceregal exemption from repartimiento labor for the silver mines of Izatlán for a year.[47] Other indigenous communities in the 1590s obtained similar reprieves from working in sugar mills, wheatfields, and mines.[48]

Not surprisingly, Spanish colonists and authorities suspected that indigenous communities were engaging in a form of disaster fraud by exaggerating or even fabricating accidents to avoid obligatory labor. For this reason, viceroys routinely ordered Spanish authorities to investigate petitioners' claims. In 1595, for example, the rulers of Jonacatlán (Central Puebla) sought exemptions in order to rebuild a damaged church. After

[46] To the consternation of Spanish miners at Tlalpuxagua and Ozumatlan, near Acambaro, 260 laborers – a quarter of all available tributaries in 1592 – were working for Franciscans. Viceregal labor exemption, Acámbaro (1592), AGN Indios, vol. 6, 2a parte, exp. 366, f. 82r.

[47] Viceregal labor exemption, Amecameca (1591), AGN Indios, vol. 6, 2a parte, exp. 120, f. 29r.

[48] Viceroy to Alcalde mayor, Tehuacán (1591), AGN Indios, vol. 5, exp. 48, f. 83r; Viceroy to Corregidor, Maravatío (1591), AGN Indios, vol. 5, exp. 982, f. 323r; Viceroy to Juez Repartidor, Atlixco (1591), AGN Indios, vol. 5, exp. 468, f. 198v; Viceroy to Alcalde Mayor, Toluca (1592), AGN Indios, vol. 6, exp. 358, f. 96r.

the corregidor verified that the local tributary count had indeed collapsed during recent epidemics – from one thousand to just four hundred able-bodied tribute-payers – the viceroy exempted them from repartimiento labor for Spanish farms in the Valley of San Pablo.⁴⁹ Petitioners in Cupándaro, in Michoacán, were not so fortunate: having petitioned for a reprieve from obligatory levies for sugar plantations in Valladolid on account of a collapsing wall in their church, the local Spanish alcalde mayor and resident friars determined that the problem could easily be solved by repairing a thatch roof that was appropriate for the church walls. The minimal labor required for these basic repairs, the viceroy concluded, did not justify an exemption from cutting sugarcane for Spaniards.⁵⁰

Yet for communities unvisited by such fortuitous accidents, there was little reprieve from the triple calamity of epidemics, famines, and overwork that unrelentingly struck in the last third of the sixteenth century. The pressures of overwork and conflicts over local resources only intensified social tensions between pipiltin (nobles) and macehualtin (commoners). Conflicts long repressed came to the surface in these years. Commoners, especially those residing in sujetos, increasingly challenged their cabecera rulers through petitions and litigation in search of relief from tribute and labor. Aware that a successful petition to the viceroy could circumvent their own rulers and missionaries, commoners make a dramatic entry into the viceregal records at the end of the century: they can be found protesting the excessive costs of wine and wax in church services, the tax levies to finance a five-hundred-peso organ, or the amount of food that a local priest demanded from a starving community.⁵¹ Protests also lept off the petitions and legal briefs and turned into open altercations. In Tlayacapa, a sujeto of Totolapa with separatist intentions, commoners attacked tribute collectors sent from the cabecera in order to prevent them from collecting tributes they deemed to be exorbitant. Pelting the collectors with stones, the macehualtin forced the cabecera officials to take refuge in the nearby Augustinian monastery.⁵²

---

⁴⁹ Viceregal exemption, Jonacatlán (1595), AGN Indios, vol. 6, exp. 1088, f. 297v.
⁵⁰ Viceroy to Alcalde Mayor, Michoacán (1596), AGN Indios, vol. 6, exp. 1165, f. 321r.
⁵¹ Viceroy to Corregidor, Jonotla (1591), AGN Indios, vol. 5, exp. 299, f. 150r; Viceroy to Corregidor, Tancítaro (1590), AGN Indios, vol. 4, exp. 785, f. 215v; Viceregal order, sujetos of Teutalco (1560), AGN Mercedes, vol. 84, f. 95r.
⁵² *Tlayacapa v. Totolapa* (1565), AGI Justicia, 176.

In Tlaxcala, as well, commoners rose up against native rulers for continuing to collect tributes that, with depopulation, had become impossible to pay.[53] The weight of "customs since time immemorial" – the catchphrase employed by native rulers, friars, and administrators in their justifications of tribute levels – mattered little to the protestors.

A lawsuit lodged in 1581 by a group of commoners in Tlapa (Guerrero) provides us with a vivid example of resistance to the increasingly heavy tax and labor burdens of indigenous polities. In that year, thirty-six commoners hired a lawyer and accused their rulers for embezzling money and products derived from extraordinary tax levies and labor drafts.[54] Leading the effort were several *tequitlatos* (tax collectors), themselves commoners, who refused to collect the extra levies and had been imprisoned and lashed for their disobedience. The tequitlatos declared that over the previous five years – precisely during the *cocolixtli* epidemic – native rulers were exacting five extraordinary levies per year under the pretext that the proceeds were needed to fund the local Augustinian doctrina. Each married household had to pay three *tomines*, two hens, one tribute blanket, and four hundred cacao beans. This was in addition to their regular tax and labor schedules.[55] While some of the proceeds supported the mission Church, the commoners alleged that their rulers were compelling them to haul cacao and tribute blankets to markets in Mexico City and the port of Acapulco. Consequently over three hundred commoners had left their households and taken to the hills.[56] The commoners did not hold back in their demands: they instructed their Spanish lawyer to call for the imprisonment of their entire ruling elite.[57]

If rulers squeezed their commoners, however, this was only partly due to greed, for the colonial tribute system was also pressuring native rulers throughout Mexico to work their diminishing populations ever harder to meet inflexible quotas. In Tenango, for example, native rulers in the 1570s were unable over the course of several years to meet their tribute demands to Spaniards, accruing a debt of eight thousand fanegas of wheat on top of their yearly obligations.[58] In Tlapa we find native rulers facing a similar predicament. There, a royal tribute collector found that native rulers had failed to raise 1,254 pesos that the altepetl owed the

[53] *Commoners of Tlaxcala v. native rulers* (1589), AGI México, 111.
[54] Commoners of Tlapa against gobernador and principales (1581), AGN Civil, vol. 695, exp. 1.
[55] ibid., ff. 3r–55r. [56] ibid., ff. 3r–8v. [57] ibid., f. 49r.
[58] Fray Juan de Córdova to Philip II (no date), AGI México 96.

crown. The collector then arrested the indigenous gobernador, don Juan López, as well as his native officials. The tribute collector only agreed to release the gobernador and local government officials after the officials agreed to raise extraordinary levies to pay off Tlapa's debt.[59] The commoners of Tlapa were unconvinced by this argument. Given the severity of the epidemics, they argued, the native rulers should have granted some reprieve. The commoners also rejected the arguments presented by the nobles of Tlapa, who justified extraordinary taxes solely on the grounds that custom had granted them the right to do so.[60] Yet depopulation, the greed of native nobles, the costs of providing for the Church, and the insatiable Spanish thirst for tributes and labor all had turned customs of taxation and deference into insufferable burdens. The tequitlatos of Tlapa called upon commoners to rebel against this order and break up Tlapa into autonomous units.[61] Their defiance of "immemorial custom" points to a desire to alter a political and economic order that the mission enterprise had done so much to cement.

Flashpoints of resistance like that of Tlapa revealed the fraying edges of the hegemony that had empowered native rulers and mendicant missionaries for decades. Yet the late-century crisis did not completely unravel the mendicant mission as an institution; indeed, it also laid the basis for its long-term survival. Even while bishops and hostile royal officials fulminated against the friars, mendicant doctrinas nonetheless received a lease on life. By the 1590s, Spanish civil authorities had come to view the indigenous towns that had grown around the doctrina monasteries as ideal nuclei for their forced resettlement programs, the *congregaciones civiles* (civil congregations). Spanish policymakers had been attempting to concentrate tribute-paying populations into Mediterranean-style nuclei in fits and starts since the 1540s, but the hollowing out of the countryside and the precipitous decline in tributes during the late-century crisis gave new impetus to these policies. Unlike the mid-century congregaciones, which had been rather piecemeal and mostly directed by local indigenous rulers, the new congregaciones civiles of the 1590s and the early seventeenth century were closely coordinated programs of mass resettlement. In some cases indigenous populations resettled themselves voluntarily. In Chalcatongo, a cabecera town near Teposcolula (Oaxaca), resettlement was a strategy of survival. In 1591, residents there reported to the viceroy that since "the majority of the population has perished" in a recent

---

[59] AGN Civil vol. 695, ff. 105r–8r.　　[60] ibid., ff. 3r–55r.　　[61] ibid., ff. 3r–5v, 55r–6r.

epidemic, they wished to transplant their town to one of their sujetos "since it has better soil, good water, a grove, and a good church." The following year, the forty remaining survivors in a village nearby asked for permission to return to their prehispanic townsite, which had water and familiar soils. Disaster forced indigenous towns of all sizes and scales to weigh the benefits of moving to new sites and concentrating their numbers there, or returning to the past – to places that had nourished their ancestors before this century of death.[62]

Yet the logic of the congraciones civiles only worked in one direction: toward concentration. For the most part, relocations were top-down affairs overseen by royal officials on orders of the viceroy. Spanish intentions were crystal clear: "those who are living scattered throughout the countryside," a royal order reads, "are to be compelled to live and make their homes in cabceras and sujetos that are governed with order and *policía*."[63] A typical congregación order can be seen in instructions that Viceroy Velasco II issued to Captain Pedro Martínez de Loaiza, alcalde mayor of the Villa de Valles (Huasteca), "to gather and resettle the Indians of the towns of Tantulanila and Macolique" to a new site near their cabecera because they were "at risk of disappearing."[64] These policies ultimately extended a lifeline to the mission enterprise, since the 277 doctrinas across New Spain served as convenient sites for resettlement. The original Spanish ideal for mission infrastructure – Viceroy Mendoza's plan of "reducing" native populations to rational Christian government by concentrating them physically in mission-centered settlements – had long been redirected by indigenous governments to suit their own purposes, largely contravening Spanish plans for resettlement. Yet what mid-century Spanish regimes could not accomplish was realized by the late-century demographic crisis, which opened the door to ambitious efforts by Spanish administrators in the first decades of the seventeenth century.[65]

Ultimately, forced removal programs opened possibilities for land acquisition for Spanish colonists. This included cash-strapped mendicant

---

[62] AGN Indios, vol. 5, exp. 698, f. 259r; AGN Indios, vol. 6, 2a parte, exp. 662, f. 152v. See also Viceroy to Corregidor, Los Peñoles (1592), AGN Indios, vol. 6, 2a parte, exp. 713.
[63] Franciscans to Philip II (1586), AGI México, 287.
[64] Viceroy to Loaiza (1592), AGN Indios, vol. 6, exp. 370, f. 99r.
[65] Ernesto de la Torre Vilar, *Las congregaciones de los pueblos de indios* (Mexico City: UNAM, 1995); Gibson, *Aztecs*, 282–6; Terraciano, *Mixtecs*, 119–20. On the more extensive resettlement programs in Andean *reducciones*, see Mumford, *Vertical Empire*.

missionaries, with the exception of the Franciscans. Alongside settlers, other corporations, and a handful of native elites, Dominicans, Augustinians and diocesan clergymen were active participants in the bonanza of post-crisis land acquisition. Throughout the late-sixteenth and early seventeenth centuries, missionaries acquired cattle ranches, haciendas, and mills. As a result the mendicant economy shifted from its earlier heavy dependence on native tributary systems to active market participation. Indigenous populations assisted in this shift: in 1582, for example, the natives of Huango (Michoacán) donated lands to their local Augustinians so that their Order could raise sheep and goats "for the friars' [own] sustenance, because [the Indians] are poor and few in number." Unable to provide for their missionaries as they had in the sixteenth-century tribute economy, residents opted to donate a new means of sustenance to the Augustinians. Similarly, the Augustinians of Yuriria-púndaro acquired a cattle ranch on the lands of an abandoned town, a former visita of their doctrina monastery.[66] Other donations to the friars included cattle and sheep ranches, cotton fields, salt pits, and lime-kilns.[67] Although diocesan opposition and royal investigations argued that mendicant property-owning violated their vows of poverty, the Dominicans summed up the position of propertied mendicant Orders in 1577, just a year after the *cocolixtli*. After "so many deaths and calamities," they informed Philip II, they only means by which they could economically sustain their mission was by reducing their dependence on diminishing populations and opting instead to live off of rents. For missionaries, then, native depopulation was also an act of God: a tragic calamity that made available a new financing model based on properties in depopulated lands.[68]

---

[66] Augustinian land titles, Huango (1590), APOAM, "Huango XVII y XVIII," no. 167, f. 1r. Land records from Michoacán acquisitions of cattle ranches through donations: Zecamembaro (1590), Yuriria XVII; Yurirapúndaro (1591), APOAM, México XVII.

[67] On Augustinian goat and sheep ranches near Tenayuca, 1582: AGN Indios, vol. 2, exp. 284, f. 70v; Augustinian cattle ranches,1594: AGN Tierras, vol. 2701, exp. 14, ff. 104r–33v; Dominicans held cattle ranches in Tehuantepec, but slaughtered the herd after local indigenous communities protested in 1592: AGN Tierras, vol. 2737, exp. 24, ff. 365r–72r. Dominican cotton plantation, Tlaquiltenango: AGN Tierras, vol. 1979, exp. 4, ff. 147r–54v. In 1581, indigenous donors transferred salt pits to Augustinians in Ocotlán: AGN Tierras, vol. 1707/1708. exp. 1, ff. 8r–15r. The viceroyalty donated lime-pits in Texcoco to the Augustinians in 1576: AGN Mercedes, tomo 10, f. 98v.

[68] Dominicans to Philip II (1577), AGI México, 283.

CONCLUSION

At the point where its expansion stammered and its once-powerful hold on indigenous politics slackened, the mission enterprise faded into the background of an increasingly complex colonial order. Mendicant missions would still be vital for indigenous communities and the rural economy, but no longer would they occupy the center stage of colonial politics as they had in the mid sixteenth century. Several indicators mark this transformation. In political terms, the Spanish politics of secularization and the atomization of indigenous polities undercut the preeminence that the mission enterprise had held in indigenous affairs since the 1530s, when its hegemony, based on hundreds of local alliances between missionaries and native rulers, extended across the central Mexican Altiplano, Michoacán, the Sierra Norte de Meztitlán, and Oaxaca, and made advances into far-off Nueva Galicia (Jalisco). In economic terms, the mendicant mission was a victim of its own early successes: its mid-century economic model, based on the convenience of harnessing tribute-paying multitudes according to indigenous customs, became strained to the point of rupture during the late-century depopulation crisis. Finally, in social terms, the costs of maintaining the mission enterprise generated tensions between indigenous commoners and the indigenous rulers, Spanish colonists, and missionaries who benefited from their labor. In the course of these transformations, missions that had stood at the vanguard of indigenous political change devolved into institutions that defended existing jurisdictions and alliances.

Despite collapsing populations, changing indigenous politics, and rising intra-Church competition, however, the end of mendicant hegemony did not unravel its institutions. Most mendicant doctrinas, especially large cabecera towns, survived demographic crises. In fact, the process of nucleation in the civil congregations sustained many doctrinas with the tributes of resettled households. Indigenous elites continued to rule through their cabildos, mendicant friars continued to influence community affairs, and the doctrina continued to serve as an anchor for the political, religious, and social life of a large swathe of the central Mexican countryside. Doctrinas survived in many areas until the end of the eighteenth century, and some even carried on until Benito Juárez delivered the final *coup de grâce* in the nineteenth century.[69] Native rulers

---

[69] Gibson, *Aztecs*, 110.

and their allied friars were periodically compelled to mount fierce defenses of their institutions and infrastructure against assaults from bishops and royal officials. This defensive posture, however, contrasted with the expansive spirit of their sixteenth-century predecessors, the friars and indigenous rulers who forged the alliances that built sixteenth-century New Spain.

8

Epilogue

Salazar's Doubt: Global Echoes of the Mexican Mission

Manila, July 1584. Fray Domingo de Salazar, the first bishop of the Philippines, wrote to his fellow bishops in Mexico, who were gathering to discuss the travails of the Church at the Third Provincial Council. Though invited to attend, he decided to pass on making the treacherous journey, opting instead to present his opinions in a letter. The council brought together veteran missionaries who had decades of experience in Mexico, but Salazar's record surpassed them all. Educated at Salamanca, he was a student in Francisco de Vitoria's seminars on the Indies before he took the Dominican habit. As a missionary he traversed the New World, even serving in Tristán de Luna's disastrous expedition to Florida. But it was in New Spain where he built his career. For twenty-three years he participated in all aspects of the mission enterprise in Oaxaca: he learned native languages, ran doctrinas, and studied the theological problems sown by colonization.[1] Now, as a bishop in Asia, he reflected on the Mexican mission and pondered its lessons for the new mission that he helped build across the Pacific Ocean.

Salazar looked back at the great edifice of the Mexican mission, and for all its apparent accomplishments, he asked what kind of salvation could be found within it. Its principal problem, he declared to the bishops, was the haste and impatience with which it was built. This was

---

[1] Lewis Hanke, *Cuerpo de documentos del siglo XVI* (Mexico City: Fondo de Cultura Económica, 1977), xxxviii–xlvii; Antonio de Morga, *Sucesos de las Islas Filipinas*, ed. Francisca Perujo (Mexico City: Fondo de Cultura Económica, 2007), xxi–xxv, 26–7; Poole, *Moya de Contreras*, 140; Ernest J. Burrus, S. J. "Salazar's Report to the Third Mexican Council," *The Americas*, vol. 17, no. 1 (July, 1960), 65–84.

especially so during its founding years. Missionaries were all too willing to accommodate worldly power in order to provoke conversions and erect churches than to converse and persuade. Ever a follower of Las Casas, Salazar despaired that this mission system negated "the principal reason why we came here, which was the conversion of infidels and the propagation of the faith." Instead, they had taken an instrumental mindset that prioritized temporal power as a precondition for preaching, helping to "extend the king's dominion [over the Indies] and ensuring that [natives] recognized him as their lord."[2] Mendicants allowed themselves to fall prey to the facile argument that Spanish conquest and subjugation would allow them to quickly convert and indoctrinate natives. Salazar warned that conquest was ill suited to evangelical work, for conquest was nothing other than "death, violence, and robberies." Under such duress, one could only say that natives had "received the faith more out of force than will."[3]

Throughout the sixteenth and seventeenth centuries, the Mexican mission became known for its the fusion of temporal and spiritual power. As an object of repute or infamy, depending on the context, observers cited it as a prime example of a Spanish colonial model in which the politics of conquest laid the groundwork for evangelization. An array of observers around the globe commented on this mission model: Spanish clergymen discussing Morisco parishes in Spain, anti-Christian Buddhist monks in Japan, Protestant polemicists in Europe, pirate-merchants in England, Puritan preachers in New England, and missionaries in the Philippines, each in their own cultural contexts and varied relations to the Spanish Empire, projected their admiration, condemnation, and rejection. This mission system, raised by Mesoamerican peoples and then exported to frontiers near and far, epitomized an era of Spanish colonization.

In Manila, Salazar acknowledged the visible successes of the Mexican mission. The mendicants' alliances with the Crown and native lords had allowed them to rapidly baptize native populations and build a visible mission Church. Yet such obvious accomplishments masked the mission's shortcomings. The source of the problem, Salazar declared, lay with the missionaries themselves, not native populations. The very density of indigenous societies in central Mexico tempted the three mendicant Orders to act as colonizers instead of apostles, fiercely competing for territory to the

---

[2] Hanke, *Cuerpo de documentos*, xlvi; Alberto Carrillo Cázares, ed., *Manuscritos del concilio tercero* (Zamora, Michoacán: El Colegio de Michoacán, 2006), vol. I, 363.

[3] Carrillo Cázares, ibid., 363, 365.

detriment of their pastoral duties. As they jockeyed to best their rivals, the Orders would entrust "a single friar or two in charge of ten or even twelve thousand Indians ... solely to promote themselves."[4] This left the Orders overstretched. Unable to attend to "innumerable Indians," they delegated their spiritual duties to indigenous deputies. By all appearances, Salazar admitted, the result was a visible, functioning mission Church: "The fiscal baptizes, cantores sing the hours each day, and Indians get rounded up to attend mass."[5] But Salazar warned against the temptation of equating such external signs of adherence with internal faith. In a similar vein, Fray Bernardino de Sahagún declared that although New Spain was "the most populated and promising part of the West Indies ... in terms of faith it is sterile soil, in which the Catholic faith has set very weak roots." Like a delicate plant, the Mexican mission could fade as quickly as it grew: "It seems to me that the Catholic faith shall persevere only for a short while in these parts."[6]

Disillusion with Mexico led missionaries like Salazar to look westward across the Pacific towards Asia. The Spanish conquests of the Philippines that commenced in 1565 attracted missionaries to Acapulco for the transpacific crossing.[7] The prospect of reaching China from the Philippines led missionaries to reimagine the Mexican mission in a global context and use its lessons for even greater spiritual victories. Even Sahagún, who dedicated his life to studying Mexico, saw New Spain as a mere stepping-stone on the way to China: a civilization of "where the people are extremely able, have excellent public order (*policía*), and great knowledge." By Sahagún's reckoning, the Caribbean, Mexico, and Peru had the sole purpose of garnering experience to one day "engage those peoples of China."[8] Missionaries held out hope that a "richer vineyard" of souls, far surpassing that of Mexico, awaited harvest in Asia. After arriving in Manila, missionary veterans of Mexico made feverish plots to convert China, dreams as far fetched as those of conquistadors who dreamed of conquering the Middle Kingdom. The Augustinian Fray Martín de Rada, a veteran of the Mexican mission who took passage to the Philippines, saw China as the next Mexico: "Through God's aid, easily and with not many people, [the Chinese] will be subjected."[9] Mexican mission experience seemed to provide lessons for the imminent conversion of Asia.

---

[4] ibid., 366.   [5] ibid.   [6] Sahagún, *Historia general*, vol. II, 811.
[7] Crewe, "Pacific Purgatory," 337–65.   [8] Sahagún, *Historia general*, 813.
[9] Martín de Rada to Viceroy of Mexico (1569), AGI Filipinas, 79, n. 1, f. 2r; Manuel Ollé, *La empresa de China* (Madrid, 2002).

Salazar was among these veterans of Mexico who intended to reach China. Indeed, with not a little presumption he called himself "Bishop of the Philippines and of China." Yet while he waited for the door to open, he focused his attention on the mission enterprise in the Philippines. Contrary to Salazar's fervent hopes to correct the mistakes of the Mexican mission, the Philippine mission had come to epitomize it. In the words of the Fray Juan Grijalva, the chronicler of the Augustinians of Mexico, the Philippine mission emulated "the Republics of Indians in New Spain ... it was planted, cultivated, and preserved in imitation of the Church in Mexico."[10] Amid the depredations of conquest, friars baptized thousands en masse, sequestered native elite children, established doctrinas in native governments (*barangays*), and exploited indigenous labor drafts (*polos*) to provide for the missionaries' sustenance. The same labor systems also built a network of imposing churches similar to those of the sixteenth-century Mexican mission.[11] As in Mexico, the mission in the Philippines secured native polities while at the same time consolidating a vital foothold for Spanish sovereignty over the archipelago.[12]

Yet the very way by which the mission was unabashedly linked to Spanish temporal conquests quickly turned out to be a liability for Spanish designs in Asia. Spanish missionaries did not abandon the techniques that had brought them rapid results in Mexico. On the contrary: American experience led them to continue with their aggressive approach, which increasingly contrasted with the Portuguese emphasis on *accommodatio* (cultural accommodation), a pragmatic strategy that minimized religious-cultural confrontations in areas where non-Christian rulers held sway.[13] Spanish provocations, together with news of their mission's central role in the conquests of America and the Philippines, presented a dire warning to observers in Japan and China about the threat that missionaries posed to their sovereignty. Most infamously, Spanish Franciscans, including veterans of the Mexican mission, were crucified in

[10] Grijalva, *Crónica*, 365.
[11] Morga, *Sucesos*, 279; Petition, Salazar (1585), *Cartas de Indias*, vol. II, 647–8.
[12] Francisco de Ortega to Philip II (1591), AGI Filipinas, 79, n. 22, f. 6v; Morga, *Sucesos*, 272–3; Luís Alonso Álvarez, "Los señores del *Barangay*: La principalía indígena en las islas Filipinas, 1565–1789," in *El cacicazgo en Nueva España y Filipinas*, eds. Margarita Menegus and Rodolfo Aguirre (Mexico City, 2005), 387–90.
[13] David Lach, *Asia in the Making of Europe* (Chicago, 1996), vol. I, 234–60, 293–300; Liam Matthew Brockey, *The Visitor: Andre Palmeiro and the Jesuits in Asia* (Cambridge, 2014), 18, 283; Joan-Pau Rubiés, *Travel and Ethnology in the Renaissance: South India through European Eyes, 1250–1600* (Cambridge, 2000), 314–25; Županov, *Disputed Mission*.

Japan after the Shōgun had allegedly heard that missionaries were responsible for bringing Mexico, Peru, and the Philippines under the sway of the Spanish crown. A Buddhist monk named Fabian Fucan, a former convert turned anti-Christian polemicist, singled out Spanish missionaries who arrived from Luzon in a treatise titled "Deus Destroyed" (*Ha Daiusu*) for their "ambition to diffuse the faith" had the ulterior goal of "subverting" Japanese sovereignty and "usurping the country." Fucan specifically referred to the conquests of "Nova Hispania and Luzon" as evidence.[14] Similarly, an anonymous Japanese anti-Christian tract around the same time warned that the Spanish mission was "a plot to take over the country without a battle fought... Right before our eyes, in Luzon and Nova Hispania, the King of South Barbary has installed his own governors... In sum, the plot consists of the design to spread religion."[15] In Beijing, meanwhile, a courtesan denounced Spanish missionaries for employing "resourceful schemes ... [to subdue] over thirty countries," including nearby Luzon.[16] And in Fujian Province, a novelist familiar with Manila attributed Spanish colonization to the missionaries' abilities to manipulate natives: "to guard the country they lack military potential; they only rely on padres."[17] The shores of East Asia thus marked the terminus of the long journey of sixteenth-century Spanish Christian universalism: it was the site where the tropics of conversion led not to a multitude of converted souls but to humiliations, limitations, and sometimes martyrdom. Instead of providing a key to spiritual and temporal victories in Asia, Mexican mission experience instead guaranteed defeat.

On Mexico's Atlantic frontier, however, the same mission institutions that Salazar criticized and Fucan vituperated were precisely what churchmen back in the metropolis still hoped to build among the Moriscos, the descendants of those who had converted to Christianity out of duress in 1500 in Granada, and in Valencia in the 1520s and 1530s. While the mission enterprise expanded rapidly in Mexico, doctrinal institutions

[14] Fabián Fucán, *Ha Daiusu* (1620), in George Elison, *Deus Destroyed: The Image of Christianity in Early Modern Japan* (Cambridge: Cambridge University Press, 1988), 283–4. Morga, *Sucesos*, 74.

[15] *Kirishitan monogatari* (1639), in Elison, *Deus Destroyed*, 355.

[16] Kenneth Ch'en, "Matteo Ricci's Contribution to, and Influence on, Geographical Knowledge in China," *Journal of the American Oriental Society*, vol. 59 (1939), 349.

[17] Risheng Jiang, *Taiwan waizhi*, in W. I. Idema, "Cannon, Clocks, and Clever Monkeys: Europeana, Europeans, and Europe in Some Early Ch'ing Novels," in E. B. Vermeer, *Development and Decline of Fukien Province in the 17th and 18th Centuries* (Leiden, 1990), 477–8; Menegon, *Ancestors, Virgins, and Friars*, 39–40.

among Moriscos languished for decades. Decades after the Moriscos' mass baptisms, barely any churches had been built, no native algua- ciles yet policed the faith, and doctrinal schools flailed.[18] The empire, it appeared, was neglecting the neophytes in its own metropole. Having heard news of advances in missions throughout the world, *juntas* (special councils) discussed ways to redirect lessons learned overseas back to this domestic mission frontier.[19] The divergence between the Mexican and Morisco missions could not have been starker: a network of over two hundred structures spanned the highlands of Central Mexico, while in Spain consensus could not be reached to build a few dozen churches, much less set up Arabic studies for potential missionaries. Yet Salazar's doubts, which sprung from the questionable motives behind the mass baptisms, could never be exorcised: not from Spain, and not from Mexico.[20] Both Moriscos and Indians shared the dubious honor of a neophyte status that placed the sincerity of their faith eternally in doubt. Just as Salazar declared that the spiritual conversion of Mexican Indians had been corrupted by the politics of conquest, so two Moriscos, with some audacity, likewise admitted to the viceroy of Aragon in 1589: "It is true that the Moriscos of Aragon were baptized with violence, without the freedom that is so necessary for this sacrament."[21] While in Mexico these lingering doubts led clergymen to argue that the process of indoctrination would require generations, however, in Spain initial gradualism towards the Moriscos gave way to systematic persecution and ultimately rejec- tion.[22] In 1609, Philip III decreed the expulsion of the Moriscos from Spain, an act that consigned tens of thousands of baptized Christians to uncertain fates in the Maghreb.

While Spaniards had failed to build an effective mission at home, the material splendor and worldly power of the Mexican mission epitomized Spanish imperial goals. Defenders and promoters situated the Mexican

---

[18] Junta on Moriscos in Valencia (1595), BNE ms. 10388, ff. 94r–6v, 108r, 110r, 122r, 126r.

[19] Bernard Vincent and Antonio Domínguez Ortiz, *Historia de los moriscos: Vida y tragedia de una minoría* (Madrid: Editorial Revista de Occidente, 1978), 170. AHN Consejos, leg. 2220, ff. 22v–4v; BNE ms. 10388, f. 129r.

[20] Diego Durán, *Historia de las Indias de Nueva España e Islas de Tierra Firme*, eds. Rosa Camelo and José Rubén Romero (Mexico City: Conaculta, 2002), 13–16; García Icaz- balceta, *Códice Mendieta*, 11–12, 25.

[21] Viceroy of Aragon, meeting with two moriscos (1589), BNE ms. 10388, f. 75r–v.

[22] José María Perceval, José María. *Todos son uno: Arquetipos, xenofobia y racismo: La imagen del morisco en la Monarquía Española durante los siglos XVI y XVII* (Almería: Instituto de Estudios Almerienses, 1997).

mission in the context of the confessional geopolitics of Europe. The Franciscan missionary-chronicler Gerónimo de Mendieta, for example, declared that the conversion of Mexico was a divine act of compensation for the loss of Northern Europe to the Protestant Reformation. Likewise, in an Augustinian chronicle published in 1569, an appendix juxtaposed a list of monasteries destroyed in Tudor England next to those that simultaneously rose in Mexico.[23] Subjects and allies of the Catholic Monarchy cited Mexico as an example of how the spiritual end justified the often-unpleasant means. In Italy, Tommaso Campanella declared in his utopian work *La città del sole* that Spanish conquests had a divine purpose of unifying the world under one law, even if avarice drove imperial expansion more than virtue. Campanella granted that abuses abounded, but this was merely an example of the fact that "we do not know what we are really doing, but we are instruments of God ... who has a higher plan." Cortés, after all, had committed acts of war but still "promulgated Christianity." Another Italian intellectual, Tommaso Porcacchi, rejoiced that Spanish arms had reduced the barbarous Aztecs to the gentle yoke of Christianity.[24]

On the opposite side of the Wars of Religion, however, the same structure that had won a new world for Catholicism attracted the jealousy and opprobrium of Spain's Protestant rivals. In seventeenth-century New England, Puritan ministers Cotton Mather and Samuel Sewall recognized Mexico's prominence as a Catholic kingdom and even dreamed rather whimsically of conquering it for Protestantism. To this end, Mather learned Spanish and published a brief Puritan catechism to "irradiate ... the dark recesses of America" with "the Pure Religion." Samuel Sewall predicted to Elisha Williams, Rector of Yale College, that the New Jerusalem would one day be raised on a "high mountain" by Protestants in Mexico, where indigenous "royalties" – he uses the Algonquian term *sachem* – would herald the end-times upon their conversion to true Christianity. Sewall even urged a Carolina preacher to hasten with this conquest: "Methinks your neighborhood should assist you in endeavoring

[23] Mendieta, *Historia eclesiástica indiana*, vol. I, 305. Hieronimo Román, *Chronica de la orden de los ermitaños del glorioso Padre Sancto Agustin, Diuidida en doze centurias* (Salamanca, 1569).
[24] Tommaso Campanella, Adriani Seroni ed. *La città del sole* (Milan: Feltinelli, 2003); Benjamin Keen, *The Aztec Image in Western Thought* (New Brunswick, NJ: Rutgers University Press, 1971), 141–63.

in this way to conquer Mexico."[25] This Puritan scheme to conquer Mexico, of course, proved as delirious as Spanish designs to seize China. In France, meanwhile, the Protestant Urbain Chauveton presaged that the "amicable" French would soon carry out the work of evangelization in the New World "better than the Spanish" because they far excelled their brash neighbors in the arts of persuasion. And in Germany, a Protestant translator of Girolamo Benzoni's work *Historia del Nuovo Mondo* lamented that the Spaniards had not done more to convert the Indians through "love and persuasion."[26] For anti-Catholic and anti-Spanish polemicists, Mexico served a prime example in their efforts to demonstrate the hypocrisy of imposing religion through temporal power.

While most European commentators tended to stay within long-running debates on force versus persuasion in evangelization, at least one European Protestant glimpsed the Mexican mission from an indigenous perspective. Henry Hawkes, an English merchant-*cum*-pirate who had spent five years as a prisoner of the Mexican Inquisition, declared to English cosmographer Richard Hakluyt that "the Indians haue the friers in great reuerence: the occasion, that is, that by them and by their meanes they are free and out of bondage." Hawkes would know: arrested alongside other shipwrecked English mariners for their Protestantism, he was sentenced to serve out his sentence laboring as foreman overseeing natives who built Augustinian monasteries.[27] From his unique vantage point, Hawkes understood that the Mexican mission rested on a promise that the Church would deliver native peoples from servitude.

While the world focused on the ethics of Spanish actions, Mesoamerican peoples fashioned the mission as a means to remake their world amid threats that could only classified as existential in nature. They engaged the mission enterprise to seek deliverance from turmoil, both temporal and spiritual: it served as their sanctuary from conquest, from enslavement, from losses of property and status, and from countless pressures to cut themselves from their own moorings. As the violence of conquest subsided, Christianity in Mesoamerica became something of a palladium, a safeguard for native polities, communities, and cultures. Yet this native mission of survival and rebuilding also had an unintended effect:

[25] Mukhtar Ali Isani, "The Growth of Sewall's 'Phaenomena Quaedam Apocalyptica,'" *Early American Literature*, vol. 7, no. 1 (1972), 71–2.
[26] Keen, *Aztec Image*, 141–63.
[27] Richard Hakluyt, ed., *The Principal Nauigations* (London, 1600).

by harnessing the mission to reconstitute their communities, they also empowered Spain's claims of sovereignty over their resources, communities, and lives. Sartre concisely defined such contradictions between local agency and global process: "[the] result achieved, when it is placed in the totalizing movement, is radically different from the way it appears locally."[28] It is a vital task for historians of colonial worlds to recover indigenous agency, but equally so to place their actions in broader context in order to understand the complexity of power relations. Indeed, so effective was the indigenous appropriation of the mission to serve their sovereignty and varied interests, that European observers came to marvel at the soaring edifice that they erected from afar, and across the Pacific Ocean, Fabián Fucan in Japan would sound the alarm based on a cursory – but fundamentally accurate – description of how and why it had risen.

Inside these sturdy structures of the Mexican mission, a myriad of vivacious and creative spiritualities arose, most of them falling somewhere between what one might initially define as Christian and Mesoamerican practices and beliefs. Memories of conquest, continued exploitation, ongoing deaths, and a colonial order that set limits to their aspirations fundamentally shaped their varied expressions and sentiments of indigenous Christianities. Their religious practices and beliefs often did not meet the orthodox expectations of doubting men like Salazar. But Mexican natives also disproved their dire predictions that the Church would collapse for lack of righteous Spaniards to guide them. Within the mission, indigenous Christianities drew energy from the determination to overcome the great calamities of the sixteenth century. The immense churches that native communities raised are testaments to this will to endure and transcend. Whatever complaints Spaniards had regarding the Indianness, alleged superficiality, or the hypocrisy of the Mexican mission, it is worth remembering that indigenous communities complained most loudly when they *lacked* a church of their own around which to congregate and rebuild their communities.

As indigenous mortality and Spanish politics stalled and then reversed the expansion of the mission, the enduring structures of the Mexican mission became, in turn, bases from which missionaries traveled onward to new assignments – to Salazar's Philippines and onward to Cambodia,

---

[28] Jean Paul Sartre, *Search for a Method* trans. Hazel E. Barnes (New York: Vintage Books, 1963), 88.

Japan, or China, or up the silver roads into the deserts of Northern Mexico. And as life in the doctrinas settled into patterns more typical of parishes, mendicant and indigenous historians gathered their sources and began to write their histories – to defend what their ancestors and predecessors had built in a seemingly distant time, in admiration of their colossal efforts to remake their world.

APPENDICES

The following data support the statistics that I provide on church construction and *doctrina* foundations in the text. This is the first data set on sixteenth-century mission activity to drawn from archival sources. The sources consist of viceregal orderbooks and trials held at the AGN, and treasury records (ramo Contaduría) at the AGI. I then cross-referenced these archival sources with the statistics provided by Ricard, Kubler, and Van Oss, which were based entirely on printed primary sources. The result is a revision of their statistics for *doctrina* foundations and church construction campaigns. In particular, the archival data has substantially revised statistics on church construction, as can be seen in Appendix 2.

Appendix 1. Foundations of *Doctrinas* by Decade

The foundation of a *doctrina* was a vital political event. Each *doctrina* foundation was the outcome of the consolidation of alliances between local rulers and mendicant friars, and it represented the attainment of autonomy for indigenous polities. The following table and list is a register of mendicant *doctrina* foundations, drawn from Kubler, Van Oss, Ricard, and Gerhard. These authors gleaned foundation dates from chronicles, correspondence, and *relaciones geográficas*. In addition, I have added several *doctrina* foundations based on accounting records in the *ramo* Contaduría at the AGI, which registered viceregal outlays for chalices for all newly founded *doctrinas*.

MENDICANT DOCTRINA FOUNDATIONS

APPENDIX TABLE A1.1 Doctrina *foundations by decade*

	1520s	1530s	1540s	1550s	1560s	1570s	1580s	1590s	16th c.
Franciscans	19	24	25	31	19	11	10	2	141
Dominicans	5	7	8	22	6	3	2	0	53
Augustinians	0	17	12	27	5	13	4	5	83
Total	24	48	45	80	30	27	16	7	277

Franciscans

1520–1529
Coatepec, Chalco, Coatlinchan, Cuautitlán, Cuernavaca, Huexotzingo, Huexotla, Mexico City, Otumba, Tepeaca, Tepeapulco, Texcoco, Tlaxcala, Toluca, Tula, Tulancingo, Veracruz, Patzcuaro, Tzintzuntzán

1530–1539

Acambaro, Ajijic, Amacueca, Atotonilco, Cholula, Cinapécuaro, Etzatlan, Guadalajara, Huaquechula, Huichapan, Izatlan, Jilotepec, Puebla, Tehuacan, Teúl, Tlahuac, Tlalmanalco, Tlatelolco, Tuxpa, Uruapan, Xalapa, Xochimilco, Zacapu, Zapotlán

1540–1549

Atrisco, Autlán, Calpan, Chapala, Chietla, Hueytlalpan, Ixtacamaxtitlán, Jalacingo, Jalisco, Jiquilpan, Juchilpila, Periban, Poncitlán, Quecholac, San Miguel Allende, Tacuba, Tamazula, Tarecuato, Tecamachalco, Teotitlán, Tlaquiltenango, Tochimilco, Valladolid, Zacatlán, Zongolica

1550–1559

Acapetlahuaca, Acatlán, Acatzingo, Ahuacatlán, Alfajayucan, Atlihuetzia, Calimaya, Cempoala, Chalco Atenco, Colima, Erongarícuaro, Iztepec, Metepec, Tajimaroa, Tampico, Tancítaro, Tecalco, Tecali, Teotihuacan, Tepejí del Río/Otlazpan, Tepexí de la Seda, Tepeyango, Teutlalco, Tlajomulco, Tlalnepantla/Teocalhuacan, Tlatlauhquítepec, Topoyanco, Zacatecas, Zacoalco, Zinacantepec

1560–1569

Apam, Atoyac, Calpulalpan, Chiautempan, Chiauhtenpan, Cocula, Ecatepec, Huamantla, Milpa Alta, Nombre de Dios, Querétaro, San Felipe Cuixtlan, Santa Ana, Sayula, Sentispac, Tequemecan, Teutitlán, Totimehuacan, Tultitlán

1570–1579

Apaseo, Atlancatepec, Celaya, Huayanamota, Hueyotlipa, Nativitas, Techaluta, Tepetillan, Totolan, Xiutepec, Zapotitlán

1580–1589

Amozoc, Cherapan, Chiauhtla, Pichataro, Purenchecuaro, San Felipe, Tecomitl, Tolimán, Xichu, Zitacuaro

1590–1599

Tecualtipan, Pachuca

Dominicans

1520–1529

Coyoacan, Chimalhuacan Chalco, Mexico City, Oaxaca, Oaxtepec

1530–1539

Amacueca, Etla, Izúcar, Puebla, Tepelaztoc, Teposcolula, Yanhuitlán

1540–1549

Chimalhuacan Atenco, Coatlán, Coixtlahuaca, Guamelula, Tehuante-pec, Tlaxiaco, Villa Alta, Yautepec
1550–1559
Achiutla, Atzcapotzalco, Cuilapan, Chichicapa, Chila, Guaxolotitlán, Huitzo, Jalapa, Justlahuaca, Nejapa, Ocotlán, Santi Afonso, Tama-zulapa, Tecomastlahuacan, Tenango Chalco, Tepapayeca, Tepoz-tlán, Tetela del Volcán, Teticpac, Tlacochahuaya, Tláhuac, Tonalá
1560–1569
Coatepec Chalco, Hueyapan, Jantetelco, Miahuatlán, Nochistlán, Texupa
1570–1579
Xaltepec, Tacubaya, Tilantongo
1580–1589
Almoloyas, Juquila

Augustinians

1530–1539
Atotonilco el Grande, Chapulhuacan, Chilapa, Lolotla, Mextitlán, Mexico City, Mixquic, Molango, Ocuilan, Ocuituco, Santa Fe, Tacám-baro, Tiripitío, Tlapa, Totolapan, Yecpixtla, Zacualpan Amilpas
1540–1549
Acolmán, Actopan, Epazoyucan, Huachinango, Huejutla, Malinalco, Tempoal, Tepecoacuilco, Tlanchinol, Yecapixtla, Zagualpa, Zempoala
1550–1559
Acatlán, Culhuacan, Charo, Chiautla, Copándaro, Cuitzeo, Huacana, Huango, Huayacocotla, Ixmiquilpan, Jacona, Jonacatepec, Jumilte-pec, Pahuatlán, Pánuco, Pátzcuaro, Tantoyuca, Tezontepec, Tlayaca-pan, Tlazazalca, Tutotepec, Ucareo, Xilitla, Ximultepeque, Xixicastla, Yuririapúndaro, Zultepec
1560–1569
Ajacuba, Chapatongo, Chietla, Huatlatlauca, Jantetelco
1570–1579
Alcozauca, Atlatlauca, Chucándiro, Guadalajara, Oaxaca, Ocotlán, Pueba, San Felipe, Singuilucan, Tzirosto, Xochicoatlán, Zacatecas, Zacualtipan
1580–1589
Atlixco, Ayotzingo, Tingambato, Tlacuilotepec
1590–1599
Parangaricutiro, San Felipe, San Luís Potosí, Undameo, Zacualpa

Appendix 2. Monastery Construction Campaigns by Decade

The following is a register of monastery construction activity in New Spain during the sixteenth century. Following Kubler, who registered building activity by tracking references in printed chronicles, letters, and indigenous annals, I did the same in the archival records of the AGN and AGI. Most indicators of building activity in archival records consist of funding requests and outlays, as registed by the viceregal chancellery. Other indicators of activity include funding for bells (indicators of a church at or near completion), disputes regarding labor or building materials, and viceregal licenses to initiate construction.

CONSTRUCTION CAMPAIGNS BY DECADE

[*]   = New construction. All other entries are ongoing projects or major repairs.

Italics = My revision of Kubler and Van Oss, based on archival records. All entries in standard font can be found in Kubler and Van Oss, and are based on published primary sources.

APPENDIX TABLE A2.1. *Monasteries under construction*

	1520s	1530s	1540s	1550s	1560s	1570s	1580s	1590s
Franciscans	5	26	23	48	35	37	26	11
Dominicans	1	3	5	26	20	20	7	8
Augustinians	0	6	18	45	27	17	5	5
Total	6	35	46	119	82	74	38	24

APPENDIX TABLE A2.2.   *New and ongoing construction projects by decade*

	1520s	1530s	1540s	1550s	1560s	1570s	1580s	1590s
New	6	32	39	77	29	43	19	6
Ongoing	0	3	7	42	53	31	19	18

1520s

OFM: *Coatepec Chalco, *Mexico City, *Tezcoco, *Tláhuac, *Tlaxcala

OP: *Mexico City

1530s

OFM: *Acámbaro, *Ajijic, Coatepec Chalco, *Cuautitlán, *Cuernavaca, *San Gabriel Cholula, *Churubusco, *Etzatlán, *Guadalajara, *Huaquechula, *Huexotzingo, *Jalapa, *Milpa Alta, *Nativitas, *Puebla, *Tepeaca, *Tepeapulco, *Teul, *Tlalmanalco, *Tlatelolco, Tlaxcala, *Tula, *Tulancingo, *Tztintzuntzán, *Xochimilco, *Zapotlán

OP: Mexico, *Oaxaca, *Tepetlaoztoc

OSA: *Chilapa, *Lolotla, *Ocuituco, *Tacámbaro, *Tiripitío, *Totolapa

1540s

OFM: *Amacueca, *Atlixco, *Autlán, *Calpan, *Chapala, *Chietla,[1] *Guadalajara, Huexotzingo, *Hueytlalpan, Mexico, *Cuixtlán, *Tacuba,[2] *Tamazula,[3] *Tecamachalco, Tepeaca, *Tlaquiltenango,[4] *Tochimilco, Tula, Xochimilco, *Morelia, *Tarecuato, *Zacapu, *Zacatlán[5]

OP: *Amecameca, *Chimalhuacan Chalco, *Coixtlahuaca,[6] *Coyoacán, *Teposcolula

OSA: *Acolmán, *Atotonilco el Grande, *Ayotzingo, *Chapulhuacan, *Huejutla,[7] *Malinalco, *Metztitlán, *Mexico, *Molango, *Morelia, *Ocuilan, *Singuilucan, Tacámbaro, *Tepecuacuilco,[8] Tiripitío, Totolapa, *Yecapixtla, *Yurirapúndaro[9]

---

[1] AGN Civil, vol. 1271, ff. 190v- 191v (1540, 1548).   [2] AGI Contaduría, 661 (1547).
[3] AGN Mercedes, vol. 1, f. 112r (1542).   [4] AGN Tierras, vol. 1979, f. 143r-v (1546).
[5] AGI Contaduría, 661 (1544).
[6] AGN Mercedes, 3, f. 189v (1550): "a mucho tiempo que está comenzado y lo que está fecho se cae e deshace." AGI Contaduría, 661 (1549).
[7] AGI Contaduría, 661 (1547).   [8] AGI Contaduría, 661 (1547).
[9] AGN Mercedes, vol. 3, f. 87v (1550, construction in progress).

1550s

OFM: *Acapetlahuacan,[10] *Acatzingo,[11] *Ahuacatlán, *Anapecora,[12] *Atlihuetzia,[13] *Calimaya, *Cempoala,[14] Chietla,[15] *Cinepécuaro,[16] *Colima, Cuernavaca, Cholula, Huaquechula, Huexotzingo, *Hueychiapan,[17] *Izatlán,[18] *Jala, Jalapa,[19] Mexico, *Pátzcuaro, *Peribán, *Quecholac, *Querétaro, Tacuba,[20] *Tampico,[21] *Tecalco,[22] *Tecali,[23]Tecamachalco, *Teotitlán, Tepeaca, Tepeapulco, *Tepexí del Río/Otlazpan,[24]Tepexique,[25] *Tepeyango,[26] Teutlalco,[27] Tláhuac, Tlalmanalco, *Tlalnepantla,[28] *Tlatlauhquitepec,[29] Tlaxcala,[30] Tochimilco,[31] *Topoyanco,[32] Tula, *Xalacingo,[33] *Xochimilco,[34] *Zacapu,[35] *Zacatlán, *Zongolica[36]

OP: Amecameca, *Chila,[37] Chimalhuacan Chalco,[38] *Coatlán[39], Coyoacán,[40] Coixtlahuaca,[41] *Guamelula,[42]*Guaxolotitlán,[43] *Iztepec,[44] *Izúcar,[45] México, *Nexapa,[46] *Oaxtepec,[47] *Ocotlán,[48] *Sant Ilifonso,[49] *Tehuantepec, *Tepapayeca,[50] Tepetlaoztoc,

---

[10] AGN Mercedes, vol. 3, f. 123r (1550); AGI Contaduría, 661 (1550, 1552); AGI Contaduría, 663B (1553, 1554, 1556); AGI Contaduría, 664 (1557).
[11] AGI Contaduría, 664 (1557).   [12] AGN Mercedes, vol. 4, parte 2, f. 324r (1556).
[13] AGI Contaduría, 663B (1554); AGI Contaduría, 664 (1557).
[14] AGI Contaduría, 664 (1558).   [15] AGN Mercedes, vol. 3, f. 175v (1550).
[16] AGI Contaduría, 664 (1557).   [17] AGI Contaduría, 664 (1559).   [18] Ayer, f. 304.
[19] Ayer, f. 282.   [20] AGI Contaduría, 663B (1553,1556).
[21] AGI Contaduría, 664 (1559).   [22] AGN Mercedes, vol. 4, f. 305r (1556).
[23] AGI Contaduría, 663B (1556).   [24] AGI Contaduría, 664 (1558).
[25] AGN Mercedes, vol. 3, f. 65r (1550).   [26] AGI Contaduría, 664 (1557).
[27] Ayer, f. 52.   [28] AGI Contaduría, 663B (1555).   [29] AGI Contaduría, 663B (1555).
[30] AGN Mercedes, vol. 4, f. 75r (1554).   [31] AGN Mercedes, vol. 4, f. 375r (1556).
[32] AGN Mercedes, vol. 4, f. 166r (1555).
[33] AGN Mercedes, vol. 3, f. 65r (1550); AGI Contaduría, 663B (1556).
[34] AGN Mercedes, vol. 4, f. 52v (1554); AGI Contaduría, 663B (1556).
[35] AGN Mercedes, vol. 4, f. 341r (1556); AGI Contaduría, 664 (1558).
[36] AGN Mercedes, vol. 4, f. 299v (1556).
[37] AGN Mercedes, vol. 4, f. 305r (1556); AGI Contaduría, 663B (1555, 1556); AGI Contaduría, 664 (1557,1558).
[38] AGI Contaduría, 664 (1557, 1558, 1559).   [39] AGI Contaduría, 664 (1558).
[40] AGI Contaduría, 661 (1552).
[41] AGI Contaduría, 661 (1551); AGI Contaduría 663B (1555).
[42] AGI Contaduría, 664 (1558).   [43] AGI Contaduría, 664 (1559).
[44] AGI Contaduría, 664 (1558).
[45] AGI Contaduría, 661 (1551, 1552); AGI Contaduría 664 (1557, 1558, 1559).
[46] AGN Mercedes, tomo 4, f. 234r (1555); AGI Contaduría, 663B (1556).
[47] AGI Contaduría, 663B (1555); AGI Contaduría, 664 (1557).
[48] AGN Mercedes, vol. 4, f. 324r (1556).   [49] AGI Contaduría, 664 (1559).
[50] AGI Contaduría, 661 (1551); AGI Contaduría, 663B (1553); AGI Contaduría, 664, (1557).

Teposcolula,[51] *Tlaxiaco, *Tonalá, *Villa Alta, *Xalapa (Oax.),[52] *Xaltepec, *Yanhuitlán, *Yautepec[53]

OSA: *Acatlán, Acolmán, *Actopan, *Ajuchitlán, Atotonilco,[54] *Cicicastla,[55] *Cuitzeo, *Culhuacán,[56] *Charo, *Chiautla, Chilapa,[57] *Epazoyucan, *Huachinango,[58] *Huango, Huejutla,[59] *Hueyacocotla,[60] *Ixmiquilpan, *Jacona,[61] Malinalco,[62] Meztitlán, Mexico, Molango,[63] *Morelia, Ocuila,[64] Ocuituco,[65] *Pahuatlán,[66] *Pánuco, *Pungarabato, Tacámbaro,[67] Tepecuacuilco,[68] *Tezontepec, Tiripitío,[69] *Tlanchinol,[70] Tlapa,[71] *Tlayacapan, *Tlazazalca, Totolapa,[72] *Tututepec,[73] *Ucareo, Yuriripúndaro, *Xilitla,[74] *Xumiltepec,[75] Yecapixtla,[76] *Zacualpan, *Zultepec[77]

1560s

OFM: Acatlán,[78] Acatzingo, *Alfajayucan, Amacueca,[79] Atlihuetzia,[80] Atlixco, *Atoyac, Cempoala,[81] *Chamacuero, Colima,[82] *Cuautinchán, *Erongarícuaro, *Huamantla,[83] Huexotzingo, *Ixtacmaxtitlán, *Nombre de Dios, *San Felipe, Puebla, Tacuba, *Tajimaroa,

---

[51] AGI Contaduría, 664 (1557, 1559).   [52] AGN Mercedes, vol. 4, f. 138r (1554).
[53] AGI Contaduría, 664 (1557).
[54] AGI Contaduría, 661 (1552); AGI Contaduría, 664 (1557, 1559).
[55] AGI Contaduría, 663B (1555).
[56] AGI Contaduría, 663B (1553, 1555, 1556); AGI Contaduría, 664 (1558, 1559).
[57] AGI Contaduría, 663B (1553); AGI Contaduría, 664 (1558).
[58] AGI Contaduría, 661 (1552).   [59] AGI Contaduría, 663B (1556).
[60] AGI Contaduría, 664 (1558).
[61] AGI Contaduría, 663B (1555); AGI Contaduría, (1559).
[62] AGI Contaduría, 661 (1552); AGI Contaduría, 664 (1558).
[63] AGI Contaduría, 661 (1553); AGI Contaduría, 664 (1559).
[64] AGN Mercedes, vol. 3, f. 215r (1550); AGI Contaduría, 661 (1552); AGI Contaduría, 664 (1558).
[65] AGI Contaduría, 663B (1553).
[66] AGI Contaduría, 663B (1555); AGI Contaduría, 664 (1557, 1559).
[67] AGI Contaduría 663B (1553, 1555); AGI Contaduría, 664 (1557, 1558).
[68] AGI Contaduría, 661 (1552); AGI Contaduría, 663B (1556).   [69] Ayer, f. 194v.
[70] AGI Contaduría, 663B (1555); AGI Contaduría, 664 (1557)   [71] Ayer, f. 192.
[72] AGI Contaduría, 661 (1552); AGI Contaduría, 663B (1555); AGI Contaduría, 664 (1557).
[73] AGI Contaduría, 664 (1558)
[74] AGI Contaduría, 661 (1552); AGI Contaduría, 664 (1558).
[75] AGI Contaduría, 664 (1559).   [76] AGI Contaduría, 661 (1552).
[77] AGI Contaduría, 664 (1557).
[78] AGI Contaduría, 671A (1567); AGI Contaduría, 675 (1569).
[79] AGI Contaduría, 664 (1560).   [80] AGN Mercedes, vol. 7, f. 92v (1563).
[81] AGI Contaduría, 671A (1567); AGI Contaduría, 675 (1569).
[82] AGI Contaduría, 664 (1560).   [83] Martínez Baracs, *Un gobierno de indios*, 232.

Tecalco,[84] Tecali, Tepeaca, Tepeapulco, *Teutitlán,*[85] Tláhuac, Tlalmanalco, *Tlalnepantla,*[86] *Tlaquiltenango,*[87] Tochimilco, Tultitlán,
*Uruapan, Zacatlán, Zacoalco, Zinacantepec

OP: Amecameca, *Azcapotzalco,*[88] Chimalhuacan Chalco, *Cuila-
pan, *Ecatepec,*[89] *Guaxolotitlán,*[90] México, *Miahuatlán, *Nejapa,
Oaxtepec, *Ocotlán, *Puebla, *Tacubaya, *Teposcolula,*[91] *Tetela,*[92]
Teticpac,[93] *Texupa,*[94] *Tonalá,*[95] Yanhuitlán, Yautepec

OSA: Acolmán, *Copándaro, *Chietla, *Chiauhtla,*[96] *Cuitzeo,*[97] Epazoyucan, *Huatlatlauca, Huejutla, *Ixmiquilpan,*[98] Jacona, *Jonacatepec, Malinalco, *Matalcingo,*[99] México, *Mizquic,*[100] *Molango,*[101]
Ocuilan, *Ocuituco,*[102] Pahuatlán, Tacámbaro, *Tantoyuca, Tlanchinol, Tlayacapan, *Totolapa,*[103] Ucareo,[104] Yuriria, *Zacualpa,*[105]

1570S

OFM: Acatzingo, Alfajayucan, Amacueca, *Apan,*[106] *Apaseo,
*Atlancatepec, *Cherapan, *Chiautla (Texcoco), Cholula, *Cocula,
Cuautinchán, *Coatlinchán, Ecatepec, *Erongarícuaro,*[107] *Huay-
namota, *Huexotzingo,*[108] Jalapa (Veracruz), Pátzcuaro, Puebla,
*Sayula, *Sentispac, *Tancítaro, *Tecali, *Techaluta, *Tecómitl,
*Tehuacán, *Teotihuacán, *Tepetitlán, *Tepexí del Río,*[109] Texcoco,
*Tlajomulco, *Tlalnepantla,*[110] Tulancingo, Tultitlán, *Xiutepec,
*Zempoala, *Zitácuaro

[84] AGN Mercedes, vol. 6, f. 567r (1563).   [85] AGI Contaduría, 664 (1560).
[86] AGN Mercedes, vol. 6, f. 310v (1563).
[87] AGN Tierras, vol. 1979, exp. 4, ff. 140v–142v (1563).
[88] AGN Mercedes, vol. 8, f. 212v (1565); AGN Mercedes, vol. 8, f. 236r (1566).
[89] AGN Mercedes, vol. 6, f. 566 (1563).   [90] AGN Mercedes, vol. 6, f. 560 (1563).
[91] AGI Contaduría, 675 (1569).
[92] AGN Mercedes, vol. 5, f. 289v (1561); AGI Contaduría 675 (1569).
[93] AGI Contaduría, 675 (1569).
[94] AGI Contaduría, 671A (1566); AGI Contaduría 675 (1569).
[95] AGI Contaduría, 671A (1566).   [96] AGI Contaduría, 664 (1560).
[97] Rubial García, *El convento agustino, table XVI.*
[98] AGN Mercedes, vol. 8, f. 139r (1565).   [99] AGN Mercedes, vol. 8, f. 92v (1565).
[100] Rubial García, *El convento agustino, table XVI.*   [101] AGI Contaduría, 671A (1567).
[102] AGI Contaduría, 671A (1566).   [103] Rubial García, *El convento agustino, table XVI.*
[104] AGN Mercedes, tomo 5, f. 261r (1561).   [105] AGI Contaduría, 675 (1569).
[106] AGN General de Parte, vol. 1, f. 38r (1575); AGN General de Parte, vol. 1,
f. 44v (1575).
[107] AGN General de Parte, vol. 1, f. 156r–156v; General de Parte, vol. 2, f. 51r (1576);
AGN Tierras, vol. 2737, ff. 324r–6v (1576).
[108] AGI Contaduría, 675 (1571).   [109] AGI Contaduría, 675 (1571).
[110] AGI Contaduría, 675 (1571).

OP: *Achiutla, *Amecameca,*[111] *Atzcapotzalco, *Chila, Coyoacán, Cuilapan, *Etla, *Hueyapan, *Iztepec,*[112] México, Oaxaca, Oaxtepec, *Tenango Chalco, Teposcolula, *Tepoztlán, *Tetela del Volcán, *Texupa,*[113] *Tilantongo, Yanhuitlán, *Yautepec

OSA: *Alcozauca, *Atlatlauhca, Culhuacán, *Chapatongo, *Ixmiquilpan,*[114] Mexico, *Ocotlán (Nueva Gal.), *Pátzcuaro, *Puebla, Tlapa,[115] *Tonalá, *Totolapa,*[116] *Tzirosto,[117] *Xochicoatlán, *Zacatecas, *Zacualpa,*[118] *Zacualtipán

1580s

OFM: Acatzingo, Alfajayucan, *Amozoc, Apan, *Calpulalpan, *Huamantla, *Huichapan, México, Tehuacán, Tlalmanalco, *Tlalnepantla, *Totimehuacán, *Xichu, Xochimilco, *Celaya, *Chucándiro, Morelia, *Purenchécuaro, *Tarímbaro, *Tolimán, Zacapu, Colima, *Tamazula, Tlajomulco, *Tuxpa, *Zapotitlán

OP: Achiutla, Azcapotzalco, Coixtlahuaca, Cuilapan, *Huitzo, Tepoztlán, *Tlacochahuaya

OSA: *Atlixtac, Atotonilco el Grande, México, *Oaxaca, Puebla

1590s

OFM: *Calimaya,*[119] *Jilotepec, México, *Pachuca, Tepeaca, Tlaxcala, Xochimilco, Zacatlán, Tzintzuntzán, Jala, Zacoalco

OP: *Almoloyas, Coyoacán, *Ecatzingo,*[120] *Jantetelco,*[121] Etla, Oaxaca, Puebla, Tacubaya

OSA: *Axacuba,*[122] Cuitzeo, *Zirosto,*[123] *Undameo, *Zacualpa

---

[111] AGI Contaduría, 675 (1571).   [112] AGI Contaduría, 675 (1572).
[113] AGI Contaduría, 675 (1571).   [114] AGI Contaduría, 675 (1570).
[115] AGN General de Parte, vol. 1, f. 141v (1576).   [116] AGI Contaduría, 675 (1571).
[117] AGN General, vol. 1, f. 166r (1575).
[118] Rubial García, *El convento agustino,* table XVI.
[119] AGN Indios, vol. 6, exp. 638, f. 169v (1593).
[120] AGN Indios, vol. 6, exp. 249, f. 63r (1592).
[121] AGN Indios, vol. 5, exp. 157, f. 113v (1591).
[122] AGN Indios, vol. 5, exp. 999, f. 327r (1591).
[123] AGN Indios, vol. 4, exp. 264, f. 90r (1590).

Glossary

Alcalde. A first-instance judge and council member.

Alcalde Mayor. Spanish chief magistrate and administrative official in charge of a district.

Alguacil. A constable. In indigenous polities, see also *topil*.

Alguacil de doctrina. An indigenous constable for the local church.

Altepetl, pl. altepeme. Nahua term for a sovereign local state in Central Mexico, with a recognizable territory and dynastic rulership. Its most visible markers of sovereignty consist of its temple (*teocalli*), ruler's palace (*tecpan*), and market (*tianguis*). The basis for most colonial indigenous municipalities and "*cabeceras*."

Audiencia. High court and governing body; presided over by the viceroy and *oidores*.

Cabecera. An indigenous "head-town" designated by Spaniards.

Cabildo. Municipal council.

Caja de comunidad. Municipal treasury in indigenous polities recognized by Spanish authorities.

Calpolli, pl. calpoltin. Nahua term for a subunit of an *altepetl*.

Cantor. Indigenous choir-members and musicians in local churches.

Cédula. A royal order.

Coatequitl. Indigenous rotary draft labor system, by which calpoltin collectively provide commoner labor for the *altepetl*.

Congregación. Resettlement of indigenous populations with the intention of concentrating them around an urban nucleus.

Corregidor. Chief Spanish judicial and administrative official in a district.

Doctrina. The principal territorial unit of the mission enterprise in sixteenth-century Central New Spain. Denotes the residence of missionaries and the site of a major church serving a large jurisdiction.

Doctrinero. A missionary.

Encomienda. A grant of tribute rendered by Indians in a given area, in exchange for providing for their indoctrination.

Encomendero. The Spanish grantee of an *encomienda*.

Fiscal. The highest-ranking indigenous church official in a *doctrina*.

Gobernador. The highest indigenous office in an indigenous municipality.

Macehual, pl. macehualtin. An indigenous commoner, whose status is characterized particularly by payment of tributes and performing obligatory labor in *coatequitl* drafts.

Mandamiento. A viceregal order.

Milpa. Indigenous term for a plot of land, especially a cornfield.

Oidor. An audiencia judge.

Pilli, pl. pipiltin. An indigenous nobleman. The plural *pipiltin* refers to the noble class.

Principal. Spanish term for a "prominent indigenous person"; a perceived member of the indigenous elite.

Provisor. The highest ecclesiastical judge in a diocese.

Provisor de indios. An assistant to a bishop in indigenous matters.

Pueblo de indios. An indigenous jurisdiction recognized by Spanish law and subjected to Spanish transformative projects in religion, politics, resettlement (*congregación*), and urbanism, to widely varying degrees of success.

Regidor. A council member.

Regular clergy. In this study, the three mendicant orders operating as missionaries in New Spain, independent of standard diocesan hierarchies.

Secular clergy. The ordinary ecclesiastical hierarchy of the Church under diocesan authority.

Tecpan. The palace of a ruler or lord; the site of community civil power in the altepetl.

Teocalli. A prehispanic indigenous temple.

Teopantlaca. The "church people": church officials and cantors.

Tepixque. Indigenous officials at the calpolli level, in charge of tribute collection and doctrinal policing.

Tlatoani, pl. tlatoque. A dynastic ruler of an altepetl.

Topil, pl. topiltin. A "staff-bearer"; indigenous constable.

Visita. 1) A subordinate jurisdiction in the mission enterprise that missionaries periodically visited to administer the sacraments and preach doctrine. Also the site of a humble church built for this purpose.

2) An inspection tour or review of an official's term in office or of the operations of a colonial institution.

Sources and Bibliography

Archival Sources

AGI	Archivo General de Indias, Seville
AGN	Archivo General de la Nación, Mexico City
AGS	Archivo General de Simancas, Simancas
AHN	Archivo Histórico Nacional, Madrid
APOAM	Archivo Provincial de la Orden Agustina de México, Mexico City
Ayer	Ayer ms. 1121, Newberry Library, Chicago, IL
BNAH	Biblioteca Nacional de Antropología e Historia, Mexico City
BNE	Biblioteca Nacional de España, Madrid
BNM	Biblioteca Nacional de México, Mexico City
BRAH	Biblioteca de la Real Academia de Historia, Madrid
LC	Krauss ms. 140, Library of Congress, Washington, DC
UT	University of Texas at Austin, Benson Library

Printed Primary Sources

Acosta, José de. *De procuranda Indorum salute*. Edited by Luciano Pereña. Madrid: Consejo Superior de Investigaciones Científicas, 1984.

Natural and Moral History of the Indies. Translated and edited by Jane Mangan. Durham, NC: Duke University Press, 2002.

Acuña, René ed. *Relaciones geográficas del siglo XVI*. Mexico City: UNAM, 1982.

Aguiar y Acuña, Rodrigo de, and Juan Francisco Montemayor. *Sumarios de la Recopilación General de las Leyes de Indias Occidentales* [1677]. Mexico City: UNAM, Fondo de Cultura Económica, 1994.

Alcalá, Jerónimo de. *Relación de Michoacán*. Zamora: El Colegio de Michoacán, 2008.

Alva, Bartolomé de. *A Guide to Confession Large and Small in the Mexican Language: 1634*. Translated and edited by Barry D. Sell, John Frederick Schwaller, and Lu Ann Homza. Norman, OK: University of Oklahoma Press, 1999.

Alva Ixtlilxóchitl, Fernando de. *Obras históricas*. Edited by Edmundo O'Gorman. 2 vols. Mexico City: UNAM, 1977.

Alva Ixtlilxóchitl, Fernando de. *The Native Conquistador: Alva Ixtlilxóchitl's Account of the Conquest of New Spain*. Translated and edited by Amber Brian, Bradley Benton, and Pablo García Loaeza. University Park, PA: Pennsylvania State University Press, 2015.

Anderson, Arthur J. O., Frances Berdan, and James Lockhart, eds. and trans. *Beyond the Codices: The Nahua View of Colonial Mexico*. Berkeley, CA: University of California Press, 1976.

Basalenque, Diego de. *Los agustinos, aquellos misioneros hacendados: Historia de la provincia de San Nicolás de Tolentino de Michoacán*. Edited by Heriberto Moreno García. Mexico City: Conaculta, 1998.

Beaumont, Fray Pablo de. *Crónica de Michoacán*, 2 vols. Mexico City: Talleres Gráficos de la Nación, 1932.

Bernáldez, Andrés. *Memorias del reinado de los Reyes Católicos*. Edited by Manuel Gómez Moreno and Juan de M. Carriazo. Madrid: Real Academia de la Historia, 1962.

Burgoa, Fray Francisco de. *Geográfica decripción*. Mexico City: Talleres Gráficos de la Nación, 1934.

Palestra historial de virtudes y ejemplares apostólicos fundada del celo de insignes héroes de la sagrada orden de los predicadores en este nuevo mundo de la América en las Indias Occidentales [1670]. Mexico City: Porrúa, 1989.

Burkhart, Louise M., ed. and trans. *Holy Wednesday: A Nahua Drama from Early Colonial Mexico*. Philadelphia, PA: University of Pennsylvania Press, 1996.

Burrus, Ernest J. "Salazar's Report to the Third Mexican Council." *The Americas* vol. 17, no. 1 (1960), 65–84.

Campanella, Tomasso. *La città del sole*. Edited by Adriani Seroni. Milan: Feltinelli, 2003.

Carrasco, David, and Scott Sessions, eds. *Cave, City, and Eagle's Nest: An Interpretive Journey through the Mapa de Cuauhtinchan no. 2*. Albuquerque: University of New Mexico Press, 2007.

Carrasco, Pedro, and Jesús Monjarás-Ruiz, eds. *Colección de documentos sobre Coyoacán*, 2 vols. Mexico City: INAH, 1976.

Carrillo Cázares, Alberto, ed. *Vasco de Quiroga: La pasión por el derecho*, 2 vols. Zamora: El Colegio de Michoacán, 2003.

Carrillo Cázares, Alberto. *Manuscritos del concilio tercero provincial mexicano (1585)*, 4 vols. Zamora: El Colegio de Michoacán, 2006.

Cartas de Indias, 3 vols. [Madrid: Ministerio de Fomento, 1877]. Madrid: Atlas, 1974.

Celestino, Eustaquio, Armando Valencia, and Constantino Medina Lima, eds. *Actas de Cabildo de Tlaxcala, 1547–1567*. Mexico City: AGN, 1985.

Cervantes de Salazar, Francisco. *México en 1554 y túmulo imperial* [1554]. Edited by Edmundo O'Gorman. Mexico City: Porrúa, 2000.

Chimalpáhin, Domingo. *Codex Chimalpahin*. Translated and edited by Arthur J. O. Anderson and Susan Schroeder. Norman, OK: University of Oklahoma Press, 1997.

Las ocho relaciones y el memorial de Colhuacan [1607–1637]. Edited and translated by Rafael Tena. Mexico City: Conaculta, 1998.

Annals of His Time: Don Domingo de San Anton Muñón Chimalpahin Quauhtlehuanitzin. Translated and edited by James Lockhart, Susan Schroeder, and Doris Namala. Stanford, CA: Stanford University Press, 2006.

Ciudad Real, Fray Antonio de. *Tratado docto y curioso de las grandezas de la Nueva España*. Edited by Josefina García Quintana and Víctor M. Castillo Farrero. 2 vols. Mexico City: UNAM, 1993.

Colección de documentos inéditos para la historia de Hispano-América, 14 vols. Madrid: Compañía Iberoamericana de Publicaciones, 1927–1932.

Colección de documentos inéditos relativos al descrubrimiento, conquista y organización de las antiguas posesiones de America y Oceanía, 42 vols. Madrid: Imprenta de Manuel B. Quirós, 1864–1884.

Cortés, Hernán. *Letters from Mexico*. Translated and edited by Anthony Pagden. New Haven, CT: Yale University Press, 2001.

Cartas y memoriales. Edited by María del Carmen Martínez Martínez. Salamanca: Junta de Castilla y León, 2003.

Cartas de Relación. Edited by Manuel Alcalá. Mexico City: Porrúa, 2005.

Cortés Alonso, Vicenta, ed. *Pintura del gobernador, alcaldes y regidores de México, "Códice Osuna,"* 2 vols. Madrid: Ministerio de Educación y Ciencia, 1993.

Cuevas, Mariano, ed. *Documentos inéditos del siglo XVI para la historia de México* [1914], 2 vols. Mexico City: Porrúa, 1975.

Díaz del Castillo, Bernal. *Historia verdadera de la conquista de la Nueva España*. Edited by Joaquín Ramírez Cabañas. Mexico City: Porrúa, 2005.

Dibble, Charles, ed. *Codex en Cruz*. Salt Lake City, UT: University of Utah Press, 1981.

Dibble, Charles. "The Nahuatlization of Christianity." In *Sixteenth-Century Mexico: The Work of Sahagún*. Edited by Munro S. Edmundson. Albuquerque, NM: University of New Mexico Press, 1974, pp. 225–33.

Durán, Fray Diego. *History of the Indians of New Spain*. Translated and edited by Doris Hayden. Norman, OK: University of Oklahoma Press, 1994.

Historia de las Indias de Nueva España e Islas de Tierra Firme. Edited by Rosa Camelo and José Rubén Romero, 2 vols. Mexico City: Conaculta, 2002.

Escobar, Fray Matías de. *Americana Thebaida, vitas patrum de los religiosos hermitaños de N.P. San Agustín de la Provincia de S. Nicolás Tolentino de Michoacán*. Mexico City, Imprenta Victoria, 1924.

Fernández, Justino, and Hugo Leicht, "Códice del Tecpan de Santiago Tlatelolco (1576–1581)." *Investigaciones históricas*, vol. I, no. II (1939), 243–64.

Focher, Fray Juan. *Itinerario del misionero en América*. Edited by Antonio Eguiluz. Madrid: Librería General V. Suárez, 1960.

Manual del bautismo de adultos y del matrimonio de los bautizandos. Edited by Juan Pascual Guzmán del Álba. Mexico City: Frente de Afirmación Hispanista, 1997.

García, Genaro, ed. *Documentos inéditos ó muy raros para la historia de México,* 45 vols. Mexico City: Librería de la Vda. De Ch. Bouret, 1907.

García Gallo, Alfonso, ed. *Cedulario Indiano,* 4 vols. Madrid: Ediciones Cultura Hispánica, 1945.

García Icazbalceta, ed. *Colección de documentos para la historia de México* [1858], 2 vols. Mexico City: Porrúa, 2004.

García Icazbalceta. *Códice Mendieta.* 2 vols. Mexico City: Imprenta de Francisco Díaz de León, 1892.

Cartas de religiosos (1539–1594). Mexico City: Editorial Chávez Hayhoe, 1941.

Códice Franciscano. Mexico City: Editorial Chávez Hayhoe, 1941.

Nueva colección de documentos para la historia de México [1892]. 5 vols. Mexico City: Editorial Salvador Chávez Hayhoe, 1941.

Don Fray Juan de Zumárraga, Primer Obispo y Arzobispo de México [1881]. Edited by Rafael Arguayo Spencer and Antonio Castro Leal. 4 vols. Mexico City: Porrúa, 1947.

García Pimentel, Luís, ed. *Descripción del arzobispado de México hecha en 1570 y otros documentos.* Mexico City: José Joaquín Terrazas e hijos, 1897.

García Pimentel, Luís. *Documentos históricos de Méjico,* 2 vols. Mexico City: Casa del Editor, 1903–1919.

Gómara, Francisco López de. *Historia de la conquista de México.* Caracas: Biblioteca Ayacucho, 1979.

González Obregón, Luís, ed. *Proceso inquisitorial del cacique de Tetzcoco.* Mexico City: Archivo General de la Nación, 1910.

González Obregón, Luís. *Procesos de indios idólatras y hechiceros* [1912]. Mexico City: Archivo General de la Nación, 2003.

Grijalva, Fray Juan de. *Crónica de la orden de N.P.S. Agustín en las provincias de la Nueva España.* Mexico City: Porrúa, 1985.

Hakluyt, Richard, ed. *The Principal Nauigations.* London, 1600.

Hanke, Lewis, ed. *Los virreyes españoles en América durante el gobierno de la Casa de Austria: México,* 5 vols. Madrid: Atlas, 1977.

Hanke, Lewis. *Instrucciones que los virreyes de Nueva España dejaron a sus sucesores.* Mexico: Imprenta de Ignacio Escalante, 1873.

Cuerpo de documentos del siglo XVI [1943]. Mexico City: Fondo de Cultura Económica, 1977.

Knab, Timothy J, ed. *A Scattering of Jades: Stories, Poems, and Prayers of the Aztecs.* Translated by Thelma D. Sullivan. Tucson, AZ: University of Arizona Press, 1994.

Ladero Quesada, Miguel Ángel. *Los Mudejares de Castilla en tiempos de Isabel I.* Valladolid: Instituto 'Isabel la Católica' de Historia Eclesiástica, 1969.

Landa, Fray Diego de. *Relación de las cosas de Yucatan.* Mexico City: Porrúa, 1986.

Las Casas, Bartolomé de. *Historia de las Indias.* Edited by Agustín Millares Carlo. 3 vols. Mexico City: Fondo de Cultura Económica, 1951.

Apologética Historia Sumaria. Edited by Edmundo O'Gorman. 2 vols. Mexico City: Universidad Nacional Autónoma de México, 1967.

Del único modo de atraer a todos los pueblos a la verdadera religión. Edited and translated by Agustín Millares Carlo. Mexico City: Fondo de Cultura Económica, 1975.

Leander, Birgitta, ed. *Códice de Otlazpan.* Mexico City: INAH, 1967.

León Pinelo, Antonio de. *Recopilación de las Indias,* 3 vols. Edited by Ismael Sánchez Bella. Mexico City: Porrúa, 1992.

Lockhart, James, Frances Berdan, and Arthur Anderson, eds. and trans. *The Tlaxcalan Actas: A Compendium of the Records of the Cabildo of Tlaxcala, 1545–1627.* Salt Lake City, UT: University of Utah Press, 1986.

Lockhart, James, ed. and trans. *We People Here: Nahuatl Accounts of the Conquest of Mexico.* Berkeley, CA: University of California Press, 1993.

López, Gregorio. *Siete Partidas,* [1555] Madrid: Boletín Oficial del Estado, 1974.

López Caballero, Paula, ed. *Los títulos primordiales del centro de México.* Mexico City: Conaculta, 2003.

López de Gomara, Francisco. *Historia de la conquista de México.* Caracas: Biblioteca Ayacucho, 1979.

López de Palacios Rubios, Juan. *De las islas del mar océano.* Translated by A. Millares Carlo and Silvio Zavala. Mexico City: Fondo de Cultura Económica, 1963.

Lorenzana, Francisco Antonio. *Concilios provinciales, primero y segundo, celebrados en la muy noble y muy leal Ciudad de México.* Mexico City, 1769.

Marín y Morales, Valentín. *Ensayo de una síntesis de los trabajos realizados por las corporaciones religiosas.* Manila, 1901.

Martínez, Hildeberto. *Colección de documentos coloniales de Tepeaca.* Mexico City: INAH, 1984.

Martínez, José Luís, ed. *Documentos cortesianos,* 4 vols. Mexico City: Fondo de Cultura Económica, 1993.

Medina Luna, Constantino, ed. *Libro de los guardianes y gobernadores de Cuauhtinchan (1519–1640).* Mexico City: CIESAS, 1995.

Méndez, Fray Juan Bautista. *Crónica de la Provincia de Santiago de México de la Orden de Predicadores (1521–1564).* Edited by Justo Alberto Fernández F. Mexico City: Porrúa, 1993.

Mendieta, Fray Gerónimo de. *Historia eclesiástica Indiana.* Edited by Joaquín García Icazbalceta. 2 vols. Mexico City: Conaculta, 2002.

Metzler, Josef, ed. *America Pontificia Primi Saeculi Evangelizationis 1493–1592,* 2 vols. Vatican: Libreria Editrice Vaticana, 1991, vol. I, 160–2 and 306–8.

Molina, Alonso de. *Nahua Confraternities in Early Colonial Mexico: The 1552 Nahuatl Ordinances of Fray Alonso de Molina, OFM.* Edited and translated by Barry D. Sell, Larissa Taylor, and Asunción Lavrín. Berkeley, CA: American Academy of Franciscan History, 2002.

Vocabulario en lengua castellana/mexicana, mexicana/castellana. Mexico City: Porrúa, 2004.

Morga, Antonio de. *Sucesos de las Islas Filipinas.* Edited by Francisca Perejo. Mexico City: Fondo de Cultura Económica, 2007.

Motolinía, Fray Toribio de Benevente. *Memoriales.* Edited by Nancy Jo Dyer. Mexico City: El Colegio de México, 1996.

Historia de los indios de la Nueva España. Edited by Edmundo O'Gorman. Mexico City: Porrúa, 2001.

Muñoz Camargo, Diego. *Historia de Tlaxcala*. Edited by Luís Reyes García. Tlaxcala: Universidad Autónoma de Tlaxcala, 1998.

Noguez, Javier, ed. *Tira de Tepechpan: Códice colonial procedente del Valle de México*. Mexico City: Biblioteca Enciclopédica del Estado de México, 1978.

O'Gorman, Edmundo. "Una ordenanza para el gobierno de indios, 1546," *Boletín del Archivo General de la Nación* vol. 11, no. 2 (1940), 179–94.

Olmos, Fray Andrés de. *Tratado de hechicerías y sortilegios: 1553*. Translated by Georges Baudot. Mexico City: UNAM, 1990.

Oroz, Fray Pedro de. *The Oroz Codex*. Edited and translated by Angelico Chavez. Washington, DC: The Academy of American Franciscan History, 1972.

Paso y Troncoso, Francisco del, ed. *Papeles de Nueva España*. 7 vols. Mexico City: Rivadeneira, 1905–1906.

Paso y Troncoso, Francisco del. *Descripción del Arzobispado*. Madrid: J. J. Terrazas e hijas imps, 1905.

Suma de visitas. Madrid: Sucesores de Rivadeneyra, 1905.

Epistolario de Nueva España, 1505–1818, 16 vols. Mexico City: Porrúa, 1940.

Relaciones geográficas de México. Mexico City: Cosmos, 1979.

Pérez Zavallos, Juan Manuel, and Luís Reyes García, eds. *La fundación de San Luis Tlaxialtemalco: según los Títulos primordiales de San Gregorio Atlapulco, 1519–1606*. Mexico City: Instituto Mora, 2003.

Puga, Vasco de. *Cedulario de la Nueva España*. Mexico City: Condumex, 1985.

Quiñones Keber, Eloise. *Codex Telleriano-Remensis: Ritual, Divination, and History in a Pictorial Aztec Manuscript*. Austin, TX: University of Texas Press, 1995.

Quiroga, Vasco de. *Información en derecho*. Edited by Carlos Herrejón. Mexico City: SEP, 1985.

Restall, Matthew, Lisa Sousa, and Kven Terraciano, eds. *Mesoamerican Voices: Native-Language Writings from Colonial Mexico, Oaxaca, Yucatan, and Guatemala*. Cambridge: Cambridge University Press, 2005.

Reyes García, Luís. "Ordenanzas para el gobierno de Cuauhtinchan, 1559," *Estudios de Cultural Náhuatl*, vol. 10 (1972), 245–313.

Documentos sobre tierras y señoríos en Cuauhtinchán. Mexico City: Centro de Investigaciones Científicas, INAH, 1978.

Cómo te confundes? Acaso no somos conquistados? Anales de Juan Bautista. Mexico City: CIESAS, 2001.

Reyes García, Luís, and Eustaquio Celestino Solís, eds. *Anales de Tecamachalco: 1398–1590*. Mexico City: Fondo de Cultura Económica, 1992.

Rumeu de Armas, Antonio. *La política indigenista de Isabel la Católica*. Valladolid: Insituto Isabel la Católica de Historia Eclesiástica, 1969.

Roman, Hieronimo. *Chronica de la orden de los ermitaños del glorioso Padre Sancto Agustin*. Salamanca, 1569.

Sahagún, Bernardino de. *Florentine Codex: General History of the Things of New Spain*. Translated and edited by Charles E. Dibble and Arthur J. O. Anderson. 12 vols. Salt Lake City, UT: University of Utah Press, 1982.

Historia general de las cosas de Nueva España. Edited by Alfredo López Austin and Josefina García Quintana. 2 vols. Madrid: Alianza Editorial, 1988.

Scholes, France V. and Eleanor B. Adams, eds. *Cartas del licenciado Jerónimo Valderrama y otros documentos sobre su visita al gobierno de Nueva España, 1563–1565.* Mexico City: Porrúa, 1961.

Scholes, France V. and Eleanor B. Adams. *The Diego Ramírez Visita.* Columbia, MO: University of Missouri Press, 1946.

Sell, Barry D. and Louise M. Burkhart, eds. and trans. *Nahuatl Theater.* 2 vols. Norman, OK: University of Oklahoma Press, 2004.

Sepúlveda y Herrera, María Teresa, ed. *Procesos por idolatría al cacique, gobernadores y sacerdotes de Yanhuitlán, 1544–1546.* Mexico City: INAH, 1999.

Solórzano y Pereira, Juan de. *Política indiana.* 5 vols. Madrid: Ediciones Atlas, 1972.

Tello, Fray Antonio de. *Crónica miscelánea de la santa provincia de Xalisco.* Mexico City: Porrúa, 1997.

Tezozómoc, Alvarado. *Códice Mexicáyotl.* Translated by Adrían León. Mexico City: UNAM, 1949.

Torquemada, Fray Juan de. *Monarquía Indiana.* Edited by Miguel León Portilla. 3 vols. Mexico City: Porrúa, 1975.

Vetancurt, Agustín de. *Teatro mexicano: Descripción breve de los sucesos exemplars de la Nueva España en el Nuevo Mundo Occidental de las Indias,* 4 vols. Mexico City: Porrúa, 1960.

Zavala, Silvio, ed. *Fuentes para la historia del trabajo en Nueva España.* 8 vols. Mexico City: Fondo de Cultura Económica, 1980.

Zavala, Silvio. *Fray Alonso de la Veracruz: Primer maestro de derecho agrario en la incipiente Universidad de México, 1553–1555.* Translated by Silvio Zavala. Mexico City: Condumex, 1981.

Una etapa en la construcción de la catedral de México alrededor de 1585. Mexico City: El Colegio de México, 1982.

Zavala, Silvio. Zavala, Silvio, ed. *Libros de asientos de la gobernación de la Nueva España (periodo del virrey don Luís de Velasco, 1550–1552).* Mexico City: Archivo General de la Nación, 1982.

Zorita, Alonso de. *Relación de los señores de la Nueva España.* Edited by Germán Vázquez. Madrid: Historia 16, 1992.

Life and Labor in Ancient Mexico: The Brief and Summary Relation of the Lords of New Spain by Alonso de Zorita. Translated and edited by Benjamin Keen. Norman, OK: University of Oklahoma Press, 1994.

Secondary Sources

Acuña-Soto, Rodolfo, David W. Stahle, Matthew D. Therrell, Tichard D. Griffin, Malcolm K. Cleaveland. "Megadrought and Megadeath in 16th-Century Mexico," *Emerging Infectious Diseases,* vol. 8, no. 4 (2002), 360–2.

"When Half of the Population Died: The epidemic of hemorrhagic fevers of 1576 in Mexico," *FEMS Microbiology Letters,* no. 240 (2004), 1–5.

Agamben, Giorgio. *The Highest Poverty: Monastic Rules and Form-of-Life.* Stanford, CA: Stanford University Press, 2013.

Álvarez, Luís Alonso. "Los señores del *Barangay*: La principalía indígena en las Islas Filipinas, 1565–1789." In *El cacicazgo en Nueva España y Filipinas*. Edited by Margarita Menegus and Rodolfo Aguirre Salvador. Mexico City: UNAM, 2005, pp. 355–406.

Anguiano, Marina. "División del trabajo en Tlaxcala a mediados del siglo XVI." In *Padrones de Tlaxcala del siglo XVI y padrón de nobles de Ocotelolco*. Edited by Teresa Rojas Rabiela. Mexico City: CIESAS, 1987, pp. 28–38.

Anguiano, Marina, and Matilde Chapa, "Estratificación social en Tlaxcala durante el siglo xvi." In *La estratificación social en la Mesoamérica prehispánica*, edited by Carrasco and Broda. Mexico: International Congress of Americanists, 1974, pp. 118–56.

Axtell, James. "Some thoughts on the Ethnohistory of Missions," *Ethnohistory*, vol. 29, no. 1 (1982), 35–41.

Bargellini, Clara. "Representations of Conversion: Sixteenth-Century Architecture in New Spain." In *The Word Made Image: Religion, Art, and Architecture in Spain and Spanish America, 1500–1600*. Edited by Jonathan Brown. Boston: Isabella Stewart Gardner Museum, 1998.

Barr, Juliana. *Peace Came in the Form of a Woman: Indians and Spaniards in the Texas Borderlands*. Chapel Hill, NC: University of North Carolina Press, 2007.

Bataillon, Marcel. *Erasmo y España*. Mexico City: Fondo de Cultura Económica, 1966.

Baudot, Georges. *Utopía e historia en México: Los primeros cronistas de la civilización mexicana (1520–1569)*. Translated by Vicente González Loscertales. Madrid: Espasa-Calpe, 1983.

La pugna franciscana por México. Mexico City: Alianza Editorial, 1990.

Bayón, Damián. "The architecture and art of colonial Spanish America." In *The Cambridge History of Latin America*. Edited by Lesley Bethel. Cambridge: Cambridge University Press, 1984.

Berdan, F. E. *The Aztecs of Central Mexico: An Imperial Society*. Belmont, CA: Thomson Wadsworth, 2005.

Berdan, F. E. Frances F. Berdan, Richard E. Blanton, Elizabeth Hill Boone, Mary G. Hodge, Michael E. Smith, and Emily Umberger, eds. *Aztec Imperial Strategies*. Washington, DC: Dumbarton Oaks, 1996.

Berdan, F. E. Frances F. Berdan, Richard E. Blanton, Elizabeth Hill Boone, Mary G. Hodge, Michael E. Smith, and Emily Umberger. "The Tributary Provinces." In *Aztec Imperial Strategies*. Edited by Frances F. Berdan, et al. Washington, DC: Dumbarton Oaks, 1996, pp. 115–37.

Berdan, Frances F. and Michael E. Smith, "Imperial Strategies and Core-Periphery Relations." In *Aztec Imperial Strategies*. Edited by Frances F. Berdan, et al. Washington, DC: Dumbarton Oaks, 1996.

Berdan, Frances F. and Patricia Rieff Anawalt, eds. *The Essential Codex Mendoza*. Berkeley, CA: University of California Press, 1997.

Bernal García, María Elena, and Ángel Julián García Zambrano. "El altepetl colonial y sus antecedents prehispánicos: contexto teórico-historiográfico." In Fernández Christlieb, et al. *Territorialidad y paisaje en el altepetl del siglo XVI*, pp. 31–113.

Bernard, Carmen and Serge Gruzinski. *Historia del Nuevo Mundo.* 2 vols. Mexico City: Fondo de Cultura Económica, 2005.

Bloch, Marc, and S. Guggenheim. "Compadrazgo, Baptism, and the Symbolism of a Second Birth." *Man, New Series,* vol. 16, no. 3 (1981), pp. 376–86.

Boehrer, George C. A. "The Franciscans and Portuguese Colonization and the Atlantic Islands, 1415–99." *The Americas,* vol. 11, no. 3 (1955), pp. 389–403.

Boone, Elizabeth Hill. "Pictorial Documents and Visual Thinking in Postconquest Mexico." In *Native Traditions in the Postconquest World.* Edited by Elizabeth Hill Boone and Tom Cummins. Washington, DC: Dumbarton Oaks, 1998, pp. 149–99.

Stories in Red and Black: Pictorial Histories of the Aztecs and Mixtecs. Austin, TX: University of Texas Press, 2000.

Borah, Woodrow. *Justice by Insurance: The General Indian Court of Colonial Mexico and the Legal Aides of the Half-Real.* Berkeley, CA: University of California Press, 1983.

Borges Moran, Pedro. *El envío de misioneros a América durante la época española.* Salamanca: Universidad Pontificia de Salamanca, 1977.

Boronat y Barrachina, Pascual. *Los moriscos españoles y su expulsion.* Edited by Ricardo García Cárcel. Granada: Archivum, 1992.

Boxer, Charles R. *The Church Militant and Iberian Expansion, 1440–1770.* Baltimore, MD: Johns Hopkins University Press, 1978.

The Christian Century in Japan, 1549–1650 [1951]. Manchester, 2001.

Brading, David. *The First America: The Spanish Monarchy, Creole Patriots, and the Liberal State.* New York: Cambridge University Press, 1991.

Brockey, Liam. *Journey to the East: The Jesuit Mission to China, 1579–1724.* Cambridge, MA: Harvard University Press, 2007.

Brumfiel, Elizabeth M. "Aztec State Making: Ecology, Structure, and the Origin of the State," *American Anthropologist,* vol. 85 (1983), 261–84.

Burkhart, Louise M. *The Slippery Earth: Nahua-Christian Moral Dialogue in Sixteenth-Century Mexico.* Tucson, AZ: University of Arizona Press, 1989.

Campbell, I. C. "The Culture of Culture-Contact: Refractions from Polynesia," *Journal of World History,* vol. 14, no. 1 (2003), 63–86.

Cañeque, Alejandro. *The King's Living Image: The Culture and Politics of Viceregal Power in Colonial Mexico.* New York: Routledge, 2004.

Caro Baroja, Julio. *Los moriscos del Reino de Granada.* Madrid: Istmo, 2000.

Carrasco, David. *Religions of Mesoamerica.* Long Grove, IL: Waveland Press, 1990.

City of Sacrifice: The Aztec Empire and the Role of Violence in Civilization. Boston, MA: Beacon Press, 1999.

Carrasco, Pedro. "The Civil-Religious Hierarchy in Mesoamerican Communities: Pre-Hispanic Background and Colonial Development," *American Anthropologist,* vol. 63, no. 3 (1961), 483–97.

Estructura politico-territorial del imperio tenochca. Mexico City: Fondo de Cultura Económica, 1996.

"Social Organization of Ancient Mexico." In *Handbook of Middle American Indians.* Edited by Wauchope et al., 349–75.

The Tenochca Empire of Ancient Mexico: The Triple Alliance of Tenochtitlan, Tetzcoco, and Tlacopan. Norman, OK: University of Oklahoma Press, 1999.

Carrasco, Pedro, and Johanna Broda, eds. *La estratificación social en la Mesoamérica prehispánica.* Mexico City: INAH, 1976.

Castro, Américo. *La realidad histórica de España.* Mexico City: Porrúa, 1987.

Castro Gutiérrez, Felipe. "Eremetismo y mundanidad en *La Americana Thebaida* de Fray Matías de Escobar," *Estudios de Historia Novohispana*, vol. 9, no. 9 (1987), 157–67.

Ceccherelli, Claudio. "El bautismo y los franciscanos en Méjico (1525–1539)," *Missionalia Hispánica*, vol. 12 (1955), 200–88.

Certeau, Michel de. *The Practice of Everyday Life.* Berkeley, CA: University of California Press, 1988.

Chamberlain, Robert. "The Concept of *Señor Natural* as Revealed by Castilian Law and Administrative Documents," *Hispanic American Historical Review*, vol. XIX, no. 2 (1939), 130–7.

Chanfón Olmos, Carlos. *Historia de la arquitectura y urbanismo mexicanos.* 2 vols. Mexico City: Fondo de Cultura Económica, 1997.

Christensen, Mark. *Nahua and Maya Catholicisms: Texts and Religion in Colonial Central Mexico and Yucatan.* Stanford, CA: Stanford University Press, 2013.

Christlieb, Fernando, Gustavo Garza Madero, Gabriela Wiener Castillo and Lorenzo Vázquez Salem, eds. "El altepetl de Metztitlán y su señorío colonial temprano." In Fernández Christlieb and García Zambrano, *Territorialidad y paisaje*, 479–530.

Chuchiak, John F. "*In Servitio Dei*: Fray Diego de Landa, The Franciscan Order, and the Return of the Extirpation of Idolatry in the Colonial Diocese of Yucatan, 1573–1579," *The Americas*, vol. 61, no. 4 (April 2005), 611–46.

Clendinnen, Inga. "Disciplining the Indians: Franciscan Ideology and Missionary Violence in Sixteenth-Century Yucatan," *Past and Present*, vol. 94 (1982), 27–48.

Ambivalent Conquests: Maya and Spaniard in Yucatan, 1517–1570. Cambridge: Cambridge University Press, 1987.

"Franciscan Missionaries in Sixteenth-Century Mexico." In Jim Obelkevich, Lyndal Roper, and Raphael Samuel, eds. *Disciplines of Faith, Studies in Religion, Politics and Patriarchy.* New York: Routledge, 1987, 229–45.

"Ways to the Sacred: Reconstructing 'Religion' in Sixteenth-Century Mexico," *History and Anthropology*, vol. 5 (1990), 105–41.

"'Fierce and Unnatural Cruelty:' Cortes and the Conquest of Mexico," *Representations*, vol. 33 (1991), 65–100.

Cline, Howard F. "Civil Congregations of the Indians in New Spain, 1598–1606," *Hispanic American Historical Review*, vol. 12 (1949), 115–37.

Cline, Sarah. *Colonial Colhuacan, 1580–1600: A Social History of an Aztec Town.* Albuquerque: University of New Mexico Press, 1986.

"The Spiritual Conquest Reexamined: Baptism and Christian Marriage in Early Sixteenth Century Mexico," *Hispanic American Historical Review*, vol. 73, no. 3 (1993), 453–80.

Comaroff, Jean and John. *Of Revelation and Revolution: Christianity, Colonialism, and Consciousness in South Africa.* 2 vols. Chicago, IL: University of Chicago Press, 1991.

Conrad, Geoffrey, and Arthur A. Demarest, *Religion and Empire: The Dynamics of Aztec and Inca Expansionism.* Cambridge: Cambridge University Press, 1998.

Conrad, Sebastian. *What Is Global History?.* Princeton, NJ: Princeton University Press, 2016.

Cook, Noble David. *Born to Die: Disease and New World Conquest, 1492–1650.* New York: Cambridge University Press, 1998.

Cook, Noble David, and W. George Lowell, eds. *"Secret Judgments of God": Old World Disease in Colonial Spanish America.* Norman, OK: University of Oklahoma Press, 1991.

Cook, Sherburne, and Lesley Byrd Simpson. *The Population of Mexico in the Sixteenth Century.* Berkeley, CA: University of California Press, 1948.

Cook, Sherburne, and Woodrow Borah. *The Indian Population of Central Mexico, 1531–1610.* Berkeley, CA: University of California Press, 1960.

The Population of Central Mexico in 1548: An Analysis of the Suma de Visitas de Pueblos. Berkeley, CA: University of California Press, 1960.

The Aboriginal Population of Mexico on the eve of the Spanish Conquest. Berkeley, CA: University of California Press, 1963.

Essays in Population History: Mexico and the Caribbean. Berkeley, CA: University of California Press, 1979.

Crewe, Ryan Dominic. "Pacific Purgatory: Spanish Dominicans, Chinese Sangleys, and the Entanglement of Mission and Commerce in Manila, 1580–1604," *Journal of Early Modern History,* vol. 19 (2015), 337–65.

"Connecting the Indies: The Hispano-Asian Pacific World in Early Modern Global History," *Jornal de Estudos Históricos,* vol. 20, no. 60 (2017), 17–34.

Crosby, Alfred W. *The Columbian Exchange.* Westport, CT: Greenwood Press, 1972.

Cuesta Hernández, Luís Javier. *Arquitectura del Renacimiento en Nueva España.* Mexico City: Universidad Iberoamericana, 2009.

Cuevas, Mariano. *Historia de la Iglesia en México.* 3 vols. Mexico City: Patricio Sanz, 1921.

DaSilva, Chandra Richard. "Beyond the Cape: The Portuguese Encounter with the peoples of South Asia." In *Implicit Understandings.* Edited by Stuart B. Schwartz. Cambridge: Cambridge University Press, 1994, pp. 292–322.

Davies, Nigel. *The Aztecs.* Norman, OK: University of Oklahoma Press, 1980.

Dean, Carolyn, and Dana Leibsohn. "Hybridity and Its Discontents: Considering Visual Culture in Colonial Spanish America," *Colonial Latin American Review,* vol. 12, no. 1 (1995), 5–35.

Deeds, Susan M. *Defiance and Deference in Mexico's Colonial North: Indians under Spanish Rule un Nueva Vizcaya.* Austin, TX: University of Texas Press, 2003.

Díaz Balsera, Viviana. *The Pyramid under the Cross: Franciscan Discourses of Evangelization and the Nahua Christian Subject in Sixteenth-Century Mexico.* Tucson, AZ: University of Arizona Press, 2005.

Dibble, Charles E. "The Nahuatlization of Christianity." In *Sixteenth-Century Mexico: The Work of Sahagún*. Edited by Munro S. Edmundson. Albuquerque: University of New Mexico Press, 1974, pp. 225–33.

Diel, Lori Boornazian. "Till Death Do Us Part: Unconventional Marriages as Aztec Political Strategy," *Ancient Mesoamerica*, vol. 18 (2007), 259–72.

The Tira de Tepechpan: Negotiating Place under Aztec and Spanish Rule. Austin, TX: University of Texas Press, 2008.

Duverger, Christian. La conversión de los indios de la Nueva España: con el texto de los *Coloquios* de Sahagún, *1564*. Mexico City: Fondo de Cultura Económica, 1996.

Agua y fuego: Arte sacro indígena de México en el siglo XVI. Mexico City: Santander Serfín, 2003.

Dyckerhoff, Johanna, and Hans J. Prem. "La estratificación social en Huexotzinco." In *Estratificación social en la Mesoamérica prehispánica*. Edited by Carrasco and Broda Mexico City: INAH, 1976, pp. 157–80.

Echenique March, Felipe I. *Fuentes para el estudio de los pueblos de naturales de la Nueva España*. Mexico City: INAH, 1992.

Edgerton, Samuel Y. *Theaters of Conversion: Religious Architecture and Indian Artisans in Colonial Mexico*. Albuquerque, NM: University of New Mexico Press, 2001.

Escalante Gonzalbo, Pablo. "El patrocinio del arte indocristiano en el siglo XVI. La iniciativa de las autoridades indígenas en Tlaxcala y Cuauhtinchan." In *Patrocinio, colección, y circulación de las artes*. Edited by Gustavo Curiel. Mexico City: UNAM, 1997, 215–35.

Farriss, Nancy. *Maya Society under Colonial Rule: The Collective Enterprise of Survival*. Princeton, NJ: Princeton University Press, 1984.

Fernández, Miguel Ángel. *La Jerusalén indiana. Los conventos-fortaleza mexicanos del siglo XVI*. Mexico: Smurfit, 1992.

Fernández Christilieb, Federico, and Ángel Julián García Zambrano, eds. *Territorialidad y paisaje en el altepetl del siglo XVI*. Mexico City: Fondo de Cultura Económica, 2006.

Fernández Christlieb, Federico, and Pedro Sergio Urquijo Torres, "Los espacios del pueblo de indios tras el proceso de congregación, 1550–1625," *Investigaciones Geográficas*, no. 60 (2006), 145–58.

Fernández-Armesto, Felipe. *Before Columbus: Exploration and Colonisation from the Mediterranean to the Atlantic 1229–1492*. London: Macmillan, 1987.

Fernández Rodríguez, Pedro. *Los dominicos en la primera evangelización de México*. Salamanca: Editorial San Esteban, 1994.

Frankl, Victor. "Hernán Cortés y la tradición de las Siete Partidas," *Revista de Historia de América*, vol. 53 (1962), 9–74.

Fraser, Valerie. *The Architecture of Conquest: Building the Viceroyalty of Peru, 1535–1635*. Cambridge: Cambridge University Press, 1990.

Frassani, Alessia. "El centro monumental de Yanhuitlán y su arquitectura: un proceso histórico y ritual," *Desacatos*, vol. 42 (2013), 145–60.

Fromont, Cécile. *The Art of Conversion: Christian Visual Culture in the Kingdom of the Kongo*. Chapel Hill, NC: University of North Carolina Press, 2014.

Galán Sánchez, Ángel. "Poder cristiano y 'colaboracionismo' mudéjar en el Reino de Granada (1485–1501)." In *Estudios sobre Málaga y el Reino de Granada en el V Centenario de la Conquista.* Edited by José García López de Coca Castañer Málaga: Diputación Provincial, 1987, pp. 271–89.

"Las conversiones en la Corona de Castilla: una visión teológica política." In *De mudéjares a moriscos, una conversión forzada. Actas del VIII Simposio Internacional del Mudejarismo.* Teruel: Centro de Estudios Mudéjares, 2002, 617–59.

Galende, Pedro G. *Angels in Stone: Augustinian Churches in the Philippines.* Manila: San Agustín Museum, 1996.

Ganson, Barbara. *The Guaraní under Spanish Rule in Río de la Plata.* Stanford, CA: Stanford University Press, 2006.

García Castro, René. "De señoríos a pueblos de indios. La transición en la región otomiana de Toluca (1521–1550)." In *Gobierno y economía en los pueblos indios del México colonial.* Edited by Francisco Gonzalo-Hermosillo Adams. Mexico City: INAH, 2001, pp. 193–212.

García Icazbalceta, Joaquín. *Opúsculos y biografías*, Julio Jiménez Rueda, ed. Mexico City: UNAM, 1942.

Don Fray Juan de Zumárraga, Primer Obispo y Arzobispo de México. Edited by Rafael Arguayo Spencer and Antonio Castro Leal. 4 vols. Mexico City: Porrúa, 1947.

Bibliografía mexicana del siglo XVI. Mexico City: Librería de Andrade y Morales, 1886.

García López de Coca Castañer, José. "Las capitulaciones y la Granada mudéjar." In *La incorporación de Granada a la Corona de Castilla.* Edited by Miguel Ángel Ladero Quesada. Granada: Diputación Provincial de Granada, 1993, pp. 264–97.

García Martínez, Bernardo. *Los pueblos de la sierra: El poder y el espacio entre los indios del norte de Puebla hasta 1700.* Mexico City: El Colegio de México, 1987.

García Oro, José. *Prehistoria y primeros contactos de la evangelización en América.* Caracas: Ediciones Trípode, 1988.

Garrido Aranda, Antonio. *Organización de la Iglesia en el Reino de Granada y su proyección en Indias, siglo XVI.* Seville: Escuela de Estudios Hispano-Americanos, 1979.

Gerhard, Peter. "El señorío de Ocuituco," *Tlalocan*, vol. 6, no. 2 (1970), 97–114.

"Congregaciones de indios en la Nueva España antes de 1570," *Historia Mexicana*, vol. 103 (1977), 347–95.

A Guide to the Historical Geography of New Spain. Norman, OK: University of Oklahoma Press, 1993.

Gibson, Charles. *Tlaxcala in the Sixteenth Century.* Stanford, CA: Stanford University Press, 1952.

"The Aztec Aristocracy in Colonial Mexico," *Comparative Studies in Society and History*, vol. 2, no. 2 (1960), 169–96.

The Aztecs under Spanish Rule: A history of the Indians in the Valley of Mexico. Stanford, CA: Stanford University Press, 1964.

Gil, Juan. *Hidalgos y samurais: España y Japón en los siglos XVI y XVII.* Madrid: Alianza Editorial, 1991.

Gómez, Wey. *The Tropics of Empire: Why Columbus Sailed South to the Indies.* Cambridge, MA: MIT Press, 2008.

Gómez Canedo, Lino. *Evangelización y conquista: Experiencia franciscana en Hispanoamérica.* Mexico City: Porrúa, 1977.

Gómez Martínez, Javier. *Fortalezas mendicantes.* Mexico City: Universidad Iberoamericana, 1997.

Greer, Alan. "Conversion and Identity: Iroquois Christianity in Seventeenth-Century New France." In *Conversions.* Edited by Kenneth Mills and Anthony Grafton. Rochester, NY: Rochester University Press, 2003, pp. 175–98.

Gruzinski, Serge. *The Conquest of Mexico: The Incorporation of Indian Societies into the Western World, 16th–18th Centuries.* Translated by Eileen Corrigan. London: Polity Press, 1993.

Images at War: Mexico from Columbus to Blade Runner (1492–2019). Durham, NC: Duke University Press, 2001.

Las cuatro partes del mundo: Historia de una mundialización. Mexico City: Fondo de Cultura Económica, 2010.

Hackel, Steven W. *Children of Coyote, Missionaries of Saint Francis: Indian-Spanish Relations in Colonial California, 1769–1850.* Chapel Hill, NC: University of North Carolina Press, 2003.

Halperin, Charles J. "The Ideology of Silence: Prejudice and Pragmatism on the Medieval Religious Frontier," *Comparative Studies in Society and History,* vol. 26, no. 3 (1984), 442–66.

Hanke, Lewis. *The Spanish Struggle for Justice in the Spanish Conquest of America.* Boston, MA: Little, Brown and Co., 1965.

Hanks, William F. *Converting Words: Maya in the Age of the Cross.* Berkeley, CA: University of California Press, 2010.

Haskett, Robert S. "Indian Town Government in Colonial Cuernavaca: Persistence, Adaptation, and Change," *Hispanic American Historical Review,* vol. 67, no. 2 (1987), 203–31.

Indigenous Rulers: An Ethnohistory of Town Government in Colonial Cuernavaca. Albuquerque, NM: University of New Mexico Press, 1991.

"'Our Suffering with the Taxco Tribute': Involuntary Mine Labor and Indigenous Society in Central New Spain," *The Hispanic American Historical Review,* vol. 71, no. 3 (August, 1991), 447–75.

"'Not a Pastor but a Wolf': Indigenous-Clergy Relations in Early Cuernavaca and Taxco." *The Americas,* vol. 50, no. 3 (1994), 293–336.

Visions of Paradise. Norman, OK: Oklahoma University Press, 2005.

"Conquering the Spiritual Conquest in Cuernavaca." In *The Conquest All Over Again: Nahuas and Zapotecs Thinking, Writing, and Painting Spanish Colonialism.* Edited by Susan Schroeder. Eastbourne: Sussex University Press, 2010, pp. 226–60.

Hassig, Ross. *Trade, Tribute, and Transportation: The Sixteenth-Century Political Economy in the Valley of Mexico.* Norman, OK: University of Oklahoma Press, 1985.

Aztec Warfare: Imperial Expansion and Political Control. Norman, OK: University of Oklahoma Press, 1988.

Mexico and the Spanish Conquest. Norman, OK: University of Oklahoma Press, 1994.

Hennessey Cummins, Victoria. "Imperial Policy and Church Income: The Sixteenth Century Mexican Church," *The Americas*, vol. 43, no. 1 (1986), 87–103.

Hicks, Frederic. "Prehispanic Background of Colonial Political and Economic Organization in Central Mexico." In *Supplement to The Handbook of Middle American Indians: Ethnohistory*. Edited by Ronald Spores. Austin, TX: University of Texas Press, 1994, pp. 35–54.

Hodge, Mary G. "Political Organization of the Central Provinces." In *Aztec Imperial Strategies*. Edited by Frances F. Berdan, et al. Washington, DC: Dumbarton Oaks, 1996.

Horn, Rebecca. *Postconquest Coyoacan: Nahua-Spanish Relations in Central Mexico, 1519–1650*. Stanford, CA: Stanford University Press, 1997.

Igler, David. *The Great Ocean: Pacific Worlds from Captain Cook to the Gold Rush*. Oxford: Oxford University Press, 2013.

Isaac, Barry L. "Witnesses to Demographic Catastrophe: Indigenous Testimony in the Relaciones Geográficas of 1577–86 for Central Mexico," *Ethnohistory* vol. 62, no. 2 (2015), 309–31.

Kamen, Henry. *Empire: How Spain Became a World Power, 1492–1763*. New York: Harper Collins, 2003, 30–2, 343.

Keen, Benjamin. *The Aztec Image in Western Thought*. New Brunswick, NJ: Rutgers University Press, 1971.

Kellogg, Susan. *Law and the Transformation of Aztec Culture 1500–1700*. Norman, OK: University of Oklahoma Press, 1995.

Kobayashi, José María. *La educación como conquista: Empresa franciscana en México*. Mexico City: El Colegio de México, 2002.

Kubler, George. "Mexican Urbanism in the Sixteenth Century," *The Art Bulletin* (1942), 160–71.

Mexican Architecture of the Sixteenth Century, 2 vols. New Haven: Yale University Press, 1948.

Lach, David. *Asia in the Making of Europe*. Chicago, IL: University of Chicago Press, 1996.

Ladero Quesada, Miguel Ángel. *Los Mudéjares de Castilla en tiempos de Isabel I*. Valladolid: Instituto 'Isabel la Católica' de Historia Eclesiástica, 1969.

"Nóminas de conversos granadinos (1499–1500)." In *Estudios sobre Málaga y el Reino de Granada en el V centenario de la Conquista*. Edited by José Enrique López de Coca Castañer. Málaga: Universida de Málaga, 1987, pp. 291–311.

Granada después de la conquista: repobladores y mudéjares. Granada: Diputación Provincial de Granada, 1988.

Lara, Jaime. *City, Temple, Stage: Eschatological Architecture and Liturgical Theatrics in New Spain*. Notre Dame: University of Notre Dame Press, 2004.

Lebroc, Reynerio. "Proyección tridentina en América," *Missionalia Hispánica*, vol. 26 (1969), 129–207.

Ledesma Gallegos, Laura. *Génesis de la arquitectura mendicante del siglo XVI en el plan de las Amilpas y las Cañadas de Morelos*. Mexico City: INAH, 2012.

Lefebvre, Henri. *The Production of Space*. Cambridge: Blackwell, 1991.

Le Goff, Jacques. *Lo maravilloso y lo cotidiano en el occidente medieval*. Barcelona: Gedisa, 1994.

Leibsohn, Dana. "Colony and Cartography: Shifting Signs on Indigenous Maps of New Spain." In *Reframing the Renaissance: Visual Culture in Europe and Latin America, 1450–1650*. Edited by Claire Farago. New Haven, CT: Yale University Press, 1995, pp. 67–80.

Script and Glyph: Pre-Hispanic History, Colonial Bookmaking, and the Historia Tolteca-Chichimeca. Washington DC: Dumbarton Oaks Research Library and Collection, 2009.

Lemistre, Anne Marie. "Les origines du *Requerimiento*." *Mélanges de la Casa de Velasquez*, vol. 6 (1970), pp. 166–81.

León Portilla, Miguel. *Aztec Thought and Culture*. Translated by J. E. Davis. Norman, OK: University of Oklahoma Press, 1963.

"Testimonios nahuas sobre la conquista espiritual," *Estudios de Cultura Náhuatl*, no. 11 (1971), 11–36.

Los franciscanos vistos por el hombre náhuatl. Mexico City: UNAM, 1985.

Leturia, Pedro de. *Relaciones entre la Santa Sede e Hispano-America*. 3 vols. Caracas: Sociedad Bolivariana de Venezuela, 1959.

Liss, Peggy K. *Mexico under Spain (1521–1556): Society and the Origins of Nationality*. Chicago, IL: Chicago University Press, 1984.

Livi-Bacci, Massimo. "The Depopulation of Hispanic America after the Conquest," *Population and Development Review*, vol. 32, no. 2 (2006), pp. 199–232.

Conquest: The Destruction of the American Indios. Cambridge: Polity Press, 2008.

Llaguno, José A. *La personalidad jurídica del indio y el III Concilio Provincial Mexicano (1585)*. Mexico City: Porrúa, 1983.

Lockhart, James. "Some Nahua Concepts in Postconquest Guise," *History of European Ideas* vol. 6, no. 4 (1985), 465–82.

The Nahuas after the Conquest. Stanford, CA: Stanford University Press, 1992.

Lopes Don, Patricia. "Franciscans, Indian Sorcerers, and the Inquisition in New Spain, 1536–1543," *Journal of World History*, vol. 17, no. 1 (2006), 27–50.

Bonfires of Culture: Franciscans, Indigenous Leaders, and Inquisition in Early Mexico, 1524–1540. Norman, OK: University of Oklahoma Press, 2010.

López Austin, Alfredo. *Educación mexica. Antología de textos sahagunianos*. Mexico City: UNAM, 1985.

Hombre-dios: Religión y política en el mundo náhuatl. Mexico City: UNAM, 1998.

López Sarrenlangue, Delfina. *La nobleza indígena de Pátzcuaro en la época virreinal*. Mexico City: UNAM, 1965.

Lundberg, Magnus. *Unification and Conflict: The Church Politics of Alonso de Montúfar OP, Archbishop of Mexico, 1554–1572*. Uppsala, Sweden: Swedish Institute of Missionary Research, 2002.

Malvido, Elsa. "La epidemiología, una propuesta para explicar la despoblación americana," *Revista de Indias*, vol. 63, no. 227 (2003), 65–78.

Martínez, Hildeberto. *Tepeaca en el siglo XVI: Tenencia de la tierra y organización de un señorío.* Mexico City: CIESAS, 1984.

Martínez, José Luís. *Hernán Cortés.* Mexico City: Fondo de Cultura Económica, 1993.

Martínez, María Elena. *Genealogical Fictions: Limpieza de Sangre, Religion, and Gender in Colonial Mexico.* Stanford, CA: Stanford University Press, 2009.

Martínez Baracs, Andrea. *Un gobierno de indios: Tlaxcala, 1519–1750.* Mexico City: Fondo de Cultura Económica, 2008.

Martínez Baracs, Rodrigo. *Tepeaca en el siglo XVI: Tenencia de la tierra y organización de un señorío.* Mexico City: CIESAS, 1984.

Caminos cruzados: Fray Maturino Gilberti en Perivan. Zamora, Michoacán: El Colegio de Michoacán, 2005.

Convivencia y utopia: El gobierno indio y español de la "ciudad de Mechucan," 1521–1580. Mexico City: Conaculta-INAH, 2005.

Matthew, Laura E. and Michel. R. Oudjik, eds. *Indian Conquistadors: Indigenous Allies in the Conquest of Mesoamerica.* Norman, OK: University of Oklahoma Press, 2007.

Matos Moctezuma, Eduardo. *Tenochtitlán.* Mexico City: Fondo de Cultura Económica, 2010.

McAndrew, John. "Fortress Monasteries?" *Anales del Instituto de Investiagaciones Estéticas,* vol. 23 (1955), pp. 31–8.

The Open-Air Chapels of Sixteenth-Century Mexico: Atrios, Posas, Open Chapels, and Other Studies. Cambridge, MA: Harvard University Press, 1965.

McCaa, Robert. "Spanish and Nahuatl Views on Smallpox and Demographic Catastrophe in Mexico," *Journal of Interdisciplinary History,* vol. 25, no. 3 (1995), pp. 397–431.

Meier, Johannes. "The Beginnings of the Catholic Church in the Caribbean." In *Christianity in the Caribbean: Essays on Church History.* Edited by Armando Lampe. Kingston: University of the West Indies Press, 2001.

Meli Piralla, Roberto. *Los conventos mexicanos del siglo XVI: Construcción ingeniería estructural y conservación.* Mexico City: Porrúa, 2011.

Melville, Elinor G. K. *A Plague of Sheep: Environmental Consequences of the Conquest of Mexico.* Cambridge: Cambridge University Press, 1996.

Memmi, Albert. *The Colonizer and the Colonized* [1957] Translated by Howard Greenfield. Boston, MA: Beacon Books, 1991.

Menegon, Eugenio. *Ancestors, Virgins, and Friars: Christianity as a Local Religion in Late Imperial China.* Cambridge, MA: Harvard University Press, 2009.

Menegus, Margarita. "La destrucción del señorío indígena y la formación de la república de indios en la Nueva España." In *El sistema colonial en la América Española.* Edited by Heraclio Bonilla. Madrid: Crítica, 1991.

Del señorío indígena a la república de indios: El caso de Toluca, 1500–1600. Mexico City: Conaculta, 1994.

"El gobierno de los indios en la Nueva España, siglo XVI. Señores o Cabildo," *Revista de Indias,* vol. 59, no. 217 (1999), 599–617.

"Los títulos primordiales de los pueblos de indios." In *Dos décadas de investigación en la historia económica comparada en América.* Edited by Margarita Mengus. Mexico City: El Colegio de México, 1999, pp. 137–61.

Menegus, Margarita, and Adolfo Aguirre. *Los indios, el sacerdocio, y la Universidad en Nueva España, siglos XVI–XVIII*. Mexico City: UNAM, 2006.

Menegus, Margarita, Francisco Morales, and Oscar Mazín, *La secularización de las doctrinas de indios en la Nueva España: La pugna entre las dos iglesias*. Mexico City: UNAM, 2010.

Meseguer Fernández, Juan. "Contenido misionológico de la obediencia e instrucción de Fray Francisco de los Ángeles a los Doce Apóstoles de México." *The Americas*, vol. 11, no. 3 (1955), 473–500.

Mills, Kenneth, and Anthony Grafton, eds. *Conversions: Old Worlds and New*. Rochester, NY: University of Rochester Press, 2003.

Miranda, José. *El tributo en Nueva España durante el siglo XVI*. Mexico City: El Colegio de México, 1952.

Moorehead, Alan. *The Fatal Impact: An Account of the Invasion of the South Pacific, 1767–1840*. New York: Harper & Row, 1966.

Morales Padrón, Francisco. *Teoría y leyes de la conquista*. Madrid: Ediciones Cultura Hispánica del Centro Iberoamericano de Cooperación, 1979.

Moya Pons, Frank. *La Española en el siglo XVI*. Santo Domingo: Editorial Taller, 1978.

Mullen, Robert J. *Dominican Architecture in Sixteenth-Century Oaxaca*. Phoenix, AZ: Center for Latin American Studies and Friends of Mexican Art, 1975.

Mumford, Jeremy Ravi. *Vertical Empire: The General Resettlement of Indians in the Colonial Andes*. Durham, NC: Duke University Press, 2012.

Mundy, Barbara. *Mapping New Spain: Indigenous Cartography and the Relaciones Geográficas*. Chicago, IL: University of Chicago Press, 2000.

Muriel, Josefina. *Las indias caciques de Corpus Christi* [1963]. Mexico City: UNAM, 2001.

Nesvig, Martin Austin. "The 'Indian Question' and the Case of Tlatelolco." In *Local Religion in Colonial Mexico*. Edited by Martin Austin Nesvig. Albuquerque: University of New Mexico Press, 2006, pp. 63–90.

Nirenberg, David. *Communities of Violence: Persecution of Minorities in the Middle Ages*. Princeton, NJ: Princeton University Press, 1996.

Nutini, Hugo G. and Betty Bell, *Ritual Kinship*. Princeton, NJ: Princeton University Press, 1980.

Nutini, Hugo G., Pedro Carrasco, James M. Taggart, eds. *Essays on Mexican Kinship*. Pittsburgh, PA: University of Pittsburgh Press, 1976.

Olivera, Mercedes. "El despotismo tributario en la región de Cuauhtinchan-Tepeaca." In *La estratificación social en la Mesoamérica prehispánica*. Edited by Pedro Carrasco and Johanna Broda. México: Centro de Investigaciones Superiores, Instituto Nacional de Antropología e Historia, 1976, pp. 181–206.

Pillis y macehuales: Las formaciones sociales y los modos de producción de Tecali del siglo XII al XVI. Mexico City: INAH, 1978.

Olivier, Guilhem. "Les paquets sacrés ou la mémoire cachée des indiens du Mexique central (XV–XVI siècles)," *Journal de la Société des Américanistes*, vol. 81 (1995), 105–41.

Olmedo Muñoz, Martín. "La visión del mundo agustino en Meztitlán: Ideales y virtudes en tres pinturas murales," *Anales del Instituto de Investigaciones Estéticas*, no. 94 (2009), 27–58.

Ortíz Macedo, Luís. *La historia del arquitecto mexicano, siglos XVI–XX*. Mexico City: Editorial Proyección, 2004.

Owensby, Brian P. *Empire of Law and Indian Justice in Colonial Mexico*. Stanford, CA: Stanford University Press, 2008.

Padden, R. C. *The Hummingbird and the Hawk: Conquest and Sovereignty in the Valley of Mexico, 1503–1541*. New York: Harper Torchbooks, 1970.

Pagden, Anthony. *The Fall of Natural Man: The American Indian and the Origins of Comparative Ethnology*. Cambridge: Cambridge University Press, 1982.

Lords of All the World: Ideologies of Empire in Spain, Britain, and France c. 1500–c. 1800. New Haven, CT: Yale University Press, 1995.

Pardo, Osvaldo V. *The Origins of Mexican Catholicism: Nahua Rituals and Christian Sacraments in Sixteenth-Century Mexico*. Ann Arbor, MI: University of Michigan Press, 2005.

Paredes, Oona. *A Mountain of Difference: The Lumad in Early Colonial Mindanao*. Ithaca, NY: Cornell University Press, 2013.

Parish, Helen Rand, and Harold E. Weidman. *Las Casas en México: Historia y obra desconocidas*. Mexico City: Fondo de Cultura Económica, 1996.

Pazos, Manuel. "Los Misioneros Franciscanos de Méjico en el siglo XVI y su sistema penal respecto de los indios," *Archivo Ibero-Americano*, vol. XIII, no. 52 (1953), pp. 383–440.

Perceval, José María. *Todos son uno: Arquetipos, xenofobia y racismo: La imagen del morisco en la Monarquía Española durante los siglos XVI y XVII*. Almería, Spain: Instituto de Estudios Almerienses, 1997.

Pérez-Rocha, Emma, and Rafael Tena. *La nobleza indígena del centro de México después de la conquista*. Mexico City: INAH, 2000.

El tributo en Coyoacán en el siglo XVI. Mexico City: INAH, 2008.

Peterson, Jeanette Favrot. *The Paradise Garden Murals of Malinalco: Utopía and Empire in Sixteenth-Century Mexico*. Austin, TX: University of Texas Press, 1993.

Phelan, John Leddy. "Pre-Baptismal Instruction and the Administration of Baptism in the Philippines during the Sixteenth Century," *The Americas*, vol. 12, no. 1 (1955), 3–23.

The Millenial Kingdom of the Franciscans in the New World. Berkeley, CA: University of California Press, 1970.

Piazza, Rosalba. *La conciencia oscura de los naturales: Proceses de idolatría en la diócesis de Oaxaca (Nueva España, siglos XVI–XVIII*. Mexico City: Colegio de México, 2016.

Pita Moreda, María Teresa. *Los predicadores novohispanos del siglo XVI*. Salamanca: Editorial San Esteban, 1992.

Poole, Stafford. *Pedro Moya de Contreras: Catholic Reform and Royal Power in New Spain, 1571–1591*. Berkeley, CA: University of California Press, 1987.

Prem, Hans J. "Disease Outbreaks in Central Mexico during the Sixteenth Century." In *Secret Judgments of God: Old World Disease in Colonial Spanish America*. Edited by Noble David Cook and W. George Lowell. Norman, OK: University of Oklahoma Press, 1992, pp. 20–48.

Radding, Cynthia. *Wandering Peoples: Colonialism, Ethnic Spaces, and Ecological Frontiers in Northwestern Mexico, 1700–1850*. Durham, NC: Duke University Press, 1997.

Ramos, Gabriela, and Yanna Yannakakis, eds. *Indigenous Intellectuals: Knowledge, Power, and Colonial Culture in Mexico and the Andes*. Durham, NC: Duke University Press, 2014.

Reff, Daniel T. *Plagues, Priests, and Demons: Sacred Narratives and the Rise of Christianity in the Old World and the New*. New York: Cambridge University Press, 2005.

Reid, Anthony. *Southeast Asia in the Age of Commerce, 1450–1680*. 2 vols. New Haven, CT: Yale University Press, 1993.

Restall, Matthew. "A History of the New Philology and the New Philology in History" *Latin American Research Review*, vol. 38, no. 1 (2003), 113–34.

Seven Myths of the Spanish Conquest. New York: Oxford University Press, 2003.

"The New Conquest History," *History Compass*, vol. 10, no. 2 (2012), 151–60.

Reyes García, Luís. *Cuauhtinchán del siglo XII al XVI: formación y desarrollo histórico de un señorío prehispánico*. Wiesbaden: Steiner, 1977.

Reyes-Valerio, Constantino. *Arte indocristiano*. Mexico City: INAH, 2000.

Ricard, Robert. *Études et documents pour l'histoire missionaire de l'Espagne et du Portugal*. Louvain: AUCAM and Paris: J. M. Peigues, 1931.

The Spiritual Conquest of Mexico. Translated by Lesley Byrd Simpson. Berkeley, CA: University of California Press, 1966.

Roulet, Éric. *L'évangelisation des Indiens du Mexique: Impact et réalité de la conquête spirituelle (XVIe siècle)*. Rennes: Presses Universitaires de Rennes, 2008.

Rovira Morgado, Rosend. *San Francisco Padremeh: El temprano cabildo indio y las cuatro parcialidades de México-Tenochtitlán (1549–1599)*. Madrid: CSIC, 2017.

Rubial García, Antonio. "La insulana, un ideal eremético medieval en Nueva España." *Estudios de historia novohispana* vol. VI (1978), 39–46.

El convento agustino y la sociedad novohispana, 1533–1630. Mexico City: UNAM, 1989.

"Tebaidas en el paraíso: Los ermitaños de la Nueva España," *Historia Mexicana*, vol. 44, no. 3 (1995), 355–83.

La hermana pobreza. El franciscanismo: de la Edad Media a la evangelización novohispana. Mexico City: UNAM, 1996.

"*Hortus eremitarum*: Las pinturas de tebaidas en los claustros agustinos," *Anales del Instituto de Investigaciones Estéticas*, no. 92 (2008), 85–105.

Rubiés, Joan Pau. *Travel and Ethnology in the Renaissance: South India through European Eyes, 1250–1600*. Cambridge, 2000.

Ruíz Medrano, Ethelia. "En el cerro y la iglesia: La figura cosmológica atl-tépetl-oztotl." *Relaciones: Estudios de historia y sociedad*, vol. XXII, no. 86 (2001), 141–83.

Sarabia Viejo, María Justina. *Don Luís de Velasco virrey de la Nueva España 1550–1564*. Seville: Consejo Superior de Investigaciones Científicas, 1978.

Sartre, Jean Paul. *Search for a Method*. Translated by Hazel E. Barnes. New York: Vintage Books, 1963.

Schroeder, Susan. *Chimalpahin and the Kingdoms of Chalco*. Tucson, AZ: University of Arizona Press, 1991.

"The Genre of Conquest Studies." In *Indian Conquistadors*. Edited by Matthew and Oudjik. Norman, OK: University of Oklahoma Press, 2007, pp. 5–27.

"Chimalpahin and Why Women Matter in History." In *Indigenous Intellectuals: Knowledge, Power, and Colonial Culture in Mexico and the Andes* Edited by Ramos and Yannakakis. Durham, NC: Duke University Press, 2014, pp. 107–31.

Schroeder, Susan, ed. *The Conquest All Over Again: Nahuas and Zapotecs Thinking, Writing, and Painting Spanish Colonialism*. Eastbourne: Sussex University Press, 2010.

Schwaller, John Frederick. *The Origins of Church Wealth in Colonial Mexico*. Albuquerque, NM: University of New Mexico Press, 1985.

Seed, Patricia. "'Are These Not Also Men?': The Indians' Humanity and Capacity for Spanish Civilization." *Journal of Latin American Studies*, vol. 23, no. 3 (1993), 629–53.

Ceremonies of Possession. New York: Cambridge University Press, 1995.

Sell, Barry D. "The Molina Confraternity Rules of 1552." In *Nahua Confraternities in Early Colonial Mexico: The 1552 Nahuatl Ordinances of Fray Alonso de Molina, OFM*, edited and translated by Barry D. Sell, Larissa Taylor, and Asunción Lavrín. Berkeley, CA: American Academy of Franciscan History, 2002, pp. 41–69.

Sempat Assadourian, Carlos. "La despoblación indígena en Perú y Nueva España durante el siglo XVI y la formación de la economía colonial." *Historia Mexicana*, vol. 38, no. 3 (1989), 419–53.

Slicher Van Bath, B. H. "The Calculation of the Population of New Spain, Especially for the Period before 1570," *Boletín de estudios latinoamericanos y del Caribe*, vol. 24 (1978), 67–95.

Smith, Michael E. "The Role of Social Stratification in the Aztec Empire: A View from the Provinces," *American Anthropologist*, vol. 88 (1986), 70–91.

Aztec City-State Capitals. Gainesville, FL: University of Florida Press, 2008.

The Aztecs. Malden, MA: Wiley-Blackwell, 2012.

Solari, Amara. *Maya Ideologies of the Sacred: The Transfiguration of Space in Colonial Yucatan*. Austin: University of Texas Press, 2013.

Sousa, Lisa and Kevin Terraciano. "The "Original Conquest" of Oaxaca: Nahua and Mixtec Accounts of the Spanish Conquest," *Ethnohistory*, vol. 50, no. 2 (2003), 349–400.

Spell, Lota M. "Music in the Cathedral of Mexico in the Sixteenth Century," *Hispanic American Historical Review*, vol. 26, no. 3 (1946), 293–319.

Spence, Jonathan. *The Memory Palace of Matteo Ricci*. New York: Penguin Books, 1985.

Spores, Ronald. *The Mixtecs in Ancient and Colonial Times*. Norman, OK: University of Oklahoma Press, 1984.

Spores, Ronald, ed. *Supplement to the Handbook of Middle American Indians*. Austin, TX: University of Texas Press, 1986.

Stenzel, Werner. "The Sacred Bundles in Mesoamerican Religion," *Thirty-eighth International Congress of Americanists*, vol. 2 (1968), 347–52.

Stevens-Arroyo, Anthony M. "The Inter-Atlantic Paradigm: The Failure of Spanish Medieval Colonization of the Canary and Caribbean Islands," *Comparative Studies in Society and History*, vol. 35, no. 3 (1993), 515–43.

Stevenson, Robert. *Spanish Cathedral Music in the Golden Age*. Berkeley, CA: University of California Press, 1961.

Suberbiola Martínez, Jesús. *El Real Patronato de Granada: El Arzobispo Talavera, la Iglesia, y el estado moderno*. Granada: Caja General de Ahorros y Monte de Piedad, 1985.

Subrahmanyam, Sanjay. "Holding the World in Balance: The Contested Histories of the Iberian Overseas Empires, 1500–1640," *American Historical Review*, vol. 112, no. 5 (2007), 1329–58.

Tavárez, David Eduardo. *The Invisible War: Indigenous Devotions, Discipline, and Dissent in Colonial Mexico*. Stanford, CA: Stanford University Press, 2011.

Taylor, William B. *Magistrates of the Sacred: Priests and Parishioners in Eighteenth-Century Mexico*. Stanford, CA: Stanford University Press, 1996.

Terraciano, Kevin. *The Mixtecs of Colonial Oaxaca: Ñadzahui History, Sixteenth through Eighteenth Centuries*. Stanford, CA: Stanford University Press, 2001.

Todorov, Tzvetan. *The Conquest of America*. New York: Harper, 1992.

Torre Vilar, Ernesto de la. *Las congregaciones de los pueblos de indios*. Mexico City: UNAM, 1995.

Tousaint, Manuel. *Arte colonial de México*. Mexico City: UNAM, 1948.

Townsend, Camilla. "Burying the White Gods: New Perspectives on the Conquest of Mexico." *American Historical Review*, vol. 108, no. 3 (2003), 658–87.

    "'What in the World Have You Done to Me, My Lover?' Sex Servitude, and Politics among the Pre-Conquest Nahuas as Seen in the Cantares Mexicanos," *The Americas*, vol. 62, no. 3 (2006), 349–89.

    "Polygyny and the Divided Altepetl: The Tetzcocan Key to Pre-Conquest Nahua Politics," In *Texcoco: Prehispanic and Colonial Perspectives*. Edited by Jongsoo Lee and Galen Brokaw. Boulder, CO: University Press of Colorado, 2014.

Townsend, Richard F. *State and Cosmos in the Art of Tenochtitlán*. Washington, DC: Dumbarton Oaks Research Library and Collection, 1979.

    The Aztecs. London: Thames and Hudson, 2009.

Traslosheros, Jorge E. *Iglesia, Justicia y Sociedad en la Nueva España*. Mexico City: Porrúa, 2004.

Trexler, Richard. "From the Mouth of Babes: Christianization by Children in Sixteenth-Century New Spain." In *Religious Organization and Religious Experience*. Edited by J. Davis. London: Academic Press, 1982, pp. 97–114.

Truitt, Jonathan G. *Sustaining the Divine in Mexico Tenochtitlan: Nahuas and Catholicism, 1523–1700*. Norman, OK: University of Oklahoma Press, 2018.

Turley, Steven E. *Franciscan Spirituality and Mission in New Spain, 1524–1599: Conflict Beneath the Sycamore Tress (Luke 19:1–10)*. Farnam: Ashgate, 2014.

Turrent, Lourdes. *La conquista musical de México*. Mexico City: Fondo de Cultura Económica, 1993.

Ulloa, Daniel. *Los predicadores divididos: Los dominicos en Nueva España*. Mexico City: El Colegio de México, 1977.

Umberger, Emily. "Art and Imperial Strategy in Tenochtitlán," In *Aztec Imperial Strategies*. Edited by Frances F. Berdan, et al. Washington, DC: Dumbarton Oaks, 1996, pp. 85–105.

van Doesburg, Bas. "The Lienzo of Tlapiltepec: The Royal Historiography of the Coixtlahuaca City-State." In *The Lienzo of Tlapiltepec: A Painted History from the Northern Mixteca*. Edited by Arni Brownstone. Norman, OK: University of Oklahoma Press, 2015, pp. 35–73.

Van Oss, Adrien C. *Church and Society in Spanish America*. Amsterdam: Aksant, 2003.

Van Young, Eric. "The New Cultural History Comes to Old Mexico," *The Hispanic American Historical Review*, vol. 79, no. 2 (May, 1999), 211–48.

van Zantwijk, Rudolph. *The Aztec Arrangement: The Social History of Pre-Spanish Mexico*. Norman, OK: University of Oklahoma Press, 1985.

Vázquez Vázquez, Elena. *Distribución geográfica del Arzobispado de México, siglo XVI*. Mexico City: Biblioteca enciclopédica del Estado de México, 1968.

Vincent, Bernard, and Antonio Domínguez Ortiz. *Historia de los moriscos: Vida y tragedia de una minoría*. Madrid: Editorial Revista de Occidente, 1978.

von Mentz, Brígida. *Cuauhnáhuac 1450–1675: Su historia indígena y documentos en mexicano: cambio y continuidad de una cultura Nahua*. Mexico City: Porrúa, 2008.

Wake, Eleanor. *Framing the Sacred: The Indian Churches of Early Colonial Mexico*. Norman, OK: University of Oklahoma Press, 2010.

Wauchope, R., G. Eckholm, I. Bernal, and J. Broda, eds. *Handbook of Middle American Indians*. Austin, TX: University of Texas Press, 1971, vol. 10.

White, Richard. *The Middle Ground: Indians, Empires, and Republics in the Great Lakes Region, 1650–1815*. Cambridge: Cambridge University Press, 1991.

Whitmore, Thomas M. *Disease and Death in Early Colonial Mexico: Simulating Amerindian Depopulation*. Boulder, CO: Westview Press, 1992.

Wood, Stephanie. *Transcending Conquest: Nahua Views of Spanish Colonial Mexico*. Tulsa, OK: University of Oklahoma Press, 2003.

Ybot León, Antonio. *La Iglesia y los eclesiásticos españoles en la empresa de las Indias*, 2 vols. Barcelona: Salvat Editores, 1954.

Zavala, Silvio. *The Political Philosophy of the Conquest of America*. Mexico City: Editorial Cultura, 1953.

La encomienda indiana. Mexico City: Porrúa, 1973.

El servicio personal de los indios en la Nueva España (1521–1550). Mexico City: El Colegio de México, 1984.

Los esclavos indios en Nueva España. Mexico City: El Colegio de México, 1994.

Zizek, Slavoj. *Violence*. New York: Picador, 2008.

Županov, Ines G. *Disputed Mission: Jesuit Experiments and Brahmanical Knowledge in Seventeenth-Century India*. Oxford: Oxford University Press, 1999.

Index